This book belongs to

Mr. William Raper
7 Veterans Way
Merrimac, MA 01860

History, Heritage, and Memories

Abbotts Creek
Missionary Baptist Church
High Point, North Carolina
1756–2006

History, Heritage, and Memories

Abbotts Creek
Missionary Baptist Church
High Point, North Carolina
1756–2006

Rufus Roy Cantrell
With valuable research and suggestions by the history committee: Zane Hedgecock, Betty Craven, Doris Loggins, Sue Foust, Libby Essick, Pearl Hayworth, and Evva Spurgeon.

Baptist History and Heritage Society
Atlanta, Georgia

Fields Publishing, Inc.
Nashville, Tennessee

*Copyright © 2008 by Abbotts Creek Missionary Baptist Church
All rights reserved. Written permission must be secured from the copyright owner to use or reproduce any part of this book, except for brief quotations in critical reviews or articles.*

Printed in the United States of America

*Library of Congress Control Number 2008927128
ISBN: 978-1-57843-051-2*

published by

Baptist History and Heritage Society
3001 Mercer University Drive, Atlanta, Georgia 30341
770-457-5538

and

Fields Publishing, Inc.
8120 Sawyer Brown Road, Suite 108 • Nashville, Tennessee 37221
615-662-1344
e-mail: tfields@fieldspublishing.com

Contents

	Dedication	7
	General Acknowledgement	8
	Personal Acknowledgement	9
	Forewords: Dr. Roy Smith and Beth Echols	11
	Preface	15
	Introduction to the Abbotts Creek Community	17
1.	The Name	28
2.	The Beginning	31
3.	Differences Between the Missionary and Anti-Missionary Groups	50
4.	The Division	58
5.	Letters from Wait and Dowd	69
6.	Abbotts Creek before 1832	73
7.	Abbotts Creek Union	97
8.	Effects of the Regulators	101
9.	A New Beginning (1832)	107
10.	Beginning The Second Hundred Years (1856)	127
11.	Abbotts Creek 1881–1901	143
12.	Beginning The Twentieth Century	159
13.	1933–1949	179
14.	The Fifties	217
15.	The Sixties	227
16.	The Seventies	244
17.	The Eighties	276
18.	The Nineties	309
19.	The Transitional Period	342
20.	June 2001–August 2006	357
21.	The Woman's Missionary Union of Abbotts Creek	385
22.	Ordained Ministers from Abbotts Creek and Ministers Licensed	388
	Epilogue	390
	Memories of Our Past	392
	Photos of Pastors	413
	Photos of Church Life	417
	Abbotts Creek Records from Liberty Baptist Association	425
	Index	434

The publication of this book
was made possible by the generous gift from
Clifton and Eva Mae (Tommie) Stewart

In Memory of Bernie and Lou Stewart

parents of
Clifton Stewart, Loyde Stewart,
The Late Pauline Stewart Eller,
and Peggy Stewart Lyda

Dedication

This book is dedicated to the memory of James Younger and other unnamed Christians who gathered first for worship in the early to mid-1750s.

To the memory of Elder Daniel and Martha Stearns Marshall whose love for preaching and winning souls enabled the church to take root and begin to grow, and to those early Christian men and women who struggled with the difficulties that demanded the reorganizations of the church twice by 1783.

To the memory of those in the late 1750s and the 1830s who gave their land and timber, sawed the logs, and built the log meetinghouses.

To the thirteen whose love for missions and Bible teaching would not allow them to remain a part of the church where they could not carry out their understanding of what the scriptures instructed them to do.

To the numerous generations who comprised the church at their particular time and continued to leave a foundation upon which the next generation could build, and who, in turn, left it for yet another generation until this very day.

To those of you who make up the present body of believers at Abbotts Creek Missionary Baptist Church and continue to carry out the purpose of Christ as exemplified by those who first gave us a heritage, history, and memories.

General Acknowledgement

Numerous individuals have made valuable contributions to the publication of *Heritage, History, and Memories of Abbotts Creek Missionary Baptist Church 1756–2006*.

Church clerks from the earliest minutes have done a creditable service with good records.

Much credit goes to a loving congregation of Christians who allowed me to serve as their pastor for twenty-four years.

In the mid-to-late-seventies, Pearl Hayworth, Daphne Moore Motsinger, Pansy Bodenheimer Moore, and her late husband, Dwight, researched the old minutes of the church and recorded numerous highlights that have been interwoven in this book.

Zane Hedgecock has collected information, stories, traditions, and facts, and he has gained an understanding of the community's history like few others. He had more knowledge about the church and community in his head than we have included in this book. Zane has collected pictures of places and people that have shown us life in the earlier community. It was, in part, his encouragement that led to the beginning of the undertaking.

The history committee has worked for more than two years searching through bulletins, newsletters, pictures, and other information to find pertinent information to be included. They have read and reread the typed manuscripts to help eliminate flaws in the writing. Committee members, in addition to Zane, were Libby Essick, Doris Loggins, Pearl Hayworth, Betty Craven, Sue Foust, and Evva Spurgeon.

A great debt of gratitude is due to Beth King whose artistic gift has provided the drawing included on the front of the book.

To our publisher, Tim Fields, Fields Publishing Inc., for the numerous questions he has answered and for the suggestions and helpful advice he has so graciously given throughout the process of putting this manuscript together.

Personal Acknowledgement

I acknowledge, first of all, my devoted wife, Linda, whose constant love and support since our marriage in June of 1956 has encouraged and challenged me throughout our ministry. I have been blessed by the encouragement of our children, David and his wife Teresa, Chet and his wife Michelle, and our son, Chris, and our daughter, Beth. Our family has been blessed to have a wonderful church and community in which to rear our children.

Evva Spurgeon has been of endless help in getting the computer to do what it would not do for me. She has spent endless hours, going far beyond the call of duty in adjusting quotes, helping to arrange pictures, and making other needed changes.

Pansy Moore has made valuable contributions by reading the material, making suggestions, and going back to her diary and the personal records she and her late husband, Dwight, kept over the years. She remembered many events and was able to add extra insight to what was written.

I give special appreciation to Betty Rose Welborn Alcon who volunteered to stay with my memory-challenged wife while I attended the numerous committee sessions. Without her help, my chair would have been vacant for many of the meetings.

Martha Teague Smith provided information allowing us to know some of the present church and community people as descendants of James Younger, our first preacher.

Jennie Counts, with the help of her husband, Howard, has read and reread the final copy, offering suggestions and making needed corrections. Without her untiring assistance, this work would have been impossible.

History, Heritage, and Memories

Forewords
Dr. Roy Smith
Beth Hayworth Echols

"Our history is important if our future is to be worthy."—Cicero
"Those who neglect their past are destined to repeat it."—Santyano

Cicero and Santyano remind us that an awareness and understanding of history are imperative for an appreciation of our past and a vision for our future.

The *History of Abbotts Creek Baptist Church* is an inspirational account of what a dedicated people can accomplish in the face of opposition, frustration, and unexpected hardships during more than 250 years of existence.

The author, a long-time pastor of the church, has encompassed the unique spirit of Abbotts Creek in a captivating manner.

Two major values emerge in each of the four centuries of the church's ministry (1750–2006).

First, the people of Abbotts Creek, along with Baptists and other Christians in the area, fought and died for personal and religious freedom. They believed that "freedom was a birthright," and that neither the Governor (Tryon) nor the King had the right to dictate religious thought and practice. The combination of "faith and freedom" has characterized the church to this day.

The second value was an unusual commitment to Christian missions. This commitment caused the "original Abbotts Creek members" to withdraw from a belligerent anti-mission, anti-education pastor and his followers in order to follow the mandate of Jesus to go into all the world with the gospel. The life of the church from that moment on reveals a most unusual commitment to and involvement in missions in the community, the association, the state, the nation, and the world. This writer has known of no Baptist church in North Carolina that has kept the "mission fires" burning as well as Abbotts Creek. This has been true despite unexpected major building expenses which could have taken the focus of the church from its commitment to missions. Regardless of the mammoth debt, untold monies were given for various mission causes and hundreds of mission volunteers went to minister in mission fields around the world.

The story of Abbotts Creek Baptist Church is an exhilarating example of how God's people triumph when they keep "the main thing the main thing." This history is a great encouragement to any fellowship that seeks to be a "Great Commission church."

—Roy J. Smith, Executive Director Emeritus,
Baptist State Convention of North Carolina

This has been an inspirational and sentimental experience for me to read this massive amount of history about my home church. I must say that at times it has been a journey mixed with sensory memories. To write that it carried me back to my childhood is an understatement. Each person who delves into any part of the book will surely come face to face with a flood of recollections and many images of persons who influenced their life.

It seems that I can still feel the fresh fall air surrounding the outdoor baptismal pool when several of us were baptized September 30, 1935. I was 11-years-old. Rev. E. F. Mumford was the beloved pastor. Of course, like a number of other "old timers," I still remember the peppermint lozenges Brother Mumford carried in his little black bag and suit pockets and gave to all us little ones.

I know, for sure, that I can still smell the artificial flowers that were on the table in our Junior Sunday School classroom. It was the room where Miss Minnie Hayworth told several decades of children how much God loved us. And, I can still feel the excitement of waiting and getting a Christmas treat of fruits, nuts, and candy in a brown paper bag. The depression of the 1920s and 30s didn't deprive those of us gathered in the Sunday School assembly hall.

Likewise, I recall the smooth feel of the seat in the outdoor toilet located at the edge of the woods. (You know, I don't think I saw a reference to when the church built indoor restrooms. Is that somewhere in the minutes? It should be!) Another remembered "fragrance" is the fresh scent of furniture oil when I recall how hard my mother and Aunt Mabel Hayworth worked to clean the sanctuary on a regular basis. My sister, Marie, and I had the job of soaking rags in the furniture oil and polishing the pews.

During the hours spent reading these manuscripts, I kept thinking about the huge oak tree that dominated the parking lot to the right of the previous church building. I wonder, did anyone take good pictures of that tree before it was cut down and the parking lot paved? I wonder what happened to all those acorns. And, what about the outdoor baptismal pool; is it still there? Is it covered with vines and filled with the detritus of many decades? Has anyone erected a marker to establish the site of baptisms for dozens of shivering junior girls and boys?

Folks, family, and friends, Abbotts Creek has come a long way since those days! To read the first several chapters will confirm what few of us knew before: we've come a long way since the recorded beginnings in the mid-1700s, several years before the Revolutionary War. This early history may be long and in some instances difficult to follow; but it is a story that must be told and preserved! It is enough to make "shouters" out of the most cynical and conservative "redeemed sinners" among us. The minutes of the meetings may be tedious to get through, but most rewarding. There are references to note and lessons to be learned from reading them. They reveal the struggles of a group of believers determined to become and remain a New Testament congregation, faithful to the high calling of God in Christ, dwelling among God's people.

For those of us who remember a childhood growing up in this community of faith, family, and religious experiences—in this place of Saturday business meetings, Cradle Roll, Sunday School, church, BYPU, and BTU—it is the last several decades that we can celebrate. The more I have read the minutes of meetings since around the 1950s and 60s, the more I have realized how important this church has been in the life of Baptist work in the state, the nation, and, amazingly, around the world.

For the most part, this church has been led by men and women who cared about people, both locally and throughout the world. This has truly been a missionary Baptist church. The minutes are filled with references to small groups, and many individuals, who ministered to families and persons in need. They followed Christ's admonition to "help the poor and the widows in their afflictions," along with forgiving those who strayed.

The Reverend Roy Cantrell, the longest serving recent pastor of the church, writes that in the last several years, small groups have gone on work missions to many states and foreign countries. They have built or refurbished church structures, often working in areas where there were no churches before. They have taught Vacation Bible Schools on remote Caribbean islands. All this was done while the local community was also being served with medical and dental clinics for migrants, the poor, and strangers in their midst; a new ministry called Labor of Love to give food and clothes to families in need; and after school programs which were a boon to working families. On and on the stories go about the caring and missions outreach of this congregation.

Brother Cantrell, who deserves the credit for compiling a lot of the history contained herein, notes that church groups have gone recently from Vermont to Alaska with many stops in between including West Virginia and Missouri. They have worked in the Philippines, South Africa, Ukraine, four countries in South America, and many islands in the Caribbean. Most of the overseas trips were done in partnership with the North Carolina Baptist Convention. Of course, the church has responded also to disasters along the Eastern and Southern coasts of North America, again in partnership with other churches in the state.

Yes, indeed, history buffs, read about the past and present of a church that was started around 1756. Join me in shouting, singing, and saying that we are glad that we grew up in the Abbotts Creek Missionary Baptist Church!

Read it and rejoice!

—*Beth Hayworth Echols, McLean, Virginia*

Preface

Since 1756, a part of the church Jesus built and Paul said was the "Body of Christ," Abbotts Creek Baptist Church, has stood as a spiritual lighthouse in the rural community near the head waters of Abbotts Creek. Services were led by James Younger as early as 1753. He and a few dedicated believers, hearing about the Separate Baptists at Sandy Creek, went in search for a spiritual leader. Daniel and Martha Stearns Marshall heard the plea of the group and dared accept the challenge. The church was organized and Marshall became pastor in 1756.

Struggles in the early years, fear of Indian attacks, Governor Tryon's determination to have no church except the Church of England, the Revolutionary War, and perhaps other factors made it necessary for the church to reorganize twice more by 1783.

Marshall served for a time before moving to South Carolina with a number of families from the small congregation to organize a church there. Elder George Pope became pastor in 1783 and served for thirty years. During this time, his zeal for missions and evangelism found him going great distances preaching and baptizing. He baptized more than 500 over this span of time.

Information is not available to allow us to know just where the earliest worshippers met. Later we know a log cabin was built. Log cabins served their purpose and then gave way to more modern buildings of planks and much later brick. Each building served its purpose until the need demanded a replacement. Early Christians lived, worshipped, served, and died, but their legacy for missions thrived and was passed down to the next generation.

By 1832, when trouble brewed with opposition to missions and Bible teaching in Sunday School, thirteen people dared to continue the practices that had been established by the founding fathers. The groups met in the same building at alternate times for two years. After those two years, and then being denied a place for worship, they moved across the road to worship in a brush arbor and were constituted as a church on July 4, 1832. A presbytery determined they were entitled to the land, cemetery and building, but they chose to leave peacefully and continued their worship.

This history allows us to follow the effort of our ancestors in being the church. We can note their long services and their strict discipline to the point of excluding members who did not live up to the church standards. As harsh as that seems, their love for the wayward was stronger and endless efforts were made to reclaim them for the church fellowship.

Financial struggles seemed constant. As time progressed, committees were named to collect funds for every need, including the purchase of a stove pipe. The salaries for the early pastors were sometimes months behind but always paid.

From time to time, differences were expressed, even dissension. Solutions were reached and the minority would always give their vote to assure cooperation and harmony allowing the membership to move on together.

Music held a priority for the church family. Funds were always provided for musical needs.

From the beginning, missions always received major attention. The first pastor moved to South Carolina with a group of families to start churches. Funds were always provided to support a variety of mission efforts. This heritage provided an adequate foundation for mission trips that have been constant since the early 1980s. Over the last few years, numerous individuals have been involved in hands-on missions. These efforts have moved beyond, but have not excluded the community and have moved across North America from Vermont to Alaska. Members have gone to South America in four or more countries. Christian workers from Abbotts Creek completed projects for the Ukraine, in Europe. The Philippine Islands of Asia needed aid that was provided by church members from Abbotts Creek as well. Several churches on various islands from Honduras to Trinidad presented opportunities that challenged many from the church family. A North Carolina Baptist Convention partnership with South Africa opened the door for some of our church members to serve on the continent of Africa.

You will be inspired reading of the "firsts" that took place throughout the years: the "first" pastor, the "first" church clerk, the "first" budget, and the "firsts" of everything. All these "firsts" opened doors to endless more that followed. Some of those "firsts" met an immediate need while others began practices that have guided the ministry and mission of the church.

Introduction to
The Abbotts Creek Community

James Younger was conducting religious services in the Abbotts Creek Community by 1756. Some sources indicate services were taking place at least three years earlier. It is documented Younger went to Sandy Creek in 1756, pleading for a pastor to come and lead the people. Who were these people? How long had they been here? Where did they originate? What was life like in the community?

By using family researched genealogies, we have been able to learn of some of the earliest inhabitants that made up the community. Some were here prior to 1756, while others took up residence during the developing years of the church. It is regrettable we are not able to learn more of some of our earliest families. We are able to learn too that several men from the community served for periods of time in the Revolutionary War.

No one kept a diary to inform us of the joys or hardships they encountered. Obviously, they carved out their livelihood from what nature provided. Homes were built from the logs taken by clearing the land. Gardens had to be prepared and crops planted to care for family needs and for the animals. Families had to produce enough to care for their family needs. Fish, wild game, and wild animals provided meat for the tables. Barns, corn cribs, smoke houses, sheds, out-houses, and other buildings had to be built with neighbors helping each other or by "swapping work." They worked together, took care of the building and farm needs, and provided some social interactions. Wells had to be dug, or homes had to be built near enough to springs in order to provide sufficient water for the family and livestock. Remedies had to be found for whatever medical needs demanded. Someone had to assume the role of midwife for the community. As time moved on, someone generally came to be known as the "specialist" to make the best plow handles, saddles, and other essentials necessary for home or farm life.

In addition to the logs used, clay and mud from the nearby streams were used in building the homes. As time allowed, the log homes were enlarged and by the early or mid-1800s, some two-storied homes were built. These homes generally had a long hall with little practical purposes except to move from one part of the house to the other. At times, the kitchen was set apart from the rest of the house. Fireplaces were built in each room for warmth with the kitchen having a larger one which was also used for cooking. Earlier sources remind us the larger meal was served at noon with the left-overs kept for supper. In many homes, the supper consisted of cornbread soaked in sweet or buttermilk. Life in the developing communities made heavy demands on family members.

Little furniture was needed or found in the homes. In addition to the table and beds, generally a large "water stand" in the kitchen provided a place for water buckets with the water for drinking, cooking, and cleaning the dishes. A smaller shelf was generally on the back porch, a place for washing dirty hands before entering the house. A towel made from a feed sack or other cloth hung nearby and was used by the entire family.

The roles of both male and female were well defined. The men and boys did the outside work leaving the inside jobs for the women and girls. Wash day was generally on Monday and was carried out by heating water in a large black pot outside somewhere in the yard. The hot water was used for washing and boiling the clothes. The soap and lye had been made by the family. Flat irons heated on the stove or in the open fireplace were used for ironing the clothes.

Having looked at some of the primitive living conditions, we turn our attention with the help of various family genealogies to meet some of our community forefathers. It is known many German settlers moved in mass to North Carolina in the 1740s and 1750s. Because of religious persecution in Germany, Queen Mary of England offered asylum in the colonies and some 30,000 arrived in Pennsylvania in the 1740s. After arriving there, many migrated south. A large group settled between Abbotts Creek and Leonard Creek in what is now Davidson County by the early 1750s. Groups, individuals, or family units were arriving from other countries as well.

Before looking at these families, we would do well to note evidence suggests Abbotts Creek community was home for Native Americans before settlers moved to the area. Numerous arrowheads have been found on the bottom lands near the creek. The Hedgecock, Orrell, Hayworth, and others families have found them, many of them well preserved. Family members still have nice collections dating back a few centuries.

Introduction to the Abbotts Creek Community

In his book, Centennial History of Davidson County North Carolina, Dr. J. C. Leonard has told us by the mid-1750s most of the Indians had retreated but some were seen occasionally, both peaceful and otherwise. "On the records of the Rowan County Court, about 1756, there is an account of a visit from a party of Indians, one a Sapona Indian, another a Susquehanna Indian, who were passing through" this part of the county.

Some sources hint to the fact that both Daniel Marshall and John Gano may have left their pastorates at Abbotts Creek and Jersey respectfully in part because of the dangers posed by warring Indians. It may have been due to these threats that the church had to disband and reorganize on two different occasions after 1756.

A history of the Davis family was written by Charles B. and Jacky Davis. It is entitled *The Ancestors and Decedents of Keziah Wheeler and William Davis*. In this history and speaking without absolute certainty, they have shared that the Davis ancestors came from Ireland and the Wheelers from Scotland. It is of interest that the Davis property was listed on the tax books of Rowan County as early as 1753. Tradition has it that the Davis family paid tax to the King of England. William Davis III continued to be listed on tax records and by 1778, "William Davis is listed as living in the Davis district of Rowan County." Tradition also had him listed as fighting in the Revolutionary War. In fact, the National Archives in Washington lists two William Davis men from North Carolina.

An incident was recorded that took place during the Revolutionary War. The Redcoats entered the home of William Davis I. The family had hidden their meat but the Redcoats took their good horses leaving the older ones. During this incident, a hole was knocked or shot in a wall of their log house. That hole is still evident in the old house.

About twenty-five years after Abbotts Creek Church was established, William and Henry Davis were given a land grant by the Governor of North Carolina. The writers of the Davis family history quote this from the land Grant Office in Raleigh: "State of North Carolina, Number 519. Know ye that we have granted unto Henry and William Davis five hundred acres of land in Rowan County on the waters of Abits Creek beginning at pointers in William Spurgeon line thence running East eighty chains to a post Oak sapling, thence North sixty-two chains and fifty links to a post Oak sapling the Southeast corner of said land lately surveyed for James Younger...." Without doubt the Davis family was in the community when services began at Abbotts Creek Church.

Another prominent family involved in the early shaping of the community and church was the Spurgeon family with various spellings during the earlier days. They arrived in the Abbotts Creek community in the mid-1750s. They were listed on the tax records by 1759 in Rowan County.

The history of the "Spurgeon Family in America" informs us two brothers, James and William, lived in Middlesex, England. Both were sentenced to a debtor's prison in a section reserved for those to be sent to the colonies. They arrived in Maryland in 1719. William Spurgeon, son of the above listed William, moved with his wife, Mary Jane, and their twelve children to Rowan County, North Carolina. He denied being a Tory although he was in favor of the King. His wife and children supported the Patriot causes during the Revolutionary War. After the war, Colonel William Spurgeon returned home but had to remain hidden because there was a price on his head. Failure to convince his wife to move with him to Canada, he headed out alone. He moved to Pennsylvania and lived there for years. While there, he married again. Four children were born to this union. He later moved to Canada as intended. His first wife, Mary, petitioned the court for several years before receiving any of her confiscated land.

The writer of the Spurgeon history had told us John Spurgeon, grandson of Colonial William Spurgeon, "farmed the land in North Carolina and became rich and prosperous. He was able to secure almost all the land his father had previously owned."

He held the office of the Justice of the Peace and later served in both Houses of the State Legislature. In fact, he introduced the bill that formed Davidson County from Rowan County in 1822.

Joseph Spurgeon went with the missionary element of the newly-formed church in 1832. The ten-room house built between 1830 and 1845 is listed in the North Carolina Historical Register. Kelly and Beverly Clinard and their two children, Kristin and Kasey, own the house and make their home at the old "Spurgeon House."

Johann Bernhart Eythe left Holland in September 1752 heading to the British Colonies in North America. After settling in Pennsylvania for a short time, he married Elizabeth (Etta) Meier. Like hundreds of others at the time, he left with his new wife and settled in the Piedmont section of North Carolina presumably to be near the Moravians in the Wachovia area. This date does not place him here when the church first began, but he seemed to be a well-established part of the community by the time the second reorganization of the church took place.

Johann operated a tavern in the Abbotts Creek area. "Here he served

Introduction to the Abbotts Creek Community

travelers between Salem and Fayetteville" according to Mattie Ruth Idol in her book, *Descendents of Barnett and Elizabeth Meier Idol*. In 1778, he received a land grant of 240 acres. As time moved on, he purchased other land and became one of the largest land holders in the area.

Neither reason nor time is given for this, but he changed his name from Johann Bernhart Eythe to Barnett Idol. County records refer to him as "Barney" Idol. Mister Idol did not participate as a soldier in the Revolutionary War but "his private papers contain an official document of his services to the North Carolina Militia by quartering the horses of American troops." Family descendents retained most of the land until 1974 when it was sold to outside interests.

The Motsinger Family Tree has been researched by Bill Keiner. His research discovered the Motzingers came from one immigrant, Felix Motzinger. However, the families that followed were very productive with some families having up to thirteen children. Felix arrived in Philadelphia with his father, Jacob Motzinger. They came from Marthalen, Switzerland. "After Jacob's death, Felix traveled to North Carolina where he bought 360 acres of land on both sides of Abbotts Creek in then Rowan County." The name was changed from Motzinger to Motsinger the first generation after Felix. Daniel, the second of three children born to John and his wife, remained in North Carolina while most of the others moved elsewhere. Though no date is given for the land purchase, Daniel, the grandson of Felix, was old enough to marry by 1792. This puts him at Abbotts Creek very early as far as church history is concerned. Some of the earlier Motsinger families were buried at the Primitive Church, others at the Abbotts Creek Missionary Baptist Church, Wallburg Baptist Church, Shady Grove United Methodist Church, and Bethany Church.

Keiner mentioned two theories about the date of arrival in North Carolina. The first suggested date was 1760. His wife died and was buried in Pennsylvania in 1765. The second theory seems more logical, indicating he moved with his four children to North Carolina in 1765 after her death.

Felix was said to be a dedicated Christian and joined the Baptist church when he arrived in Rowan County. Although not a resident when James Younger was first preaching and seeking a pastor for the church, this person was at Abbotts Creek during some of those earlier struggles and the reorganizing of the church.

A note of interest concerns Felix and his first son Jacob. They "reportedly fought with Francis Marion, the 'Swamp Fox' in North and South Carolina, during the Revolutionary War." Felix provided supplies for the horses and spied on the Tories. Jacob, a fast runner, would run long distances delivering messages.

The Raper family had tremendous influence in the community and the early life of the church. We gather our information from a book written by Rebecca Holton Raper Austin, *Descendents of William Raper, 1725–1795*. William Raper was born in England, in 1725. His name was not listed on the passenger lists of those who sailed from 1740–1755. He probably traveled on a trading vessel, *The Sarah*. His father had a business interest in the ship and in Charlestown, South Carolina. Mister Raper had purchased land in the Abbotts Creek community as early as 1755. It appears, he like others, may have purchased land and waited until it seemed safe from the Indians before taking up residence. A speech was given at the Raper Reunion at Abbotts Creek Church, September 9, 1928. From this speech, we have learned the Raper family had been in the area of Abbotts Creek for more than 150 years.

The Raper family was not in the community when the church was first established but were here shortly afterwards. The Raper name is found frequently in the minutes of the church long before the division. The church records contain a copy of a deed where Joseph Raper had been paid eight dollars for land deeded to the trustees for land including the "Missionary Baptist meetinghouse…containing one acre be the same more or less." This took place in August of 1837.

We learn of the surname Bodenhamer/Bodenhammer from a genealogy book published by Herb Eaton, Inc. Charlotte, North Carolina, and Walsworth Publishing Company, Marceline, Missouri. They hold a copyright to this publication. Due to the briefness of this work, we will not deal with the various spellings of the name. The family origin was Germany but they traveled to the New W orld in the 1740s–1750s when thousands of others were migrating. At least three Bodenheimer brothers left Bodenheim, Germany, for Pennsylvania and nearby New Jersey. Some lived there for as long as twenty-five years. Agnes, the wife of the second son of Christian and Charity Bodenheimer, states she came to North Carolina in 1774. This would have been prior to the first reorganization of the church. Records indicate they purchased land on both sides of the Abbotts Creek. In pension papers dated in April of 1846, Agnes Bodenheimer is listed as the widow of Peter Bodenheimer who served in the Revolutionary War as a private.

Christian and Charity Bodenheimer were of the German Reform Church in the United States. It seemed logical they continued to worship in their faith but since there was no German Reform church to attend in

Introduction to the Abbotts Creek Community

their new home, Rowan County seemed to dictate for them the need to attend another church. They became a part of the Abbotts Creek Church. It is known that Charity was attending the church meetings in the early 1800s.

For our purpose, we are not trying to follow family lines but simply learn of the arrival of the earliest families making up the Abbotts Creek Community.

The genealogy of William Hitchcock I tells us he left England for the colonies and settled in Maryland in about 1670. He died of fever in 1684 as a prosperous man in Cecil County, Maryland. A son, William II, survived, "Whose progeny became the foundation of the Hitchcock, Hedgecock, and Hedgcock family in America." It seemed the name Hitchcock stayed with those in Maryland while the spelling Hedgecock was kept by the family in North Carolina. The name Hedgcock continued as the name of those who migrated to Illinois in 1834.

After the death of William II, most of his land had been sold five years later by William III. By this time some of the family began to migrate to both North and South Carolina. William and his wife, Susannah, stopped attending the St. John's Parrish on a regular basis. When questioned about this by the Elders of the Parrish, they responded by saying "they no longer received spiritual comfort from the church." They attended the Quaker meetinghouse. Records do not indicate they were members, but they were closely associated.

William III died leaving a wife and seven children. His nearest of kin was his widow, Susannah and Isaac, the oldest son. William IV could not be administrator because he was listed on the Debtor Book and had tax problems. Isaac was given money to pay the tax debt by his uncle, Ashael. It was done with the understanding he would go to North Carolina "where his uncle John Hitchcock had migrated in 1738. He and his two brothers moved to North Carolina in 1776." We note this is about the time of the first reorganization of the church.

Isaac Hitchcock, the oldest son of William III, was granted 258 acres of land in Rowan Country in 1793 "on Abbotts Creek and Richfork." This gives us enough information to help us understand the Hedgecock family was here soon after the second reorganization of the church.

The following information helps us to place the Welborn family in the Abbotts Creek community at the time of the organization and reorganization of the church. The first membership roll of the church in 1783 gives the names of James, William, and Isabel Welborn. James Welborn arrived in Rowan County in 1752. While riding his horse through the area later known as Salem, Indians shot his horse. After running several yards, the animal fell dead. Mr. Welborn was able to free his leg from under the horse and escaped his attackers by running. He settled on the headwaters of Abbotts Creek in what later became known as Davidson County.

About this same time many Moravians were moving to the area, as well as Daniel Boone, who was arriving in a nearby county. Gene Welborn has researched the Welborn history and recorded it in his work, *Welborns and Related Families in North and South Carolina*. In his work he states, "The Boones and Welborns were not only neighbors but had a lot in common. Both families were pioneers, blacksmiths, farmers, and public office holders.

James Welborn purchased several tracts of land in 1762, and later deeded them to William Spurgeon in 1771. They were deeded back to Mr. Welborn in 1772.

The first dated membership roll for Abbotts Creek was in 1783. Among the eighty-two names listed, we have Charity Swaim, Martha Swaim, and William Swaim. In addition, John Swaim is listed two times or there were two by the same name. The same is true for Mary Swaim. That first roll had either five or seven members by the name of Swaim. This family was from Dutch origin, Lierson, Holland and migrated to the New World in 1759 and 1776. John, and his father, William Swaim, and his brother, Michael, moved to North Carolina about 1740. John and his wife had five or six children; one was named William who was born in Rowan County in 1745–1747. He purchased land in the present-day Abbotts Creek area. By 1765, he had sold the land and moved to Surry County (now Yadkin). Two children born to him and his wife, Charity, are listed as William Swaim, born 1745, and Rachael Bess Swaim. They are both listed as living in the Abbotts Creek community.

The late Ethel Swaim Teague has researched and documented that the John Swaim family had moved to the Abbotts Creek section of Rowan County by 1740. Mrs. Teague's grandfather was Hyram D. Swaim. The story passed from one generation to the other has it that Hyram was to be married on Christmas Day, 1876. Heavy snow prevented his arrival by train from Winston-Salem to High Point on time. Two days later, he was married to Eliza Robbins but always teased about being late for his wedding.

From the information provided by Patrie Swaim Smith, under the third generation of the Swaim family, Ashley Swaim (1782–1856) is listed. Beside his name, a notation was given: "...a Baptist minister in Davidson County, North Carolina." We know Ashley Swaim as the pastor of Abbotts Creek Church when the division took place.

Browntown

We would not dare discuss any history of the Abbotts Creek Community without including Browntown. The story has developed from various sources. In 1928, a group of at least a dozen people researched the traditions and stories that had been and were being told. Their collections were recorded by Colonel W. A. Blair. Mrs. Jean Davis Brown drew the sketch of the town as remembered by the older residents. Other information at hand was written by Millard Bodenheimer who gives credit to at least eighteen sources (people). Art Hedgecock provided other information concerning "Davidson County's Forgotten Town." Much of the information of the latter two probably came from the 1928 group.

Traditions handed down have informed us that a widow, Elizabeth Brown, came from Pennsylvania with her six children just before or during the Revolutionary War. She settled at the intersection of the Salem to Fayetteville and the Salisbury to Guilford County Roads. Browntown was said to be the first stop of the stage coach between Salem and Fayetteville "where the passengers were given delicious cakes and a most wonderful refreshment called 'cider rile,' a mixture of cider and brandy."

A post office existed in Browntown long before the one opened in High Point in 1855.

Browntown was incorporated by the North Carolina General Assembly on January 26, 1843. It is of interest to note Winston-Salem was incorporated in 1856 and High Point in 1859. The Act of Incorporation included this: "That Dr. Alfred M. Folger, Austin Raper, Absolom Brown, Ezekiel Hedgecock and William Shields, and their successors be, and are hereby appointed, commissioners for Browntown in County of Davidson." Art Hedgecock adds, "The limits extended a quarter of a mile in every direction from a point called the crossroads. The town was incorporated in a circle. Absolom Brown was the first and only known mayor of the town."

From the crossroads, the line of the town limits extended one fourth of a mile for the complete circle. This incorporation took place sixty years or more after Mrs. Brown moved to this northeast section of what is now Davidson County. Mrs Brown was a part of the Abbotts Creek Church and went with the missionary element of the congregation in 1832, when the church divided.

At the time of incorporation, Browntown included "thirteen dwellings, three stores, a post office, one hatter's shop, one shoe shop, two cabinet-makers' shops, one saddler shop, two blacksmith shops, and one tailor shop." The old churches at Abbotts Creek and the old Evans Mill were just outside the corporate limits. Forty years later, the Census lists eight hundred people living in the Browntown area.

Traditions continue to exist that General Nathaniel Green camped (this may be historical rather than traditional) in the area on his retreat from the British forces. The tradition adds General Green rested his horse in the shade of a large oak tree which stood near the intersection of the roads at the center of town. This tree became famous and was called the "Election Oak." Political meetings were held there and the men leaving to join the Confederate soldiers gathered and left from this point during the Civil War.

An interesting story compares the town to others in this section of the state. In 1859, John Robertson selected Browntown to be the site of the circus he was bringing to North Carolina, one of two places in the state. On the eve of the grand opening, neighbors had gathered waiting with excitement. Hundreds of people came by wagons, buggies, horseback, or walked great distances to see the circus. The demand for food for these

The Browntown community store

"out of town" guests used up about all the food the town folk could supply.

A story associated with this concerned a large elephant which had been tied to a farmer's corn crib. The hungry animal pulled a log from the crib, "inserted his trunk, discovered a barrel of threshed oats and ate this together with some corn and other grain."

The citizens of Browntown and the area were skilled in making the tools necessary for survival. The following list apparently was first given by the group in 1928.

"A list of industries is a surprising one. Furniture, chairs, buckets, barrels, looms, wagons, buggies, saddles, harnesses, bridles, shoes, cutlery, cradles, scythes, plows, and hats were all manufactured there. Knives, hammers, sewing awls, pegging awls, nails for building, horseshoes, horseshoe nails, scissors, candle snuffers, and various other articles were produced by the skilled blacksmiths. Ropes for bed cords, well buckets, and harnesses were made from flax; and cloth of various kinds was woven in the looms. Shoepegs were made from maple, persimmon, dogwood, and apple trees; and the lasts for shoes were made from the same wood or from poplar. Thread for sewing shoes and harnesses was spun from flax. There was a grist mill, a sawmill, a power plant, two photographers, two nurseries, and a distillery."

The Browntown tales and traditions carry many exciting stories of the individuals who made up the Abbotts Creek Community. Many of these people were a part of the two churches existing at the time. These stories are very interesting but would not add to the intent of this book and must wait for other ways before being told again.

CHAPTER ONE

The Name

Early Baptist historians tell us while Shubal Stearns and Benjamin Miller were preaching at Sandy Creek and Jersey Baptist churches, respectively, religious services were being led in the Abbotts Creek community by James Younger from Welsh Neck, South Carolina.

Abbotts Creek was mentioned as a thriving community, but where did the name originate? There are two leading thoughts concerning the name. The influential Raper Family held a reunion at Abbotts Creek Church on September 9, 1928. A speech was given and partially published in the *High Point Enterprise*. The article was entitled "Abbott's Creek Church and The Raper Family." The paper indicated this was a "Historical Address Before the Raper Family Association." Reference was made to a history of North Carolina Baptists, written some years earlier by Rev. C. B. Williams. Williams names the oldest Baptist church in North Carolina as being Shiloh, in Camden County. The speaker was quoted as saying, "In 1765, Rev. Henry Abbott, son of John Abbott, canon of St. Paul's in London, went to Shiloh Church as pastor." The article quoted the speaker as saying, "It is a logical supposition borne out by many evidences that the name Abbott was selected because of the reputation and success of Rev. Henry Abbott of eastern Carolina." Other information was given about Abbott stating he was a member of the Halifax Convention in 1776. He even served on the committee to help prepare the Constitution and worked on the section dealing with the guarantee of religious freedom. "Here doubtless, we find the source of the name Abbott as applied to the church and the Creek of Davidson County."

The second explanation was given with a much earlier date. *Homespun* magazine published for schools in Davidson County, Volume 9, Spring of 1982, reminds us that many communities were named after some earlier settler who resided there. The same could be said for the way streams were named. Abbotts Creek is one of the largest creeks in the county. Early sources tell us that this creek provided water for more grain grinding than any other creek in the county. According to this article, Abbotts Creek "received its name from an early settler, William Abbott, who with Matthew Rowan (for whom Rowan County was named) ran the dividing line between the lands turned back to the King of England by the Lord's proprietors in 1729."

The reasoning of the creek's name is given but still leaves unanswered exactly how the church was named. It should be noted that both persons mentioned had the last name Abbott not Abbotts. Grammar would seem to dictate adding a creek or church to the name would require an apostrophe thus showing possession, such as Abbott's Creek. The spelling has created endless discussion over time. There seems to have never been a consistent spelling of the name in the minutes of the church. Clerks have spelled it as they understood the name, such as Abet's Crick, Abot's, Abbotts, Abbott's, and perhaps other ways. During the years 1881–1932, the minutes of the church used the spelling Abbotts Creek. When we quote in this work, we will use the spellings as the sources give. We keep in mind when historians make references to the church, they may have been thinking of the grammar that seems to demand the apostrophe without regard to how the church people were spelling it.

Various spellings are found in the Liberty Baptist Association's minutes. For the most part the name is spelled with the apostrophe through the 1919 minutes and from then on, the "s" is included but no apostrophe. The minutes of the church do not tell us if the spelling was fixed or if it became generally accepted to be spelled as: Abbotts.

Since the division in 1832, the church has always added Missionary to its name. No other church in the Liberty Association adds the missionary part though all are considered missionary Baptists. This has caused confusion to some not acquainted with the church's history. Missionary distinguishes it from the Primitive Baptist Church located across the road. At times, the churches have been referred to as the Upper or Lower church. The Primitive Church is located across the road and just down the hill, thus identified as the Lower Church. Lower is never used with other connotations. It is simply a matter of location.

It seems appropriate to give some history relative to the name. Baptists at Abbotts Creek, like in other places, were called by one name, Baptists. After the churches began to split, a problem seemed to emerge. What will we call ourselves? Names began to be used such as "The Old Baptists," "The-Old-Sort Baptists," "The Old-School Baptists," and "Baptists of the Old Stump." Others names were "Ironsides," "Hardshell," "Square-Toed

Baptists," "Hard–Rind Baptists," and "Predestinarian Baptists."

The Biblical Recorder, the Baptist State newspaper of North Carolina, carried an article in the November 1871 issue regarding these names. A quote was given in reply to a paper from the anti-mission groups called the Primitive Baptists.

"It is true that this sect is called by many names. Its own ministers have not been able to agree on their name. ...Is it any marvel that outsiders find difficulty in naming those who have never been able to name themselves?"[1]

In 1898, an article appeared in the *Baptist Historical Paper*, "The Baptists in the Forks of the Yadkin," describing the feelings of the people at the time of the splits. Such descriptive feelings there seemed to picture what was taking place elsewhere as the splits occurred. "The anti-mission element was very bitter...and tried to hold on to the church," meaning the building and property.[2] Such an attitude was surely seen in the history of Abbotts Creek. The missionary element pleaded for harmony and peace. A deaf ear was turned.

The word "primitive" was never found in any of the church histories prior to 1825. In the Abbotts Creek Union meeting in 1879, we read, "the following item was adopted: The association agrees that the words Primitive Baptist be added to the third article of the act of Convention of 1825."[3] This was fifty-four years after the article had been adopted. The question has to be asked; why would one have to change names if there had been no change in doctrine or practice?

The title missionary is an honorable name added only to make the distinction between two practicing groups. However, it must be noted throughout all Baptist histories, the missionary Baptists were the ones actually following the practices that were in place before the split. At times, the majority of members from a particular church became anti-missions and retained the building while at other times the mission group was stronger and able to remain in the building. At Abbotts Creek, the minority was forced to leave the others. It appears in many churches, the Primitive element was in the minority. With this in mind, Henry Sheets asks, "Whoever heard before of a body of four fifths seceding from one fifth?"[4]

Endnotes

1. Sheets, Henry. *A History of Liberty Baptist Association* (Edward and Broughton Printing Company, 1907) 81.
2. Ibid., p. 175.
3. Ibid., p. 177, footnotes
4. Ibid., p. 179

CHAPTER TWO

The Beginning

The pioneer settlers and church people of the Abbotts Creek community faced untold hardships, which are left mostly unknown. More than two decades before the Constitution of the United States was signed and the Revolutionary War was fought with the Mother Country to carry out the intent of the signed document, Abbotts Creek was a budding community. The neighborhood was composed of people with Scotch-Irish, German, Welsh, English, and other descent.

> The people living now have little conception of the trials and hardships which the pioneers of our Baptist Zion had to undergo in planting the Banner of the Cross in sparsely settled districts, and where, too, in many instances they were rudely insulted, unmercifully beaten and jailed like common felons.[1]

Obviously, the Divine hand was guiding as we hear of the disadvantages and hardships under which the preaching of the gospel was first carried out. Success arose above the many obstacles. This would be nothing short of miraculous guidance. "Men of God went into the world, preaching under brush arbors, in private residences, and often in the open air."[2]

Just when the preaching first took place at Abbott's (Sheets' spelling) Creek may not be known. Sheets shares a belief that many individual Baptists had lived scattered across the country of whom no account has ever been given. He gives this further date for work nearby.

Membership Role of Abbotts Creek Baptist meetinghouse

1783
Pastor, George Pope
Abraham Teague
Samuel Spurgin
John Ledford
Thomas Green
Danniel Silliven
Moses Craner
Christopher Vicory
Isaac Teague
Cadvolender Jones
James West
John Swaim
Thomas Kook
Samuel Coart
William Swaim
James Helton
Isaiah Teague
Joseph Morey
James Welborn
J----- Wetherly
John Swaim
Mary Pope
Isabel Welborn
Sary Davis
Jane Mash
Eve Lowery
Elizabeth Morris
Ann Brown
Mary Helton
Lille Kook
Debran Stack
Sarah Bisinton
Elizabeth Strauhorn
Mary Buller
Mary Teague

----- Pope
Susannah Kimbro
Ruth Mash
Ann Grassum
Oliva Pope
Dillen Chaplin
Margaret Silliven
Sary Cranen
Hanar Green
Lary Harenton
Elizabeth Wetherton
Anne Swaim
Sary Spurgin
Mary Swaim
Rachel Moris
Hanah Moris
Ann Kook
Mary Williams
Margaret Chipman
Mary Parr
Elizabeth Robins
Elizabeth Jones
Mary Swaim
Anna Evens
Charity Watson
Elener Cartswell
Marthe S-------
Frana Richason
Rebecca Helton
Widow Gutrugs
Charity Swaim
Sister Easter
Negro Grace
(END 1783)

Names in minutes but not in membership roll:
Richard Grissom
Brother Younger

Dated Sat. 2-Nov.—1783
Sary Moris now Sary Grissom

Ann Fields
Sarah Cradleboh
Margaret Davis
Mary Green
Jeremy Shelle
Dorcus Rush
Brother Morgan
Mary Lusk
John Rich
Sarah Jones
William Barron
Frances Barron
Sary Spoolman
Jacob Idol
Mary Garson
Rachel Smith
John Roberson
Mary -------
Tomson Smith
Ann Right
Jason Teague
Tamer Lowe

All of the above were refered to as members.

The first organized Baptist work in North Carolina was in the Eastern part of the state. In the middle section, Shubal Stearns came to Sandy Creek in the latter part of 1755. Benjamin Miller was preaching at the Jersey Settlement a little earlier in the same year. He was followed by John Gano, who constituted the church there, probably in 1757.[3]

THE BEGINNING

In the same reference, Sheets added "And while these men were at work on their respective fields, James Younger was preaching at Abbott's Creek." It is regrettable that we know so little about a man to whom we are indebted so greatly. Sheets refers to him as a man, "under God, first began a work which has resulted in bringing that vast section of country almost wholly under Baptist influence."[4]

According to the *Rowan County Record of Deeds* (book 10, page 155), we learn that Younger bought eighty acres of land with one edge of the property being "some nine chains to the corner of the meetinghouse." This land was referred to as being "on the cool waters of Abbits Creek [sic]." We remember Abbotts Creek was still a part of Rowan County at this time.

With our limited information we have learned that eighteen years after Younger was influential in the start of the church and had helped to secure the first pastor, his name is mentioned again in the early minutes of the church. Just prior to February 1784, the church in conference appointed members to labor with Brother Younger and get him to the next church meeting, which was to be held in February. The minutes of that meeting note: "A church meeting opened in course at Abets Crick [sic] on the first Saturday in February, 1784. The church agreed to make a declaration against James Younger for breaking our constitutional order and receiving ordination without our consent and contrary to our fellowship." Just what is meant by this and what became of it, we are not told. We would like to know more about the person who made such a significant contribution to the religious life of our community.

From an unpublished notebook of Morgan Edwards, who spent several months gathering information from Baptist churches and groups in North Carolina in 1770, we have learned of written documents reminding us that Abbotts Creek was the first church organized from the Sandy Creek Church. The following was stated while speaking of the Sandy Creek Church:

> The word went forth from this sion [zion], and great was the company of them who published it, in so much that her converts were as the drops of the morning dew. The first church that sprang hence was Abbot's Creek, then Deep Creek, Little River....[5]

The Sandy Creek, (now Randolph County), Abbot's Creek (Davidson County, then Rowan), and Deep River (Chatham County) churches had reached a membership of over nine hundred within the first three years of their origin. There were several branches or arms of these churches reaching as far away as Brunswick County.

The above information is given again in George W. Paschal's book, pages 271-272, with the spelling Abbot's Creek.

The events leading to the constitution of Abbotts Creek Church cannot be overlooked in Baptist history. "The events that led to the constitution of this church are characteristic and reveal one of the most important causes of the rapidity with which Separate Baptist churches sprang up all over North Carolina."[6]

On the same page, Paschal shared the exact opinion as Sheets reminding us in many areas there were people who seemed to have been holding to Baptist principles and may have even belonged to some Baptist church elsewhere.

> We know that this was true of the church in question, that at Abbott's Creek; and of the church at Lockwood's Folly, of that at New River, and on the Neuse. Being without a minister, some pious man or woman yearning for salvation for himself and family and neighbors, after hearing of the work of grace at Sandy Creek would either come himself or send a messenger begging that a preacher be sent among them.[7]

James Younger was living and preaching in the Abbotts Creek community before the arrival of the Separate Baptists. He had come by way of the Welsh Neck settlement in South Carolina. Very little is known about him except he did have a family in the community including a daughter, Anna, who married James Evans. She died in 1843 at the age of ninety-seven and is buried in the Primitive Baptist Church cemetery. During her lifetime, she assisted many mothers in childbirth while serving as a midwife. Little is know of Mr. Younger after the establishment of the church.

Some helpful information was found in a book, *Welborns and Related Families in North and South Carolina*. In this book, published in 1994, we learn that James and Anna Nash Younger had two daughters, Rebecca (born April 1767), and Elizabeth (born March 1772). Rebecca married James Welborn, Jr. Elizabeth married Aaron Welborn. Aaron and Elizabeth seemed to have moved to Anderson, South Carolina, while James and Rebecca moved to Missouri. There are many Welborn families in the Abbotts Creek area of Davidson and Forsyth counties, and perhaps some of them may be linked to James and Anna Younger.

We have positive evidence of several families who do have that direct connection with the first preacher (not pastor) in the community. Martha Teague Smith has given us valuable information in regards to this. The Teague genealogy record lists James Evans, Sr., (born in 1745) as being a land owner near the headwaters of Abbotts Creek. He received a land grant in 1760 and bought more land as it became available. He married Ann Younger, daughter of James and Anna Younger. James, their son, the grandson of James and Anna Younger, married Ann (or Anna) Teague. James and Ann Evans' daughter, Martha, married Moses Teague. She was the great-granddaughter of James and Anna Younger. Evans had a son, Moses, a great-great-grandson of Mr. and Mrs. Younger. Moses and Martha's son was Abraham O. P. Teague, a great-great-great-grandson of the first preacher at Abbotts Creek, who was married to Jane Jones. Their child, Noah Richardson Teague, would have to call James and Anna Younger his great-great-great-great-grandparents. The son born to Noah and his wife, Victoria Swann Teague, was Thomas Carrick Teague. He would have to add another "great" to the name of James Younger as grandparents. Carrick Teague was married to Ethel whose children would add the fifth "great" dating back to the pioneer preacher at Abbotts Creek.

Noah Richardson Teague had four sisters. One sister, Eudora Bell Teague, married Jeffrey Traynham. Christian Jane Teague married Sanford Hayworth. Flora Augusta Teague married Charlie Davis. The other sister, Julia Eliza, married George Motsinger. Their only child died at birth. She was the step-mother to George's children.

Many descendants in the community still carry the name Teague, Davis, Hayworth, or Traynham. They can claim to be a part of the James and Anna Younger heritage.

James Younger seems to have had little education but was blessed with the rare ability for giving thorough and earnest exhortations with such a plea he enabled his neighbors to realize the claims of God upon their lives. It became very evident he was not an ordained minister at the time the church's first pastor was ordained. Upon the arrival of Daniel Marshall as pastor, Younger was not allowed to be the second ordained minister needed to assist in ordaining the pastor. The early historians refer to him as an Andrew, who was not able to preach as he wished but sought one more able than he. Younger urged the people to seek out a pastor who could be their spiritual leader. Having heard of the fame of the work at Sandy Creek, a group from the unorganized congregation, including Younger, went to the

Sandy Creek Baptist Church where Elder Shubal Stearns was preaching and a great spirit of revival prevailed.

Daniel Marshall, brother-in-law of Stearns, heard the pleading request and accepted the challenge to become pastor at Abbotts Creek. There are no minutes to document this, but it is believed that Stearns himself came and assisted in the work; certainly it was he who, as the only ordained minister of the area, baptized the new converts.

> At first in accordance with the plan of organizations that [was] followed by the Separate as well as the General and Particular Baptists, the group at Abbott's Creek became a branch of the parent church at Sandy Creek. But soon, probably as early as 1756, it was found desirable that Abbott's Creek be constituted as a distinct church.[8]

Paschal tells us more about the church's first pastor.

> Daniel Marshall, though not possessed of great talents, was indefatigable in his labors. He sallied [sic] out into the adjacent neighborhoods, and planted the Redeemer's standard in many of the strongholds of Satan. At Abbot's Creek, about thirty miles from Sandy Creek, the gospel prospered so largely, that they petitioned the Mother church for a constitution, and for the ordination of Mr. Marshall as their pastor. The church was constituted: Mr. Marshall accepted the call and went to live among them.[9]

The request for ordination became a problem. However, from this problem, we learn more than we might have known otherwise. For ordination to take place, "It required, upon their principles, a plurality of elders to constitute a presbytery."[10]

The Sandy Creek pastor could not do this alone but found himself as the only ordained minister in the area. Learning of some Regular Baptist preachers living along the Pee Dee River in South Carolina, he requested their assistances for ordination of Marshall, the new pastor at Abbotts Creek.

The minister Stearns had contacted sternly denied such a request. He refused to have fellowship with Stearns' party in that "he believed them to be a disorderly sect; suffering women to pray in public; and permitting every ignorant man to preach that chose; and that they encouraged noise and confusion in their meetings."[11] Not to be outdone, Stearns turned to a Rev. Henry Ledbetter asking and securing help for the ordination. Ledbetter, a brother-in-law of Marshall, was a pastor serving in Lynch's Creek, Craven County, South Carolina. The two ordained Marshall to care for the new church.

Having to seek assistance for this ordination in South Carolina helps fix the date of the organization of the church.

> It must have been while the church at Jersey settlement was yet without a pastor, that is, before Rev. John Gano had taken up his work there, which was not later than 1757. If Gano had been there when Stearns was seeking ministerial help for the ordination of Marshall he would doubtless have turned to him, and in all probability would not have been rebuffed, for Gano was only too ready to court Baptists of other names. ...Accordingly, it seems certain that the Abbott's Creek church had already been constituted and secured a pastor on the arrival of Gano at the Jersey [sic] settlement in 1757.[12]

The earliest Baptist churches, in what is now Davidson County, were Jersey, listed as Regular Baptists, and Abbotts Creek, called Separate Baptists. They were similar to other Baptist churches moving toward the South during that same period of time. Both Separate and Regular Baptists had good strong dedicated men leading in the establishment of churches. Sheets tells us, "They were true Baptists, but out of harmony as to the best methods of conducting revival work."[13]

Earliest records of the churches make no mention of the two with any correspondence between them. Though Jersey existed when Daniel Marshall was ordained at Abbotts Creek as pastor, no mention is made of Shubal Stearns contacting the pastor there for help with his ordination. Though the distance between the two churches is about twenty-five miles, "They chose to leave each other severely alone without any formal recognition, and evidently for no other reason than Jersey was Regular and Abbotts Creek was Separate."[14]

In consideration of this, we are able to see Baptists as Baptists in the New World who came from England. Even the English Baptists had two names, Particular and General, and maybe for no solid reason. "The Particulars received their name from the fact that they were Calvinistic in their views of theology, claiming that the atonement of Christ was particular in its application to God's elect."[15]

> On the other hand, the General Baptists were Arminian [sic] in their view of the doctrines of grace. And, notwithstanding this, the General Baptists were much more numerous and influential than the Particulars. But in the course of time these distinctions gave way in large measure; for the Particulars had to a great extent absorbed the General Baptists, and all were known as Baptists.[16]

Separate Baptists came from the New England Congregationalism except in Rhode Island. Baptists paid heavily for their beliefs. One writer even says this lasted for 175 years. Some were whipped, required to pay a fine, or banished while others were placed in prison.

> In Congregationalism, the believer was required to tell of his or her "experience of grace." Later one could list this in writing rather than verbally. After some period of time, such requirements were dropped and "all forms of giving an experience of grace was abandoned."[17]

> Thus the spirituality of the membership composing the churches was at such a low ebb that church life was almost extinguished. And it was believed that a majority of their preachers were strangers to the power of saving grace. This seems to have been the real condition of church life about and this low spiritual condition of the churches prevailed amongst Baptist to a large extent as well as amongst others.[18]

In 1740, George Whitfield came from England with an unheard-of evangelistic spirit. For two months, he preached with a great revival spirit moving over the area.

> Multitudes of church members, as well as many preachers, professed conversion under the soul-stirring sermons of Mr. Whitfield. The churches were beginning to feel the throb of new life. But a majority of the church members and preachers opposed this great work. But, while this was so, there were some of the

> preachers of the State churches, and among them the talented and pious Jonathan Edwards, who did all in their power to promote it, believing it to be a work of divine grace.[19]
>
> The government gave strong opposition. "Men and women were fined and imprisoned for the crime of favoring and otherwise encouraging revival measures."[20]
>
> Being thus persecuted, and believing that the great work was of the Lord, they separated from the old churches and former pastors and set up churches for themselves. These were called "Separates" because they had separated from the established churches. The old organizations were called Regular because they were established by law. In this manner the term Regular and Separate first came to be applied to the churches.[21]

Separates took this name about 1744 and although persecution increased rapidly, the preachers continued to preach with great zeal and intense earnestness. Crowds were coming and did not let distances hinder them. They were hearing messages declaring that each person must feel conviction and "experience a sense of relief from the burden of sin, through faith in Christ, which resulted in joy for those experiencing such faith."[22]

Such a movement in North Carolina cannot be discussed without the names of Shubal Stearns and Daniel Marshall. Stearns became convicted that infant baptism was an act of "futility." Elder Wait Palmer immersed him in May of 1751. Marshall was being converted to Baptist views to the extent that he refused to have his infant son baptized which led to his departure and separation from his old church even though he had served as a deacon for twenty years.

> While this was taking place, "Regulars were performing a task which by no means can be overlooked. They stood firmly by the doctrines of grace, ever precious to God's dear children, and preserved them pure as given and accepted everywhere in all our confessions of Faith."[23]

After years of bitterness between the Regulars and Separates, their differences began to be of less significance and were eventually dropped. About 1787, there was a spirit of reconciliation and both groups accepted each other in love. By 1810, A. B. Semple in his history of Virginia Baptists stated, "This union has now continued upwards of 22 years without any interruption. The bands of union are apparently much stronger than at first."[24]

A religious awakening in religion was sweeping Europe in the early 17th century. This was especially true in Great Britain and the Protestant churches throughout Europe. The movement spread to America with its earliest manifestations in the Middle Colonies involving the Presbyterian and Reformed congregations. Without much delay, it moved to the New England states in the established Congregational churches.

> "As the first general revival of religion in America, the Awakening profoundly affected the life of the colonies, introducing a new religious earnestness, purifying and elevating moral and ethical standards, and contributing markedly to the nonconformist character of American religion and idealism."[25]

Some twenty years later, the Awakening reached the colonies in the South. Such a movement was of no concern to the Baptists already in the South and had been prior to 1755. They were called "regular" Baptists.

> It was, rather, the work of a handful of rugged, single-minded, enthusiastic colonists from Connecticut who, for their 'irregularity' were known as 'Separate' Baptists. These settled at Sandy Creek in central North Carolina in 1755 and immediately introduced the phenomenon of revival to the southern frontier.[26]

Prior to this time, Baptists in the South were very insignificant for the most part and were seen as a despised "sect." Within twenty years, Separate Baptists had planted themselves as a rapidly growing population. Baptist historian William A. Lumpkin tells us, "They were destined in the providence of God to serve as chief instruments for planting the Christian faith along the southern frontier of early America."[27] This gives us some background and understanding of the religious influences on the lives of both Shubal Stearns and Daniel Marshall. Stearns and Marshall, the first pastors of Abbotts Creek, were influential in bringing revival to the South.

Daniel Marshall was born in Windsor, Connecticut in 1706. He was reared by pious parents and at the age of twenty, experienced conversion that was described as "profound." As a young man he was elected as deacon

The Beginning

in the First Congregational Church of Windsor and served in this capacity for about twenty years. He became a prosperous farmer during these years and married Hannah Drake on November 11, 1742. Hannah died shortly after giving birth to their first and only son. It appeared Marshall was beginning to accept the views held by Separate Baptists. His refusal to allow their infant son to be christened was evidence of this. At this time, Daniel had not been baptized. This had made him "odious" to the church. Odious means "causing or deserving hatred or repugnance." Lumpkin gives us this sad account.

> After he had served as deacon for twenty years, the church found opportunity to retaliate when Marshall's wife died. As the people assembled "to witness the funeral ceremony the pastor of the church refused to perform the usual service, upon which the people dispersed leaving the rev. widower to bury his deceased spouse himself." This cruelty would have made Marshall a confirmed Separate at least, making his final break with the old church.[28]

On June 23, 1747, Marshall married Martha Stearns, sister of Shubal. He seemed to have been holding and preaching Baptist doctrines by conviction. His becoming a Baptist may have been hurried along by his marriage to Martha. At this early-unknown date (about 1750), Marshall's sister, Eunice, who had taken upon "herself to exhort and preach Baptist doctrines; was ordered to desist, but not obeying, was (although pregnant at the time), thrown into jail."[29]

Both Marshall and Stearns were leading dissenting groups from among the Congregational church. This created a very hostile atmosphere for them. They were facing criticism and were being ostracized for their strong convictions. This failed to deter them from preaching the gospel.

Marshall and his wife were two of the sixteen members when the Sandy Creek Church was constituted. The following sketch of his life is taken from a biographical notice prepared by his son, Elder Abraham Marshall:

> He was born in 1706, in Windsor, in Connecticut. He was religiously educated, by respectable and pious parents, and being hopefully converted at twenty years of age, joined the Presbyterians in his native place. He was for eighteen months a missionary among the Mohawk Indians, and labored with much

success, which position he had to abandon on account of war among the savage tribes. He lived a while at Connogogig, in Pennsylvania, and thence he moved to Winchester, Virginia. Here he became acquainted with Baptists, and after an impartial examination of their faith and order, he and his wife were immersed, in the forty-eighth year of his life. He moved from Virginia to North Carolina, and settled for awhile on Uwhary; he afterward moved to Abbott's Creek church. He was ordained pastor of this church in the fifty-second year of his age, by Elders Henry Ledbetter and Shubal Stearns.[30]

History indicates the leaders of Sandy Creek had some type of missionary strategy that remained a secret, "but a careful plan for overspreading the entire surrounding country with gospel preaching evidently was set in motion."[31]

Marshall's direction initially seemed to have been northward. Historian Lumpkin quotes a Moravian as saying "the Baptists are the only ones in the country who go far and wide preaching and caring for souls."[32] Marshall was described as not having great talent but was "indefatigable in his labors."

While serving as pastor at Abbotts Creek, Marshall was untiring in his efforts elsewhere. He would preach at any gathering. While preaching at a location in Virginia, he baptized several people including James Read. Though without education, Mister Read soon began to preach, which led to great things in Virginia. Marshall led a revival and baptized forty-two persons at one time. This led to the first Separate Baptist church in Virginia and is described as the mother church for many other churches. Both Marshall and Stearns later revisited some of the thriving congregations.

The Abbotts Creek's pastor was invited to the Grassy Creek section (near Oxford) of North Carolina. Lumpkin gives us a view of his preaching mannerism.

> A tireless emissary, he did not hesitate to use extraordinary methods to gather a crowd. He would preach at a muster, a sale, a wedding, or a barn raising. Conversions, and entire communities stirred by his preaching almost always followed. The Grassy Creek Church was revived and began to grow rapidly. People were attracted to the church from distances of fifty miles or more; some were residences of Virginia.[33]

The pastor from Abbotts Creek was constantly preaching in distant places. In addition to Grassy Creek, he preached at numerous places across the state line in Southern Virginia. He along with Stearns and a third ordained minister, Philip Mulkey, traveled and preached in the eastern part of North Carolina. Mulkey and a group moved to the Broad River section of South Carolina in 1762. Historians give us the nearest accurate dates as possible but Lumpkin shows Mulkey going to South Carolina in 1762, saying Marshall followed him later and then gave the date as 1760.

> Within a year after Philip Mulkey went to South Carolina, Daniel Marshall and a good portion of his Abbott's Creek membership moved to the same state. Marshall left Abbott's Creek not only because he felt circumscribed by the Sandy Creek Church and the Moravians at Wachovia but also because of unsettled political conditions.[34]

Mention is made of "unsettled" political conditions, but the fear of Indians was being felt more and more at this time. As white settlers continued to move in, the Indians were threatened to lose their hunting grounds. Such grounds needed to be protected from their standpoint. Just how much this affected the population in the Abbotts Creek community is not clear, but we do know people were moving on to what they considered safer areas. More serious situations occurred west of the Yadkin River. The Moravians have this recorded in Volume One on page 230 of *Records of the Moravians in North Carolina*. "In March of that year (1760) Elder John Thomas of Toisnot Baptist Church (in the present Wilson County) while on his way from Bethabara to Abbott's Creek was killed by the Cherokee Indians who a few days before had reached the Yadkin." It is known that some churches had to reorganize after the Cherokee War of 1759–1761. It was about this time John Gano left the Jersey Settlement and Daniel Marshall left the Abbotts Creek congregation going to South Carolina.

It appears Marshall moved on to his new work in South Carolina before the end of 1760. Then in 1772 his company moved on to Stevens Creek, where they built a meetinghouse ten miles from Augusta, Georgia. Marshall continued to itinerate, establishing churches on Beaver Creek, and across the provincial line in Georgia. Stevens Creek was constituted in 1766, by Marshall, who by that time had gathered and inspired a promising group of young preachers, including his son Abraham, Benjamin Harry, Saunders Walker, and John Herndon. The elder Marshall, Harry, and Walker were very active itinerants.

Immigrants from Virginia and North Carolina were moving into the back country of South Carolina. Marshall and his Separate Baptist fellow pastors were waiting for their arrival, and more churches were springing up.

> Their churches extended to within a hundred miles of Charleston.... By 1772, the Separates claimed fully half of the Baptist membership of the province, although the Regulars had been there nearly a century ahead of them. Within twenty more years the Separates were to be far in the lead.[35]

The first mention of Marshall going into Georgia was not well received. The Lieutenant Governor gave a charge or challenge to the Anglican minister in Augusta. The words of the governmental official were: " Preach in New Windsor, hoping 'it will effectively put a stop to the progress of those Baptist vagrants, who continually endeavor to subvert all order, and make the minds of the people Giddy, with that which neither they nor their teachers understand.'"[36]

Marshall was still making his home in South Carolina. While preaching in Georgia, he was arrested and convicted and ordered to cease preaching in the state of Georgia. Such an order did not silence the minister. It seemed to have fueled his intent.

> Not only did he continue but also his wife asserted that the authorities were interfering with the preaching of the gospel, quoting Scripture to sustain her view. A young man named Cartledge was convicted by her words and became a minister. Also the arresting constable and even the magistrate who had tried Marshall were soon converted and baptized.[37]

Such success was experienced and the possibilities so great, Marshall moved from his South Carolina home to Kiokee Creek in Georgia, 1771. "There he formed the first Baptist Church in Georgia at Appling in 1772."[37] Twelve years prior to this, nine of the first sixteen members of Sandy Creek Church had moved south to live. By the time the first church was formed in Georgia, all nine were residing within the state.

Abraham Marshall tells us his father was a "friend" of the American cause during the revolutionary war and was placed in prison under heavy guard:

> ...but obtaining leave of the officers, he commenced and supported so heavy a charge of exhortation and prayer, that, like Daniel of old, while his enemies stood amazed and confounded, he was safely and honorably delivered from this den of lions.[38]

Paschal, an outstanding church historian, tells us that Marshall and his family spent the rest of their lives living in Kiokee. He did not leave the area, as did most of the other ministers as the British approached. Neither the army nor other difficulties caused him to retreat.

Author Loulie L. Owens gives information concerning Marshall in South Carolina. In her book, she is dealing with the growth of Separate Baptists in that state and not where Marshall was before settling there. She has Marshall leaving Sandy Creek and going to Beaver Creek near the present-day Winnsboro. In speaking of the growing numbers of believers, Owens says, "Almost as fast as the settlers erected their cabins, they joined the Separate churches."[39] On a page later she noted, "Marshall moved on across the Savannah River and became the father of Georgia Baptists." With Marshall and Phillip Mulkey (whom Owens mentions first at Broad River), we read of the lasting contributions of Separate Baptists, "They were the first American religious movement to affect South Carolina Baptist life."[40]

In this work, we will quote often from Elder George Purefoy whose book, *A History of Sandy Creek Association*, was published in 1858. He has preserved the rest of the dying testimony written by Marshall's son, Abraham.

> After a life of extended labor and usefulness, he, at a good old age (78 years), fell asleep in Jesus. His last words (as taken down at the time) were as follows: 'Dear brethren and sisters, I am just gone; this night I shall probably expire; but I have nothing to fear; I have fought the good fight; I have finished my course; I have kept the faith; and henceforth there is laid up for me a crown of righteousness. God has shown me that he is my God; that I am his son; and that an eternal weight of glory is mine!' He then said to his dear wife and faithful assistant in all his labors, who was sitting by his side, bedewed with tears: 'Go on my dear wife to serve the Lord. Hold out to the end. Eternal glory is before us.' After a silence of some minutes he called his son, and said, 'My breath is almost gone. I have been praying that I may go home tonight. I had great happiness in our worship this morning, particularly in singing, which will make a

> part of my exercise, in a blessed eternity.' He then closed his eyes in death, at the dawn of the 2nd day of November, 1784. His funeral was preached from the above named text ("I have finished my Course,"&, c), by Elder Charles Buffey.
> Tho' no proud pile, learned pen, nor lettered stone
> His virtues rare to late posterity reveals
> He'll ever shine, and waxingly has shone,
> Through rolling years, in ministerial seals.[41]

Though we have mentioned his death, we need to pick up some additional aspects of his life. After the birth of Daniel Marshall's son and the death of his wife, he later married Martha Stearns. Seven sons and two daughters were born to them. The sons were Abraham, John, Zaccheus, Levi, Moses, Solomon and Joseph. The daughters were Eunice and Mary.

Mrs. Marshall was a great asset to her husband's ministry. In fact, it seems obvious it was a team effort. Historians remind us of the valuable involvement of women in the aggressive movement of Separate Baptists. Martha Marshall was a leader among the women. We have already called attention to the time she quoted the scriptures showing the governmental officials they were interfering with the preaching of the gospel when they arrested her husband near New Windsor, Georgia. This was prior to any mention of freedom of religion in the colonies. A young man was converted while hearing her exhortations and later became a minister of the gospel.

Paschal reports how great crowds gathered to hear Stearns and Marshall preach in both North Carolina and Virginia as well as in Georgia. The manner, gestures, tone of their voices and the excitement with which they spoke had never been heard before. People came from miles. Some came to make fun, some for curiosity, while others came for serious purposes.

> They trembled; they cried aloud for mercy, they found their strength too frail and fell upon the ground in collapse. A spirit like that of Pentecost was among the Christians. It seems that nearly every member of the little church, men and women, preached or exhorted or prayed. Daniel Marshall and Joseph Breed, although not ordained as pastors of Baptist churches, were already preachers, Mr. Marshall having spent several years as a Presbyterian missionary among the Indians. Marshall's wife, Martha Stearns, a sister of Shubal, was hardly less powerful in these meetings than her famous brother. Of her we are told that,

> "without the shadow of an usurped authority over the other sex, Mrs. Marshall, being a lady of good sense, singular piety, and surprising elocution, has, in countless instances melted a whole concourse into tears by her prayers and exhortations."[42]

When Younger traveled to Sandy Creek bent on bringing a pastor of his Abbotts Creek community, he found Marshall. Historians tell us he was the Andrew-type follower of Jesus. He sought and brought one more able to preach the gospel than he was.

> On his return, he brought with him that indefatigable missionary pioneer, Daniel Marshall. As a result of the labors of this earnest and fervent evangelist, in which he doubtless had the assistance of his saintly and gifted wife, Mrs. Martha Stearns Marshall, great numbers turned to the Lord.[43]

A more recent work places great value on the ministry of women in planting churches as the religious fervor continued to move south.

> Planting churches was but one area in which early Baptist women in America served; some also preached and served as exhorters in worship services. Many of these women belonged to Separate Baptist churches, which originated during the First Great awakening of the 1730s and 1740s and were known for their evangelistic preaching, boisterous worship services, and emotional conversion experiences. The most prominent Separate Baptist woman was Martha Stearns Marshall, who often prayed and preached during worship services. Although her leadership in worship scandalized many Virginia Baptists, Martha's husband and pastor, Daniel, considered her preaching to be a perfectly acceptable way for her to exercise her spiritual gifts. The early Virginia Baptist historian Robert Semple claimed that Daniel's successful ministry in Virginia and North Carolina was largely due to Martha's "unwearied and zealous co-operation."[44]

When Marshall was to be ordained as pastor of the Abbotts Creek church, two other ministers had to be involved. Mention has been made earlier of the necessary steps Stearns had to take to carry out the ordination of his brother-in-law.

Much has been said about Martha Stearns Marshall, wife of the first pastor at Abbotts Creek. The Baptist Women in Ministry declared February 4, 2007, as the First Annual Martha Stearns Marshall Day of Preaching Celebrating Women Preaching. In making this announcement about such a beginning, we read from the publicity informational sheet:

> Martha Stearns Marshall was an eighteen-century Separate Baptist preacher. She often stood alongside her brother Shubal Stearns and spoke at Baptist meetings. She also assisted her husband Daniel Marshall in his churches and preached to his congregations. In 1810, Virginia Baptist historian Robert Semple" wrote of Martha's contributions to Baptist work: "Mr. Marshall had a rare felicity of finding in this lady, a Priscilla, a helper in the gospel. In fact, it should not be concealed that his extraordinary success in the ministry is ascribable in no small degree to Mrs. Marshall's unwearied and zealous co-operation. Without the shadow of a usurped authority over the other sex, Mrs. Marshall, being a lady of good sense, singular piety, and surprising elocution, has, in countless instances melted a whole concourse into tears by her prayers and exhortation!"

"In the late 1750s, the Marshalls founded a Separate Baptist Church at Abbott's Creek in North Carolina. There Martha served alongside her husband and 'was noted for her zeal and eloquence,' and her preaching 'added greatly to the interest of meetings conducted by her husband.'"

Endnotes
1. Sheets, Henry, *A History of Liberty Baptist Association* (Edward and Broughton Printing Company, 1907), 81.
2. Ibid.
3. Ibid.
4. Ibid., 82.
5. George W. Paschal, *History of North Carolina Baptists*, Vol. 1. (Edwards and Broughton, 1930), 227.
6. Ibid., 290.
7. Ibid.
8. Ibid., 291.
9. Ibid., 275.
10. Ibid.

11. Ibid.
12. Ibid., 292
13. Sheets, 145.
14. Ibid.
15. Ibid., 146.
16. Ibid., 146.
17. Ibid., 147.
18. Ibid.
19. Ibid., 147.
20. Ibid., 147-48.
21. Ibid., 148.
22. Ibid.
23. Ibid., 150.
24. Ibid.
25. William L. Lumpkin, *Baptist Foundations in the South* (Nashville: Broadman Press, 1961), p.v.
26. Ibid., v-vi.
27. Ibid., vii.
28. Ibid., 22.
29. Ibid., 23.
30. Purefoy., 294.
31. Lumpkin, op. cit., 47.
32. Ibid.
33. Ibid., 47-48.
34. Ibid.
35. Ibid., 54.
36. Ibid., 55.
37. Ibid.
38. Purefoy, op. cit, 296.
39. Loulie Latimer Owens, *Saints of Clay, The Shaping of South Carolina Baptist* (Columbia, SC, The R.L. Bryan Company, 1971), 42.
40. Ibid., 44.
41. Purefoy, op. cit., 296.
42 Paschal, op. cit., 289.
43. Ibid., 291.
44. Pamela and Keith E. Durso, (eds.) *Courage and Hope, The Stories of Ten Baptist Women Ministers (*Macon, Georgia: Mercer University Press, and Brentwood, TN: Baptist history and Heritage Society, 2005), 6.

CHAPTER THREE

Differences between the Missionary and Anti-Missionary Groups

Elder Ashley Swaim was pastor at Abbotts Creek when the church divided. Elder Swaim had major differences of opinion with Samuel Wait. Elder Wait was greatly involved in the issues that divided the missionary and anti-missionary groups, including Abbotts Creek. Samuel Wait was born in 1789, in White Creek, New York. He grew up in Granville in that state and later moved to Middletown, Vermont. His grandfather was a minister but his parents were not "professors of religion." Samuel was baptized on March 12, 1809. Thirty years later, he baptized his parents into the fellowship of the same church. Upon feeling the call for ministry, he began to prepare by studying Greek and Hebrew at Salem Academy in Washington County, Vermont. He was licensed to preach by the Baptist Church in Middletown and in 1816 accepted the call to be pastor at the Baptist church in Sharon, Massachusetts. Two years later, June 3, 1818, he was ordained by the same church. While serving there, he met Sarah (Sally) Merriam of Brandon, Vermont. They were married two weeks after his ordination.

In correspondence with a cousin, he wrote, "I have great work to perform and I am anxious to begin it. It is an arduous and tiresome work to get ready, but I dare not begin until I feel some strength to meet the infidel on his own ground, and this strength at this day must be derived from study." This was the driving force that sent him to enroll in the Theological Institute of the Baptist General Convention to study with Dr. William

Stoughton. His wife Sally waited back in New England and ran a millinery to support her and to send money to Samuel for his support and education.

In 1821, Dr. Stoughton became president of Columbian College, which is now George Washington University. Wait followed his teacher to his new work. Wait was employed as a tutor and by the winter of 1822, Sally was able to join her husband. It was the first time they had seen each other in over two years. The Columbian College did not award degrees but Waterville College (now Colby College) awarded degrees to students who were attending schools still awaiting accreditation. Wait did receive an honorary degree from Columbian College in 1834.

The needs for funds to support the college were great. The trustees sent the president and Samuel Wait south to try to raise funds to keep the school open. While on this journey, a freak accident occurred that had at least some part in Wait staying in North Carolina. The horse pulling the wagon was spooked and caused the wagon to wreck. While it was being repaired, Thomas Meredith, another of Stoughton's students, sent a letter of introduction for Wait to the First Baptist Church in New Bern. He was invited to preach and was so popular with the congregation he was asked to serve as minister. He wrote his wife explaining their need to be here by saying, "To tell the whole truth, I do not know of a more important opening. The state of the ministry all around in that region is deplorable."

He was one of only five educated ministers in North Carolina, in 1827. These men were in anguish over the lack of education for ministers. They could see North Carolina was losing the brighter young men as they observed a flight to other states in search for education. "The general indifference and conflicting beliefs among many North Carolina Baptists only hardened the resolve of these five ministers, and in March of 1830 at the Anniversary of the Benevolent Society in Greenville, the North Carolina Baptist State Convention was formed."

After some time, Wait began to be disappointed in that the church at New Bern did not give him enough to support himself. This, plus he was not getting to preach in the surrounding areas as he had anticipated, caused him to resign with the intent of going back to New England. Before he left, "he attended the meeting in Greenville and was appointed General Agent of the Baptist State Convention."

While he was traveling and preaching on behalf of the newly-formed convention, Sally received word that her only sister was seriously ill back in Vermont. Even though she had recently given birth to their second son, William Cary Wait, she went to care for her ailing sister. Shortly after the sister's death, William Cary contracted a fever and died suddenly on January 1, 1831. Samuel did not learn of his son's death until April. He wrote asking his wife to return to North Carolina. For the next three years, he traveled by wagon all over North Carolina trying to raise funds for the Convention, whose intent was to establish a school to train young ministers.

Some land was purchased in Wake County and in 1834, seventy students enrolled in Wake Forest Manual Labor Institute. Even after being elected as the first president, he worked in the fields beside the students teaching them "industrious habits." This later became Wake Forest College and Wait was selected to be the first president of the college.

The desire to organize the churches into a single organization with the stated goal "intellectual improvement" did not happen.

> There were differences among and within the churches regarding the Convention's goals, the education of ministers, compensation for pastoral service, and the Tract and Missionary Societies. The Kehukee Baptist Association first raised their objections in 1826 and in 1827 issued the order to 'discard all Missionary Societies, Bible Societies and Theological Seminaries, and the practices heretofore resorted to for their support, in begging money from public. ...'"
>
> "The disagreement over the Baptist State Convention literally tore churches in two. ...Many of the issues that divided Baptists in North Carolina over the establishment of the Convention appear in an episode from the records of Abbot's Creek Primitive Baptist Church and Abbot's Creek Missionary Baptist Church, both in Davidson County, North Carolina.[1]

With Wait serving as General Agent for the Baptist State Convention,

> Wait visited Abbot's Creek Baptist Church of Christ in 1832. The controversy surrounding Wait's visit and events following it eventually caused the church to split into the two separate churches.[2]

There were other issues at stake during the 1830–1835 years.

> There was much opposition in this section to the system of Home and Foreign Missions, which was being practiced in Yadkin and the adjoining associations, to which the term 'Missionary System' is applied. The churches were so much opposed to the 'new system' they refused, not only to send contributions for Missionary purposes, but also refused to sit in conference with, or to fellowship those who did."3

> They were not opposed to the spread of the gospel. It seems they strongly supported such an effort. "But their objection was that, if a compensation in dollars and cents is offered, and he who goes is sure of such compensation, there is not only danger, but great danger of men, who are not only not called of God to preach, but designing men who know nothing of the grace of God, going out under the title of Missionaries, and preaching such doctrine as would burden his people.

> The system of High Schools or Colleges for the preparation of young men for the ministry was also objected to strongly, on the grounds that many might take the advantage of such opportunities, not for the truth's sake, but to benefit themselves.4

This was taken to such an extreme that many of the churches left off helping their own pastor.

> And some of the members came to the belief that it was wrong to give to a preacher who was worth more than the giver, no matter what his sacrifices might be. Thus the ministers, few in number, and all poor men, had a hard struggle to serve their churches. The supporting scripture for this as they interpreted it was found in First Timothy chapter five and verse eight 'But if any provide not for his own, and especially for those of his own house, he hath denied the faith, and is worse than an infidel.'"5
> "They claimed that God was not dependent on any conditions, means, circumstances, or environments for the preaching of the word; that if his work demanded an educated man he could call one, as he did Saul (Paul) of Tarsus; or if it demanded ignorant and unlearned men he could call them, as in the case of Peter and John; that he was not dependent on Schools of Learning to tame

the hearts of sinful men and women, but that he writes his laws in the hearts of men of his own will and pleasure.[6]

To note the anti-mission group was opposed to eduction for ministers clearly shows a change in what had been in Baptist life. Henry Sheets says on page 191: "long before the split, Baptists favored ministerial education." The new position was justified by saying people who are in danger of dying don't have time for ministers to get years of education before preaching for such souls.

As far back as 1250, in England, schools existed for training ministers and were supported by contributions from the churches. For a period of time in the middle of the 17th century when such schools were not available, some ministers privately instructed the young would-be pastors. One hundred and ten years before the split in Baptist churches in the Philadelphia Association, young men were sought out and recommended for ministerial training. In 1756–1757, the same association went on record urging churches to give generously toward a Baptist college to be built in Rhode Island. It was built over the next few years. Yet one of the strong arguments supported by the anti-mission group was in the negative toward training for ministers.[7]

Another strongly expressed difference between the two groups concerned not so much the compensation for ministers but the manner in which it was carried out. The anti-mission group referred to ministers who were paid as hirelings. "With them there must be no agreement as to what the pastor must have for his support."[8] Sheets is using the view of Elder John M. Watson without defining his own position. Watson adds, "It is strange that this should be so in regard to pastoral support and not practiced in any other calling in life."[9]

A reader can almost feel the ire of Watson when he uses the illustration of a carpenter of the anti-mission group. Would a carpenter among the anti-mission group agree to build a house and be paid like he felt the minister ought to be paid? He continues by saying if ministers agreed on what wages they would be given for his ministerial services, they would at once be "branded as 'money hunters' or preaching for 'filthy lucre.'"[10]

It seems the opponents of an understanding between the church and the minister are willing to ignore Paul's statements such as "The workman is worthy of his meat" or "the laborer is worthy of his hire." Watson translates Paul's words in this manner. "Have I committed an offense in abasing myself that ye might be exalted, because I preached unto you the

DIFFERENCES BETWEEN THE MISSIONARY AND ANTI-MISSIONARY GROUPS

Gospel of God freely? I robbed other churches, taking wages of them, to do you service."[11] The intent here is not to justify adequate pay for ministers but to show the reasons behind the opposition. Watson goes so far as to place blame on all ministers for not dealing with the scriptural teachings about this in honesty to the congregations.

Getting back to the anti-missions position, he states,

> It seems that 'wages, reward and hire' are not contrary to the genius of New Testament teachings on this subject, but fully in accord with it. The trouble with our 'Anti' brethren is that they have made a hobby of this, while they are receiving money in handshaking and on the sly generally. If a church or churches ought to support a pastor, there can be nothing wrong in understanding what would be sufficient to support him.[12]

In citing this, it brings to the writer's memory something that had taken place at Abbotts Creek while I was pastor. Paul and Jane Morris attended our church while visiting their daughter's family several times before joining the church. On a few occasions, Jane would shake my hand and leave a ten or twenty dollar bill laughing as she said, "I am being Primitive Baptist today."

Leaving that topic, we look at some opposition to Sunday Schools. From the time of the Exodus of the children of Israel, God's people have been commanded to obey the instructions He had given. The book of Deuteronomy specifically states, "These commandments that I give you today are to be upon your hearts. Impress them on your children." How any religious group could express opposition to such a clear Biblical statement of teaching is difficult to understand. Henry Sheets describes it this way.

> There have been many foolish and unwise things said about this great work by our Anti-mission brethren. They have treated the Sunday School and its work as though it were an engine of the devil. But such a thing as abuse of this institution was unknown till our brethren split off and set up opposition to this work.[13]

On the same page a footnote is included of a conversation between Sheets and Deacon John Teague of Abbotts Creek. Of Teague, Sheets says:

> In his old age he told the author that he was born August 18, 1815; and was therefore about seventeen years old when the split took place in the old church. He said that he attended Sunday School at Abbott's Creek regularly before the split there. He recollected well that the large meetinghouse would sometimes be nearly full of Sunday School scholars. About the time of the division in the church the people were gathering for school as usual on the Sabbath. Someone who knew remarked 'you need not go to school today, the doors are nailed up and you can not get in'. All of which was found to be true. That ended the Sunday School work in that house."[14]

In an associational session in 1821, a circular letter was adopted giving strong commendations for Sunday School work. The letter stated:

> Let there be stated periods which we will devote wholly to their instruction. And those of you, brethren who can afford no other time, we advise to teach them (the children) before and after the ordinary exercises of public worship (preaching). It is lawful to do good on the Sabbath day. Then take them to the house of God with you and you will lessen one of the crying sins of the land, Sabbath breaking. They may be taught also in Sunday Schools, an institution which has been blessed of God to the salvation of many souls, both of children and parents— we earnestly solicit your attention to these schools, and beg you to establish one in every neighborhood.[15]

With the above evidences, how can one suddenly be opposed to Sunday Schools and still claim to be true to their heritage or practices? In this history, while trying to be honest to the anti-mission position, the writer has searched with diligence trying to find a stated cause for such opposition. This search has been in vain.

Endnotes

1. Notes from Samuel and Sara Wait Collection, Z. Smith Reynolds Library at Wake Forest University.
2. Ibid.
3. Ibid.
4. Ibid.
5. Ibid.

6. Ibid.
7. Sheets, 193
8. Ibid., 194
9. Ibid.
10. Ibid.
11. Ibid.
12. Ibid., 195
13. Ibid., 197
14. Ibid., 197
15. Ibid., 198

CHAPTER FOUR

The Division

The years preceding the division between the missionary and the anti-missionary groups in the church must have been trying and frustrating for both groups. About fifteen years before the division, in spite of the bitter feelings of the anti-missionary group, the church delivered this decision as recorded by Sheets.

> The church took into consideration the glory redounding to God to join in union with our sister churches that have joined the Missionary Band of Mission in America; to send the gospel to the heathen in America and elsewhere, and for our Trustee to receive voluntary contributions in the church; and without the church we appoint our deacon, William Raper, to receive what money may be put in his hands for that purpose, and correspond with such missionary as is and may be appointed from the Sandy Creek Association.[1]

Elder George Pope, having served as pastor for thirty-one years, left the church in 1813, going to South Carolina. It seems the church was without a pastor until March of 1819, when Elder Ashley Swaim was chosen and remained as pastor until the division in 1832. He continued to pastor the anti-mission group afterwards. It was reported his feelings and attitude bearing toward the brethren was not "of a kind to beget love and confidence."[2] Brethren seems to imply those who leaned toward being missionary in spirit and practice. His bitterness was strong toward those who had the courage to differ with his persuasion in regard to this. His feelings and actions tended to divide the people of the church.

He used all his power and influence against organized work. About the time he assumed pastoral control, "The church took into consideration the nature of foreign and domestic mission, and unanimously rejected the foreign, and agreed that our representative report to the Association that they think favorable of the Union, but want time to consider more on the subject; and for the tuition of young men we totally reject."[3]

Elder Swaim seemed successful in persuading the people. A church that had heard nothing but glowing success on the part of their previous pastors with a missionary and evangelistic zeal was now being fueled with discord. Much bitterness existed between this time and the actual division. Swaim and his supporters were "unreasonable, and would hear to nothing only the intensest [sic] opposition to Missions, Sunday School, etc. This spirit was carried so far that pastor, Elder Swaim, attempted to injre [sic] the good name of Samuel Wait by insinuating that his life was immoral."[4] The letters in the next chapter will explain this further.

The mission element came to be in the minority and pleaded with the majority to allow them to remain in fellowship, even thought they favored mission work, Sunday Schools and "other agencies that tended to the furtherance of the Redeemer's kingdom in the world."[5] Even after they were declared in nonfellowship, they petitioned the church to withdraw their declaration of nonfellowship that they might live in peace and fellowship as formerly. This was denied and these same Christians were not allowed to unite with any other church fellowship except "they had declared against the Baptist State Convention."[6]

The second petition failed by a ten to one margin and the anti-missionary spirit prevailed in the church. This majority held the property. Elders Eli Phillip and William Dowd were called from the association to look into matters as a presbytery. They examined carefully the church situation and concluded:

> We are unanimously of the opinion that the majority is clearly in the state of disorder and have forfeited their right as members of the church by their oppressive, unchristian and ungodly conduct. But the minority, as we believe, being orderly in their conduct and orthodox in their principles, have remained on the old ground and are clearly the old church. We therefore recommend to all associations, churches and brethren to recognize the mi-

Report of the Presbytery

We the undersigned being called on by the minority who withdrew from the majority of abbots creek church do certify that wee met at abbots creek ch. on the 4th July 1832 and then and there examined in to the situation of that church & unanimously are of opinion that the majority is clearly in a state of disorder and has forfeited their right as members of the church by their oppressive unchristian and ungodly conduct and we believe the minority were commanded to withdraw from them as disorderly brethren the apostle paul says "now we command you brethren in the name of our lord jesus christ that ye withdraw yourselves from every brother that walketh disorderly. 2nd thes. 34:—6th Consequently, weare bound to view the minority properly speaking as the abbots creek church the majority having forfeited their right to member ship by disorderly conduct cannot in the eye of the gospel be viewed as a church at all but the minority as we believe being orderly in their conduct & orthodox in their principles have remaind on the old ground & is clearly the old abbots creek church we do therefore recomend to all associations churches and brethren to receive the minority as the abbots creek church & view the majority as disorderly people entirely unconnected with the Baptist denomination

C. B. Philips
William Doub

nority as the Abbott's Creek Church, and view the majority as disorderly people, entirely unconnected with the Baptist denomination.[7]

This decision gives a sufficient base for the Abbotts Creek Missionary Baptist Church to declare and retain 1756 as the date of beginnings. This procedure by the presbytery was in keeping with an earlier decision of the association. At the 1815 associational meeting at Rock Springs meetinghouse in Chatham County, Abbotts Creek was represented by Elder Daniel Robbins, Isaac Odel, and J. Chaipman. During this session, the question came to the attention of the body from a sister church, "If members of the church are laid under censure, and afterwards one part considers them excommunicated, and out of fellowship, and the other party still holds them in full fellowship, what shall (be) the redress of the aggrieved party?"[8] The answer the body gave followed immediately on the same page, "Call for help in the neighboring churches." As previously stated, this procedure was followed in that the association sent a presbytery which investigated before making a decision. The majority did not adhere to this. In fact, there seems to be no evidence of any response in this matter. The minutes of the Primitive church do not mention a presbytery being called, much less the decision rendered.

The facts collected are not kind to Elder Swaim leading up to the division. It appears to this writer that his stubborn personality could have been more influential than any other differences within the church. How could a church move from a strong statement concerning sending the gospel to the heathen under the long and strong leadership of Elder Pope to change and vote ten to one against missionary efforts in a matter of fifteen years, shortly after Elder Swaim became pastor?

The history of the Jamestown Baptist Church (later changed to First Baptist Church in High Point) speaks with information supporting this claim. The church was an arm of Abbotts Creek for several years before being constituted into a church September 3, 1825. Ashley Swaim was chosen as pastor in October of that same year. It seems he had been serving the role as pastor even prior to the constitution of the church. In 1819, they had ordained and sent out William Burch to preach. The church was not numerically strong, and had only thirty-two members. Sheets shares this about Swaim.

> "He began to sow seeds of discord among the membership. Few men were more bitter than he, against the work of missions, and general development of church work. He would not reason;

> he would hear nothing except that which suited him. Much of his conduct was unbecoming a Christian, to say nothing of a gospel minister.[10]

He had been critical of other ministers and was accused publicly and charged with "casting gross reflections" upon them in order to destroy their influence, because they stood for order and method in the Lord's work.[11]

Elder William Dowd brought this complaint and entered the charge against him at the church where he (Swaim) held membership (Abbotts Creek). He was charged with "gross, immoral conduct, and offered to prove him guilty by church evidence."[12] Swaim used every effort to prevent the church from hearing this evidence. Sheets informs us:

> ...the public mind was impressed that he was guilty, and 'the church at Abbott's Creek, of which he was pastor, showed a disposition to protect him in his disorderly conduct.' Living witnesses have testified that they have seen him so intoxicated while trying to preach, that he had to steady himself by holding to the "book-board."[13]

Writer Henry Sheets apologizes for having to record such information but does it to show "how the chief leader in the split in this section demeaned himself as a minister. He was the pastor who used his influence to wreck this once prosperous and happy little Church."[14] While this was taking place, he was pastor of both Abbotts Creek and Jamestown. The test came at the Jamestown Church and he carried with him all members except nine. The nine were excluded from that fellowship for being disorderly in that they favored the great work of missions. In the Jamestown situation, the nine members were recognized as the true Jamestown Church and retained the church property and minutes.

Elder Swaim was also pastor of Liberty Baptist Church when it split, just three years after its date of organization in 1829. In that church, Swaim and Elder Eli Phillips disagreed on numerous points, to the extent Swaim walked out inviting all who agreed with him to follow. Some six or seven followed leaving the church property and records with the missionary supporting group.

The problem confronting Baptist churches was not limited to one local congregation. We must look at the particular situation at Abbotts Creek. The church records have been kept by competent clerks. Copies have been made of the originals. The Samuel and Sarah Wait Collection of Baptist records can be found at the Z. Smith Reynolds Library at Wake Forest University including minutes from the two churches called Abbotts Creek. Pansy Moore and her late husband, Dwight, and his sister, Daphne Moore Motsinger, have carefully copied some of those minutes and collected other records where they can be read more easily. For the most part, their copies are being used here dealing with the split at Abbotts Creeks that had been recorded in the original minutes.

We find and list here brief sketches of the reasons for the split in the church at Abbots Creek in Davidson County, North Carolina. At the February meeting in the year of our Lord 1832, Elder William Dowd, pastor of New Friendship Baptist Church, presented a complaint against Ashley Swaim, pastor of the church at Abbots Creek, in the following manner:

> 1. For attempting to ruin the character of a brother minister Samuel Wait without any just cause.
> 2. For saying he had heard bad reports about Samuel Wait, that he had been to the neighborhood where they originated, made inquiry, and had received information in a way that he believed the report was true, but when called on said he was informed by a Miss Mann who was not a professor of religion and whose character he did not know.
> 3. For acting directly contrary to the gospel by receiving accusation against an Elder without a single responsible witness.
> 4. For giving publicity to a scandalous report about an Elder without speaking to him on the subject or taking any gospel steps which complaint was received and entered on the record and was carried over by the vote of the church til the next church meeting. At the March meeting Brother Dowd came forward and informed the church that he was prepared to prove the charges contained in the above complaint and when he was denied the privileges, he then pleaded with the church to hear his evidence, and said he could prove the charges in the above complaint by members belonging to the Abbots Creek Church. He was then informed by the moderator that the church had nothing to do with him nor his complaints, and without hearing him nor his complaints, and without hearing any evidence in the case either for or against the above charges, the vote was taken to throw the complaint out of the church, which was car-

ried by a majority, to the great grief and mortification of us who were in the minority, to think that our pastor must lie under such weighty and grievous charges. We plead that the case should undergo a fair investigation in order that if our pastor was not guilty that his innocence might appear so as to stop the mouths of gainsayers but in order to shut the door against any possible chance to bring it to an investigation. The pastor took deceptive measures to get the church to declare an unfellowship against the Baptist State Convention and all its aiders [sic] of which Elder William Dowd was a member. We say deceptive measures because it was done in a way that many who were counted as voting against the convention never thought there was any such thing intended til it was all over. This caused us to entertain strong suspicion that Elder Swaim was not as clear as we wished him to be. At the April meeting, we the minority petitioned the church for a relief of our grieviances [sic] and requested them to withdraw their declaration of unfellowship against the other Baptist churches that we might live in peace and fellowship as formally. They refused to allow us to unite with any Baptist church except they (the church) had declared against the Baptist State Convention.

At the May meeting we again petitioned the church to grant us our former privileges than what had been tolerated and practiced by the Baptist churches ever since our first acquaintance with them (until very lately) and if this cannot be granted we wished to know to what extent the Declaration of unfellowship against the Baptist State Convention would extend without breaking the fellowship between the members of our church. The pastor Ashley Swaim informed us that we should not aid the convention in no way, neither with our hands nor our tongues, that we should not pay our money into their funds, nor use our tongues in a way to influence others to think favorable of the institution, upon which the vote was taken and carried by a majority of thirty four to eleven, and they had let us know that the Bible societies and Sunday Schools were as much out of their fellowship as the Baptist State Convention. Taking these things together they composed a burden too intolerable for us to bear; it was impossible for us to travel with them in union and having no hope of any relief of our grievance and to think of being separated from the church was no small trial to us.

At the June meeting we concluded to make one more effort to try the church to see if they would condescend to hear our grievances and in order to amid any controversy and that they should not be mistaken in our view and wishes, we committed them to writing and signed our names to it in the words following: We, whose names are undersigned composing part of the church of Christ at Abbots Creek, have felt and do feel at this time greatly distressed and burdened upon the account of your Declaration of unfellowship against the Baptist State Convention and all its aiders [sic]. In as much as we do not feel at liberty to go with you in these extraordinary measures, we therefore do most earnestly pray you for this liberty, as from a sense of duty and for the sake of liberty of concience [sic] which is so dear to us as our lives. We shall be under the painful necessity of withdrawing from the majority who we dearly love, and some of us have long been members. Signed by: (The names were listed without punctuation).

- Alexander Thomas Hannah Thomas
- William Raper Heziah Raper
- James Evans Anna Evans
- James Odell Elizabeth Brown
- David Raper Elizabeth Pain
- Stephen Guesford Sarah Guesford
- Phebe Horney
- Mary Evans
- Martha Teague

After the meeting was opened we offered them the above paper in writing and requested them to read it and they refused to take it, and then added that they could not tell whether they would receive it or not without they knew the contents of it. Alexander Thomas told them the contents. Alexander Pearce, one of their preachers, arose and said that he would to God that all those that trouble us were cut off. So we having no hope of anything being done in our favor and to avoid contention we quietly withdrew out of the house and Elder Ashley Swaim said he thanked God that we have showed ourselves.

After a short consultation we agreed to meet at Abbots Creek meetinghouse on the fourth Saturday in the present month for the purpose of forming ourselves into Church Order and to contract such business as may appear necessary."

June meeting A.D. 1832

Church meeting opened at Abbots Creek meetinghouse on the fourth Saturday in June by singing and praying by Alexander Thomas and proceeded as follows:

1. Those members who had signed their names to the above paper were informed that if they wished to turn back, they were at liberty and Stephen Guesford requested his name and his wife's name be taken off of the paper which was granted. The July 1832 minutes in the lower church's record indicates they came back before the church and gave satisfaction and were restored to the membership.

2. It was agreed that we call on Elders Thomas D. Armstrong, Eli Phillips, and William Dowd to attend with us at this place on the fourth day of July, next in order that we may undergo a proper examination and if found in order and in possession of the necessary qualifications that we may be established as a church, in Order then adjourned, prayer by Elder Wm Busch.

A presbytery was called to assist the small group. The minutes of the church carried the report. We, the undersigned being called on by the members who withdrew from the majority of Abbots Creek Church, do certify that we met at Abbots Creek meetinghouse on the fourth day of July A.D. 1832, and then and there examined into the situation of that church and unanimously are of the opinion that the majority is clearly in a state of disorder and has forfeited their right as members of the church by their oppressive unchristian and ungodly conduct. (It is interesting to note the word withdraw is used here whereas the minutes of the lower church uses the term excommunicated.) And we believe the minority were commanded to withdraw from them as the disorderly brethren. The Apostle Paul says, "Now we command you, Brethren in the name of our Lord Jesus Christ that you withdraw yourselves from every Brother that walketh disorderly," 2nd Thessalonians 3rd chapter and the

6th verse. Consequently we are bound to view the minority properly speaking as the Abbots Creek Church. The majority having forfeited their right to membership by disorderly conduct, cannot in the eye of the Gospel be viewed as a church at all, but the minority, as we believe being orderly in their conduct and orthodox in their principles, have remained on the old ground and is clearly the old Abbots Creek Church. We do therefore recommend to all Associations, Churches and brethren to recognize the Minority as the Abbots Creek Church, and view the Majority as disorderly people entirely unconnected with the Baptist Denomination. Eli Phillips and William Dowd signed this.

The minutes of the Abbots Creek Primitive Baptist Church taken from the Z. Smith Reynolds Library at Wake Forest University deal with this matter as well. The February meeting held on the first Saturday of the month mentions the complaint of Brother Dowd against Brother Swain. Three charges were given with this notation. "The case of Brother Swain (the spelling here has n rather than m) was called and liad [sic] over to the next meeting."

"Church meeting opened at Abbots Creek meetinghouse the first Saturday in March 1832 and proceeds as follows:

Brother Pierce Moderator:
The case of Brother Swain was called and after investigation the business of the church says that in their opinion the complaint was not brought in a legal manner and therefore have dispensed with it on that account."

The May quarterly meeting was opened "and proceeds as follows:

Pastor Moderator:
The church have this day publicly declared an unfellowship with the Baptist State Convention of North Carolina its system and its aiders as we believe it to be repugnant to the word of God."

The pastor is again listed as moderator for the June 1832 meeting with this being given as the business.

There being a dissatisfaction expressed by some members of this church relative to the declaration of unfellowship with the State

Convention its system and advocates made by this church at our last meeting and one of the members expressing a wish to present a paper to the church and without ever waiting for a decision of the church whether they could receive and read their paper of not the same members arose and addressed the other members who stood with him to follow him to the stand alleging that they could not be heard. The church have unanimously excluded here the names of the excommunicants [sic] as follows:

Alexander Thomas, William Raper, James Evans, Stephen Guesford, James Odell, Davis Raper, Ann Evans, Heziah Raper, Hannah Thomas, Martha Teague, Mary Evans, Sara Guesford, Elizabeth Brown and Phebe Horney.

We pick up now at the November meeting, "the first Saturday in November 1834 and proceeds as follows. No mention is made as to the Moderator.

Whereas there has been some threats by certain persons of erecting another meetinghouse or building on the lot owned by the Abbots Creek Church and on which our meetinghouse now stands. The Church direct their trustees should such an attempt be made to preserve this lot unviolated [sic] and sacred to the church at the expense of the church.

Endnotes

1. Sheets, 85.
2. Ibid.
3. Ibid., 86.
4. Ibid., 84
5. Ibid.
6. Ibid., 85.
7. Ibid.
8. Purefoy, 101.
9. Sheets, 119.
10. Ibid.
11. Ibid.
12. Ibid.
13. Ibid., 120.
14. Ibid.

CHAPTER FIVE

Letters from Wait and Dowd

A letter dated Tuesday, January 24, 1832, was addressed to the Abbott's Creek Baptist Church of Christ, Davidson County. N.C. It was from Samuel Wait, Tarboro, N.C.

> Dear Brethren:
> In consequence of what took place about the time of my visit to Davidson, you will of course expect to hear from me again. I was told when among you, that a short time before my arrival, your Pastor informed you or, some of you that he had heard certain reports, seriously affecting my moral character, that when he first heard them, in June last, he paid no attention to them, but that he had since made further inquiry, and found them to be true; or words to that effect. I was also informed that, when urged by the brethren while in the meetinghouse to let them know what it was that he had heard, he refused to tell, saying, that the report was too bad to be repeated: or something to that effect, and further, that when two, or more of the brethren, saw your Pastor, a day or two after, at some place, perhaps at a mill they again urged him to tell them what it was that he had heard against me and he declined telling. The tendency of this was, as you will perceive, to raise curiosity and expectation to the highest pitch, and make the more unfavorable impression on all around. I state these things just as I heard them; if there be any mistake in my statement you will be able to correct it. Knowing, as your Pastor must, the value of a good character to a minister of the gospel,

I cannot but feel the deepest regret that he should have thought proper to pursue the course that he did. And especially that he should have ventured to tell you that he had examined the reports and found them to be true, or words implying the same thing.

Those of you who were present when I preached in the School house will recollect that I denied the truth of these reports. And now for further information, I refer you to Elder William Dowd. It is proper that I should here state, in order to prevent any mistake that Bro. Dowd has done in relation to the investigation that has taken place in Montgomery, and also in what he is now doing in presenting the result to you; he does solely at my own request. As I am so far from you that I cannot, with any convenience, call and see you at this time myself, I hope that no one will consider him as being too officious or meddling in this matter. Allow me, now, dear brethren, to remind you of two or three passages of scripture. 1 Timothy 5:19, "Against an elder receive not an accusation, but before two or three witnesses." But in this case, there was not even one witness. There being, from your Pastor's own statements, only a flying report, entirely destitute of any responsible author. And yet, it was upon such ground as this, that you were told things adapted, if true, to destroy my character forever.

Again, look at the directions of our blessed Saviour in Matthew 18:15-17. "Moreover, if thy brother" &.e. In my judgment, your Pastor ought to have been silent in regard to what he might have heard until he had seen me; especially as I was expected so soon. We never ought to depart from the directions of our Lord in the 18th chapter of Matthew.

But once more, Matthew 7:12. "Therefore all things whatsoever ye would that men should do to you, do ye even so to them; for this is the law and the prophets." Do you think that your Pastor has done by me, as he would be willing that I, or any other brother, should do by him? But to conclude—So far as I am personally affected by what your Pastor has done, I can, if I know my heart, forgive him. Indeed, I did forgive him before I left your county. I have, I confess, been grieved to think that, while I was peaceable pursuing what I believed to be a course of duty and before he had even seen my face, your Pastor should have allowed himself to take a step, whatever may have been his motives, adapted to do me this greatest injury I could possible sustain on earth. For of what account is a minister when once his moral character is gone? But although I forgive, I think the good of the cause of Christ requires that I should simply lay this matter before you. It is now in your hands. May the Lord direct you that you may act in regard to this matter, in such a manner, as will be pleasing to him.

As I design by this letter only to make such a statement as I would make to you verbally, if permitted I could be present with you, I request that, after it is read, it may be handed back to Bro. Dowd.

Providence permitting, I hope to see you again before the next meeting of the convention: probably the last of June or the first of July. Of this, however, you shall have due notice.
May the Lord bless you all
As ever your friend & brother.
Sam'l Wait, Tarboro, Jan 24, 1832.

The second letter printed here was addressed to Samuel Wait, Fayetteville, N.C. It was dated Tuesday April 24, 1832 and is from William Dowd, Cedar Grove, N.C.

Dear Brother Wait:
I have been long silent, & now feel unwilling to disturb your mind with unpleasant matter, and without going into particulars would only say, that the Abbots Creek Church refused to even hear your address alledging [sic] that the accused and the accuser must be face to face, tho they did not know what you had written, they also refused to let me read the certificates which I had obtained in Montgomery, but suffered Swain in the publick congregations to bring gross and unfounded charges against you and me. When he sat down, I rose but strange to tell they refused to permit me to reply, not being

disposed to act out of order and the church being in session I sat down but next day (Sunday) after Swain had _____ worship, I attained the attention of a large assembly endeavored to explain the whole matter and read all the certificates in vindication of your character, which I believe was generally satisfactory to the congregation but I learn that since Swain has sent_____ of his members to Montgomery to obtain certificates to prove what he said to be true but I presume they made but a pore [sic] out tho I tell the people that they fully confirm all that he said and what he has said is of a very _____ nature and clearly actionable, some of your friends here think you ought to make him suffer the penalty of the law.

Tom Creek Church have turned out all their missionary brethren and sisters without alledging [sic] any accusation against them except their being favorable to benevolence these and other things my Brother are of a disturbing nature but God reigns and we must submit, he moves in a mysterious way his wonders to perform and while he moves he rides on the storm and commands a calm at his pleasure.

The other parts of the letter have to do with the health of his wife and the death of friends but nothing to do with our subject. The letter is signed, Your in gospel bond, William Dowd.

CHAPTER SIX

Abbotts Creek Church before 1832

Trying to read the oldest preserved manuscripts of the church records proves to be most difficult; some of them are impossible. In many instances, the records simply state the church met in conference but lists no more. For example, starting in September of 1784, we read "a church meeting opened in course at Abets Crick on the first Saturday in September 1784." The meeting before and following has the same statements except a change of dates. The November meeting has the same but adds, "The church having received complaints against Samuel Spirgin and John Ledford for neglecting church meetings and of worship." Someone was appointed to "labor with them for the neglect and bring them to the next meeting." Unfortunately, the next few meetings are not readable. One can make out words like labor but not the persons involved. However, on the first Saturday in June 1785, the minutes state the church "proceeds to labor with Samuel Spirgin and agrees to wait till the next church meeting."

We follow this a bit longer showing the longsuffering of the church or the unwillingness to give up. The July meeting reads "the church took into consideration the labor with Samuel Spirgin and appoints Isaac Teague and Cad Jones to labor with him and cite him to the next meeting." The same was said of Brother Ledford. The same two were assigned to cite him to the next meeting. The August meeting tells us Brother Spirgin was restored to the church. Ledford appeared at the same meeting but the January 1786 meeting still has the church laboring with him. It was reported in the February meeting the appointed ones had not been able to talk with him and would make a report the next meeting. The next meeting, the same thing took place. As best we can make out the church received a satisfactory report and he was restored at the October 1786 meeting. The matter came to the attention of the church in November of 1784 and was settled October 1786. The minutes of the next few meetings were impossible to read but the February 1787 meeting informs us Brother Ledford was laid under suspension. Samuel Spirgin was restored to the unity of the church having been excommunicated prior to this date. John Ledford was restored again at the March 1787 meeting.

The membership roll of Abbotts Creek Baptist meetinghouse, 1783.

Pastor, George Pope, Oliva Pope, Abraham Teague, Dillen Chaplin, John Ledford, Thomas Green, Samuel Spurgin, Danniel Silliven, Moses Craner, Christopher Vicory, Isaac Teague, Cadvolender Jones, James West, John Swaim, Thomas Kook, Samuel Coart, William Swaim, James Helton, Isaiah Teague, Joseph Morey, James Welborn, J…Wetherly, John Swaim, Joseph Phillips, Elijah Raper, Moses Strauhorn, William Welborn, James Evans, Mary Pope, Isabel Welborn, Sary Davis, Jane Mash, Eve Lowery, Elizabeth Moris, Ann Brown, Mary Helton, Lille Kook, Debron Stack, Sarah Bisinton, Elizabeth Strauhorn, Mary Buller, Mary Teague, _____ Pope, Susannah Kimbro, Ruth Mash, Ann Grassum.

Margaret Silliven, Sary Craaver, Hanar Green, Lary Harenton, Elizabeth Wetherton, Anne Swaim, Sary Spurgin, Mary Swaim, Rachel Moris, Catron Pope, Elizabeth Gilum, Widow Moris, Ann Kook, Mary Williams, Margaret Chipman, Mary Parr, Elizabeth Robins, Elizabeth Jone, Mary Swaim, Roda Mash, Mary Evans, Mabel Kimbro, Sary Wearenton, Margaret Low, Martha Swaim, Anna Evens, Charity Watson, Elener Cartswell, Marthe S_____, Frana Richason, Rebecca Helton, Widow Gutrugs, Charity Swaim, Sister Easter, Negro Grace.

The following names were given with the notation, "some names in minutes but not on membership roll. Richard Grissom, Brother Younger, (Dated Sat. November 2, 1783). Sary Moris now Sary Grissom, Ann Fields, Sara Cradelboh, Margaret Davis, Mary Green, Jeremy Shelle, Dorcus Rush, Brother Morgan, Mary Lusk, John Rich, Sarah Jones, William Barron, Frances Barron, Sary Spoolman, Jacob Idol, Mary Garson, Rachel Smith, John Roberson, Mary _____, Tomson Smith, Ann Right, Jason Teague, Tamer Lowe."

Information for the next several meetings simply listed the date but no business was mentioned. Without any explanation the church agreed to send George Pope, Isaac Teague, and James Welborn "down Chatham to hold church meetings on difficulties that has rose with some of (the) members down there." This is listed as October 1787 and adds Joseph Spigin [sic] was cited before the church. The meeting one month later, he was suspended because he neglected to hear the plea of the church and was excommunicated. No other reference is found concerning who the members were in Chatham, what the difficulties were, where they lived, or action taken if any. Sandy Creek Associational minutes with this date that might have dealt with this had been destroyed in a house fire in the home of William Lightford.

As the monthly meetings continued, others were mentioned who were brought before the church for disposition. This constituted the business of the church for several meetings except for the mention of those being sent to Chatham. The records show some were brought before the church, labored with, suspended, excommunicated, or received back into the church family.

It seems impressive that the church did not hesitate to bring people before the church for discipline, but the membership tended to go to great lengths to restore the wayward. An example of this can be seen in the case of William Williams when the church received a report at the April 1789 meeting of his getting drunk and the church "judged it to be worthy of church dealings." Two were appointed to cite him to the church for the next meeting. He did not give a satisfactory answer and the case was laid over until the next meeting. It was the September meeting before he was restored. At the same meeting some were appointed to labor with Mary Green for "unfellowshipping [sic] her own church and joining with disorder," which seems she was attending elsewhere and had united with that church. If any disposition was made for or against her, the minutes are not readable.

Such a practice seems to have continued in Baptist churches for many years. My personal knowledge of such happening with churches was taking place as late as the early 1970s. While serving on the Cherokee Indian Reservation during 1970–1974, I observed that if a member of some Baptist church joined a church of another denomination, he or she was removed from the church for "adhering to false doctrine" without any acknowledgement to the church of which the person joined. In some churches, there were also other disciplines practiced such as a girl being "churched" or excluded for becoming pregnant without being married or a person "churched" for getting drunk.

The minutes of Abbotts Creek recorded on June 1791, "church meeting opened in course at Abets Crick the first Saturday of June 1791." That is the extent of the notation. However, the minutes dated a year later, June 1792, tell us this: "The church this day agree that last June they united in the belief that it was the gospel duty in supporting the ministry and that they are yet in the same principle and intends with the Lord's help to be found in the practice thereof."

It seems good to see action and hear of things other than the discipline parts and in February 1793, James Welborn was appointed to act for the church in what seems to be getting the deed for land and the meetinghouse. If more was said about it, the minutes are too blurred to read. George Pope and Christopher Vickery were appointed to attend the May associational meeting.

In August of 1796, Alexander Thomas was received into the membership by experience. In November 1796, "the church proceeded on the difficulty with Mary and unites in her excommunication for taken up and going away with another woman's husband."

Occasionally, we read where "after divine worship," certain ones were received by "experience." It does not seem to list each time this happens but from time to time, we find such information. Of the fourteen churches listed in the Sandy Creek minutes in 1816, Abbotts Creek reported the largest number of members at 101. The Mother Church, Sandy Creek, listed 75. We note the previous year, the Sandy Creek minutes listed twenty-two churches. A notation on the side informed us the number of churches had been reduced because some churches were dismissed to join the Pee Dee Association.

The first Saturday in April 1798, "The church unanimously agree that the ministers and members of the several arms of our church meets [sic] at Abet Crick the first Saturday in June to labor on the desent [sic] that is between our ministers." At the June meeting, "after divine worship" the church considered the desent [sic] of our preachers and "agree that making the report and receiving of it in the church not be good conduct and therefore give our voices against all that we did heretofore."

Without knowing the nature of the problem mentioned, or much of what was taking place in the church, one could speculate without noted evidence. Others sources tell us about the great missionary work of Elder Pope. In revival services, he baptized over five hundred new believers. Could the problem have been related to his being away preaching rather than caring for the flock at home? Could it have been he was baptizing in areas other ministers considered their territory?

It is difficult to tell if this was what came back to the church in 1802. Much information between these dates is not clear enough to read. At this time, the church "proceeds on the former difficulties and the church agreed to draw the censure and to forgive injuries done endevor [sic] to love as brethren." It is impossible to follow up on this over the next several meetings due to the unreadable print.

In July of 1804, the church considered the resolution made at the last associational meeting, and sent the pastor, George Pope, and James Welborn to "sit with them in the committee and labour [sic] for a communion of saints." Just what this problem involved, no hint was given in our minutes and we have no recording of the Sandy Creek minutes at this date.

In September of 1804, second Saturday, the clerk records this: "Meet [sic] today to consider ways and means to raise a necessary fund to defray the expense of the meetinghouse." Complaints were given on this day against certain members for "letting horse run for money and leaving a meeting of worship on the Sabbath and turning deaf ears to the discipline." Others disciplines were considered against one for "not paying for corn," another for "drinking to excess," and one for confessing fornication, and all were excommunicated. At the same time, "the church took into consideration the remote distance of some of our members who live near Hunts Fork meetinghouse and for their convinces [sic] we appoint an occasional church meeting to be held there once in ever three months beginning on the fourth Saturday in July of 1805, and so on as long as may be convinces [sic]."

In 1805, Sister Mary Pope, daughter of the pastor and his wife, was cited before the church and excommunicated from privileges as a member for being disobedient to parents. In several matters mentioned earlier, the church tended to be extremely patient with those cited to the church for discipline. One has to wonder in the case of Mary Pope, was the excommunication so quickly done because her disobediences were so extreme, or could it have been because she was the daughter of the pastor and therefore more was expected of her? One source tells us Mary was a headstrong child. Going against the wishes of her parents, she ran off and attended a dance. Her mother went for her and brought her home. This helps us conclude the exclusion may have been pushed by her parents more so than by the congregation.

It was quarterly meeting time again in February 1806. Brother George Pope, pastor, brought allegations against Brother James Welborn. No statement was given as to the nature of the problem. However, Brother Welborn "said in open conference that it was the opinion of the world and the church in general that Brother Pope's aim was for money and such like." A word that seems to be "jealousy" starts the next sentence. "Jelesy [sic] entering the minds of many of the members they publickly [sic] demonstrated the same by rising in vindication of the charge which Brother Pope denied and they failing to support the accusation the church laid them under censure."

We move away from the minutes long enough to pick up a very interesting story. Elder Pope, though born in England, was very much for the American cause in the Revolutionary War. This created some dislike toward him by those still supporting the Mother Country.

Some guests approached his home (later identified as Tories) requesting through Mrs. Pope a meeting with the pastor at the school house. (This information is credited to the late Raymond Pearce.) He learned their intent was to kill him but he asked for permission to preach once more before his death. In the delivery of his sermon, which was one of great power, "some were convicted and all were more or less wrought upon. At the close they told him to go home that they would never brother him again."

We continue to rely on Pearce for this information regarding Elder Pope. He was not a poor man, for he gave all his sons a good tract of land, and yet notwithstanding his ability to do this, he, like the Savior often walked to appointments. One day walking on his way to church he passed a man notorious for wickedness; the man called to him, offering him a horse and saddle, which he accepted. When he got back he returned them. "No," said the wicked man, "as good a preacher as you are ought not to walk to his appointments, and I now make you a present of the horse and saddle."

Moving back to the minutes, other "cases" were brought to the attention of the church. One was "laid over to the next meeting." In the other situation the church was satisfied that B. Jackson (?) was guilty of drinking to excess, "quarling [sic] and offering to fight and not coming to make satisfaction;" therefore he was excommunicated from membership.

The church assembled at the March meeting and "could not go on in business for lack of union." Over the next page or so in the minutes but prior to the June 1806 meeting, which is clearly written, some labored with the members who dissented the March meeting. It states, "by judging the censure that was laid at the February meeting to be illegal and proceeded to take account of the names of those that is under censure with James Welborn which are these: John Welborn, William Welborn, John Teague, Ezekiel Teague, Jacob Idol, Archabel Johnson, Wheeler Chadwich, and William Teague."

At what seemed to be the May meeting members "came forward to make a recantation of their sin in vindication of the jealousy they obtained against B. Pope. Those who did so were Ezekiel Teague, Joseph Spirgin, and Jacob Idol, Mary Johnson, and Archabald Johnson. The names were called of those who were censured and absent. Some were appointed to go visit the others and cite them to church for the next church meeting. One such person being sent was Ezekiel Teague who had just been restored to the church after having been put under censure about two months earlier.

Anna Evans, remembered as the daughter of James Younger, was mentioned here. The church needed to know her standing. Her sin had been aggravated by her "unfellowshipping" [sic] Brother Pope for more than a year and kept it from him to the reason of the cause, therefore the church thought her ripe for excommunication as a truce breaker."

The following few meetings had people coming before the church that had said negative things or voted against Brother Pope. For instances, the July meeting had Jacob Bodenhamer coming forward acknowledging the jealousies he had against Brother Pope. This was to the satisfaction of the church.

James Evans and Anna, his wife, were called and examined. "They remained in an impetinent [sic] state and still entertained the same opinion of Brother Pope. Feeling they were ripe for excommunication, they were removed from the church as members." In the October meeting, Anna Evans was received back into the fellowship of the church.

In the August meeting, John Teague was "called and on trial made for excommunication was held over for want of union." Two members were to cite him to the next meeting. John Welborn had been cited and did not appear. The church thought him ripe for excommunication since he did not appear to give a satisfying response for his "supporting the false declaration against the world, the church, and Brother Pope." The voice vote agreed to remove him from membership.

This seemed to continue and in August, John Roberson's case was called for and in his absence he was looked on as ripe for excommunication "for the sin of supporting false declaration against the world, the church, and Brother Pope and by neglecting the church he aggravating his crime and was disowned accordingly."

The October meeting tells of William Teague coming forward making confession of his conduct in "supporting the wrong declaration against Brother Pope the world and the church. He was received back into the fellowship." No idea is ever given as to why some changed their minds about their opinion or charges against their pastor.

At this meeting, Elijah Hitchcock came forward informing the church against himself for getting too much to drink. The church laid him under censure and then received him back as he repented to the satisfaction of the church. This action tends to speak of the harshness and tenderness of the people. We can see their strong stance against what was wrong and their willingness to be forgiving.

The church dealt with "a difficulty being between Joseph Spirgin and Anthony Hincle [sic] in some trade being between them and Hincle refusing to abide by the judgment of the committee appointed by the church laid him under censure." At the November meeting he was not present but not being satisfied with the judgment of the committee the church "agreed to suffer him a rehearing at the next church meeting by the same committee and more if required."

The cases of Tabitha Ledford and Elizabeth Montgomery were brought before the church in that they were not married and said to be pregnant. Two were cited to investigate. The report being true, both were excommunicated at the January 1807 meeting for the "sin of fornication." The same was the fate of Elizabeth Evans who confessed to this as true. She was excommunicated in April of 1807.

It is of interest to follow some of these cases. For instances, we note the case involving Joseph Spirgin and Anthony Hincle was brought up but laid over until the next meeting. At the same time John Teague was cited and excommunicated for supporting the sin of accusation against the world, the church, and Brother Pope. It just does not seem to die.

The January meeting of 1807, found Anthony Hincle and Joseph Spirgin coming before the church to say their differences were settled to the satisfaction of the church.

The September 1804 meeting included discussion on raising funds for the meetinghouse. No more was mentioned (if so, not readable) about it until the June 1807 meeting, when two members were appointed to labor with John Ledford "for not giving satisfaction in respect to his part of the assessment pay toward the meetinghouse." The August meeting called the "case" of another person, whose name was unreadable, for neglecting to pay his part of the assessment. The monthly meetings that took place during this time had one "case" after the other of members being called to give the church a satisfying answer for their wrong doings. One was called for having said a female member had a lying tongue. Pastor Pope brought charges against a fellow member who had failed to pay him for corn he had purchased. Mention was made earlier of one being "labored" with for swearing and offering to fight. It was brought up again. Another one informed the church against himself for drinking and being disorderly. He informed the church of "conviction and pardon." The church excommunicated him and received him again.

The person whose name was unreadable from the June meeting was mentioned again. When his case was called for, those assigned to labor with him brought his answer which was "when he had paid his own debts, he might pay the church requirements for which the church laid him under censure." Someone was appointed to call him to the next meeting.

The October meeting seems to refer to something that had happened earlier. A couple of people, it was reported, had taken a water million [sic] and ate half of it. "The church concluded that had the appearance of evil and admonished them and concluded for the future such conduct shall be censurable."

Reading such action two hundred years later might appear amusing yet it gives insight into the idea of purity among the membership. It appears one might be afraid to attend the meeting for fear of having some conduct exposed. In our present day, we wonder if people would even return to the services. From all indications, they did repent of their evil and wanted to be restored to the fellowship. In the same meeting, one was brought up to be excommunicated but was held over for "want of union."

The October 1807 meeting has a complaint against "John King's servant man in getting drunk and swearing for which the church laid him under censure." The servant man was mentioned as being black. We will hear from him again.

Similar things were recorded in the meetings over the next few years. The November 1807 meeting on Saturday lists a couple of things that took place and then tells us "John King's servant man came to a meeting at Hunt's Fork on Sunday, the first Sunday in November and made satisfaction to the church" for which the church had laid him under censure.

The first church meeting in January of 1808 found the church appointing representatives to visit one who "joined another church and leaving her own."

The unnamed person mentioned earlier who had been placed under censure for not paying his assessment on the building came and made satisfaction and agreed to pay his part and was restored to fellowship.

A couple of months later, in the March meeting, Wheeler Chadwick appeared confessing to "shooting a squirrel on the Sabbath for which the church laid him under censure." No mention is made that someone brought this matter to the attention of the church so we assume it was his own confession. In the April meeting, he made "satisfaction" to the church and was received back into the fellowship. The May meeting gave us this notation. "John Ledford was called and not being present but entirely neglecting to hear the church for so long a time till the church's patience was entirely worn out," the church excommunicated him as a member.

The July meeting placed a Squire Spirgin under censure for belonging to a society which the church felt to be of principles which "is after the rudiments of men and not the commandments of God and when called on by the church he behaved somewhat in an unscriptural manner in rebuking an elder." The case was "laid over to the next meeting." Later, the November meeting found his "case laid over again." Mention is made of it again in the February 1809 meeting. This time it was laid over because he was sick. He failed to appear at the March meeting. Someone was appointed to labor with him and bring him to the next monthly meeting. When he wasn't present, someone was sent with the message the next time would be his last. By this time, he was "ripe for excommunication." His case was heard the next time and the church received "some satisfaction" and laid the case over until the next time "in hopes he would get better satisfied with himself." The April conference only mentions he was excommunicated "for the allegations he was charged with and not appearing to give Christian satisfaction to the church." Much later, August 1914, one was cited before the church for his involvement with the "free masons" but the above mentioned society is not identified at this point. It may or may not have been the "free masons."

Several meetings have been listed with one after the other being cited to the church, labored with, placed under censure, or excommunicated. Yet another charge is presented at the November (1808) meeting. Brethren were appointed to "inquire into the report of Elijah Hitchcock in being at a shooting match and found him to be a partaker with them." He was placed under censure.

As the months moved on and more meetings were held, we continue to read of similar things already noted: drinking to excess, offering to fight, neglecting to attend the meeting of the church, getting angry, and other similar charges.

The church met in August 1807 and considered the case of Isaac Jackson. The church heard the case "against Isaac Jackson and he confessing to the same that in an argument with his wife and family in which he behaved very disorderly and called a neighboring woman who was present a lying bitch for which the church laid him under censure." He did not appear at the next meeting.

At the associational meeting, at Caraway meetinghouse in September 1807, a Negro man was excommunicated from the Abbotts Creek Church for the sin of "fornication." Two and a half years later, March 1810, "A black woman belonging to John (?) was disowned from this church as a member for the sin of fornication."

It seems that two women, one of whom was the wife of James Younger, were placed under censure at the April 1810 conference for "upholding James Younger in his disorderly stand and cited to the next meeting." There is no other mention of this in the later minutes. However, it is known that the church placed him under censure at a later time for being ordained without the consent of the church.

During twelve months, beginning April 1810 through March 1811, not one mention is made of any additions to the church, and no other significant and positive experiences were listed. Cases were brought against certain persons for fighting with a brother, fighting, and drinking to excess. This is mentioned at least three times. Four separate times, one or more were cited to the church for "unfellowshippping" with Brother Pope, one being accused of doing it in a "dishonorable manner." Drinking to excess is mentioned again and profane swearing was the crime of at least two separate ones. Some were censured for not hearing the church. A member was cited for some wrong he had done, and he "aggravated his crime by neglecting to hear the church." The statement was given about the church "being grieved" that one of our brethren "is belonging to a sister church." An attending member was appointed to carry a letter of grievance to the sister church. At a latter meeting, the one carrying the letter of grievance to the sister church returned with no satisfaction from the church.

The cases of nine listed persons were laid over to the next time for the second time. During these twelve months, some were censured and even excommunicated while others were restored after giving satisfaction to the church.

From several early Baptist histories, we read about Elder Pope preaching in many places and baptizing as many as five hundred people. For the first time in the minutes, the March 1810 meeting, we find the church giving approval for Brother Pope to go to the "lower part of the state by a request from Brethren that sent a letter for him to preach the gospel of our Lord and Savior Jesus Christ."

The year 1812 opens with us reading of the meeting being held and "proceeds [sic] as following." Each meeting has this recorded but nothing else until the June meeting. It is not even clear what this meeting concerned, yet it was the only matter to be mentioned until the September meeting. With the activity of some of the earlier years, this must have seemed quiet and a welcomed relief.

As best as we can ascertain, the December 1812 conference had to do with some differences between Abbotts Creek and a sister church (Cross Roads). A group of members was appointed to seek a satisfactory solution. Without understanding just why, Abbotts Creek declared "unfellowship" with the sister church.

In September of 1813, long-time pastor George Pope resigned his tenure as pastor at Abbotts Creek. Just how Elder Pope offered his resignation is not explained. The minutes read this way: "Elder George Pope and Sister Mary Pope his wife hath this day made application for letters of dismission [sic] which was reluctantly granted. In hopes that Brother Pope's business as related to this church by him in regard to his call to leave this church and remove to South Carolina is from God. Wherefore Brother and Sister Pope is invited to call on the clerk of this church when they are ready to move for letters and the clerk authorized to write the same."

We have no way of knowing if the church did any expressing of appreciation for his long years of ministry for the church and community. In previous minutes we have indicated from time to time problems he and the church endured. But his pastorate without question gave stability to the church for over three decades. To this day, his pastorate is several years longer than any other. It does seem appropriate for us to record here the last song he sang at the church. It comes from the book of *Primitive Hymns*, 1906, page 493.

A Thought of Death

1. Hark! From the tombs a doleful sound
My eyes, attend they cry:
Ye living men, come view the ground
Where you must shortly lie.

2. Princes, this clay must be your bed,
In spite of all your towers;
The tall, the wise, the Rev'red head,
Must lie as low as ours.'

3. Great God! Is this our certain doom?

And are we still secure?
Still walking downward to the tomb,
And yet prepared no more!

4. Grant us the power of quick'ning grace
To fit our souls to fly;
Then, when we drop this dying flesh,
We'll rise above the sky.

Pope's leaving did not slow down the "censorship" method of the congregation over the next several months. Representatives were sent to visit some who were "neglecting the meetinghouse." Another was sent to cite John King's black man because he was "of a long time living in adultery." The next meeting he was present and was laid censure "for the above."

Again George, John King's black man, came before the church and was found guilty of the "crime laid against him for which the church laid him under censure." The next monthly meeting, George was back but "failed to give a satisfactory answer and his case was laid over."

In the March 1813 meeting, "Sister Isabelle _____being inadvertently overtaken by drinking too much the church condemns her conduct and she makes acknowledgement and is received." This was the first such mention of a female drinking. It seems to be so carefully worded, almost as to excuse her. Mention had been made numerous times of one being cited before the church for drinking to "excess." Never was the word "drinking" listed alone. One can only speculate as to what is meant by such wording.

Mr. King's George had his case called again in the February 1814 meeting. His answers were not given in a way to satisfy the church so the case was laid over. In the April meeting, George did not fare as well and was "excommunicated from this church for the sin of adultery and aggravating his crime by running away and for disobedience to his master."

In the March meeting, Sister Isabel _____ was before the church for drinking. The wording for her was exactly as it was worded just one year earlier; "being inadvertently overtaken by drinking too much the church censured her conduct and she makes acknowledgment and is received" back into the church's fellowship.

The matter of James Pope came to the attention of the church at the November 1814 meeting. James along with John Teague and others were "on a journey with his wagon to South Carolina" last spring. He was guilty of ungodly conduct and language "in words and actions." Four persons were appointed to visit with him and cite him to the next meeting. Suggestions were made allowing them to call on John Teague and the others if it was necessary. This was laid over to next time during the December meeting.

The committee calling on James Pope gave their report at the January 1815 meeting. Mention was made that Pope "Is guilty of buying corn of a Negro slave last spring on his way to South Carolina." The church laid James Pope under censure and the case was left over until next time. He did not appear at the March meeting and again the case was laid over. Some report was given about him in April. The same two were to cite him to the next meeting. He made his appearance at the May meeting and requested the case to be held over and it was granted. In June, the case was called on and held over for "want of union." The July meeting records that Pope was "ripe" for "excluding" but was laid over to the next meeting at his request. A similar appeal was made in August and the case was laid over yet again. First mentioned in the previous January meeting, Pope appeared before the church in September and the record tells us he "spoke contempable [sic] to the church and especially to Brother _____ for which he was censured for the church agreed in his excommunication."

Still during the January meeting, the church appointed "James Teague and William Raper to purchase from James Evans the plot of ground the meetinghouse stands on and take a deed for as much as they can contract for not less than two acres and a half and the church agrees to pay for the said land."

On April 15, and at many other times, matters were brought to the conference for disposition which could not be made because of "the want of a union."

Trustees were appointed at the May 1815 meeting. They were Brother William Raper, Brother James Teague, and Brother Solomon Davis. They were asked "to keep the deed made to them to get it recorded in court tho the deed made to them is to secure the land belonging to Abbotts Creek meetinghouse."

At the December meeting, Elizabeth Evans returned to the church and giving "satisfaction" was restored to the fellowship. She had been excluded for acknowledging she was unmarried and pregnant. By now at least three women had been expelled from the church for being pregnant but nothing is recorded as being said in reference to the fathers of these unborn babies.

Brother Daniel Robbins was laid under censure of the church in August 1814 because he was "manifesting a belief to join the free masons in becoming a member of their society." A year and a half later, he reported to the church in a manner that was "of satisfaction" and he was restored to membership.

For several months, we have seen where meetings were held but no information other than the date being mentioned. However in February 1817, Brother George Clambet (?) came forward "and complained against himself for Sabbath breaking and drinking." He was laid under censure. His case was laid over at the next monthly meeting because he was not present. In April it was brought up and "laid over." In May he appeared and "made full satisfaction to the church for the crimes he was laid under censure for." However, the story does not end here. Minutes mentioned again and again his case, his censure, and were laid over. He got drunk again, told the church, and was censured with the case being laid over. This went on until the March 1818 meeting when he was restored to fellowship again.

During the November, 1817 meeting, the records indicate money is being taken for missions and appointed Deacon William Raper to receive what dollars may be given for that purpose.

In March of 1818, "the church appoints James Evans, John _____, Jacob Teague and Isaac Odell as a committee to interpret old church book and transfer such rules and documents _____ as they may think proper and inject them into the new church book together with the names of the members and make report to the next church meeting."

The book of minutes had this recording at the end of the April minutes:
"North Carolina, Davidson County
The 5th of July 1818 (and what looks like S. C.)
The church made this book in the year of 1783 (and it seems to be Y. C.)."

The above initials could be of the church clerk who recorded the minutes and the ones who signed the book. The handwriting is not the same.

The second book of the old minutes starts with 1818. It seemed to be routine for notes to be taken stating the meetings were held on a certain Saturday but no business is listed. The cases of individuals were called, dealt with or carried over to be brought back to the attention of the church later.

From the information given in the records, at the February or March meeting of 1819, Ashley Swaim was called to be pastor. The church agreed to send for help "in order to solemnize the same, agreed to call on the Timber Ridge church for their pastor and Elder Christopher Vickery and to Tom's Creeks for their pastor to meet at this place the first Saturday in May next."

The May meeting can be read with interest: "The church having this day unitedly [sic] agrees that the deacons in the future shall have full authority to call on members of the church for such sums of money as they think they ought to pay for the purpose of supporting the gospel and to pay the expense of the church...."

The following January, the Rules of Decorum were adopted.

Rules of Decorum

1. First, meetings of all business shall be opened with singing and prayer.
2. Second, the moderator shall be chosen by the election of the members present whose duty it shall be to invite members of sister churches to sit with us.
3. All difficulties touching fellowship shall be attended to before the reception of members.
4. The eighteenth chapter of Matthew shall be a rule for all private offences. But public transgressions may be handed into the church by any member who having first notified the trangressor [sic] that a complaint will be handed in against him the next meeting.
5. Any male member wishing to speak shall first arise and address the moderator by the name of brother moderator whose duty it shall be to answer said applicant in token of the same. But the female may speak standing or sitting and without addressing the moderator. The moderator shall have equal privilege of speak as any other member provided the seat be filled but not to vote except in case the church be equally divided.
6. The reception of new members shall be the unanimous concent [sic] by the church. Exclusion of members shall be by a majority of two thirds of the church and the minority shall be amenable _____. In case of one or more members being grieved, it shall be the duty of the church to give them a candid hearing and to labor to keep the unity of the spirit in the bonds of peace.
7. No person shall speak more than three times on any one subject without leave of the church and shall strictly attend to the subject before him casting no reflection on any person having spoken before.
8. It shall be the province of any member of this church to bring any business forward by a motion. All motions made and sec-

onded shall have the voice of the church before a vote.

9. No male member shall leave his seat in time of public business without leave of the moderator. But the female member may withdraw without leave.

10. No person shall be interrupted in time of public speech unless he departs from the subject. Then it shall be the duty of the moderator to reprove all such offenders.

11. That the former rule adopted by this church of meeting at eleven o'clock and breaking at three be strictly attended to.

12. That such rules undergo a revisal at any time when the church shall deem it expedient.

13. It shall be the duty of the clerk at each church meeting immediately after making any record to read the same distinctly and the sense of the church to be immediately taken by the moderator.

No mention was made as to how these guidelines were formulated or who presented them to the church. We are not even told they were adopted but we must admire the wisdom of the church and the attempt to be fair with whatever business claimed the attention of the church family. The very next thing mentioned was one being restored to the fellowship of the church.

The August meeting found the presbytery that had been named to examine Brother Swaim present with their findings. They were called on "to set apart as the pastor of this church and after due labor in examining him and the church they unanimously agreed in his being set apart in that office and he is hereby set apart accordingly."

A month after the pastor had been approved, a sexton was chosen. "James Evans was unanimously appointed sexton for this church and the graveyard at this place for one year and as much longer as he and the neighborhood shall think proper." Evidently, he served well in this capacity and continued serving until July of 1821. At this time, the records indicate the appointment of Nathan Teague as sexton of the church "in the place of James Evans and (and that he) continue as long in that office as the church and neighborhood and himself shall think proper."

At the same time, the church adopted rules that said, "In observance of Baptism and sacraments days, baptize before sermon at all other meetings after sermon."

Elder Swaim had been pastor a very short time before the October 1819 meeting. "The church took into consideration the nature of foreign and domestic missions and unanimously reject the foreign and agree that our representative (at the Associational meeting) report to the satisfaction that they think favorable of the former but want time to consider more on the subject for tuition of young men for ministry they totally reject."

Meeting after meeting, cases were cited and disposed of or the date of the meeting is simply given. At each meeting a moderator was elected. Sometimes it was the pastor but not always. From time to time we read where one or more were accepted to the church membership by experience. Some reported their own "offences" while other members brought charges against others members. Most any of us would wonder what might have been going on when a case was brought against one for some grievance and at his or her own request the case was held over until a later meeting. For instance, how can one give an explanation for "drinking to excess" one month better than he or she can one month later? The church took into consideration certain members who had been notably absent. Someone was appointed to cite them to the next meeting. Routinely the minutes help us to see where a member had been placed under censure for moving to another community without asking for a letter of dismissal.

The handwriting of the clerk changes with minutes taken in November of 1822, but no mention is made of the fact a different person might be taking the minutes. We are not told who took the earlier minutes or what necessitated the change. In some matters the one doing the job kept it as long as the person felt it proper. The mentioned change was temporary since the old penmanship returned but for only a few sessions of business.

Just prior to the October 1823 associational meeting, to be held at "Falls Creek meetinghouse in Chatham County," members were appointed to attend with instructions for expressing "our dissatisfaction with regards to the standing presbyter." We are given no indication as to what this was. With what transpired later, does this suggest Pastor Swaim had his grudges against certain leaders in the association?

At the October meeting, the way was opened for "experience" and four people were received as members. The very next meeting six people were received by "experience."

The next month members took into consideration those who lived great distances from the church. Action taken was worded in this manner, "took into consideration the disadvantage of the church book being at such a great distances." We are not given what else was said, if anything, about this but the very fact of distance may have given birth to the idea of another church.

Solomon Davis was elected as clerk and Brother Joseph Davis assistant clerk. Again we find the handwriting changing.

In September of 1825, "a petition was handed in by Brother Beeson requesting the eldership of this church to meet them at Jamestown the second Saturday in this month to inquiry into the qualifications in order to become a constituted body which petition was granted and appoints Elder Ashley Swaim, Solomon Davis, Alexander Thomas and _____ Spirgin [sic] to attend to same."

Still, case after case occupied the attention of the church as recorded by the clerk. Some new names appear but numerous persons are named again and again. Another complaint was given at the September meeting. A complaint was given against Nancy Teague "repeating an ought (she) held against some members of the church." Someone was appointed to cite her to the next meeting.

For several meetings the case involving her had been called and laid over. However, in April of 1826, and "after a long debate the church decided that she has a right to demand a private acknowledgement from sister Teague but not a public one." The matter was laid over. The next meeting found her absent thus laid over again. The case claimed the attention of the church in July 1826. The situation was not settled. The action of the church was to petition the eldership of the Jersey settlement, Big Creek, and Tom's Creek to meet this church to "labor with the said difficulties and meet with this church at the August meeting." Brother Pierce was appointed to make sure she was present.

Before this matter was reviewed at the August session, Joseph Spirgin handed in a complaint against himself for "getting angry and making use of unbecoming language" for which the church laid him under censure. The very next matter mentioned informs us he came "forward and made the church satisfaction for which the church restored him to fellowship."

Only after this did the Nancy Teague matter get mentioned in this manner. "The help having come forward according to this petition sent out at our last meeting and having labored faithfully on the difficulty on which sister Nancy Teague was under the censure of this church she is thereby restored to full fellowship again." First mentioned in September of 1825, she was restored in August of 1826.

Apparently some disagreement had arisen in the church prompting this: "The church agreed to send to the following churches for help to settle a difficulty existing in this church and agree to send to the following churches viz [sic] Timber Ridge, Tom's Creek, Big Creek, and Jersey Settlement to meet at this place on the third Saturday of December." Persons were named or appointed to contact the listed churches. The next minutes are written but in bolder script on top of them so as to make those words unreadable, a notation, which seems to say the request from the former meeting, should not have been made and is signed by Solomon Davis "by order of the church." It remains unclear what those difficulties involved.

The January 1827 session opens with certain members living near Charles School House "having petitioned us for help to constitute them in order as a church we have answered their petition by appointing the elders of this church to attend them on the fourth Saturday of the month." The report was given the next month "they attended according to the petition from the members near Charles School House and they were constituted." No name is given for the church and it is not clear if this was an "arm" of Abbotts Creeks at the time. From other sources, we learn that the group "near Charles School" actually became New Friendship Baptist Church.

Some disagreement of two neighbors involving a tract of land was reported with some persons appointed to "labor on the matter" with them. One meeting later, the committee was dissolved. At the same meeting, two members reported another member had moved without paying what he "justified owed them." The absent member was placed under censure and the two lenders were told they were at full liberty "to get their money any where or any how they can according to law." The case was called at the church meeting in June. It does not state the member present but does record "after conversation on the subject he was excommunicated for moving away without paying a just debt."

In the August meeting, the censured one "came forward (without being expected) and made the church "full satisfaction for the crime he was disowned for and was restored to fellowship again." However, when he requested a letter of dismissal, the clerk was ordered to withhold this until he had paid the two fellows what he owed them.

At the March 1827 meeting, it was unanimously agreed "hereafter any member making a motion to adjourn business after three o'clock shall be in order and the church shall lay all business of the church over til the next meeting."

The May conference dealt with preaching funerals. It was decided funerals would not be held on the monthly, quarterly, or yearly meeting day, except on the request of the family involved.

Pastor Swaim brought a claim against Sister Ruth Payne, at the July 1827 meeting, "for accusing him of moving a quantity of manure from another plantation to his own in a slanderous manner and when attacked on the subject denied the same also that Brother Thompson Craven was trying to cheat her out of the rent on the place Craven lives on and that he, Swaim, was the cause of it." On the same day, the church accepted Black Alice on "experience."

At the next meeting Sister Payne was laid under censure for the "charge and allegations" brought before the church at the last conference.

James Evans who had been out of church for a number of years came before the church and made full satisfaction and was restored to the fellowship at the September meeting.

At the November 1827 meeting, at least thirteen members living in Randolph County requested letters of dismissal to form their own church.

The church heard again from Elder Swaim with another accusation against him at this same November meeting. He reported "A certain David Morgan" from Indiana was in this section of the country and was circulating scandalous things such as this: "that he was charged of having a child by a certain woman." Some other unclear matters were mentioned that made Swaim "guilty of very things that mankind could be guilty of except horse stealing and murder." He further reported this man has received some of his so-called "information from his brother Ezekiel Morgan." Three members were appointed to go with Elder Swaim to visit Ezekiel Morgan "in order to make inquiry" of what his brother David had said to him.

This was not the first matter of the next meeting, January 1828. Joseph Spirgin (as spelled) was disowned from the church. Two years earlier in open church he had "called on the Great God of Heaven to bear witness of his innocence in contradiction of a report out there in the world of his being the father of a bastard child since which time his lawful wife having deceased he in a short time thereafter married the mother of said child for which cause the church unfellowship and excommunicated him." Another member replaced him on a committee which was to go on a petition in Randolph County to help constitute a church.

The report was then given by the committee members who were to see Ezekiel Morgan. He denied telling his brother "any such things as was stated." Other matters were heard. Brother Pierce was placed under censure "for neglecting the church and moving his family and goods on the Sabbath day." Sister Polly Ann Campbell was "excommunicated from this church for the sin of absenting herself from this church for near three years and removing out the bounds of this church without carrying a letter of demission."

At the February meeting, the committee appointed to constitute a church in Randolph County had done so for the members dismissed from this church. Still there is neither indication of the exact location nor the name of the newly-constituted church. This tends to follow a pattern where members of the Abbotts Creek Church living some distances from the community would petition the membership to allow them to establish their own church. We find this mentioned several times.

Before this meeting was over, "The church appointed Brethren Joseph Davis and _____ Idol to assist Brother Swaim in drawing a paper to present to the church at their next meeting to contradict David Morgan's report against Brother Swaim so that it can be put in the public papers or otherwise disposed of." A month later, the committee's report failed to satisfy the church and was to continue. They were told to "take sure effective measures as shall be thought sufficient to support said report and have the same committee to _____ from under the hands the persons whose names Morgan had made use of and report to next meeting." This case was continued at the April meeting. In the May meeting, "the measures taken by the committee were not satisfactory to the church. The church has let the matter drop."

The way was opened for "experience" and "the church received Black Hannah, servant of Squire Ledford, by "experience." "Also Black Nancy free woman of color formerly servant of John Pitts (?) who was once a member of this church and having laid out a number of years was received into full fellowship again."

In June of 1828, "The church took into consideration the necessity of having some person appointed to raise the hymns in time of public worship and named Barnet Idol, Joseph Davis, and James Evans to hold their own trial until one of them shall be selected by the choice of the majority of the church to fill that place." The July meeting came but the matter was continued to the August meeting at which time it was continued yet again. The matter came to a conclusion at the next meeting when Barnet Idol was selected "to raise the hymns for the future."

In the January 1830 meeting, they adopted an agreement saying any male member absent three successive meetings would be cited to the church "to give account of his non attendance." A month later, Brother Joseph Davis was elected regular clerk and Samuel Craven as assistant.

A resolution was passed at the February, 1831 meeting. "No members of this church shall join the State Convention Bible Society of North Carolina except by the union of the church."

The action of the December 1831 meeting was for Sister Elizabeth Evans to be paid the sum of two dollars and forty cents a year "for sweeping the meetinghouse." This was to be "commencing on the first of January of 1832." She was to be paid monthly the sum of twenty cents.

The February meeting had Brother William Dowd entering a complaint against Elder Swaim. Chapter four deals with the division of the church concerning these matters and will not be included here. However, the May meeting gives the record of the church declaring unfellowship with the Baptist State Convention. This meeting was followed by the June meeting where certain ones stood and left. Again, these matters are discussed in the division chapter, but we note the church excommunicated them in a unanimous way.

As if no major or unusual event had taken place, the next meeting proceeded with one being appointed to visit Sister Elizabeth Payne trying to know "whether she has withdrawn from this church or not." It is not stated if this person might have left to be a part of those excommunicated or had simply been absent from the meetings. Ansel Hedgecock was appointed as trustee to take the place of the excommunicated former trustee, William Raper. Heretofore, the church had expressed concern enough with members who were absent or committed a "crime" to appoint one to check on the wayward member. No such concession is made concerning those who left and helped to constitute the newly-formed church.

Information was given by two members that another church (Middle Fork?) had asked about what had taken place and wanted to hear the "true statement of the affairs of the church." Certain ones were appointed to go with a "copy of our records and give them as much verbal information as they may be in possession of for the helping the minds of our brethren."

Two members who left or were excommunicated, Stephen Guesford and his wife Sarah, "gave the church full satisfaction for the charge for which they were disowned and was restored to fellowship again."

In an effort to speak to what has actually begun the split of the church, we find this recorded:

> Whereas a diversity of opinion existed in the minds of many in consequence of an event which we believe the enemy of the truth has for some cause been permitted to make among us.
> 1. Resolve that we feel deeply affected on account of the situation of the Zion of God and that rent and divisions are making inroads among the churches ("s" is added but not clarified if it means other churches or this one plus the split off) to the wounding of the cause in many instances.

2. That we would recommend to our Brethren to receive the admonition of our Savior in searching the scriptures, and try and do it with prayerful heart to be directed into all truth.
3. To labor to keep the unity of the spirit in the bonds of peace and with Paul to know nothing but Christ and him crucified.
4. That we believe it to be the duty of every professor of Christianity to use their united efforts in trying to preserve a union among the brethren and not be endeavoring to sow discord but on all occasions where rents have been made and a union can be effected on the plan the scriptures direct to use all possible means for accomplishing the same.
Finally brethren pray without ceasing that Israel's God would again visit his Zion and elsewhere and pour him out such a blessing as they could not contain."

It has to be very apparent this was intended for the group who left or were excommunicated and not their own intent to practice. Failure to see this "resolve" had already occurred when the ones who left tried to work out where the two groups of difference opinions could still worship together.

The next few meetings kept things going with one being excluded and other complaints being given. The church appointed "delegates" to the next associational meeting and referred to one messenger as "our beloved Pastor Elder Swaim."

At the November meeting, in 1832, the "church has directed their trustees to take legal measure to possession the lot on which our meetinghouse stands." No other mention is made regarding this over the next two years. The meeting in November, of 1834, opened and proceeded as following. "Whereas there have been some threats by certain persons of erecting a meetinghouse or building on the lot owned by the Abbots Creek Church and on which our meetinghouse now stands. The church directs their trustees [that] such an attempt be made to preserve this lot inviolated and sacred to the church at the expense of the church."

We leave the records of what later became known as the Abbotts Creek Primitive Church and deal with the excommunicated group, which was declared by an outside presbytery to be the true Abbotts Creek Baptist Church. The records of the lower church make no mention of a presbytery being called much less of the decision that was rendered.

CHAPTER SEVEN

Abbotts Creek Union

In June of 1758, the Sandy Creek Association was organized as the fourth Baptist association in America. Abbotts Creek, Sandy Creek and Deep River were the churches making up the association, which was the first in North Carolina. Abbotts Creek remained a part of that association until the Abbotts Creek Union was organized in November of 1825, except for one year in the Yadkin Association.

We turn our attention now to Abbotts Creek as a part of the new association. In 1825, "on Saturday before the fourth Sabbath," Sandy Creek Association, in session at Friendship meetinghouse in Moore County, had Elder Ashley Swaim, Joseph Spurgeon and William Raper as representatives from the Abbotts Creek Church. The church reported twenty-six baptisms with total membership of 167. During the session, a mission offering was taken that totaled $14.95.

At this meeting, Timber Ridge and Jamestown joined Abbotts Creek in requesting and were granted "letters of dismission [sic] to join a new association about to be formed more convenient to them."[1] Delegates from the association were appointed to meet with them for assistances as needed at the appointed time. They were Elders William Dowd, Isaac Kirby, Eli Phillips, and P. W. Dowd. This was set for Saturday before the second Sunday in November at Liberty meetinghouse in Davidson County. The new association was called the Abbotts Creek Union.

One year later, in October of 1826, at the Sandy Creek Association meeting, William Dowd was elected moderator and was selected to preach the sermon. In doing so, attention is called to the fact that Elder Dowd, following his divine commission to preach and teach the gospel and to baptize, had baptized a number of persons outside the association. In doing so, "he had injured the feelings of Elder Ashley Swaim." The Abbotts Creek Union was represented by Joseph Spergen [sic] and Michael Swaim. It seemed evident that Dowd was preaching and baptizing in a territory Swaim thought should be left to him, otherwise why would it be hurtful to him? Elder Dowd reported this and no mention is made that Swaim was present. Swaim was still pastor at Abbotts Creek but now in the new association, the Abbotts Creek Union. Since he was not an appointed representative from the Abbotts Creek Union, he would have only been a visitor had he been present. Dowd requested an opinion from the group. The disposition was determined after a "full and fair investigation" with the associational body expressing "the firm belief that Brother Dowd had acted entirely agreeably to the gospel, and bid him God's speed."[2]

By the year 1829, when the association met with the Jersey Baptist Church, eleven churches with their numerical membership were named. They were Lick Creek 45, Jersey Settlement 64, Abbott's Creek 135, Hunt's Fork 24, Timber Ridge 45, Big Creek 47, Tom's Creek 53, Jamestown 32, New Friendship 51, Mount Tabor 14, and Liberty 26, making a total of 536. The churches reported fifty-five baptisms for that year.[3] Sheets also points out, "All was peace and harmony. Not one word of discontent recorded. To show the condition of the group just three years before the split occurred, "one sentence from the Circular letter tells the story: 'The utmost harmony, unanimity of sentiment and brotherly affection prevailed'."[4] Three years later, dissension over missions sharply divided that spirit. Leading personalities of the two opposite sides were a part of the group. All who favored missions, Sunday Schools, and certain other unmanned things were ruled out of order in the September 1832 meeting. "This body also 'rejected the messengers of correspondence' from the Sandy Creek Association because the body was 'friendly to missions'."[5]

The rejected group being in the minority had to leave. They gathered outside in a tent and organized the Liberty Baptist Association. "This little body was strong in the faith and determined to press on in spite of all opposition." [6]

Without knowing much about what was taking place with the churches in the new association, we have to look back to the Sandy Creek Association to see what was happening in Baptist churches. No doubt some of the same things were taking place. Abbotts Creek Union had to deal with these in one way or the other. The 1830 session of the Sandy Creek Association, gave strong approval to some resolutions concerning the organizational efforts of the State Convention of North Carolina. Support was voiced also in this manner "that we recommend a paper, about to be published under the direction of the convention, to the patronage of our brethren and friends."[7]

A bit earlier in 1827, Elders M. Swaim and Isaac Beeson were listed as the messengers of correspondence from the Abbotts Creek Union to the Sandy Creek Association. How interesting to note that at this meeting, similar messengers were appointed to attend other associational meetings. Two messengers were sent to Flat River, Raleigh, County Line, Pee Dee, and Yadkin. But when Abbotts Creek Union is mentioned, four messengers are listed with no mention as to why twice those were sent to the other association. The next year, three were appointed and sent to the Abbotts Creek Union. One cannot help but wonder: were the added numbers due to the close distance or was it an effort to know what was taking place in the old association?

Along the same line, an inquiry is made at the 1828 meeting indicating some kind of a struggle was taking place. The question was raised, "What course should be pursued by the churches when a few of the members stand in opposition to the body in any manner whatsoever?" The answer was given, "We recommend to each church, so situated, to endeavor to obtain disinterested helps; give the matter a fair investigation; and if such members are found wrong deal with them as transgressors."[8] It was further stated that if it seemed that a fair settlement did not look probable, the churches should call in "judicious helps from sister churches."[9] We take from that if a church is facing the possibility of being split, the church was urged to postpone any decision until this outside help could be secured.

Whatever prompted that inquiry may have been carried over to the next meeting when the session was held at Lick Creek. We have noted already that Lick Creek was listed in the Abbotts Creek Union that same year. A resolution was passed at this meeting that seems significant when we remember some of the problems relating to the splits taking place. The resolution was this:

> Resolved, that this association recommend to the several churches of which it is composed, to use their best efforts for the promotion and extension of religious knowledge, by encouraging the benevolent institutions of the day, either by contributing their pecuniary aid, by forming Bible and tract societies, or in any way which they, in their wisdom, may think best calculated to answer the designed purpose.[10]

We know Abbotts Creek was no longer a part of the Sandy Creek Association but such questions and resolution being asked at Sandy Creek may hint at what could have been going on in the churches of the Abbotts Creek Union as well. Since we have no records of such meetings where Abbotts Creek was now a part, nor how they were dealing with such questions if they were being asked, we can only note this while being fully aware that these hint at some of the later reasons given for the split in the church.

At the 1832 session, no mention is made of a representative from the Abbotts Creek Union; however Joseph Spergen [sic], Davis Raper, and Elder Burch are listed as being present from Liberty Association of which Abbotts Creek is now a part. At the same meeting, seven names were given of those who were to attend the next Liberty Association's meeting as messengers of correspondence.

Endnotes

1. Purefoy, 131.
2. Ibid., 135.
3. Sheets, 3.
4. Ibid., 4.
5. Ibid.
6. Ibid.
7. Purefoy, 146.
8. Ibid., 140.
9. Ibid., 141.
10. Ibid., 143.

CHAPTER EIGHT

The Effect of the Regulators on the Church

The early minutes of Abbotts Creek Church tell us the church was organized in 1756, and reorganized in 1777, and yet again, in 1783. We have neither direct explanation of this nor do records help understand any reason. Doubtless, there were countless hardships experienced by our forefathers, which may give us some understanding as to the need for reorganization. One Baptist historian reminds us that the first pastor, Daniel Marshall, left Abbotts Creek, and the political situation may have had some bearing on his leaving.

Prior to the reorganization in 1783, the Revolutionary War had taken place, and the colonies had gained their independence from the Mother Country. It is not known how the war affected the Abbotts Creek community or if several men were a part of the activities. We do know about one soldier from the community. We have information that Jacob Idol, the great-great-great-grandfather of Sue Foust, a present member of Abbotts Creek Church, served in the war. The community was still a part of Rowan County at the time. Mr. Idol enlisted at the age of nineteen. For three months during the war, he served as a private in Captain James Billingsly's company of the North Carolina mounted militia. The next year, he enlisted again and served a month as a private in Captain William Davis' company and was captured by the Tories. After his escape, he enlisted again in the summer of 1781, serving three months as First Sergeant in Captain Lopp's company, as a part of Colonel Smith's North Carolina Regiment. This information was gathered from the headstone at the cemetery of the Abbotts Creek Primitive Church.

Several family genealogies mention those who served their country in battle. Sometimes, it seemed farmers would serve for short durations and return to care for the crop.

Information is available that informs us of the activities of the Regulators just two years after the church was first constituted. Just what bearing if any this had on the Abbotts Creek community is not spelled out for us. However, M. A. Huggins in the *History of North Carolina Baptists 1727–1932,* gives this insight as he quotes from Paschal: "The turbulence of the Regulation period caused a reorganization of the Abbott's Creek Church in 1771; and again the period of the Revolution produced some changes which led to reorganization in 1783 or 1784."[1] During the following years, Moravian missionaries traveled and preached to Baptists as well as other groups.

Some writers tell us the persecution taking place was akin to the persecution that drove the early Christians from Jerusalem. Morgan Edwards relates the Sandy Creek Church went from sixteen members to 616 in seventeen years but at this time was reduced to fourteen and was in danger of becoming extinct. Edwards did say the numbers were not known but it is certain that many left from Abbotts Creek and other churches.

The Regulators were an organized group of citizens trying to get taxes regulated. Lord Granville's chief surveyor William Churton arrived at Bethabara from his Salisbury headquarters with this statement: "The 'mob' about seven hundred strong had formulated its demands into certain Articles. One Article demanded that the Vestries should be abolished and that each denomination should pay its own ministers."[2] Mob was another term used for the Regulators.

In 1752, no white settlers in large sections of North Carolina were able to own any land. The number of Regulators had reached about 700 six years later (1758). They met demanding some corrections be made regarding political and religious rights. At the time, citizens were paying tax including support for the ministers of established churches. By 1767, the number of citizens paying tax in Rowan County was the second largest in the state. Small farmers expressed their grievance to the unmerciful taxes in this way, "…taxes and rents, half of which was stolen or unaccounted for, were so high that 'poor people in order to pay such taxes, found it necessary to sell their beds and bed clothes, yea even their wives' petticoats.'"[3] This included such a high tax to obtain a marriage license that couples could hardly get

The Effect of the Regulators on the Church

enough money together to pay such a fee. Rather than paying a high fee to the state, young men and women were being married by the services of the justice of the peace or Baptist ministers who were described by Governor Tryon as "itinerant preachers." This did not constitute marriage as recognized by the state.

Tryon's appointed minister, Therodorus S. Drage, reported the Separate Baptists as being his chief opponents. They were insisting that each clergy ought to be paid by the volunteer contributions of the members one served rather than with tax money. These Separate Baptists created opposition and frustration for the Governor Tryon's plan for an established church. The strong animosity of the governor caused him to wreak havoc with the Baptist neighborhoods in the Jersey and Bethabara communities. He looked at Baptists as "avowed enemies of (the) Mother Church."[4]

With Tryon's well-trained army of one hundred strong men from the best of families, he marched them from the ocean to the North Carolina Blue Ridge Mountains. Crossing through Rowan County did not win friends from the Baptist corners. The Moravians gave strong support to Tryon except taking up arms, which for them was not permissible. Their records show this was done to the offence of their neighbors. The government against the Regulators caused a great exodus of Baptists from the area. Many went to Tennessee and established the first Baptist church there and organized the Holston Association. They found the freedom they desired to worship as they chose to do since they were no longer in Tryon's jurisdiction. He intended to gain his terms of peace with all insurgents to the extent he would wage war. Tryon's plans for this cause was to be helped by two thousand soldiers from England and with the arrival of newly-appointed Governor Josiah Martin. Tryon left to become governor of New York. The soldiers were never sent to North Carolina even after Martin became governor.

Tryon had plans to use stringent means to subdue the untrained and mostly unarmed settlers. It would be slaughter without mercy. The new governor, Martin, shortly learned the settlers were a peaceful group of people who needed relief from Tryon's abuses more than anything else. His government allowed such to be achieved.

Before Martin arrived, Tryon's army traveled to Alamance Creek, some few miles Southeast of Burlington. The Regulators, 2,000 strong, met them. The governor refused an audience with them as long as they possessed arms. He gave them an hour to lay them aside and move out. They refused and a two-hour battle took place. At least nine were killed on each side. Tryon had sixty-one wounded while an unknown number of the Regulators were wounded. "Twelve regulators were tried for treason and convicted; six of whom were hanged and six were pardoned by the governor."[5]

After the battle of Alamance, Tryon turned his fury against Separate Baptists in other places. His army moved on to Sandy Creek, the center of Baptist work in the state. Some days were spent there but little harm done. Some reports indicate that Stearns had encouraged his people not to take up arms, and Tryon seemed to have that information. From there, the army moved on to the plantation of Benjamin Merrill some four miles south of Lexington. The three divisions of the army, believed to be about 3,000 to 3,500 strong met at the site of the plantation. This was the largest gathering of troops in North Carolina prior to the Civil War. This took place during the last days of May, in 1771. The governor has a well-devised plan "for the final operations of his campaign against the Regulators and the Baptists near Jersey Baptist Church. It was central for Baptist populations in all directions—eastward on Abott's Creek and the Uwharrie and Caraway Creek. ..."[6] A week passed as this was taking place.

According to the Moravian records, we learn that Merrill was captured, convicted and sentenced to die. Chief Justice Howard pronounced the death sentence in this way:

> I must now close my afflicting duty by pronouncing upon you....The awful sentence of the law, which is that, you, Benjamin Merrill, be carried to the place from which you came; that you be drawn from thence to the place of execution, where you are to be hanged by the neck; that you be cut down while yet alive; that your bowels be taken out while you are yet alive and burnt before your face; that your head be cut off, and your body divided into four quarters, and this to be at his Majesty's disposal; and the Lord have mercy on your soul.[7]

Governor Tryon allowed Mrs. Merrill and eight of her ten children to watch and actually allowed Merrill's last request to be carried out by allowing the family to retain the plantation. This plantation was in total waste but for many others, the homes were burned and animals turned loose on the crops. This happening in June meant the year's harvest had just been aborted before having a chance to grow.

This horrible quote is given to let us see Abbotts Creek was not spared from these atrocities. A nineteen-year-old son of Benjamin Merrill, Merell, was captured but soon released. From the Moravian records, Paschal records this for us:

> Toward evening Merell, from Abbots Creek, came in much distress, seeking his father, who is outlawed. The Governor has given until the 7th of next month, June, promising pardon to all who submit, outlaws excepted. Merell had been pardoned, and had begged for his father.[8]

Communities and churches hardly had time to settle down from the hostility against the Regulators and Baptists, until attention had to be turned to war with our Mother Country. Statements we read involving Baptists show their willingness to give obedience to the law, pay taxes, and pray for their leaders. They expressed a willingness to take an oath. "Their religion allows them to bear arms in defense of their life, liberty and property. This society has maintained themselves to be true friends to civil liberty ever since the commencement of the war. ..."[9] George Washington in 1789 said because of that, "I cannot hesitate to believe that they will be faithful supporters of a free yet efficient general government."[10]

Baptists in North Carolina had resisted Governor Tryon's intent to have an established church. Ministers were assigned to certain churches and some churches refused to accept them as their pastor. They considered religion and civil freedom their birthright. As the constitution began to be worked out, the Rev. Henry Abbott, mentioned earlier in Chapter One concerning the name of Abbotts Creek, is credited with preparing the article concerning religious liberty. In addition, a resolution by Abbott presented to Congress was passed giving ministers of all denominations the right to officiate at marriages.[11]

We are able to glean a bit more about community life during the war days. We will quote a lengthy paragraph taken from the *History of Rowan County* written by Rev. Jethro Rumble and published in 1881. This was republished by the Elizabeth Maxwell Steele Chapter Daughters of the American Revolution, Salisbury, N.C.

Just prior to the battle at Martinville (Guilford Courthouse), General Green moved from:

> Trading Ford on to Abbotts Creek meetinghouse, still in Old Rowan, and halted for two or three days to rest his troops and await further developments. During his stay there he made his

headquarters at the house of Colonel Supurgen [sic], a Tory, who, of course, was not home to receive him. But his wife, Mary Spurgeon, was as true a Whig as her husband was a Tory, and like Mrs. Steele in Salisbury she showed him all the kindness in her power. While staying there he was naturally anxious to know whether the British were still in Salisbury, or whether they were moving up the river. In this state of perplexity, he inquired of Mrs. Spurgen [sic] whether she knew anyone whom he could trust to send back to the river for information. Mrs. Spurgen promptly recommended her son John, a mere youth, as perfectly trustworthy. After convincing himself that this was the best he could do, he mounted John on his own horse, directing him to go to Trading Ford, and if he could not hear of the British to go up the river until he could gain information. John went, and hearing nothing at the Ford went several miles up the river. Still hearing nothing he returned home and reported. Green started him off again, and told him, that he must go as far up as Shallow Ford, if he could hear nothing before that time. John took the road again, and actually went as far as Shallow Ford, some thirty miles from home, where he saw the British crossing the river. Hastening home with all speed he reported his discovery to the General. Instantly Green ordered his horse and was off for Martinville, where he met General Huger and the eastern division of his army, as mentioned above, on the evening of the seventh of February.[12]

Endnotes

1. M.A. Huggins; *A History of North Carolina Baptist, 1727–1932.* Raleigh: General Board of the North Carolina Baptist State Convention, 1967), 70.
2. Paschal, op. cit., vol. 1. 42.
3. Huggins, 60.
4. Paschal, op. cit., vol. 2, 52.
5. Higgins, 60.
6. Ibid., 68.
7. Paschal, vol. 1, 76.
8. Ibid.
9. Paschal, vol. 2, 446.
10. Ibid.
11. Ibid., 207.
12. Ibid.

CHAPTER NINE

A New Beginning

The break had been made! By a majority of thirty-four to eleven, the vote had been taken in opposition to Bible societies, Sunday Schools, and aiding the Baptist State Convention in any way. "Taking these things together, they composed a burden too intolerable for us to bear. It was impossible for us to travel with them in union and having no hope of any redress of our grievance and to think of being separated from the church was no small trial for us." This was recorded in the first record book of the church just after having listed the reasons for the split.

A request hoping to live in peace with each other had been made at the June 1832 meeting. The minority carried this hope.

> "We whose names are under signed composing part of the church of Christ at Abbots Creek (note the spelling) have felt and do feel at this time greatly distressed and burdened upon the account of your declaration of unfellowship against the Baptist State Convention and all its aiders [sic]. In as much as we do not feel at liberty to go with you in these extraordinary measures, we therefore do most earnestly pray you for this liberty. As from a sense of duty and for the sake of liberty of conscience, which is as dear to us as our lives, we shall be under the painful necessity of withdrawing from the majority who we dearly love, and some of us have long been members. Signed by these whose names are listed: Alexander Thomas, William Raper, James Evans, James Odell, Davis Raper, and Stephen Guesford. The other column lists Hannah Thomas, Keziah Raper, Anna Evans, Elizabeth Brown, Elizabeth Pain, Sarah Guesford, Phebe Horney, Mary Evans, and Martha Teague."

The preceeding information was offered to those who remained with the anti-mission group.

> After the meeting was opened, we offered them the above paper writing and requested them to read it and they refused to take it, and then added that they could not tell whether they would receive it or not without they knew the contents of it. Alexander Thomas told them the contents. Meredith Pearer (or Peaser) one of their preachers arose and said that he would to God that all those that trouble us were cut off. So we having no hope of any thing being done in our favor and to avoid contention we quietly withdrew out of the house. And Elder Ashley Swaim said he thanked God we had showed ourselves. After a short consultation we agreed to meet at Abbots Creek meetinghouse on the fourth Saturday in the present month for the purpose of forming ourselves into Church order and to transact such business as may appear necessary.

In June of 1832, the group met at the Abbots Creek meetinghouse. They had singing and prayer led by Alexander Thomas, and the following business was carried out.

First, "Those members who had signed their names to the above paper were informed that if they wished to turn back they were at liberty and Stephen Guesford requested his name and his wife's taken off of the paper which was granted."

> It was agreed that we call on Elders Thomas D. Armstrong, Eli Phillips and William Dowd to attend with us at this place on the fourth day of July next in order that we may undergo a proper examination and if found in order and in possession of the necessary qualifications that we may be established as a church in order, then adjourned, prayer by Elder Wm Burch.

Among those present at the July meeting was Elder Samuel Wait.

The report of the presbytery was included in these minutes, which recognized the minority as the Abbots Creek Church. This report was included elsewhere, but the minutes of the "anti-mission" church makes no mention of the presbytery.

The group at the August meeting unanimously agreed to adjourn and start meeting the third Sunday of the month. Brother Alexander Thomas, William Raper, and Davis Raper were appointed at the September meeting to attend the Abbotts Creek Union meeting. They would be the first messengers sent by the minority, already declared to be the true Abbotts Creek Church.

The infant group received their first additional members at the October meeting. They were Phillip Horney, Margaret and Hannah Raper. They united with the church by "experience" and were welcomed. At the same meeting, Joseph Spurgin [sic] and Jane Jones were restored to fellowship. They had been excommunicated prior to the division of the church. It seems obvious these two had gone with the original fifteen but were not members in that they had been excluded prior to the division. Three were appointed and would be the first messengers to attend the newly-organized Liberty Baptist Association. Those messengers were Alexander Thomas, William Raper, and Joseph Spurgin. The appointment of Spurgin [sic] tends to suggest for us the group's feeling about the report that had caused Brother Spurgin [sic] to be excommunicated in the first place. He had just been restored to the church and immediately was appointed as the church's representative to the associational meeting.

The first of many things is recorded for the December meeting. After the meeting was opened with singing and prayer, the following is recorded:

> First, whereas we have been deprived of our records in consequence of a split in the church, and Brother William Raper having been one of our deacons for many years past and regularly ordained and being found blameless, it is unanimously agreed that he shall be continued as a deacon of this church.
> Second, Agreed that Brother Phillip Horney be appointed as our writing clerk and Brother Davis Raper assistant clerk.
> Third, agreed that Brother Joseph Spurgin be appointed singing clerk.

At the next meeting, "Sister Rachel (colored) woman is restored to fellowship with us." She too had been excluded from membership some months prior to the split. She was the first named black person to be accepted by the minority church group. To this writer, it seems significant that three of the earliest members of this group had been excommunicated previously. The fact is, according to the minutes of the anti-mission group, the first fifteen members had been excluded. The minutes of the Primitive church use the word "excommunicated" but the records we have in our minutes use the term "withdrew." The minutes are clear: the withdrawal took place prior to the excommunication. This was never acknowledged by the anti-mission congregation.

Elder Eli Phillips preached at the February 1833 meeting. After singing and prayer, his was the first recorded sermon for the separated group who was continuing the ministry of Abbotts Creek Church. The scripture was taken from Matthew 13:30. "We then unitedly [sic] agreed to call him to preach for us for one year." The next day, he preached from Proverbs 18:28 "to a large and attentive congregation." How large? No hint is given. The next meeting records "Elder Phillips attended his appointment at this place." At the same meeting, the Liberty Baptist Church requested help to settle a "difficulty existing in that church." Any church within fifteen or twenty miles surely knew what had taken place here, but the request came to the missionary group.

The Saturday meeting in May of the same year, Elder Phillips preached, and then Josiah (?) Wiseman preached. The sermons increased the next day with Eli Carroll preaching from Proverbs 3:16. Paul Phifer preached "from Solomon Songs 5:3." They were followed by Pastor Eli Phillips' sermon from John 7:37. Elder Phillips and Elder Wiseman served the first communion that day.

Exactly one year after the minority withdrew, the conference dealt with the matter of the split. After the prayer, the following information was before the group.

> Whereas there appears to be a controversy between the two churches who occupy this meetinghouse and lot. We appoint Brother Joseph Spurgin and Phillip Horney to attend their church meeting on the first Saturday in July next with the following instructions.
> "Whereas there is controversy between the two churches who occupy the meetinghouse and lot at Abbots Creek Davidson County respecting the privileges and benefits of the said house and lot, therefore we the Baptist Church at Abbots Creek being a member of the Liberty Association do hereby certify that we as a church have not nor even has had any intention to hinder or deprive any church society or individual from the full enjoyment of such privileges and benefits in said house and lot as justly belongs to them. Neither are we willing to be shut out of the afore

said meetinghouse and intirely [sic] excluded from the enjoyment of such privileges as we believe justly belongs to us. And in order for the aforesaid controversy may be speedily and amieably [sic] adjusted without the tedious and vexations prosecutions of law suits, we have appointed our Brethren Joseph Spurgin [sic] and Philip Horney to attend the church meeting of the other party to be held at the aforesaid meetinghouse on the first Saturday in July next with authority from this church to received or offer proposals for the purpose of effecting a speedy and amieable [sic] adjustment of the matter in dispute as above stated on principles of justice and equality. Doing to others as we would they should do to us. And our prayer is that the whole of the business may be transacted in the fear of the Lord, to the Honor of His cause and the good of His churches.
Signed in behalf of the church, P. Horney, Clerk. June 15, 1833.

Of interest is the fact that this group from the missionary element of the division, following the conclusion of the presbytery, had declared themselves to be the church and even mentions "the other church." There is no information as to how the wording of this came together so quickly. It just seems impossible that one would suggest we word this in such and such a way so quickly and have it so meaningful and well thought out.

Of course, we must include what transpired at the next meeting. The following, again, is quoted from the minutes:

> The committee appointed at last meeting to attend the church meeting as aforesaid with the foregoing instruction being called on to report as follows, that we attended the meeting and informed their clerk and their trustees the import of our business before their meeting commenced and when they got through their business we presented them a copy of the above instructions which they received and took the vote of the church whether to read it or not. It was decided in the affirmative by very large majority. The moderator then requested us to inform them of the contents. We done so. He then without taking any other vote on it handed it back to us without it being read. No other reaction was given.

A month later, at the August meeting, two matters demanded the attention of the body. William Raper, James Evans, and Phillip Horney were appointed to act with the brethren from Jamestown and New Friendship churches "for the purpose of procuring a preacher to attend the three churches for the next years." The Lord's Supper was the second order of business. At the next meeting, a change was made for their monthly meeting to be on Saturday before the third Sunday of each month.

Things were taking place as, sermons preached, someone censured, another person excommunicated or taken back into fellowship after they gave satisfaction to the church with a repentant attitude and testimony. Some were added to the church by experience while still others were cited to the following meeting to answer before the church body matters that had been brought to the attention of the church. The list goes on.

In October 1833, it was agreed that messengers to the associational meeting would be decided by secret ballot. This decision was to become "a uniform rule." Joseph Spurgin was chosen to act as a trustee along with the already-elected William Raper. Mention was made on different occasions where the preaching was taking place "before a large and attentive congregation."

In the December 1833 business meeting, nothing is said of the weather but "after preaching administered the ordinance of baptism to Hannah E. Mock and Nancy Vickery."

The assignment to draft the Rules of Decorum and report back to the next meeting was given to Mathew D. Freedman, Joseph Spurgin, and Phillip Horney. Such was the extent of the business part in April 1834. The worship part featured singing and prayer in addition to the sermon. A month later some were united with the church by experience while yet another, Sister Dinah Atkinson, was received as a "tracient" [sic] member.

The committee of three had done their homework for the Rules of Decorum. The rules were presented and adopted as following in June of 1834.

Rules of Decorum
(from minutes of the church)

1. The church when assembled shall open their business with singing and prayer by the moderator or by some other person at his request.

2. The pastor of the church shall be moderator except the church think best to appoint some other person, whose duty it shall be to invite all brothers and sisters of sister churches, who are present and are in good fellowship at home to sit with this

church, also to put questions and announce decisions.

3. The first business that shall be entered upon by the church shall be an inquiry into the fellowship and orderly conduct of all the members and if there be any disorder, or cause of grief, it shall be brought forward and acted upon.

4. Then all differences shall be brought forward and acted upon.

5. It shall be the duty of each member to attend all church meetings by the hour of eleven o'clock and any male member, not prevented by known bodily infirmity failing to attend two meetings in succession shall be cited to come forward and show cause why he has done so, and if any female member not prevented by infirmity or disease repeatedly neglect to attend a church meeting, there shall be some person or persons to inquire the cause.

6. All members shall keep their seats during the meeting nor shall any male members withdraw without leave of the church neither by laughing nor talking in time of conference.

7. Every male member upon going to speak shall rise from his seat and address the moderator and members generally.

8. No person shall speak on the same matter more than twice without leave of the church and while speaking shall avoid casting any reflections calculated to wound the feelings of any member, and shall confine himself closely to the subject in question.

9. When two members rise at the same time the moderator shall decide who shall speak first.

10. All matters before the church shall be determined by majority union of the members then present.

11. All motions made and seconded shall be attended to except withdrawn by the mover.

12. It shall be the duty of each member at all church meetings and times of communion to take their seats otherwise it shall be deemed disorder.

13. There shall be a clerk regularly elected by the church whose duty it shall be to record the proceedings of the church, to do the reading, and to report such member as have by repeated absences violated the provision above mentioned for securing functual [sic] attendance at church meetings.

14. There shall be a trustee regularly appointed by the church whose duty it shall be to receive and transmit funds in behalf of the church and preserve a correct account of his proceedings

and render a written report of the same to this church at least once a year bearing his signature. In the margin beside this article, we read this "the fourteenth article is recinded [sic]. We call attention to this because we will hear from it again.
15. The Lord's Supper should be administered at least once in three months.
16. The clerk shall at the close of business read over the minutes of the proceedings, that if any thing needs correction it may undergo that correction before dismission [sic].

During the June meeting, others were mentioned as being baptized which seems to be more frequent than it had been before the division or at any time since that had occurred. At the next regular meeting one month later, "the church took into consideration the provision of the fourteenth article of the Rules of Decorum which is continued to the next meeting." In addition, Brother Freeman, who had been listed as preaching on several occasions, was asked to write Samuel Wait and "request him to send us a copy of the complaint that Brother Dowd enlisted against Elder Ashley Swaim to the church at Abbots Creek." Just what had produced such a request at this time is not known (Wait and Dowd's letters are included in chapter five of this book). The minutes of the July meeting list Samuel Wait as giving the opening prayer. Nothing else is given as to what questions were asked or of any explanation as to why he was there or what answers were given to the satisfaction of the church. The next conference reminds us that Thomas' letter to Elder Wait is "complied with and satisfactorily answered" with no other explanation, not one word to hint what this concerned.

The August minutes pick up on the discussion of the fourteenth article of the Rules of Decorum. The body rendered a decision saying the trustees are to continue, "to discharge the duties required in the fourteenth article in the Rules of Decorum."

Nothing had been mentioned since the August 1833 meeting about the committee joining with New Friendship and Jamestown to find a preacher for the churches. Brother Thomas had preached often as had Eli Phillips and a few others especially when there were multi-preachers at the services. At the January 1835 meeting, Jonathan Welch, Joseph Spurgin, and William Raper were appointed to "call a preacher to attend us the present year and report at the next meeting." Rather than hearing a report, the minutes state the committee's report "is continued." The same was true for the next two meetings, and at the third (May) meeting "the committee appointed to procure a preacher is continued and the church unites in applying to Elder Eli Phillips." In the June meeting, the committee reported they had agreed with Elder Phillips to "attend us once in two months for the remaining of this present year." The church approved this at the June 1835 session.

We pick up a significant and extremely interesting matter at this point. "On Friday the nineteenth of June, Elder Eli Phillips preached in the new meetinghouse" from John 5:39. Since the division of the church in June of 1832, the minutes always state the church met at the Abbotts Creek meetinghouse. The minutes have been carefully reviewed by several of us, and nothing can be found as to the need for a different building, funds being raised to build, no mention of the purchase of land, or the kind of structure that was to be built. We know the two groups met in the same building at different times for a couple of years. Over the years, traditions or facts were passed down for us allowing us to know the group crossed the road and built a brush arbor. Information leads us to believe the building mentioned here was a log church. The minutes remain silent about the facts but this clearly states a new "meetinghouse."

Henry Sheets gives this bit of information. "The two organizations, the Regular Baptists and the Anti-mission, have their houses of worship in the same beautiful grove—some little distant apart."[2] This still does not give us any details helping our search for the construction of our very first building.

The next mention of the meetinghouse for the Abbotts Creek worshippers was during the time Elder George Pope was pastor.

> While Mr. Pope was pastor it is said that he preached in a small log house a few yards east from the present old one, which, it is said, was built early in the nineteenth century. The house being small and the congregation large, the people often had to stand on the outside of the house to hear the preacher.[3]

As to why a separate building was needed in the first place, we find Henry Sheets talking with Deacon John Teague, who was elected clerk at Abbotts Creek ten years after the division of the churches. He served as clerk for thirty-seven years "until the infirmities of age demanded his resignation."

Deacon John Teague, of Old Abbott's Creek church, in his old age, told Sheets that he was born August 18, 1815; and was therefore about seventeen years old when the split took place in the old church. He said that he attended Sunday School at Abbott's Creek regularly before the split there. He recollected well that the large meetinghouse would sometimes be nearly full of Sunday School scholars. About the time of the division in the church, the people were gathering for school as usual on the Sabbath. Someone who knew, remarked, "you need not go to school today, the doors are nailed up and you can not get in." All of which was found to be true. That ended the Sunday School work in that house.[4]

The new building was used for the first time in May 1835, so we note what happened after the July 1832 organization of the church. In June, the minority left the church when it was evident there was no way for the two groups to worship together. After a brief conference outside, they agreed to meet in July at which time they were constituted into a new church and determined to remain true to the previous practices of the old church. They continued to be the Abbotts Creek Church. But, on May 19, 1835, the first sermon was preached in the new meetinghouse.

We know they continued to meet in the same building as the anti-mission group for something like two years. We do not know anything of their meeting place or places between the times they were "nailed out" until the May 19 session in the new facility.

The old minutes allowed us to know they met every month except November of 1832, when mention was made that the session was omitted in order to attend the Liberty Baptist Association's meeting. Notations are given that tell us the meetings were held, some brother was selected as moderator, or there was singing and prayer. Nothing else was mentioned on several different occasions. Time and again, we read where complaints were called for but none given. In fact, it was February of 1833 before any mention is made of a preaching service involving the new group. On Saturday, Eli Phillip preached using the text from Matthew 3:30, and the next Sunday, he preached from Proverbs 18:24. Evidently preaching was taking place, though not mentioned, because in the October 1832 meeting, Phillip Horney and Margaret and Hannah Raper joined the fellowship by "experience." Joseph Spurgin and Jan Jones were restored to the fellowship. They had been excluded from the old church. The following Elders delivered the sermons during a span of thirty-five months: Eli Phillips, Paul Phillips, Joseph Wiseman, Eli Carroll, Paul Phifer, M. D. Freeman, Elder Lanier and Elder Richards.

Those elders delivered sermons from twenty-seven different books of the Bible. John's account of the gospel was used seven times while Matthew's writings were used five times. Four times Proverbs from the Old Testament provided the sermon text. Three sermons came from Luke. Twice the Elders went to I John, Revelation, Ephesians, I Timothy, II Corinthians, Genesis, Jeremiah, and Psalms. The Old Testament books of Isaiah, Malachi, Ezekiel, II Kings, and Ecclesiastes were used for one message each. Galatians, I Corinthians, Mark, Titus, I Peter, Romans and Acts were the New Testament books used as the scriptural basis for different messages one time each.

Rachel, always referred to as a colored woman, was restored to fellowship in January of 1833 (excluded from the old church), and later she was excommunicated because she "joined another society."

In September of 1833, James Odell, one of the original members, was cited to the church because of his non-attendance but restored the next month. The November meeting mentions that Nancy Vickery, Hannah Mock, and Heziah Wheeler had joined the church by experience. In March Heziah Raper came by experience. At the same meeting Betty Evans was restored but there had been nothing said about her becoming or being a member or of her being censured. In May, Polly Welch and Jonathan Welch came by experience. The same was true for Ester Wood and Polly Miller. Ruth Payne (listed earlier as Ruth Pain) was restored, but there had been no record of her being censured.

Baptismal services were mentioned for the first time at the June 1833 meeting when Huldah Motsinger and Ann Crouch were received by "experience." They along with Polly Miller, Jonathan and Polly Welch, and Heziah Wheeler were baptized.

The first letter of dismissal was for Polly Miller in September of 1834. Four months later Betty Evans was excommunicated for "joining another society not in fellowship with this church" thus becoming the second one to meet this fate.

For the next several meetings, we note, "the way was opened for complaints but none were offered."

In September of 1835, preaching started on Saturday prior to the third Sunday and continued the next day. Monday, Elder Phillip followed by Elder Richardson preached and a way was opened for "experience." Phebe Teague, Ester Bodenhamer, Christiana Evans, Eliza Raper, Ann Charles, John Teague, Solomon Motsinger, and Alexander Delap [sic] "came forward relating their experiences and were received into the church." Elder Phillip baptized them the very next day. Two months later, Delap [sic] asked for a letter of dismissal. On Friday, October 2, it is mentioned Elder Freeman preached and Richard Couch came forward and was received into the church and was baptized. Whether the meeting that started on Saturday prior to the third Sunday in September was still going or not, we are not told.

Elder Phillip agreed in December of 1835 "to attend us for the year 1836...to commence in March and continue throughout the year."

Worship services continued to take place with preaching, prayers, and singing. Each session opened the way for complaints, but for many months, none had been heard.

The church at the March 1836 meeting had this recorded. "Brother Charles informs this church that Friendship Church acquiesces in the camp meeting being held at Abbots Creek to commence the Friday before the third Sunday in September." No other mention is made of the camp meeting.

We have noted, a few by this time had asked for a letter of dismissal without explanation. At the April meeting, "Sister Frances Atkins handed in a letter of dismissal and was received into fellowship with this church." It seemed she had requested it from somewhere else and brought it with her. Much earlier, prior to the split, we recall some were excommunicated for moving away without asking for a letter of dismissal.

It was not unusual for two or more to preach during the Saturday and Sunday meetings each month. Concerns had been expressed about some financial help for those who traveled to preach. This was not limited to Abbotts Creek. In September of 1836, the church "took into consideration the propriety of imploying [sic] traveling preachers in the bounds of the association and subscribed five dollars for that purpose." James Evans was appointed to meet with other delegates from the churches at Holloways "to fix a plan for that purpose." He reported the next time he had attended that meeting. It was called to the attention of the church at the July 1838 business session that $1.80 was sent to the associational meeting for "corresponding preachers."

In October and November of 1836, baptismal services took place for some who had joined the fellowship of the church by experience. While that was taking place, the minutes kept recording "no complaints offered." The next year in April, it was recorded like this, "inquired for the fellowship of the church all well."

During the same April meeting, "At the unanimous request of the church Elder Wiseman agreed to attend at this place for the remainder of this present year." At the next monthly meeting Elder Phillips preached twice and Wiseman preached once. Together they served the Lord's Supper.

Several meetings had taken place with no complaints being given. Someone was granted a letter of dismissal while others had joined by experience. An occasional new name appears as preaching for the Saturday or Sunday services, sometimes for both days. For the first time since the new meetinghouse was used, John Teague was appointed; "to attend to shutting the doors of the meetinghouse for one year." This was done in August 1838. The clerk was so exact in giving the scriptural text for the sermon. More than one time saying, in these words: "the latter clause of the verse." In December of 1838, the business session heard a motion made to settle with Elder Wiseman for his services for the past year. The motion was that William Raper was "to pay Brother Wiseman the amount in his hand."

The Sunday meeting of March 1839 was held and preaching took place. However, for the Saturday meeting, "The member was prevented from attending in consequences of incessant rain that fell that day." The meeting three months later had this recorded for another business meeting, "but few attended and there was no business."

Over the next two years, June 1840-42, Elder Wiseman preached for several services in December with one or two others mentioned with preaching by Elder Benjamin Lanier.

January, February, and March meetings were recorded, but no preaching was listed until April of 1841 when Elder Lanier began preaching. No mention is made of the church calling him to care for the church until June of 1842 when the membership voted for him to continue with them though January of 1843 "under the same conditions."

During these months complaints were called for but none given. One was listed as joining the fellowship and one was excommunicated for joining another group not in friendly cooperation with the fellowship of Abbotts Creek.

In May of 1842, the church "took into consideration the necessity of visiting Sister Anna Evans in her afflictions" and appointed three people to visit her and report back at the next meeting. The visiting persons reported back without any recording of their report and were discharged of their assignment by "laying over the case till the next meeting." No details were included but the case was dismissed the next time because the church was "satisfied that she will be taken care of for the future."

Elder Lanier made a motion at the April 1843 meeting:

> That there be a committee appointed to attend the churches at

Jamestown and New Friendship to inform them that we look in consideration the weakness of the churches and have appointed Brother William Raper and Joseph Spurgin to the Jamestown church and Brother J. Teague and J. Spurgin to New Friendship.

What the concerns were or what was meant by weakness is not spelled out for us. Their report was given at the next meeting and they were discharged of their responsibilities. It always seemed important for a committee to be discharged by vote of the church after doing what the church had asked to be done. The very next line in the minutes tells us John Teague was elected as clerk.

It appears that Elder Lanier did the preaching during the time of his call through January of 1843. The minutes were dated through October of 1842 and the November conference is dated 1843. This seems to be a misprint rather than a gap because Elder Lanier was still preaching and we have gone from the December 1843 meeting back to March of 1843. For a few months, no preaching was mentioned. It probably was taking place because on more than one occasion, "the way was opened for new members."

In January of 1844, the church "unanimously agreed to call Elder Hammer to preach for us." The next meeting he attended and "consented to attend the ensuing years." Things seemed to move on without complaint even though there was no mention of new members. December 1845 the church called Elder Hammer to "preach for the church the insuing [sic] year."

The Rules of Decorum adopted in the earliest days after the constitution of the church were called for to be read at the February 1845 meeting. The church agreed to alter the fifteenth article by striking out the number five and part of six. It was also agreed to strike out article fourteen. It can be noticed the clerk began to write "after divine worship" the conference opened.

The September 1845 minutes read, "A camp meeting was held at this time and place." Four persons were named who "came forward relating their experience and received the ordinance of baptism."

We cannot be specific about camp meetings and their influence at Abbotts Creek, but historians tell us about the nature of camp meetings in general. Churches were scattered and transportation was by walking, horseback, or by wagon, and church people came together and camped for days to attend services. Reports stated people traveled up to eighty miles to attend. Henry Sheets tells us "Later on, small log huts were built, many of them, where the people cooked, ate and slept. Nearly all the old churches had these small buildings (called tents), one belonging to each family."[5] *Paschal* (Vol. 2, 362-63) gives information from Benedict's *History of Baptists*, helping us see the picture of families or church groups traveling great distances, and were encouraged by their ministers to come prepared to care for their own needs. The local people would help and provide some refreshments but were not able to care for numerous congregations over a period of time. Besides this, they should not be hindered from assembling with the worshippers themselves. Camp meetings were generally held near a grove of trees providing shade for the crowds. The meetinghouses were small which meant groups had to wait, often under the shade trees, before taking their turn to enter the place of worship. The Abbotts Creek minutes gave no indication of what took place. We only know the camp meeting was in progress "at this time and place."[5]

As churches began to multiply and distances were not as great, camp meetings gave way to "protracted meetings." Dates were set and invitations were sent to the churches and ministers within reasonable distances. All of this seems to have been a forerunner to what were later called revivals. In these protracted meetings, ministers were all seated near the front of the crowds, thus letting all know who would be preaching their turn. Some were not known as good preachers and rather than the local pastor having to tell them they could not preach, a committee was formed to weed out the weaker ones. They seemed to do this by informing certain ones that the desired number of speakers had already been chosen. Often times the ones not chosen would simply leave without staying for the meetings.

"To make a choice of a pastor stands postponed to the January meeting in consequence of not many members present" was recorded at the December 1845 meeting.

Again in September of 1846, we read a camp meeting was held "at this time and place." Five people related their experience and received the ordinance of baptism. A month later, the church selected Elder Lanier as pastor for the "ensuing year."

For the first time in many months, in March 1847, a committee of three was appointed to visit a sister. No reason was given. The report was continued at the next meeting but at the next meeting, the report was given and the committee discharged but there still was no hint of the substance of the report. During the fall months of August and September of 1847, several members were added by experience and were baptized.

The February 1848 business meeting mentions the church "eunanumously [sic] agreed to call Elder (no name is given) for our pastor if we fail to agree, call Elder Turner." I take the missing name to be Elder Lanier but the March minutes simply state, "Failed to get either of the above named Elders." Brother Spurgin was chosen to get a pastor for the remainder of the year. At the next meeting, we learned Brother Spurgin "reported satisfactorily" but what he reported was not named. A couple of meetings later, Elder Lanier was mentioned as the leader.

In the May meeting of 1848, the church instructed the clerk "to write to Sister Martha Raper and inform her of unfavorable reports that were being circulated and notified her to appear at the next meeting. This was not mentioned again until the March 1849 meeting and then it was referred to the next meeting. However, as the congregation gathered for the April meeting, the church agreed to write her a letter requesting her to appear at the next meeting. She failed to report as requested and Brother Teague was to visit her and bring his report for the next meeting. At the same meeting, four people were received into the church and baptized by Elder A. Jacobs. At the June 1849 session, the church "eunanimously [sic] agreed to exclude Martha Raper." The reasons were still not listed but the situation was first mentioned thirteen months earlier.

Camp meetings had been mentioned at least twice before and were mentioned again as taking place in September 1848. One person was baptized that month and one the next month. It appears when one came for membership by experience, he or she was baptized the same day. In December of this same year, Elder Lanier was called to the "pastoral charge of the church."

In January and February, members were appointed to visit certain sisters without details of their mission. They and the church understood this purpose to the extent their reports were given at the next meeting and the members of the committees were discharged.

Another camp meeting was held in September. Twenty-seven names were listed of persons who "related their experience and were baptized by Elder Lanier." No mention was made of how long this lasted nor who did the preaching. The months following, Elder E. Dobson preached and administered the ordinance of baptism to three others. The cool days of November did not hinder Elder Williams from baptizing four other new members.

Elder Lanier was again elected as pastor and he agreed to be at the December 1849 business session.

The first month of the New Year, 1850, after some years of no complaints being offered, Ephraim Brown brought one to the attention of the congregation. The stated complaint was "against Brother James Crouch for having joined the Masonic Lodge." Motion was made to refer this to the next meeting. The moderator at the next meeting, interestingly enough, started the business session by asking about the "health of the church." The second matter was "the case of Brother Crouch." The third matter on the agenda states the case was "laid over until the next meeting."

The very next line of the minutes read, "demanded Brother Crouch lisins [sic] he refuses to hear the church." A motion was then made for a committee to be appointed to "labor with Brother Crouch and try to bring about a reconciliation and report" at the next business meeting.

A month later the committee reported that Brother Crouch "still refuses to come to terms with the church and the committee was discharged." Crouch was called on "to know if there was any change in his mind and he answered there was not." "It was then moved and seconded that we take a final action on Brother James Crouch's case." Seemingly it did not take long for a decision, for the church "eunanimously [sic] agreed to expel James Crouch for joining the Masonic Lodge after he joined the church and then refusing to hear the church."

A couple of months later, we were able to learn that the last of that matter had not been heard. The June 1850 meeting minutes have given us this record.

> The moderator informed the church of the standing of Brother J. Crouch and Sister A. Crouch and took up the case against them for declaring an unfellowship against the church at the March meeting for excluding James Crouch for joining the Masonic Lodge and refusing to hear the church. Brother Crouch declared the church could show no sin in it and the blood would be on there [sic] own shirts.

The minutes continued with this which seems to have been written in haste because of the spelling and few marks of punctuation.

> The church thinking they acted in hast [sic] and that they would reflect an [sic] return and ecknowledge [sic] there [sic] error at the April we found them no better Brother Crouch offered a complaint against the whole church which we refused to hear

but still hoped that time and reflection would bring repentance and continued up to the present being called on said there [sic] was no change."

J. Spurgin, Wm Raper, and J. Jones make up the committee to "labour" [sic] with them.

The July meeting simply stated that Brother and Sister Crouch gave satisfaction to the church. There was nothing to indicate if Brother Crouch gave up his membership with the Masonic Lodge or if the church accepted him without requiring him to do so. At the same meeting, a letter was received from Brother and Sister Ledford inquiring of their "standing in the church." Again no explanation but a motion was made to inform them of their standing with the church.

So seldom in a church history do we find anything negative given about the church. The clerk, including a complaint against the church, has to be applauded for giving us honest history. The statement was even given to allow a month's time to pass allowing the church family time to reflect on the decision they had made and all the time hoping for reconciliation.

The previous Septembers had proven to be good months for the church. No mention was made of a camp meeting, but eight people shared their experience and were received as candidates for baptism. Elder Lanier administered the ordinance of baptism.

Another Crouch was mentioned in the October 1850 meeting. Whether he was of of the same family was not added. The church agreed to "Exclude Elizabeth Crouch a single women [sic] who is found to be in a state of pregnancy." Elder Turner was called as pastor for the next year in the same business meeting. However, at the next meeting, the minutes informed us "having failed to get Elder Turner for our pastor called Elder Lanier."

When the "health of the church" inquiry was made, a complaint was offered against Brother John Nickles for being intoxicated." That case was laid over and one was appointed to cite him to the next meeting. The one to cite him gave his report and the case was referred until the next time. Someone else was to "labour" [sic] with him until the next meeting.

The past November meeting reported Elder Turner would not be pastor and Elder Lanier accepts. However, at the January 1851 meeting, "Elder Turner consented to take the pastoral care of the church."

The church was informed at the December 1851 session: "There is a report in circulation against Sister Lucy Bodenhamer that is derogatory to a

Christian character." Two sisters were appointed to inquire and report back. The next meeting found Sister Bodenhamer present "acknowledging her transgression, believing that God had pardoned her ask [sic] the church to forgive her which was granted."

The April meeting had Levi Hollon in disorder and the church laid him under censure. Two months later, he was not seen as being repentant and was excluded. The May meeting heard the report, "Olive Slone (?) in a state of pregnancy" which resulted in her being excluded.

Moving on to August of 1852, E. Brown informed the church a report was circulating against him and it was false. The church advised him to "remain silent until further circumstances occur."

Camp meeting time rolled around in September of 1852. Six persons are named as "confessing of their faith in Jesus Christ" and were baptized. The next month, four were baptized. In addition Barnabas Pain [sic] returned and not joining another church "returns his letter to the clerk."

John Robertson agreed "to the pastoral care of the church for the year 1853" during the November 1852 session. In January, he was "present and excepts [sic] the pastoral care of the church for the ensuing year."

The first mention of financial help for a member was given in February of 1853. Deacon Clinard informed the church James Odle [sic] was in "circumstances that called on the church for substance aid." The church responded by offering to "defray the expense of movin [sic] him to his sons provided that it should be his desire." Again, Deacon Clinard was connected with the situation to the extent he informed the church at the next meeting Mr. Odle desire was "to stay with us" and the church "proceeds to make arrangements for his sustenance." The church further agreed "to deposit provisions with Mr. Starbuck for Brother Odle to be delivered to him, as he may need."

In the past, we have observed how certain ones were placed under censure and later restored or excluded. A new twist appears in the March 1853 business session when Brother E. D. Brown, who approached the church the past August saying false reports were circulating about him and was advised to remain silent until further circumstances developed, requested that he be expelled. The request was granted. This leads one to believe that the earlier "false" reports may not have been false at all.

Elder Lanier was chosen to assume the pastoral role at the September 1853 meeting. He accepted the call at the October meeting to serve for the ensuing years. At the same meeting, Charles Teague was elected treasurer.

September found the church busy with another camp meeting. Eight people were listed as being added to the church by baptism.

Several business sessions were reported without any complaint being given or action taken. In February of 1855, it was mentioned Elder Turner "excepts [sic] the pastoral care of the church." There was no mention of a September camp meeting in 1855.

In January of 1856, a committee was elected and asked to report on the "salary we pay our pastor." The congregation was informed we pay the pastor fifty dollars a year. Conferences continue to be held with only a few lines being recorded concerning each. August found a couple of people asking for their church letter and they were granted. A report was given informing the church of Mary A. Brown who was in "disorder and she was excluded" but no mention is made either of her being censured or of anyone appointed to talk with her. Elder Turner was called to "the pastoral care of the church for the ensuing year."

Endnotes

1. Sheets, op. cit., 164.
2. Ibid., 83-84.
3. Ibid.
4. Ibid., 197.
5. Paschal, op. cit. vol. 3, 362-63.

CHAPTER TEN

Beginning of the Second Hundred Years

One hundred years had passed from the time James Younger and a few others began worship services in the Abbotts Creek community. The early years of struggling to survive had been rewarded. No records have been available for the most difficult years when the church was organized and re-organized twice during the first twenty-five years. Reports indicate the earlier records were burned in a house fire. Troubled by conflicts with Governor Tryon's determination to establish the Church of England involved attempts by the Regulators to resist such an effort. Citizens of Abbotts Creek seemed unable to escape being involved to some degree. Punishment and threats seemed to scatter some of the members, but history records they went elsewhere establishing churches as they settled. Fear of Native American attacks and the approaching Revolutionary War no doubt left marks, though not spelled out for us. Surely this left many of the people in an unsettled state, but their efforts to maintain a center of worship for their people resulted in the Missionary Church and the Primitive Church continuing to influence the religious life of the community.

The division of 1832 was now twenty-four years past. The church had lived in harmony with a limited number of complaints. Many had joined the church, some moved away, and a few had joined churches of other denominations. Very few had been excluded. If any celebration took place for a centennial, it was not mentioned. By this time, the church had left the Sandy Creek Association, been a part of the Yadkin association for one year, helped to organize the Abbotts Creek Union, later was a part of the organization of the Liberty Baptist Association, and seems to have elected messengers to attend each time there was an associational meeting.

Abbotts Creek again called Elder Turner to lead the church in 1857. During March and April, the notations in our church records tell us there were no conferences held. In August, someone was expelled for "unchristian conduct," though no mention had been made that he was called before the church or censured. Elder Turner was called to pastor the church for the next year in October but informed the church he could not do so in 1858. The minutes would lead us to believe there was much harmony among the people. The year ended with the church calling A. Weaver (?) as pastor for the next year.

In April of 1858, after no complaints were offered, "on motion agreed to protract the May meeting." The May meeting mentions three people joined the church by letter. Later, a couple asked for their letters of dismissal and two others were baptized and became members. During the final month of 1858, the church "Resolved that we be governed by the plurality vote in choice of a pastor, maid [sic] choice of Elder Turner for pastor."

The New Year (1859) opened with Elder Turner giving a negative answer to this call. The clerk was authorized "to write to Elder Lanier having received the next highest votes." No answer is given, but a couple of months later, Elder Lanier is listed as moderator of the business session "after divine worship." In July of this year, six people were granted letters of dismissal at the Saturday conference. Two more were granted at the Sunday worship, with yet another letter granted the next month. Nine persons removed their membership over a period of two months yet the minutes still lists "complaints called for and none offered."

No conference was held in December of 1859 nor the first two months of 1860. The same was true for June and July 1860. At the September conference "Sister Eliza Brown presented a Bible for the use of the church." The church made a choice of a pastor for the ensuing year during the October conference. The choice was Brother Jackson but a notation informs us "failed to get Elder Jackson."

The year 1861 opened with a committee being appointed to get a new pastor. There was no February conference but the committee reported in March and had "secured the services of Elder Noah Richardson as pastor."

September followed with no business meeting the previous month. The "doors of the church being opened," it was mentioned that one came forward and "was considered a fit subject for baptism." John Robbertson [sic] baptized the new Christian. Later, we see his name spelled with one "b," which was probably the correct spelling. "Being without a pastor the church went into the election of a pastor which resulted in the choice of John Robbertson." We had not seen any notation of dissatisfaction among the congregation, no complaints had been offered, nor any mention of the resignation of Elder Noah Richardson who was announced as pastor in March. There have been other times where the pastor did not serve the length of the call, usually a year or the remainder of the current year. No other information has been read to help us understand if this was a unique situation or a common practice. For several business sessions preceeding the September date, Robbertson became pastor and the minutes afterward continued to read, "Complaints called for, non [sic] offered." The very next month, three new members were baptized.

"On motion agreed to revise the list of church members" is the only business recorded during the June 1862 conference. No criteria were listed for this undertaking and no one was specified as the one or ones to attend to this job.

The October meeting listed one excluded, one female only, for fornication. No male is mentioned. The decision was unanimously rendered. The next item of business was to elect Elder John Robertson (only one "b" now and afterwards) as pastor. With his being present, the church received an affirmative answer. For the rest of that year and until December of the next (1863), the only business mentioned was the representatives elected for the Liberty Baptist Association's meeting. This was done annually prior to the scheduled associational meetings. Abbotts Creek Church was always very active and supportive of the ministry of the association. The church at the December meeting "proceeded to make choice of a pastor for 1861 which resulted in the choice of J. B. Jackson."

The next complaint came in June of 1864 when Sister Juliann Hedgecock was reported for "disorderly conduct." The next meeting she was excluded for being "guilty of adultery." At the September meeting, "R. Quincy Teague was excluded "for having joined the Society of Friends." At the same time, four were received for baptism. The year closed with the December meeting at which time Elder Jackson was selected as pastor and agreed to the same for the next year.

A new twist is seen at the March 1865 meeting. No mention has been made of the Civil War taking place, but "the doors of the church being opened Newel W. Beeson came forward and was received on certificate from the army." Five months later, at what seemed to be the next voted action, found "Ester Brown excluded from the fellowship of the church

HISTORY, HERITAGE, AND MEMORIES

for adultery." No mention had been made of a previous censure on the part of the church. The tenure of Brother Jackson as pastor was nearing an end but he was re-elected at the November 1865 session for business.

In February of 1866 the church excluded Wm. Carter "for using profane language." Earlier he had been called before the church. Seven business meetings in succession are listed where the only matter presented was the appointment of the messengers for the Liberty Baptist Association.

At the October session, "The meeting was protracted and on the fourth Lord's Day the list of eighteen persons was baptized." We have not always listed the name of each one who joined the church (sometimes the names were not given), but we do this time because of so many at the same time. They were: Charles Watkins, G. W. Charles, Roan Charles, A. R. Jackson, Jeffrey T. Traynham, John Hedgecock, William R. Hedgecock, D. H. Bodenhamer, Thomas Beeson, Lucy A. Traynham, E. L. Traynham, Mary Teague, L. F. Clinard, C. J. Clinard, Elizabeth Crouch, Flora Pitts, Melissa J. Charles and Eliza A. Spurgin.

The choice for a pastor for 1867 resulted in the selection of Brother Jackson again. This took place in November of 1866. N. B. Orrell and Elizabeth Payne were received into the church by letter. R. L. Teague was restored to full membership. With no mention of the cold November weather, the following people were baptized: Emory E. Pitts, J. J. Jones, Christina Orrell, Martha Shields, W. Idol, L. K. Raper, and G. H. Spurgin. The next baptism listed took place in May of 1867. In October, two others joined the church and were "received as fit subjects for baptism." Another one came and was baptized in November.

A committee made up of Emory Pitts, Wm. Clinard, and C. J. Watkins was elected in December of 1867 to "raise funds for the purpose of building a new church."

The February 1868 meeting has this notation as business: "On motion associated Eld [sic] J. B. Richardson with Eli Jackson as pastor of the church." The next minutes state, "Brother Richardson does not except [sic]. This is hard to clarify but seemingly the church voted on two persons at the same time with one declining. No mention is made of which one had the most votes after the voting had taken place.

The June meeting starts off by saying, "The church in fellowship received Simeon Shoseraft (?) colored on a relation of his experience as a candidate for baptism. He was baptized the next Sunday along with William Spurgin and his wife Emily." With the slaves being freed by this time, he is the first to be listed as a "colored" person without mention of an owner.

October 1868 finds the church electing a new pastor. Brother J. B. Richardson was unanimously elected to this position. He accepted the call in December. From all indications, the church prospered during the days Brother Jackson served the church. The relationship between pastor and people must have been good. The following resolution was adopted upon his resignation. This was another first for the church.

> Whereas Elder J. B. Jackson has been the faithful and devoted pastor of the harvest, and whereas, he has made known to us the necessity of leaving us and going west, and thereby breaking up the relation that exists between, as pastor and church.
> Resolved, that we part with him in sorrow, remembering his self denial, and meek deportment while he went in and out before us.
> Resolved, that we recommend him to the church and people wherever God in his providence may direct him, as a faithful and devoted minister of the Gospel, and our prayers go up before God for his success and that our Christian sympathies may cluster around him.

January 1869 started with the church decision to have "services twice a Month, appointing the fourth Sabbath in each month for the second service." The conference minutes the next month referred to a letter from the former pastor, Brother Jackson. The letter was read and the present pastor led the prayer as the "church unified in prayer."

In addition to the letter, "on motion a committee consisting of Brother Wm. Clinard, P. W. Raper, and Moses Teague were appointed to see if services at this church on the fourth Sabbath would seriously conflict with appointments of any other church. On motion church conference adjourned."

The Rules of Decorum stated earlier that the clerk was to read the minutes of the business session before the conference was dismissed. If any error was detected, it could be corrected on the spot. However, at the March 1867 meeting we see for the first time "proceeding of last meeting read and approved." The decision was made for this to be done in the future and in parenthesis beside the statement "(after they are recorded on the church book)."

No mention had been made in earlier records of a starting time for the services. At the above mentioned meeting, "On motion, agreed that 11 o'clock be the hour for commensing [sic] services at our meetings." The committee also reported the decision to add fourth Sunday services would not conflict with services of any other church.

Sabbath preaching was taking place in May of 1869 by the pastor. An evening service is mentioned at which time Brother Wightman was preaching. A notation is made "congregation large." We further note the minutes with this information: "Fourth Sabbath preaching at 11 o'clock to the white and at 2:30 o'clock to the colored."

Three months later, in August, the pastor preached followed by Brother Harmon. "After intermission, Brother Hammer preached from Romans 5:7."

A month later, "Sister Phebe A. Carter returned her letter with a note informing the church that she had joined the Methodist church for which she was excluded." The next line tells of another person who was excluded "for fornication." Both were excluded for totally different reasons. This seemed to have taken place at the Saturday meeting because the Sabbath meeting is mentioned next with "congregation large." The pastor preached at eleven o'clock followed by Brother Harmon. Then we read "after intermission" William Hammer preached at the two o'clock service. No mention is made that the congregations were segregated for these services. For several consecutive services, the pastor preached followed by another preacher.

No explanation was given but in November 1869, the Sabbath preaching by Brother Harmon was followed by Brother Richardson, "congregation large." Monday services are mentioned with no business listed, complaints were not called for and there was no mention of adjournment. Two letters of dismissal were granted followed by the pastor's message on the prodigal son. On Tuesday, Elder Turner preached.

We move from the mention of the Tuesday service into the next month where "oweing [sic] to enclemency [sic] of the weather, the church did not meet on Saturday." Sunday's note may imply the pastor did not live near enough to make it to church in the worse type of weather. "In the absence of the pastor, services were conducted by Brethren Harmon and Brown. We can read between the lines that the church did not allow the situation to keep the congregation from worship.

The first two months of 1870, services were held but no business mentioned. The March meeting opened with what seems to be a new person preaching, Brother Carie, followed by Brother Harmon. We note the previous year had ended and a new one beginning with no mention of the

Beginning of the Second Hundred Years

church making a decision regarding a pastor. After the preaching was over, the church "met in conference. Proceedings of the last meeting approved." This group of people who believed Bible teaching was important was now thirty-eight years away from those who opposed Sunday Schools. The minutes have informed us of their decision. "On motion appointed a Sunday School Convention. Resolved, that we cordially invite the churches of the Liberty Association to meet with us in a Sunday School Convention on Saturday before the fifth Sunday in May. Resolved, that we earnestly request Brother B. W. Justice to be with us in said convention." Previous minutes have made no mention of the church ever being invited to attend such a "convention" which leads one to believe Abbotts Creek was the first church to make such an emphasis on Sunday School. The May conference occurred before the scheduled date of the "convention." The June meeting is silent about such an event if indeed it took place. The results remain unknown. Of course, had that taken place without it being a conference time, the clerk would not have included it as a part of the business session. No doubt many good things took place in the church at non-conference times and are not recorded for us.

Four or five members had been absent for a number of church meetings. The August 1870 meeting had others appointed to contact them and report back at the next session. The pastor was absent for the "Sabbath Day "service but two of the brethren led in a prayer meeting. It must have been a powerful service for we note what took place in the September meeting.

"The meeting protracted ten days, the pastor assisted by Brethren Turner and Harmon three days and by Elder Jordan two days. The Lord was with us during the meeting. A number of persons professed faith in Christ and the members of the church revived. The Lord has done great things for us whereof we are glad, to his name be all the glory. On Monday the last day of the meeting from inability of the pastor, Brother F. M. Jordan baptized into the fellowship of the church the following persons: Peter R. Bodenhamer, Joseph M. Raper, Sanford Spurgin, Hyram Clinard, John Cadell, Montalva Mendenhall, King C. Beeson, John Q. Teague, Henry Traynham, Henry Harris, Pleasant Horney, Orville Raper, Larkin Charles, Phebe W. Horney, Sarah E. Bodenhamer, Eliza J. Teague, Mary Clinard, Sarah Lou Clinard, Elsie G. Charles, Jane Brown, Elizabeth Peake, Eleanor Charles, Phebe Mendenhall, Sarah J. Raper, Alice Richardson, and Mary Banks Traynham.

George W. Brown was accepted by letter and two other were baptized, 'Minerva and Lucinda, colored.'"

The following month the pastor preached and the previously mentioned Brother Carie led the prayer. The committee reported on those who had been visited to the satisfaction of the church. Two other candidates for baptism were named. The next day, Sunday, "met at the water. The pastor Elder Richardson baptised [sic] Dr. Dillard, Meranda Dillard, Jane E. Teague, Emma Spurgin, Crissa Carter into the fellowship of the church." Leaving there, they "repaired to the house, the pastor preached and the Lord's Supper was administered."

The next item mentioned what else took place. "Sunday preaching by the pastor, then repaired to the water and baptized Joseph Charles, Levi Brown, Jesse Clinard and George Traynham colored into the fellowship of the church." With present-day inside baptismal pools, it is easily understood how in earlier days some came to be baptized at the morning service and others at an afternoon service. However, it appears their service started at the water after which they went to the church for the morning service and then back to the water. This must have created great excitement among the church people.

We have seen many times where persons were chosen and ordained as deacons. However, in November of 1870, a presbytery composed of Pastor J. B. Richardson and B. G. Covington "proceeded to set apart Newell W. Beeson and Mose Teague to the office of deacons by the imposition of

Pastor Mark Holler is shown baptizing Molly Gibbons in the old outdoor pool.

hands." Much earlier, we were informed of a presbytery which had been involved in the ordination of a minister but never mentioned for deacons. After this, the church "repaired to the water" where they witnessed four others who were baptized.

The year 1870 closed with nothing being said concerning the election of a pastor. Attention is called to this because for a number of years, every nine to twelve business meetings, the election of the church's pastor was determined by the church. In March of that spring, Pastor Richardson "tendered his resignation through the clerk." Two meetings earlier, he had missed the Saturday meeting but preached on Sunday. In consideration of a pastor, the church "referred it to the April meeting."

A committee was appointed at the May meeting "to visit Red Bank Church in reference of pastoral service of Elder Turner." G. W. Harmon was called to serve as "supply for the balance of this year." Numerous preachers had preached and some seemingly several times in a row, but for the first time one was actually voted on to be called the supply pastor.

In August, the committee appointed to visit Red Bank reported. Period! What was the report? It must have been "just wait" because it was January of 1872 before we read, "The members present vote unanimously for Elder Turner pastor." The next few minutes included a reference to preaching by the pastor, but it was not until March that Elder Turner was actually mentioned as that pastor.

Elder Turner served Abbotts Creek for many years. Our records show he served from 1872 through 1889. In a few of those years someone else was listed pastor. Some other records list him serving at Abbotts Creek for thirteen years, eighteen years, and still another list sixteen years. Rev. John Pace has written a book, *History of New Friendship Baptist Church*. In that book published in 2007, he refers to Elder Turner saying he "must rank near the top of a list of ministers who served in this area." At the age of seventy three, he was still serving as pastor at New Friendship, Abbotts Creek, Lick Creek, and Holloways Baptist churches at the same time. "During the last years of his life, probably eight or nine, he was so afflicted he had to sit on a high stool and preach, but none the less effective because of this."

It was known that he had said he preferred dying "in the harness" rather than "outliving his usefulness." On April 6, 1889, he preached a short message at New Friendship Baptist Church where he had served as pastor for thirty nine years, and while traveling home "fell in his wife's arms and expired." (Pace, 231).

N. B. Orrell gave a personal confession to the church at the May 1872 meeting. He "reported to the church he had violated the third commandment (name of the Lord in vain), that it had caused him deep sorrow [and that he] hoped the Lord had forgiven him and [that he had] asked forgiveness of the church, which was granted."

The pastor preached on Saturday as the church met in October. On Sunday he preached again as did Elder Crutchfield. Numbers were never given but the statement was made "the congregation was large." Then we read, "meeting protracted three days." Elders Crutchfield and Jordan assisted the pastor. Two were received for baptism.

Though the church received African-Americans as members, it seems they were always noted as "colored." One such person was Jesse Clinard who was cited to the church for being intoxicated. He failed to be present for the next meeting. The "church believed him guilty of the charge and withdrew fellowship from him."

The Saturday meeting in January of 1872 was not held, "the weather unfavorable." At the Sunday meeting the church gave Thomas L. Beeson a "letter of recommendation for the purpose of aiding him in getting an education."

Back in December "some evil reports" concerning Sister Mary Carter were brought to the attention of the church family. In April this matter was heard and the three sisters who visited to investigate reported she pleaded innocent. However, five male members were appointed to investigate further. Their report given at the May meeting resulted in the church withdrawing fellowship from her. At the same meeting a letter of dismissal was granted to Thomas Beeson, which leads us to believe he had left the community to pursue his education. This is the first indication that anyone from the church had left the community for educational pursuits.

At the August 1873 gathering, the church met at the creek and two new members were baptized "after which the congregation assembled at the house" where the pastor brought the message. It seems safe to assume "house," which has been mentioned several times before, means the church meetinghouse.

Brother Daniel Taylor preached at what was reported to be a "divine service" at the September 1873 gathering. A meeting was protracted which started on Thursday. Five people were listed as "fit subjects for baptism" at the October meeting. The following day, the congregation "met at the water" for a baptismal service before the group returned to the house of worship.

Beginning of the Second Hundred Years

Another unexplained item surfaced at the July 1874 time for worship. "Preaching by the pastor, funeral for Peter Brown's children." Reading such facts makes one wonder: Were the children newly-born twins? How did they die? Why isn't the mother's name mentioned?

In the fall (October), "owing to inclemency of the weather, no meeting was held on Saturday. Sabbath, pastor preached the funeral of Mrs. A. Payne, Large congregation." It is recorded during the same meeting, "preaching and church conference as usual." Then as if picking up in the middle of something without explanation, we read, "the meeting continued five days, the pastor assisted by Brethren Harmon and Dodson...."

The December meeting took place without the pastor who was "excused from preaching on Sabbath to preach the funeral of Brother Nisen at Freedland."

There was no business meeting in February because the pastor was ill. Neither was there a March meeting. We are not always told why a meeting was not held, but the thoroughness of the clerk surely made notes of the lack of a meeting. A note in point, the September conference was not held "oweing [sic] to inclement weather." What constituted this is not known and we are not told how such word spread. Again in March of 1876, the Saturday business session took place, but the service for the Sabbath day involved the pastor preaching the funeral service for Moses Teague.

Late spring and summer the minutes noted little business was conducted. A four-day protracted meeting was decided on as the September group gathered. The former pastor, Benjamin Lanier, and F. W. Jones assisted the pastor.

Again in May of 1877, a funeral was "held on meeting day, the Sabbath." Afterwards the Lord's Supper was administered. This writer wants to ask, did they do this in the presence of the deceased or did they carry out the grave service and then return to the meetinghouse? Did this take place at the hour scheduled for worship?

The meeting was protracted again in November of 1877. Elder Brown assisted the pastor. One person was received "as a candidate for baptism."

From January through June neither business matters nor complaints were listed in the minutes. A couple requested letters of dismissal and another person was received by letter. Attention is called to the fact the pastor preached the funeral service for William Raper on Monday after the May Sabbath meeting.

Messengers were appointed for the associational meeting during the July gathering. Such constituted the rest of 1877, until November, at which time the minutes recorded there was preaching and "church meeting." It is then noted, "Monday the pastor and Elder R. H. Moore preached."

In January of 1872, the church had given Thomas A. Beeson a letter of recommendation to further his education. Now, December 1878, his name surfaces again. "Thomas A. Beeson formerly a member of this church and dismissed by letter to join another church of the same faith in California and said church being scattered, he could not get a letter and on application for membership is unanimously received as a member of this church." At such an early date, one wonders what educational pursuit might have demanded a trip across the country. How could one even learn there were educational institutions that far from the rural life of Abbotts Creek?

Short statements tell us the church family gathered for worship and business and we read more than once, "prayer and the usual order of business attended." In August 1879, the church agreed to "protract the September meetings."

On Saturday, the pastor preached. On Sunday, Elder H. Jones brought a message. Jones H. Brown and Brother Richardson assisted the pastor in the meeting that continued through Saturday. On Wednesday of that week, Elder Turner baptized four people. In the absence of the pastor, Elder Jones baptized more on Saturday.

The group started the service in October with singing and prayer even though the pastor was absent for the Saturday service. The pastor was back by the next day and the activities that took place were listed. "Sabbath morning in the presence of a large congregation, Elder Turner married C. A. Rominger to Nevada Spurgin also at the same time Luther Stewart to Haritha S. Rominger."

Two months later, in December, "Elder Turner resigned the pastoral care of the church." In July of 1879, Brother J. B. Richardson was the congregational choice for the next pastor. In February, the church asked someone else to serve until "We get a pastor, having failed to procure the labors of Elder Richardson." The church moved right on and in March, the committee reported "they have procured the labors of Elder Moore for the present year."

The April 1880 conference shows the congregation understood the task of the entire fellowship. "The church assembled a committee of the whole to visit the members that repeatedly neglect to attend church meetings." They were also charged to make a "suspension list of those who never attend."

We note, too, that the clerk understood the minutes and the record book of the church belonged to the church, and he was not at liberty to change anything without church vote. The following is recorded on the same April day. "On motion ordered the clerk to change the last names of the married sisters that they may be known by their proper names."

John Teague resigned as church clerk in July of 1880, and "Wm R. Hedgecock elected clerk of the church."

Two significant actions took place at the August 1880 conference. Each action received one sentence by way of explanation. "On motion the church voted their willingness to have an organ in the church. On motion the church instructed their delegates that they would assist in supporting a missionary in the destitute point in the association." One would note there were no funds discussed for an organ. Neither was there a motion to purchase one, simply a "willingness" to have one.

For years, the church always appointed messengers for the Liberty Baptist Association, including an alternate if one of the elected ones could not attend. No mention is ever made as to what was taking place as far as what the other churches were doing together until September of 1880. Even then we don't know what was said, but "after some remarks by the delegates concerning the association the meeting adjourned." Since the Liberty Association was formed, Abbotts Creek had been a strong supporter.

The September business concerned a protracted meeting: "Brother Weaver was with us four days, J. B. Richardson four days. Brother Conrad preached four nights and two days. Also Brother Baldwin preached two sermons." The clerk then added, "there were some conversions and the church was somewhat revived."

The previous month, information was given that a collection was taken for the "board of education." The amount was four dollars. The October meeting may explain that more fully. Seven dollars and thirty-five cents was given in "cash and subscription toward the education of ministers at Wake Forest College."

In November of 1880, the church voted to elect Brother Conrad as pastor for the next year, 1881. A letter from the newly-elected pastor was read in which he stated he would accept and at the same time, he would serve the church for $125. It was moved and a second was given "that the church pay the salary. The vote was taken, resulting in yeas twelve, nays eleven." Brother Beeson was to write the result of the voting to Elder Conrad. Some years back, the congregation inquired as to what the pastor was being paid and the answer was given as fifty dollars. The agreement with Elder Conrad seemed to be the first time any minister had known in advance what his pay would be.

The long-standing policy of the church requiring the minutes of the business acted on by the church to be read by the clerk before adjournment is now officially being changed. From now on by vote of the church, those minutes would be read at the beginning of the next conference. Actually, this had been done for several months but not by church vote. It was being deliberately changed. It was decided that "a subscription paper" be given to each member "for them to subscribe what they can for the pastor's salary." Pastor Conrad was present and preached the next day.

The February meeting called for and had the Rules of Decorum read for the congregation. Some change in wording was suggested and after what seemed like much discussion, a committee was appointed to submit suggested changes at the next meeting.

The clerk then read the list of male members who had not attended meetings in quite some time. We note too for the first mentioned time, "the church adopted the use of the Baptist hymn and tune book in church services."

The committee working on changes in the Rules of Decorum reported back at the next meeting listing the suggested changes. "Rules laid over until the next meeting for further reflections." During the March session, the rule was changed to elect two trustees. Some discussion took place as other changed not specified were adopted.

We come to the close of the first book of minutes dating from 1832 through June of 1881. The last pages of the book list the membership with notations such as excluded or deceased. Even though the clerk had beautiful handwriting, some of the initials are hard to distinguish. For instance, T and J look almost alike. We need to remember where some names are listed as excluded, it could mean they were "kicked out" or simply had joined a church of another denomination.

Male Members

John Teague, Jesse Jones, Moses Teague, A. O. T. Teague, Aquilla Teague, Solomon Teague, dismissed; Charles Teague, Phillip W. Raper, excluded; William Carter, excluded; William Clinard, Barnabas Pain, 9-1850, William T. Raper, deceased; Joseph C. Teague, deceased; R. I. A. Teague, excluded; Andrew Livengood, James, colored (this was marked through); John Hepler, Newell W. Beeson, David Essee, dismissed; Charles T. Watkins, dismissed; George W. Charles.

Poan C. Charles, A. P. Jackson, Jeffrey T. Traynham, John L. Hedgecock, dismissed; Mrs. P. Hedgecock, dismissed; David A. Bodenhamer, dismissed; Thomas L. F. Peasons, dismissed; Emory E. Pitts, excluded; P. T. A. Teague, dismissed; J. J. Jones, dismissed; Anderson Crocack, N. B. Orrel, Valentine Harman, Wilson Clinard, deceased; Simon Shocraft, colored (marked thought), William Spurgin, John Sells, Peter R. Bodenhamer, Joseph M. Raper, Sanford Spurgin, Hyram Clinard.

John Cadell, dismissed; Montalva Mendenhall, John T. A. Teague, deceased; Henry Traynham, King C. Beeson, deceased; Henry Harris, excluded; Pleasant Horney, Orville W. Raper, Larkin Charles, George W. Brown, deceased; Dr. George Dillard, Servilas King, dismissed; Jacob A. Clinard, Wilson Payne, Charlie H. Teague, Willie H. Root, Wm. R. Hedgecock, William R. Hedgecock, by letter, Thomas L. Beeson, letter, Jeffrey P. Traynham.

Female Members

Margaret Raper, deceased; Phebe Horney, deceased; Martha Teague, deceased; Mary Evans, deceased; Nancy Vickery, excluded; Heziah Raper, Christina Evans, Eliza Raper, Frances Atkins, deceased; Sarah Raper, deceased; Mary G. Idol, Mary Brown, dismissed; Alethe Jones, Sarah Spurgin, Anna Teague, dismissed; Almira Teague, Elizabeth Brown, dismissed; Mary Crouch, excluded; Mary Philips, deceased; Mary J. Pain.

Hannah E. Teague, Jane Carter, Hatharane B. Ledford, Sara J. Wall, Sarah A. Jones, Esther Hayworth, Susanna Proctor, excluded; Margaret Bodenhamer, deceased; Lucy Bodenhamer, Rachael Weavil, Elizabeth Glusseck, Martha Rigans, deceased; Mary Idol, dismissed; Emaline Teague, deceased; Sarah Craver, Louisa Idol, dismissed; Jane Haworth, deceased; Ester Brown, excluded; Julian Hedgecock, Louisa Spurgin, dismissed.

Lety Brown, Emaline Hedgecock, Martha J. Teague, (then we have listed) Martha Teague, Matilda C. Teague, (a name I cannot make out, dismissed), Huldak Charles, Melissa C. Charles, Jane Horney, Sophia A. Teague, Lucy A. Traynham, Elizabeth T. Traynham, Mary E. Teague, Elizabeth Crouch, Flora T. Pitts, Melssa J. Charles, deceased; Crissa J. Clinard, Eliza A. Spurgin, Laura K. Raper, Sara G. A. Spurgin.

Loreta F. Clinard, Hesak Idol, dismissed; Charlema L. Orrel, Martha C. Shilds, Elizabeth Idol, Destimones R. Charles, excluded; Christenie C. Walls, Lotitia Pitts, Alberta Spurgin, Sarah Charles, Sarah Brown, deceased; Emily Spurgin, Rebecca Horney, Susan Sells, deceased; Nancy Teague, Elizabeth Motsinger, Jeanette Sapp, Phoebe A. Horney, Sarah E. Bodenhamer, Eliza I. Teague.

Mary Clinard, Louisa Clinard, Elsie G. Charles, Jane Brown, Elizabeth

Peake, Eleanor Charles, Phebe Mendenhall, deceased; Sarah J. Raper, deceased; Alice Richardson, dismissed; Mary Banks Traynham, deceased; Emma G. Spurgin, Jane E. Teague, Crissa Carter, deceased; Meranda Dillard, Desdemona R. Clinard, Carolina E. Richards, dismissed; Clarissa Charles, Elizabeth H. Clinard, Louiza N. Spurgin, Bettie J. Hedgecock.

Martha J. Walker, Eliza J. Clinard, Mary J. Teague, Rebeca Harmon, Lou Ann Teague, Cora E. Raper, Mary Heare, Martha Bodenhamer, Crissa J. Hayworth Naney K. Bodenhamer, Debby B. Bodenhamer, H. Banks Teague, Lena G. Charles, Lena L. Potts, Sarah T. Traynham, Eudora B. Teague, Crissa J. Teague, Margaret J. Clinard.

Colored Males

James Spurgin, dead; Simeon Shocraft, Joseph Charles, Levi Brown, George Traynham, Jesse Clinard, excluded; Louis Sowers, excluded.

Colored Females

Manerva Wood, excluded; Lucinda Clinard, dismissed; Letty Spurgin, Rose Raper, Selina Raper.

CHAPTER ELEVEN

Abbotts Creek 1881–1901

The minutes of book one have carried us from the time of the division of the church until 1881. The second book begins with the July business meeting. However, a notation prior to this reminds us of the Order of Business.

1. The calling of the roll. Penciled in beside this is the note "suspended."
2. Reading of the proceedings of the last meeting.
3. Invitation to visiting members.
4. Opening of the doors of the church for the reception of new members either by experience or by letter.
5. Unfinished business.
6. New Business
    Reports of committees (Treasurer's Report)
    Resolutions
    Motions
    Miscellaneous business
7. Adjournment

Early in the life of the church, Rules of Decorum were given. A couple of times since they were adopted, discussions were mentioned concerning such rules, but nothing to spell out what changes had been made if any. Much more took place in those changes than the few lines recorded. Since these rules tell us the understanding of the church family as to how the church would operate, it seems wise to include the new set here.

Rules of Decorum

1. Conferences shall be opened and closed with singing or prayer.
2. The pastor of the church, or in his absences, any brother whom the church may appoint, shall act as moderator and in all meetings for the transaction of business.
3. It shall be the duty of the moderator to keep order, state and explain propositions, and put questions to the house for decisions.
4. He shall suffer no second motion to be entertained until the one under consideration has been disposed of, except motions to amend, postpone, adjourn or put the main question.
5. No person shall speak on the same subject more than twice without permission from the church and while speaking shall avoid casting any reflections calculated to wound the feeling of any members, and shall confine himself closely to the subject under discussion.
6. The moderator may speak upon any subject under discussion, by inviting a brother to preside in his place.
7. In putting forth questions the moderator shall rise, unless prevented by infirmity.
8. Every member who wishes to speak shall rise and respectfully address the moderator.
9. Every proposition presented for the action of the church must be introduced by the motion of one member and seconded by another.
10. No male member shall withdraw from conference without the consent of the church.
11. All laughing and talking calculated to disturb the transaction of business shall be deemed disorder.
12. When two members address the moderator at the same time, he shall decide which shall speak first.
13. The roll of male members shall be called at each regular business meeting, and all absentees marked, and the roll of female members shall be called at each quarterly meeting.
14. These rules shall be read quarterly, March, June, September, and December.
15. The Lord's Supper shall be administered quarterly; and it shall be the duty of each member to partake of the sacraments and thus commemorate the suffering and death of our Savior.
16. The election of the pastor shall be held annually at the regular

meeting in November. Or the church may, if they prefer, elect a pastor who shall serve them as long as both parties are satisfied; and in case of dissatisfaction three months notice shall be given by the dissatisfied party.

17. The church shall elect deacons by a majority of at least three fourths of its members present at any regular duly notified meeting as often as it may render necessary.
18. It shall be the duty of the deacons to seek out such members of the church as need pecuniary assistance, and to use the alms of the church for their relief, to assist the sick, to prepare and distribute the elements of the Lord's Supper, to take a general supervision of the temporal interests of the church and cooperate with and assist the pastor in the performance of his duties.
19. The ordination of deacons shall be preceded by one year's trial. They shall continue in service as long as satisfaction shall be given.
20. A treasurer, clerk, and two trustees shall at the regular business meeting in November be elected by ballot by a majority of votes. In case of any omission to hold the election as above, it shall be held at the next regular meeting for business. In case of death, resignation or removal of either of the said officers, an election shall be held to fill the vacancy at the first regular meeting following that at which such vacancy shall have been announced as having occurred.
21. It shall be the duty of the treasurer to receive all monies, and pay them out as directed. He shall keep a true and fair book of accounts, and annually at the said meeting for business in December shall lay before the church as statement of the monies so received and paid, which a committee appointed by the church shall examine with the necessary vouchers.
22. The clerk shall call the roll, keep a fair record of the proceedings of the church in their meetings for business, take charge of all records, and keep a register of all the members of this church.
23. It shall be the duty of the sexton to keep the church in order, furnish wood, make the fires, and have a general supervision of affairs, and shall received $5 per year for his services.
24. It shall be the duty of the trustees to hold the deed to the property of the church and see that the same is registered and secure from any encumbrance whatever.
25. There shall be a standing committee elected annually at the

regular business meeting in November, which shall consist of seven of the most judicious members, including the deacons of the church.
26. It shall be the duty of the standing committee to look after the discipline of the church, for instances, if a brother or sister has been guilty of any misdemeanor, the committee shall visit if possible, if not write to the offending member; and if said member satisfies the committee, the committee shall report the same to the church and no further action shall be taken. But if the offender manifests no Christian spirit, and does not satisfy the committee as to his or her conduct, the committee shall recommend to the church the expulsions of the offending member, and the church may without debate withdraw fellowship from the same.
27. The regular meeting for business shall be held on Saturday before the third Sunday in each month.
28. Ten male members of the church shall constitute a quorum; and all business transacted without a quorum shall be null and void.
29. All questions shall be decided by the vote of the majority except the cases mentioned in either section of these rules.
30. It is the duty of every member of this church to be present at all its meetings; and any member violating by continued absence shall be considered an offender, and shall claim the attention of the standing committee.
31. It shall be the duty of every member of this church to contribute regularly to the support of the gospel unless prevented by infirmity; and any member failing in this respect shall be considered an offender.
32. Resolve it is an insult to God to chew tobacco and spit on the floor of his house.
33. At the regular meeting of business in November, there shall be an auditing committee appointed by the moderator, whose duty it shall be to examine the treasurer's book and report to the church at the next meeting.

Immediately below these statements of decorum are some amendments, some are not dated. They are copied as given. Amendment one, the reading of the rules is hereby dispensed with unless called for. Two, the calling of the roll is hereby suspended with except quarterly. Rule three; no deacon-elect shall enter on his duties until he has been fully set apart to the work by the church.

Item sixteen was amended by the church in conference October 4, 1950. Then we read Amendment four. "Item 16 in Constitution to read as follows: The Board of Deacons recommends to the church that in the future the pastor gives us thirty (30) days notice if he desires to resign. Also, church gives him thirty (30) days notice. Passed by the church in conference June 36, 1949."

The July 1881, business session was a busy one. The church withdrew fellowship of one because of repeated absences. A special offering was taken for Sister Jane Carter, which amounted to $1.70. Another offering was taken "for the benefit of the poor amounted to $1.40." September was the decided date for the protracted meeting.

Messengers were appointed to attend the next associational meeting, and the pastor was excused from that time at the church in order to be in attendance at the Liberty Baptist Association's meeting.

The delegates who attended carried a letter adopted at the August meeting. It read, "The delegates were instructed to state to the association that this church will do its proportional part in the supporting a missionary to labor, half of his time, in the destitute parts of the association."

The protracted September meeting started with "three good sermons by our pastor," and the meeting was protracted for the next nine days. Rev. Jordan came on Tuesday and preached with "simplicity and great power." On Tuesday of the week, he baptized nine new converts. The summary of the ten days lists this, "The meeting was indeed a season of refreshing from the presence of the Lord." The protracted meeting is recorded and simple followed by these words, "no record of business because of the affliction and death of W. R. Hedgecock."

In October, the church voted against employing a missionary for the association full time. At the morning services four people were baptized. "We then met at the arbor, as the congregation was very large."

The November meeting meant it was time to select a pastor for the coming year. "The election resulted in the choice of Rev. S. F. Conrad, at a salary of $125 per year." A second motion was that the call be indefinite. It seems strange that the pastor was to be paid that salary, which was the most ever by the church to this point, when Brother Jordan had received $28.60 for preaching at the protracted meeting, which was less than ten days. Brother Waff and Brother Conrad reported they had pledged ten dollars for state missions from Abbotts Creek to the Baptist State Convention, while they attended the meeting in Winston-Salem. During these months the conferences involved calling the roll, marking absentees and other business, which seemed to be routine at every business session.

The year 1882 started with a good financial report being given. This is the first full treasurer's report listed in the minutes.

Treasurer's Report

Received and paid in full Salary	$125
Received and paid in full Associational Missions	$8.81
Received and paid in full Foreign Missions	$1.36
Received and paid in full State Missions	$7.81
Received and paid in full Orphan Asylum	$4.40
Southern Baptist Theological Seminary	$3.11
Received and paid in full The Poor of the church	$1.70
Received and paid in full Rev. Jordan	$28.60
Received and paid in full W. A. Brown	$2.30
Balance on hand	$1.40
Total expenditures for the year	$183.09

The auditing committee found all of this in order. One year later, the report shows total expenditures as $108.29.

From time to time, the clerk gives statements such as "preaching by the pastor," "after divine worship services," or other such description of the times of worship. March 1882, we read, "after a practical sermon by the pastor. ..." At the same meeting our interest is stirred again by the remark, "A good little talk by Brother John Teague, urging the church to pray over the difficulty now in the church (Brother G. W. Charles and J. M. Raper being the offending members)."

The pastor "presented the claims of the church at Lexington, desiring to build a house there for the Lord" at the April meeting. The Lexington church is not named in the minutes.

The next month Brother Conrad gave his resignation to take effect in three months. The reason given was "the church (a part of it rather) was not in accord with his ideas of doing the Lord's work, and was lax in its discipline, therefore he felt compelled to offer his resignation." The next line mentions the Sunday Sermon, "the pastor preached an excellent sermon. Quiet [sic] a large congregation."

It was the next month before the church accepted the pastor's resignation. That took place only after some of the brethren spoke on the condition of the church.

A copy of a letter on a sheet of tablet paper is included to show us how church business was done. August 18, 1882, "At Brother Waff's request a letter of dismissal was granted him. Dear Brethren, This is to certify that brother W. B. Waff is a member in good standing with us. And that he will be dismissed from our membership when we are informed of his reception by any church in like faith and order. Done at his request and by order of Abbotts Creek Baptist Church. H. Morton, Moderator, Charlie H. Teague, church clerk." That letter was dated August 19, 1882. Since it is still in the book of minutes, it is obvious it was never mailed.

About this time, offerings were taken for various causes and at most every meeting, the associational offering, foreign missions, state missions, education, or home missions. The roll was called and regular matters were discussed and recorded in the minutes. In the fall, September, the Saturday meeting was canceled "owing to...the busy season." Brother Beeson was appointed to correspond with "some brothers in relation as pastor." The next month, which was November, the church "proceeded in the election of pastor, resulting in the choice of Brother S. H. Thompson at the salary of $100 per year."

In April, the decision was made to continue the May meeting. At the Sunday worship it was announced this meeting would continue for the next nine days. "Brother Thompson preached the word with simplicity and great power. The church seemed revived and fourteen souls gave evidence of the new birth in Christ." The church received eight new additions.

For the second time in the minutes on the church, the arbor is mentioned. This was in June of 1883, going from a baptismal service, "the congregation repaired to the arbor and Elder Turner preached the funeral service of Brother T. H. Packard."

The standing committee assigned to care for the church discipline was not mentioned but in September of 1883, Brother J. M. Raper requested fellowship be withdrawn for him due to his non-attendance. In November the pastor was absent but was reelected pastor.

Another first is recorded in August 1884. "On motion the delegates were instructed to pledge to try to raise next year the following: Education; $5. State missions, $10; Associational missions, $15; Foreign missions, $5." At the same meeting, Pastor S. H. Thompson resigned. This was to take place in November. Two others assisted him in an eight-day meeting in August. The two together were paid $23.20.

Ten unnamed people were "appointed to raise means to build a new church" in October of 1884. During conference the next month, the church elected as their new pastor the former pastor, S. H. Thompson. There were no meetings in December, "the weather being inclement."

It was January of 1885 before the pastor-elect stated he could not serve as pastor. Elder William Turner was chosen. There was no February meeting but March minutes noted "preaching by the pastor Elder William Turner. The second Sunday in August was set aside for the next protracted meeting."

Months earlier, the church family decided in conference they would not object to organ music at the worship service. Sister C. B. Beeson was selected as organist at this January business meeting. No information was given to enlighten us as to what the organ cost, if one had been secured, or even if the church had decided to purchase one. Brother J. H. Mills gave a lecture on Christian charity the next day at the Sunday worship.

As the months went by, the congregation collected monies for associational missions, state missions, and other mission objects of concern to the church. The discipline of members had not been forgotten. The August meeting found membership withdrawn from a sister for fornication. As the church gathered in November 1885, the treasurer's report was listed without any mention of an organ or money for such.

In May of 1886, delegates were appointed for the union meeting. It had appeared that "union" and "association" had been used for the same meeting, but the July conference the next year has three persons being appointed for the union meeting and three for the associational meeting. Generally, before the associational meeting an offering was taken and sent by the messengers. The very next line of the minutes reads, "On motion the trustees were authorized to receive any land that might be given as church property by W. M. Raper's heirs and take a deed for the same." The number of trustees was brought to five at the next meeting when the names of J. P. Traynham and John Sell were added.

With a protracted meeting planned for November, the pastor appointed three people at the September meeting to "secure ministerial aid to protract the November meeting." That meeting started on Sunday, continued the entire next week, and ended the following Wednesday. Collection at this meeting was to pay Brother W. L. Wright for his services and twenty dollars was collected. During the July meeting in 1887, a motion was made to protract the September meeting. At the same time, "on motion, the colored people were granted the privilege to preach under the arbor." The scheduled protracted meeting set for September was canceled, "owing to the sickness of Brother Wright's family."

Bad weather eliminated the December conference and also the January 1888 meeting. February and March had five people asking for letters of dismissal, which were granted. The April gathering reported letters were granted to the E. E. Beesons after "the case had been investigated." Offerings were constantly being taken amounting to sums in the range of $1.70, $2.10, $1.75 and sometimes even more.

From time to time, we have noted certain sisters being excluded for adultery or fornication or even being with child while unmarried. For the first mentioned time, a male, J. C. Teague had fellowship withdrawn "on a charge of fornication." At the same meeting, it was announced that an offering would be taken for "Kernersville church." The offering the next day amounted to $1.90. Again, the name of the church was omitted. This could imply everyone knew the church or it could mean, the church at Abbotts Creek was willing to help any church with needs.

A meeting took place in September with Elder Turner preaching. Among others who were baptized during that week was Daniel S. Hayworth. His reputation as a devout churchman has been long-lived. A Sunday School class in the church continues to be known as the Dan Hayworth class. He was baptized along with other on October 21, 1888.

For the past few years when officers were to be elected, the minutes read, "On motion, the present officers were continued." This was a statement noticed prior to this time and for months later. For the first time in November of 1888, certain individuals were appointed "collectors on missions." Grace Spurgin was responsible for state missions. Others were C. H. Teague for education; Flora C. Raper, foreign missions; Julia Teague, associational missions and C. W. Davis for the orphanage.

The first two months of 1889, there were neither conferences nor worship services due to "weather inclement." In April of that year, the treasurer requested that the next meeting be designated to raise money for "the back salary."

> The death of pastor Elder Turner brought great sorrow to the church family. He died while on his way home from New Friendship Church. A resolution was passed which showed the high esteem the Abbotts Creek congregation had for their pastor. We include the resolution passed by the church, in April of 1889.
>
> "Whereas it has pleased Almighty God in his wisdom to take from us our dear pastor Elder William Turner who died on his

way home from his regular appointment at New Friendship, on Saturday April 6, 1889 in his seventy-third year.

Resolved first, that the church at Abbotts Creek has lost a faithful and devoted pastor, and which our hearts are saddened at his vacant seat. Yet are we comforted in believing that he was ripe for the harvest.

Second, that while our loss is great we should not wish him back believing he has fought a good fight and the Righteous Judge has given him a crown of rejoicing, but that we should learn lessons from his life and death and strive to met him in that better land.

Third, that his bereaved wife and children have our deepest sympathy and fervent prayers.

Fourth, that a copy of these resolutions be spread upon our minutes and a copy sent to his bereaved family.

Done in conference April 20, 1889."

Elder J. N. Stallings was elected to serve as pastor for the remaining of the year, dated May 1889. In September of the same year, "it was agreed that the church support the Sunday School and that the pennies collected of the school be applied to the orphan and missions." The church evidently had not paid Elder Turner his entire salary so "the remainder of Elder Turner's salary $23.60 was secured." The minutes reiterated the protracted meeting was held with Elder Henry Sheets assisting the pastor for ten days. Twenty-four persons were received as candidates for baptism; twenty-three were baptized at the close of the meeting. This is the same Sheets who was quoted so much in the beginning of this research.

In November of this year, 1889, one male member had fellowship withdrawn for "dealing with liquors." Two members were appointed to "examine the stove and make such changes as needed." Elder Stallings was selected as pastor.

The very next meeting, six members were appointed "to examine the house and report some plans for its enlargement." They were given a week and were to report at "a called meeting next Saturday." The committee was ready and the report stated, "The committee reported to plans of which the second was received to build a room twenty-six by forty-two feet to the east end of the old house. On motion a building committee of five were appointed, M. A. Tesh, J. P. Traynham, A. C. Teague, J. S. Spurgin [sic] and C. W. Davis." The next meeting, January of 1890, "the entire work of finishing the house was left to the committee. Nothing was mentioned in either of these meetings as to cost or any arrangements for paying for the building.

Grady Green, born in 1895, remembered some of it and shared it in a personal interview with this writer on April 26, 1976. He relates how his father sawed the timber for "the first framed church at Abbotts Creek before the years of 1890-95. He sawed it with an old water mill. ...These trees that he sawed for this timber to build this church, the neighbors and friends cut it in their neighborhood and hauled it to his mill and he sawed it and they built the first framed Missionary Baptist Church."

When asked who helped to construct the building, he replied, "Well, this building was built by the Spurgeons who donated labor, and the Hayworths, The Rapers, and Bodenheimers, them old citizens. I don't remember anyone else."

A Sister Steed at the May 1890 meeting gave a Bible to the church. In August, "a committee was appointed to examine D. S. Reed's chandeliers and if suited collect monie [sic] and purchase." J. P. Traynham, M. A. Tesh, and J. S. Spurgin made up the committee. The next month, a couple of male members were appointed "to collect money and purchase stoves." Three were appointed to purchase lights.

The new building, according to an interview with Mary Willie Orrell (1976), was constructed on the end of the present church building making it in a 'T' shape. She had drawn a picture showing this. The pulpit was in the center of the newer part. On the right of the minister in the pulpit were the "singing choir" and a classroom for the young married couples or singles. On the left side were the "amen corner" and the class for adult men and women. Between the minister and the choir, Mrs. Orrell has marked a place for the organ. She shows steps on both sides of the raised pulpit area. Near the communion table, she notes "old organ." On one end of the new part, the "front door" is drawn with a door on the other end labeled "back door."

The October business session reflected a decision to hold "dedication services at the next meeting." We must assume it was for the new addition including the lights and stoves. The next month, those committees for the stove and lights reported and were dismissed of their responsibilities. After this a statement is given, "total receipts and disbursements of $23.65. J. H. Lambeth assisted the pastor for the dedication service."

C. W. Davis was appointed to "raise money for Denton church" in February of 1891. This is not the first time money was raised for another church. As before, the specific church is not given.

The Rules of Decorum required the name of male members to be called every month. The minutes always included this being done. The female names were to be called each quarter. That was changed in November of 1891 and the sisters' names were to be called at every meeting. At the same November meeting, we see a committee of three women: Lula Raper, Loucinda Hayworth, and Phobe Bodenhamer appointed to raise money for the protracted meeting. The meeting lasted Sunday through Sunday, and Elders J. N. Stallings and J. K. Fant were paid ten dollars each.

For the past year or more, a transportation committee had been mentioned. Names of committee members are given and from time to time one needed to be replaced and a new name was added. This was mentioned in 1892 (February) and previously. What was done or how was not specified.

At the March meeting, the trustees reported $4.60 received from rent of land, expended $1.25 leaving a balance of $3.25. The reported balance is given as $3.25 rather than $3.35.

During the August 1892, "letters of dismission [sic] were granted the following to help constitute a church at Wallburg, C. M. Wall, Christina C. Wall, Emma E. Wall, Minnie M. Wall, and Cora E. Welborn."

For the September protracted meeting, Henry Sheets was asked to come again and assist the pastor. The clerk evaluated the meeting as "resulting in a general revival to the church and many souls were made to rejoice in the Savior's love." Eleven persons were listed as being received "as candidates for baptism."

Many months earlier, the church voted to add fourth-Sunday services. However, in reading the minutes, such services were not mentioned except a few times when a vote was taken. In May of 1893, "on motion the colored people were [sic] granted the use of the church for fourth Sunday in June."

In May, June, and July of 1893, the pastor brought the messages for worship. However, in August, Brother N. B. Orrell did the preaching. When the meeting for business came on Saturday morning, "having received notice of Elder Stallings' resignation, a pastor was considered resulting in the choice of Elder Henry Sheets." The next day, N. B. Orrell preached at eleven o'clock service and Brother Fielder at the two o'clock service. Fourth Sunday preaching service was by Pastor Elder Stallings who had decided to remain as pastor for the "balance of the year."

The September meeting was protracted with Brother Sheets invited to aid the pastor. At the September business, the church was informed that Brother Sheets could not serve as pastor. D. S. Hayworth, J. P. Traynham, and William Clinard composed the committee "to seek who could be secured." In October, the church voted to call Rev. J. M. Hilliard as pastor for the ensuing year at a salary of $100. Rev. Hilliard was notified of the vote and reported to the church in November that he would serve. Elder Stallings preached his farewell sermon at the Sunday meeting in December 1893.

In January of the New Year, 1894, the treasurer gave the church a report noting the church was out of debt and had a ten-dollar balance on hand.

Big things seem to be taking place in June of 1894. The treasurer reported $11.60 balance on hand. "On motion agreed to underpin the church with brick." Three months later at the business meeting, the building committee requested "some sisters be appointed to secure means to purchase brick." Eliza Bodenhamer and E. G. Spurgin [sic] were the two appointed. At the same meeting, the members "granted use of the house for school."

The protracted meeting took place in November. C. W. Davis had been appointed to raise money for the visiting brother. The services lasted through Friday. Eight people were received into the church as candidates for baptism. The minutes make no record of the amount of money collected or paid to the visiting minister. Brother Thomas Carrick was asked to aid the pastor but could not. Elder J. M. Bennett was available to help.

In May of 1895, the report was given saying the house was complete and the church dismissed the building committee. The next month, the request was made that each one who had helped in the repair of the "house make out a report of work done or material furnished or money given and report it to the treasurer of the building committee." The request was carried out and the "chairman reported $275.42 received and paid out." That seems to be money given and the dollar cost of "work done or material furnished."

In July, a decision was made to protract the November meeting. Three months later, "remarks were made by the brethren on the pledge plan of raising pastor's salary." The next month, November, D. D. Orrell and N. R. Teague were elected as "collectors for the church."

Brother Carrick assisted the pastor for the November meeting. Some were "restored" and seven were received for baptism.

In January of 1896, it was "agreed to donate the old stove and unused brick to the free school house."

During August of the same year, Dr. John Mitchell gave a "brief reminiscence of his travel in Palestine."

In January of 1897, "on motion Brother Davis was instructed to secure music books for the church."

In the spring of that year, Mr. Carter had his name withdrawn from the church fellowship for carnal punishment to his wife and unfaithfulness to the church "as he felt unworthy of church membership." Still another one was received into the church "by restoration." He had been excluded from New Friendships "without sufficient cause and at his request."

The church adopted a form letter of dismissal as printed here.

Letter of Dismissal

Good for Six Months
To any church of like faith and order greetings:
Dear Brethren:
This is to certify that _____ is a member in good standing with us and that they will be dismissed when informed of their reception by another church of like faith and order.
Done at _____ request and by order of Abbotts Creek Baptist Church.
This the _____.

In July of 1897, the church selected three men to "prepare a place for baptism." The next month a partial report was given. In September, E. B. Fitzgerald and wife were received by letter. Brother Fitzgerald, being a deacon, was received as a deacon and added to the deacons at Abbotts Creek. Elder J. B. Brown preached at the Sunday morning service of the November protracted meeting. Elder H. Morton led the afternoon service. Brother Morton continued through Friday "preaching the power of God unto salvation of souls." Ten persons joined the church.

The year 1898 started with C. H. Teague, Thomas Cridlebough, A. O. Raper, and E. B. Fitzgerald being "appointed committee to solicit funds for the enclosure of the graveyard." We note Brother Fitzgerald has been a member for about six months but that did not keep him from being asked to serve on a new committee. The said committee was "to confer with committee of old yard and if agreeable cooperate for the enclosure of both."

In March of the same year, "trustees were instructed to secure deed for vacant land."

The church was informed at the September meeting that the committee on the graveyard made a final report, which was received, and the committee dismissed. The very next month, a committee of five was appointed to raise means "for the painting of the church." The committee was instructed by the membership to go forward with the painting at the April 1899 meeting. However, it was one year later before we read "the committee was instructed to have the inside painting done."

In February of 1899, a letter was read from Brother A. M. Simms "in regard to furnishing a room of the female university." Meredith College is not mentioned by name but we must assume that was the one considered. The amount needed to furnish the room was $42.50. A committee was appointed to raise such, which included both men and women.

Another first is seen in July 1900, when a decision was made "on motion was agreed to have the graveyard cleaned by hired help." Later in the year, October, it was agreed to meet and repair the roof of the meetinghouse the first Saturday in November.

Sunday School has been emphasized in the church over the years. A couple of Sunday School conventions had taken place. In November of 1900, a committee was appointed to draft "resolutions in regard to Sunday Schools."

In January of the next year, "a committee of five brethren was appointed to classify the church roll in regard to those who do not attend and report at next meeting." This committee reported back in February and thirty-two names of person not attending were given to the spiritual committee. At the same meeting, the minutes noted this interesting information. "On motion agreed to ask the legislature to incorporate the Abbotts Creek Church." At the very next meeting "Brother Willard reports on incorporation 'as favorable.'"

Back in February of 1899, a committee was appointed to draft a resolution on the life and death of John Teague. John Teague was the young man whose statement informed the missionary element that the church doors had been nailed closed forcing them to meet elsewhere rather than sharing the same building with the anti-missionary element. Somehow in sending that copy to the *Biblical Recorder*, the Baptist state newspaper, the resolution was lost and never published. The church adopted the resolution but a notation was given saying it was lost. Two years and two months later, a committee was appointed to write a resolution in regards to the life and death of Sister Eliza Bodenhamer. That resolution was adopted in May of 1991. Reading this tribute helps us understand the respect and love the people seemed to have for each other.

A Tribute

Died near Abbotts Creek North Carolina on the thirteenth day of March 1901. Sister Eliza Bodenhamer in her seventieth years.

Few women have been more faithful in the home and to her church than she ever alive to all the interests of the church, given of her means to the different objects of benevolence.

For a number of years she was a consistent member of Abbotts Creek Baptist Church rairly [sic] ever missing a monthly meeting.

While we feel keenly the loss of our dear sister, yet we know that god [sic] doeth all things well; therefore we submit to His will, hoping that every member of this church may imitate her example of faithfulness.

We know our loss is her gain.

Her great desire was for all people to do right; often speaking of her great burden of her heart wich [sic] was the welfare of the church and the conversion of sinners.

She often exhorted sinners to make their peace with God.

Respectfully Submitted,

E. G. Spurgin

Dora B. Traynham

C. W. Davis

E. G. is later listed as Grace Spurgin.

The protracted meeting in October with Brother J. A. Garret preaching for the week went well. The clerk describes the services: "Brother Garret did some excellent preaching that aroused the members and sinners to repentance." Twenty-two people were listed as being ready for baptism. Brother Garret was given twenty-five dollars for his week of work.

CHAPTER TWELVE

The Beginning of the Twentieth Century 1902–1932

Discipline had not been forgotten, though carried out more by the spiritual committee than the entire congregation. In April of 1901, one presented herself for membership by letter. There were some objections necessitating a committee to investigate the charges. After investigation, the committee reported at the next meeting, "the charges are of such a character that her reputation would be detrimental to the church. Report received." Her desire for membership was denied.

Back in February of 1899, the report had been given concerning the need of funds for the female college. Now in September more than a year later, we read that the moderator appointed a committee "to raise money for the female institute."

The spiritual committee reported on two members in June of 1903. One was for "drinking and general rowdiness" and the other for "profanity and non attendance." The recommendation was for their exclusion, and it was carried out.

From time to time, the weather caused the conference to be left off even though the preaching service took place. Whether they did not have a number required for a quorum or just felt the numbers were too few for business is not clear.

In February of 1904, the church accepted the recommendation of a committee appointed a month earlier to secure a sexton for the church.

Brother P. F. Rothrock was employed at the salary of $10 for the year. A month later and for the first time mentioned, "The deacons arranged among themselves and appointed one to act as an usher."

Mysteries continue to be mentioned but not revealed. As a side note to the minutes of this date (March 1904), we read, "owing to disturbance no preaching." The report of the church meeting in April sheds no more light. The "committee reports on disturbance at last meeting the offender made satisfaction acknowledgment and was excused."

In November, of the same year, an appointed committee informed the church members that Thomas Carrick and John R. Miller were both "excessable [sic] as a prospective pastor. The church vote showed Carrick getting twenty-nine votes and Miller getting seventeen. The church then voted unanimously to elect Thomas Carrick. The December preaching service is recorded with this notation, "This ends the labor of eleven years pastorate of Elder J. M. Hilliard with this church. May the Lord's blessings attend him."

We have two separate interviews concerning Rev. Hilliard. Both were recorded in 1976. Mary Willie Orrell says:

> The Reverend J. M. Hilliard was the first preacher I remember. He would ride home from High Point with my Father, Andrew Bodenheimer, and spend the night with us. He wore a long frock tailed suit coat and always carried pecans and Lozenges candies for all us little folks in his long coat pockets. He would always sing a bunch of songs before and pray before we went to bed.
>
> He wanted to always be on time for church services. He preached good. He would walk all over the neighborhood visiting everybody. We loved him.

Grady Green remembers Rev. Hilliard as well. Since he served at Abbotts Creek for eleven years, there is no need to see these two as contradictions to each other. In his interview, he remembers:

> Mr. Hilliard, J. M. Hilliard, at one time was pastor and was living at the orphanage at Thomasville. And he would walk on Friday morning, would walk from the orphanage to Abbotts Creek Church. At that time, we lived at the old Pinnix place

The Beginning of the Twentieth Century 1902–1932

and he would stop there and get him some fresh water and talk with my mother (her husband was deceased). Of course, they would have services Saturday, business meeting. That was every third Saturday and then Sunday evening some of the members would take him back to the orphanage.

The year 1905 started with Brother Rothrock being reelected sexton for the ensuring year. The next month, his salary was increased to one dollar per month. The very next month, we are told the church secured W. F. Hanes as sexton. He kept this work until May of the next year, when Henry and Jeffrey Traynham were elected to carry on the work of sexton.

The church decided in March of 1906 to call the roll of church members in May and November rather than every month as previously decided.

No recent mention had been made of the pastor's salary but the report is given "pastor's salary, $130."

A committee was appointed in June 1907, "to look after the rebuilding of the pool." A month later they reported "brick as best in their judgment." The committee was authorized "to collect the money and proceed to rebuild."

Mrs. P. S. Vann was present and invited to speak at the November 1907 business time. She made "statements in regard to her work with reference to collecting money for the infirmary at Thomasville orphanage." The church endorsed the work and appointed a committee to collect funds.

Brother P. S. Vann "spoke in the interest of the school at Wallburg." The membership voted to allow the church building to be used for "probation (the word here and elsewhere in this paragraph should be prohibition) causes for speaking." This was done in March of 1908, and in May, "Brother S. N. Avritt delivered a strong lecture on probation." After the intermission, the pastor "made a strong plea for probation."

For several months, we see repetitive notes in the minutes. The meetings are protracted, certain ones join the church, others are granted letters of dismissal to go elsewhere, officers are reelected, and members are appointed to attend the union or the associational meeting, or even the state convention. Those attending gave reports. It would have been of interest had we counted the times that the same officers serving were reelected as a group to continue their work for another year. Financial reports were frequently given showing the pastor's salary and what was given for the various mission causes and other expenses.

Surely not all deaths are mentioned but from time to time a committee was appointed to write the memorial for a beloved deceased member. We include two such reports as stated in the minutes to show the faithfulness of our ancestors who helped to make Abbotts Creek a strong and thriving congregation.

Memoriam of Dora B. Traynham

It is always sad to _____ the death of one of our members. But more than sad to lose one who is cut down in the midst of an active and useful life. These sad words have gone forth: "died of pneumonia at her home March 25, 1909." Mrs. Dora Bell Traynham, the daughter of Mr. and Mrs. A. O. P. Teague and wife of Mr. J. P. Traynham. She leaves an aged father, a husband, one daughter and two sons to mourn their loss. Her mother passed over the river of death a few days before her. Our sister has gone to be with her mother in glory land.

Sister Traynham had been a member of Abbotts Creek Baptist Church for about thirty years. Educated at Thomasville Female Coledge [sic], cultured, refined, affectionate, self-sacrificing, and Godly in her life. She was one of the best and most useful women in our church and community. She will be greatly missed in her home and the circle of her friends.

Resolved; that we deeply deplore our loss in the death of our sister.

That this small tribute to her memory be spread on our church record and that our heartfelt sympathy be extended to her family.

Respectfully submitted, D. S. Hayworth, W. S. Spurgeon, W. L. Hayworth

We continue to copy the exact words from the minutes.

This has been a year of more than usual loss to Abbotts Creek Baptist Church. Sister Jane Teague full of years and labor in her church was the first to go then following soon her daughter, Dora Bell Traynham, then on July 18, 1909, these sad words went forth: "Dan Orrell is dead."

The Begining of the Twentieth Century 1902–1932

Daniel Dieator [sic] Orrell was born August 29, 1868, and died July 18, 1909. Our brother has always been afflicted but bore his affliction with patience. Brother Orrell joined the Baptist church at Abbotts Creek, in the fall of 1892, and was a faithful member having never missed a Saturday meeting except on account of sickness. His last work on earth was in the interest of his church.

He was married to Miss. Ada F. Hedgecock on December 15, 1898, and to this union they were blessed two sons, one having died in infancy. He leaves a wife one son and aged mother two sisters and one nephew to mourn their loss (this is printed as written).

Brother D. D. Orrell was a devoted son, a kind husband, an affectionate father, a thoughtful brother and a helpful neighbor. As a church member he was quiet but ever willing with heart, hand and purse to do his part. We shall greatly miss him from our church and community.

Resolved: That these words in memory of our beloved brother be spread on church record and that we extent to the loved ones our hartiest [sic] sympathy.

Respectfully Submitted, D. S. Hayworth, W. D. Spurgeon, W. L. Hayworth

In December of 1909, a committee was appointed, "to devise some financial plan by which all members may be induced to bear their part of the finances." Three months later, we have this mentioned again. The church had gathered "for preparing wood and sanding the yard." A resolution was adopted, "That the delinquent members shall be given notice to attend the church conferences or contribute regular to the support of the church or show sufficient (by letter or other communication) to the church. Failure to comply with the above for three months will be considered sufficient cause to forfeit their membership."

Minutes mentioned several times when large numbers of people were baptized but there was no mention of a total number of members. At the May 1910 business meeting the roll was called. Fifty members were present and 114 were absent.

The January 1911 meeting continues to deal with finances. "On motion the treasurer was ordered to make report at the November meeting the list of members with amounts they gave for pastor's salary together with a list of those who don't contribute." One year later when the treasurer's report was given, the "treasure read a list of delinquents."

The next month "Brother N. R. Teague suggests that the church bear the expense of Sunday School literature." This was left open until the next meeting when the church agreed to do so. Blanche Spurgeon and Flora Traynham were named "collectors" for such funds.

The church appointed Lillian Hayworth and Ettie Teague in May of 1911, to "raise means for a new carpet." Three months later, the pool is mentioned again. The committee was instructed to raise money and complete the baptistery.

Nothing had been mentioned regarding the Liberty Piedmont Institute located at nearby Wallburg until May of 1912. "On motion, it was agreed by the church that as a church it would not assume the amount allotted to it by the committee on the debt of Liberty Piedmont Institute but would recommend and urge that individual members subscribe stock to the amount allotted to the church."

In May 1914, two members were appointed to "solicit funds for the Wake Forest Church." Though the word church is given, one is made to wonder if it should have been for the college; but in February 1916, collecting money for the church is mentioned again.

The Piedmont Liberty School was located at Wallburg. Originally, it was a framed building erected in 1902. The school was a co-educational boarding school for children primary through high school. The building was destroyed by fire in 1907.

The Begining of the Twentieth Century 1902–1932

We find a very strong word used in the August 1914 meeting, "ordered that we meet Tuesday before third Sunday in September and clear off grave yard and grounds."

W. D. Spurgeon resigned as treasurer in December 1914 and N. R. Teague was elected to take his place. At the same time, "on mention resolution, in regard to delinquent members rescinded."

C. W. Teague ended his service as clerk in October of 1915, after serving thirty-three years and six months. W. D. Spurgeon became clerk the next month. The pastor announced his resignation at the same time. D. S. Hayworth, W. R. Spurgeon, J. R. Phillips, Andrew Bodenheimer, and W. S. Hayworth were announced as the pulpit committee.

The treasurer's report in January of 1916 shows the pastor was paid $138.50 but was still owed $11.50. The church voted to pay that. The pulpit committee announced they were not ready to report. In February upon their recommendation, Pastor Carrick was asked to serve the "balance of the year."

Delinquent members were not forgotten. During May of 1916, the church sent a committee out to "see the ones who could attend and have not."

November 1916 was the time to elect a pastor for the ensuing year. "No one received a majority of votes. On motion adjourned." A month later, a motion was made that the present pastor be paid "before another one is called." The committee met to discuss forming a "field of work for a preacher." J. M. Hilliard was elected "as supply pastor" in May of 1917. In December, he was elected "pastor for the coming year."

In March of 1918, J. P. Traynham was appointed to buy two brooms for the church. The report in May shows $1.50 paid for the brooms. The church voted on this day to purchases forty songs books. The next month's meeting happened on a stormy day. We read "religious exercises conducted by the pastor reading Psalm 71." There was no conference "since only five people were present."

A motion was made at the September 1918 conference to "extend thanks to the ones who bought and arranged the carpet for the church." At the same session, a committee of one was appointed to collect subscriptions for the *Biblical Recorder*. Still other matters were considered. C. E. Spurgeon and Andrew Bodenhamer were "appointed to collect money and buy two stoves for the church." At conferences three months later, it was announced $29.50 had been collected for the stoves that cost $25.50 leaving a balance of $4. There were no services in October "owing to an epidemic of influenza."

History, Heritage, and Memories

The New Year, 1919, opened with a financial report showing the pastor had been paid $130.75 and $13.75 paid out for missions. Ivey Orrell was appointed to collect money to pay for sweeping the church. The needed amount was to be $4. It was also noted that subscriptions were taken to pay the balance of the pastor's salary.

No further mention was made to collect for any other specific cause. However, the minutes report a high increase over the next three months. The amount for missions in March was $20.76. April shows an increase and was listed at $26.05. One month later, the listed amount was $76.

In May of 1918, the records shows baptismal services were held for John Welborn, Maggie Welborn, and Gladys Welborn. The congregation went from the water to the church. After the preaching services, the right hand of fellowship was extended to them. Attention is called to this because the same three are listed as being baptized in May of 1919, including the church giving the right hand of fellowship. The earlier date seems to be more likely because all three were "received as candidates for baptism" in November of 1917.

Kara Lee Motsinger was recorded as being baptized in September of 1919. She died as Kara Dean in 2006. At the time of her death, she was the oldest member of the church and had the distinction of having been a member longer than any other person in the church. Some of her memories are listed in the memory section of this book.

When a need became evident, someone was selected to meet that need. One such committee was referred to as the "stove pipe committee." This group made a report in February of 1920, which is not included in the minutes, but the committee had done their job and the committee members were dismissed.

Months passed with little more in the minutes than regular exercises conducted by the pastor, minutes read and approved, pastor's salary and contributions listed along with gifts for missions. The Lord's Supper was observed at regular intervals. Messen-

The oldest lady of the church at the ground breaking, Mrs. Kara Motsinger Dean.

gers were consistently appointed to attend the union and associational meetings. The church was always involved in Baptist life, including messengers to the Baptist State Convention. Time and time again the church voted to "elect the present officers to serve for another year." In the September 1920 report, the minister who assisted in the protracted meeting was paid $52, the largest amount paid to this time and more than one third of what the pastor received for the entire year.

Earlier conference minutes included nothing concerning the Woman's Missionary Union or Society. The November 1920 conference reports $80 for missions with the notation, "twenty dollars of the above mission money was paid by the WMS."

At this date, members were still being excluded for non-attendance, immoral living and at times names were listed as being removed without a stated cause whereas until recently, the cause was always given. It is not specified if the Spiritual Committee did this without informing the membership of the cause or gave adequate information to the church.

The notes from the February 1921 meeting had this information: "paid $146.10 to famine strickin [sic] district in the far east." No hint is given to clarify "far east." For the first time any mention has been made of a gift to the pastor, the same meeting has a notation $55 was given to Brother Hilliard for a Christmas present. This was more than a third of what had even been listed as being paid for his salary.

J. P. Traynham, N. R. Teague, C. H. Teague, and D. S. Hayworth "were appointed to look into the resources for the building of a new church," in May of 1921. The committee reported back to the church the following month, "The committee appointed to look into the resources to build a new church reported unfavorable."

The protracted meeting in September of 1921 resulted in a number in the high teens being received as candidates for baptism. The meeting lasted for twelve days and the minister; Rev. Black, was paid $105. We note again this amount compared to the pastor's salary for the year, which was $119.75.

December 1921 was a time to elect officers for the next year. The ones presently serving were reelected except for R. Bodenhamer who was replaced by Brother A. M. Bodenhamer. It must have been so obvious to the church family the clerk felt no need to record what position was involved.

The clerk moves on as if one thing is as important as another to tell us "N. R. Teague, Willie_____, and Minnie Hayworth were appointed to secure an organ for the church." The rest of the lines read, "C. E. Spurgeon was appointed to repair the window frames." The next meeting his report on the repair job was received. We were also told Pastor Hilliard received a Christmas gift of $62.50.

The clerk inserted here, the November 1921 minutes, where the roll of members was called and the absent members were marked. The February meeting of 1922 is recorded next.

Ninety years after the division of the two churches, the church "on motion" in May of 1922, "C. E. Spurgeon, N. S. Hayworth, and N. R. Teague were appointed to cooperate with the lower church in regard to building two dressing houses at the pool." To this point, the minutes had never mentioned anything the two churches had done in cooperation with each other.

Fifty-seven years later, the spring of 1979, the present writer and his family lived in the parsonage and along with other neighbors were harassed by a neighborhood young man with a drinking problem. Late one Saturday night, a stone was thrown breaking out a storm door at the parsonage. The Davidson County Sheriff's Department was called and responded. They were told who the suspect was and that he would probably return after a short time. The officer drove his car behind the Primitive Church to wait and noticed windows had been broken there as well. After waiting a short time, the suspect walked back up and was arrested. The officer asked that we notify the Primitive Baptist church officials and have them call the department. This was done early on Sunday morning before any of their congregation arrived. We received a letter of thanks from the church for the information and help. This was the first recorded correspondence from the Primitive Church to the Missionary Baptist Church.

After preaching by the pastor, in October of that year (1922), the conference opened. "A committee was appointed to take subscriptions for a new $15,000 brick veneer church. If not enough subscribed for a new church then the present building be repaired. C. E. Spurgeon, D. S. Hayworth, W. S. Hayworth, Minnie Hayworth, Flora Raper, and Mary Lee Charles were named to the committee." A month later, N. R. Teague "tendered his resignation as treasurer of the church."

No mention is made if this resignation had anything to do with the just-mentioned decision of the church. However, it seems obvious that all did not agree for the building of a new church. In January of 1923, the sum of $208.50 was reported for the repair of the church. The amount for the new church was listed as $7,404. Without understanding the reason-

The Begining of the Twentieth Century 1902–1932

ing as far as the minutes are concerned, the church voted for the third Saturday in February to be the day for "recovering the present church building." It must be assumed that the church was not fully in agreement to construct a new building in the immediate future.

The next conference in February has three listed as appointed "to collect money, buy shingles and recover the church. Brother Hilliard who had been supplying the church announced he would "cease to preach after the third Sunday in March." The committee charged with the covering of the roof of the church reported and the members were released a month later.

In April of 1923, the church was informed of the "dressing rooms at the pool" and the committee was released. A committee was named to search for a minister for the rest of the year. E. L. Mumford was chosen with this added, "On motion pay pastor at the rate of $200 per year. The church decided at the same time to allow the $15.75 left over from the funds to recover the church was to be used as the church directed. In July, there were members appointed to collect funds and paint the church. In October, it was reported $110 had been paid out to paint the building.

Money was collected in February of 1923, to help pay the hospital bill of a brother, W. C. Hines. In January, of the following year, it is mentioned again that the church helped to pay more on Brother Hines' hospital bill, whether the same bill or a new one was not defined.

Mission funds were always mentioned with any type financial reports being given. These offerings generally were very strong compared to other church expenditures. In the April 1924 business meeting, three members were "appointed to encourage missionary in the church." The meaning of this is not clear.

Christian education always had the attention of the congregation. In June of the same year, the amount of money collected for that cause was to "be paid to the Liberty Piedmont Institute." In August, the amount given was $262. A month later, $366.40 was listed as being given.

A couple of times earlier, it has been observed an active mission organization was at work in the church with notes of certain listed offerings supported by a sizeable contribution from the WMU. For the first time mentioned in the minutes, Minnie Hayworth is listed as WMU director. Another first is seen in that N. R. Teague was named publicity director.

C. E. Spurgeon, Minnie Hayworth, and Mrs. Mary Willie Orrell "were appointed to collect money and buy a communion set for the church." This was in December 1924. The next September, mention is made "collected $3.40 balance on communion drinking cups." A month after the committee was chosen to get communion cups, N. R. Teague, Frank Spurgeon, and Mozell Bodenhamer were appointed to collect money and buy one hundred song books for the church."

Interesting events occupied the church at the May 1925 meeting. "On motion, the Church sustained the action of W. D. Spurgeon in having the timber cleared from the cemetery. On motion W. D. Spurgeon appointed to get someone to cultivate part of the cemetery cleared." The pastor was given the month of June off for a vacation—another first!

With the approach of winter, the second Saturday in November was set aside to "get wood for the church."

With the church calling the roll of the membership in May and November of each year, the November 1925 meeting had Minnie Hayworth and Grace Spurgeon "appointed to write each member inviting them to be present at the roll call the third Saturday in May of 1926."

The next month the pastor and other officers were elected for another year.

"On motion building committee be appointed to build a new church. D. S. Hayworth, E. E. Cridlebough, A. M. Bodenhamer, Ivey Orrell, and Jeffrey Traynham were appointed building committee." Talk of the new building seems to have been taking place. Earlier, we noted a committee was appointed and their report was given and marked "unfavorable." Then a vote was taken to raise $15,000 dollars for a brick veneer building. Nothing more was mentioned but then we read a new roof was to be done. Now, a group is named the "building committee." At the same conference, the church decided to ask the pastor to preach at another service once a month "at double the pay he is now receiving." The church was informed the next month the pastor declined to preach the added time.

This time the building idea seemed to be on go. In February of 1926, "on motion finance committee be appointed. Charlie Raper, Minnie Hayworth, Charley Bodenhamer, John Welborn, and Mrs. Ivey Orrell were appointed to collect funds for the new church. On motion D. S. Hayworth appointed to have pledge cards printed to be used for subscribing cash work on lumber for new church." Mrs. Orrell remembers, "I was put in to collect money and collected $2,133 cash. A lot of people gave lumber and work."

The minutes continued to tell us the events taking place in the church. The normal church things were in place, protracted meetings were carried out, and reports were given along with other church business. Of-

The Beginning of the Twentieth Century 1902–1932

Abbotts Creek Church c. 1928

ferings were taken and committees appointed to care for the details of sustaining the church. New members were baptized and given the right hand of fellowship. Occasionally a letter of dismissal was given and a name was dropped because the person had joined a church not of the "same faith and order."

In June of 1927, "C. H. Teague was appointed to write a history of Abbotts Creek Baptist Church from its organization to the present time." If this was ever accomplished, no record of it has been found.

As a side note, the clerk inserts information from the July 1927 conference. The building committee was "authorized to dispose of old church as they see fit."

The protracted meeting ended on October 1, 1927 with sixteen persons being baptized. The visiting minister was given $101.53 and the pastor, Brother Mumford was given $70. The next month, the pastor, Brother Mumford, was elected for another year. The vote was 100 percent in favor of retaining him.

At the same November meeting, a motion was made to have worship services on the first and third Sunday of each month. It was determined the deacons would decide what amount the pastor would be paid. It was also obvious discipline had not died. D. S. Hayworth and Floyd Teague reported they had talked with a sister in the church and that "she said she had (not) done anything she was sorry for and if the church wanted to turn her out all right." The pastor asked a committee to get some light on what to do about this. The next month, fellowship was withdrawn "because of having been convicted in the coart [sic] of certain charges." Immediately following this, the conference agreed to pay the pastor one thousand dollars "for salary."

The New Year, 1928, started with Ivey Orrell assigned the job of finding someone to build the fire in the stoves on the days of services. The building committee along with Minnie Hayworth, Victoria Teague, and C. H. Teague were to serve to decide on a musical instrument for the sanctuary. In the April and May conferences, Clarence Moore, Perry Hayworth, Floyd Teague, and Charlie Teague were appointed ushers for the church.

May 19, 1928, the Saturday conference took place after the "religious exercises" were concluded. The next day, May 20, dedication services for the new church were held. The 11:15 a.m. services took place after the Sunday School hour. "Talks by former pastors on history of the church" were given. At one o'clock, "dinner on the ground." The laying of the cornerstone took place at the 2:30 p.m. services. No names were given of the former pastors who spoke but Dr. John R. Jester of Winston-Salem preached the "dedicatory sermon."

An interesting fact can be observed though not explained. In February, Carrick Teague was granted his letter of dismissal. Four months later, he was received back into the church by letter.

The decision was made at the September conference to "saw large poplar trees that stand east of the church." A month later, the church voted that "wire or rope be put around the pool." A vote determined also that a wood shed be built at the church. The shed was built back of the church and on the wood cutting days would be filled with wood for the winter. The roll call of members took place in November and those absent were so marked.

Over the next few months, the minutes were short. The minutes explained payments for sweeping the floor of the church, naming those who were appointed to attend the associational meeting, and information concerning the state convention. One has to be impressed by the involvement of the church in the state convention and the associational meetings. The treasurer gave reports as to how the money was being paid out. In March of 1929, Andrew Bodenhamer was to collect money to pay for tin on the new wood shed."

The June 1929 meeting minutes note: "D. S. Hayworth was appointed to buy four trays for bread and wine." Prior to using the trays and cups, Mary Willie Orrell remembers, "They (the deacons) used two glass goblets at first for communion and they carried them when in the old church. Everyone would take a sip of the Welch grape juice. They got new communion sets."

Brother B. Towsen helped with the September protracted meeting, which continued for twelve days. Twelve persons were baptized. After this meeting, the visiting minister was paid one hundred dollars. The following month, Clarence Moore and John Spurgin were appointed to repair the heaters and Charley Bodenhamer was appointed to look after sawing wood for the heaters.

In January of 1930, the pastor was paid one thousand dollars, probably the remaining salary owed from the previous year. The collection for the orphanage was $293. "Ivey Orrell, W. S. Hayworth, J. R. Phillips and C. E. Spurgin [sic] were appointed to place tolets [sic]." The necessity for these would not be questioned though such had never been mentioned in the minutes prior to this date.

The March session gave a strong clue of what was taking place in the community. "On motion church go on record to take electrick [sic] lights if the line comes this way." Charlie Bodenheimer was appointed to "look after securing lights for the church." On August 15, 1931, this information was given: "on motion, the church pay for lights on the installation plan." In September, the treasurer's report listed $1.05 for lights. In October, $8 was paid for "taping (sic) fee for lights." The next month, $2.10 was listed for lights.

Prior to this time, as far back as 1927, the church was using a Delco system for electricity powered by a gas engine generator.

Back to April of 1930, "Arthur Hedgecock and Ivey Orrell were appointed to inform people where to bury in the cemetery."

Plans were being made for the future during the June meeting. The protracted meeting was being planned for September (it was changed to October). At the same time, the treasurer was instructed to pay Willie Paul Hedgecock for building fires at the church on Saturdays. In August, the minutes stated he was paid $15. This seems to have been for the past winter. With no explanation to what is involved or implied, Sanford Hayworth and D. S. Hayworth were appointed to the "entertainment committee."

No mention has been made of exclusions for many months but the spiritual committee had not been eliminated. Three months earlier Minnie Green and Minnie Hayworth were added to the Spiritual Committee. At the conference day in August, fellowship was withdrawn from a member for "misconduct."

Brother J. C. Canipe came on Monday night of the protracted meeting and preached for ten days. Brother Canipe was another noted Baptist minister to preach at Abbotts Creek. When a roll call is given of leading ministers who have made significant contributions to Baptist life in North Carolina, many of those have preached at Abbotts Creek, including Canipe.

Back in June of 1927, C. H. Teague was appointed to write the history of the church. November 11, 1930 was the beginning of "Fellowship Week." The church covenant was read, as was the history of the church.

At the same meeting, an every member canvas was discussed. Ten members were appointed to contact every church member to see what they would contribute for the work of the church for the coming year.

The presbytery determined in 1832 that the minority membership were continuing the previous practices of the old church and should therefore be seen as the true Abbotts Creek Baptist Church. However, in February of 1932, the minutes stated, "on motion church celebrate the one hundredth anniversary the third Sunday in June." A century of ministry had been concluded giving great cause for celebration. Since the presbytery had followed Baptist procedure of the day in declaring the minority the true church one hundred years earlier, we must use the 1756 date as the beginning of the Abbotts Creek Baptist Church.

The word "Missionary" was added later to distinguish between the two churches.

In the financial report given March 19, 1932, among other things mentioned was this: "bonds $45.45." This was the only mention of "bonds." A month later, $8.34 was listed as "paid Industrial Bank." This was listed for several more months, but nothing had been recorded in the minutes where the church decided to, or had to, borrow money from the bank. In September, the amount paid was reduced by a few cents, from $8.34 to $8.26. Other business in the March meeting named Charley Bodenhamer as treasurer of the cemetery committee.

On June 20, 1932, the "church celebrated the one hundredth anniversary Sunday morning." Here again, a renowned man in Baptist history of North Carolina preached at Abbotts Creek. "Charles Maddry preached Sunday afternoon. Herman Stevens gave a lecture on the history of the Baptist denomination after which former pastors made short talks."

J. Clyde Turner preached during the protracted meeting, this time in July rather than the fall as in the past. Pastor Turner served for long years as pastor of First Baptist Church in Greensboro. He was paid $82 for his help in the protracted meeting. We also note "paid Chism (later we find the spelling as Chishalm) sisters $20 for singing."

The church was always involved in Baptist life. Messengers were appointed for the associational meetings and yearly to the Baptist State Convention of North Carolina. There were several times when messengers were chosen to attend the Southern Baptist Convention.

The year 1932 ends with the Saturday conference not held because of "heavy snow." On Sunday, the pastor preached and a note is recorded telling us the pastor was paid one thousand dollars for the year.

The church voted to get insurance, which was mentioned for the first time June 26, 1932. Farmer's Davidson County Mutual Fire Insurance Company insured the church for four thousand dollars. "Entrance fee to be paid out of the church treasury."

The picture of the Hedgecock Service Station at Horneytown was taken in 1928. The men standing are Carl Hedgecock and Emerson Idol. The Idol peach orchard can be seen on the right.

Sunday School class in the late 1920s.

Pine Stump School, located near the intersection of Curry Road and Horneytown Road. Grace Davis, Gary Idol, and Carey Davis attended here.

The Begining of the Twentieth Century 1902–1932

The Delane School was located at the intersection of Old Mill Road and Johnson Street. The picture was taken in 1919 or 1920 with Ada Wheeler seen as the teacher. Others pictured, second row from the top, third on left, Fleta Motsinger Burton. Third row from top, second from left, Kara Motsinger Dean. Fourth row from the top, second from left (bow in hair) Elva Motsinger Hedgecock.

The Boston School was located near the intersection of Lexington Avenue and Chestnutt Street Extension. Front row, (left to right), Myrtle Yokley, Harvey Hayworth, Norman Kanoy, Jake Bodenhamer, and Mae Craven Bodenhamer. Second Row: Louis Hayworth, Unknown, Unknown, Unknown, Sanford Hayworth, Emma Lee Tise, Unknown, Unknown and Ara Green Spurgeon. Third row: Unknown, Unknown, Hobert Garrison, ? Davis, Perry Hayworth, Teacher, Maude Bodenhamer, Pauline Willard, Charlie Bodenhamer, and teacher Floy Smith.

History, Heritage, and Memories

The Clifton Grove School was located on Abbotts Creek Church Road and the intersection of Mock Road. Pictured (front row, left to right): Milton Teague, Gete Bodenheimer, Early Yokley, Willie Yokley, Curt Motsinger, Burney Bodenheimer, Charlie Hedgecock, Early Hedgecock, Fred Hayworth. Second row: Cathleen Snyder, Chester Smith, May Hedgecock, Bessie Spainhour, Ollie Clodfelter, Eric Bodenheimer, Rosie Glassco, Vera Kanoy, Stella Bodenheimer, Velena Teague, Fanny Newsome, Burley Bodenheimer, Lewis Sells and Florence Newsome. Third row: Mat Glassco, Hosey Snyder, Lou Teague, Alverta Hayworth, Annie Green, Maggie Teague, Blanch Hines, Chester Spurgeon, Ida Craver, Jessie Motsinger, and Carvin Spainhour. Back row: Marvin Smith, Robert Green, Ester Smith, Vera Snyder, Frank Spurgeon, Sadie Bodenheimer, teacher Mabel Hayworth, Sula Sells, Willie Snyder, Charles Kanoy, Charles Teague and Clarence Hayworth.

The Clifton Grove School — Pictured from left: Row 1: Fletcher Fields, Colman Hilton, Clyde Craven, Fella Sink, Clarence Craven, Frank Brown, Belvin Craven, Carmel Craven, Gilbert Stroud, Roy Griffin, Raymon Craven, Otis Cecil, Chippy Perryman, Walter Moore, Malcom Tuttle, Mitchell Wade, Row 2: Vincent Perryman, Fred Swaim, ??, Johnson, Thurman Hilton, Ora Gray, Mattie Fields, William Kennedy, Moore, Swaim, Merle Ring, Faye Payne, Bryon Criddlebaugh, Pierce Criddlebaugh, Violet Payne, Vera Moore, Colon Haynes, Lillie Moore, Charles Carmichael, Myrtle Wade, Roosevelt Carmichael, Flora Carmichael, Jacob Cecil, Lola Tise, Minnie Craven, Row 3: Teachers Gaither Balick, Mitler Long, Rose Johnson, ? ?, Charles Haynes, John Haynes, Ward Cecil, Robert Hayworth, Emory Ring, Louise Snyder, Roby Craven, Bessie Swaim, ?, Florence Snyder, Elma Ring, Wade Cecil, Laura Hammer, Mary Moore, Cletus Hayworth, Blanche Moore, Cory Wright, Rae Moore, Row 4: Ina Mae Craven, Stanton Moore, Ola Cecil, Myrtle Sink, Esther Sink, Edith Sink, Nina Kennedy, Annie Craven, Tereva Moore, Bertha Moore, Cora Hayworth, Nally Carmichael, Edith Boles, Paul Cecil, Lema Tise, Blaudie Craven, Cleva Boles, Della Varglera, Bertha Ellmore, Naiara Cecil, Garsey Sink, Row 5: Etta Boles, Thawer Craven, Cletus Cecil, Cletus Sink, Barney Moore, Stamey Cecil, Carl Craven, Avery Swaim, Julus Craven, Clarence Moore, George Moore, George Craven, Walter Hammer, Roscoe Moore, Roy Carmichael, John Glasco.

CHAPTER THIRTEEN

1933–1949

The New Year opened with the January 1933 business being conducted. The church was informed that the roof of the new building was leaking. The old building committee was asked to care for this. A month later, the church learned the cost for doing repairs would be twelve dollars. The offering taken to cover this came up to be $1.70 short. The church also elected Miss Mattie Teague as treasurer after learning John Welborn had resigned of that task. Miss Teague was the first female to hold this position.

What may have been the first missionary speaker for the church is cited at the February service. "Mr. J. L. Heart, from Brazil, South America, spoke to us in the afternoon giving us some interesting facts about South America as well as giving us an inspirational message." On May 6, Mr. Gallimore, "our missionary to China" spoke to the church about his work in China. The church voted in July to let their mission money go to help Brother Gallimore get back to China.

Two meetings had passed in the New Year when the church was informed of the need for a new record book "since the old one was filled." The church did not want to be extravagant so Carrick Teague was chosen to "make an investigation in regard to prices of a church record book and report the same." The clerk was instructed to order the book at the March conference. No cost was listed. At the same conference, the pastor suggested "the little patch of ground near the graveyard should be cultivated" and further suggested some young people cultivate it and "let the proceeds go to church work."

A letter from D. W. Weston, pastor of a small church near Guilford College, requested permission to hold a revival meeting at Abbotts Creek to help pay his way to attend seminary. Such a decision was postponed but in March the church voted seven to five to invite him to preach for the meeting scheduled for July. The pastor said, "He would obligate himself to write Mr. Weston and ask him to come." In June, without explanation, the meeting was postponed.

In April, the pastor announced "we would have a gold and platinum offering the third Sunday in April to go for a special mission offering." The April meeting mentioned it was taken but no specifics were given.

Two weeks later, "Floyd J. Teague then announced that the Will of Milton Teague's was being tested and that according to the will the church was entitled to some money from the estate." Three members were selected with the aid of the pastor to "do what they think best or wise in defining the will, since the church voted to protect the will." When such a decision was made is not clear since no earlier mention had been made regarding the will.

The Southern Baptist Convention was promoting a campaign encouraging every member of Baptist churches to contribute one dollar a month for one year to help raise one hundred thousand dollars to have relief from its debt. The pastor made an announcement to this effect, but the church voted not to participate with the effort.

Pastor Mumford announced on Sunday, August 20, he was to preach the associational sermon, which was to take place at Lick Creek Baptist Church on September 5 and 6. He requested all who could to attend.

With the revival meeting scheduled, the pastor brought up the question about "remunerations for help in the meeting." It was decided for him to appoint a committee to collect money and that a free will offering be taken. The minutes read, "The pastor appointed the following girls on the committee: Cora May Welborn, Miss Cassie Bodenheimer and Miss Ruby Bodenheimer." At the time of this writing in 2007, Cassie Bodenheimer Teague was in her early nineties, which means this "girl" would have been approaching twenty years of age.

On Sunday, November 12, 1933, after Sunday School was over, the congregation was reminded the delegates for the state convention had not been selected. The pastor requested a conference be called and it was "duly called." The delegates were selected to attend the convention, which was to be held in Greensboro's First Baptist Church. The following Saturday at conference, the roll of members was called. It was decided to send the church covenant cards to all "inactive members of the church to remind them of their duty they owed to their God and to their church."

The pastor called a meeting of the deacons plus D. S. Hayworth and Carrick Teague for three o'clock on November 19, 1933. A month later, the church officers were elected for the New Year. Over the past few years nothing had been mentioned about a yearly re-election of the pastor, but this was included in this December meeting. The church clerk and treasurer, Carrick Teague and Mattie Teague, were reelected for their respectful positions.

We learn here also what the previously-mentioned three o'clock meeting concerned. The deacons with the pastor decided at that time to present to the church the need to elect two additional deacons, bringing the total to five. The church elected Grady Green and John Welborn, both of whom were ordained January 21, 1934. This seems to have been a big thing for the church and was carried out in style. The pastor led the service and was assisted by M. O. Alexander, pastor of the First Baptist Church in Thomasville. Doctor A. B. Conrad, pastor of First Baptist Church in High Point, and The Rev. John Arch McMillan, editor of *Charity and Children* (Baptist Children's Homes publication), assisted in the service.

For numerous business sessions, the clerk simply records them taking place, briefly mentioning minutes read and approved and from time to time, financial reports were given listing money collected and applied to pastor's salary, and other expenditures. The sermon topics were always listed and the scripture given. The church had agreed on the salary for the pastor, yet we note different amounts listed as pastor's salary. The salary was listed on June 20th as being $91.65. Earlier in February, it was listed as $40.33. At the same time, the treasurer showed $1.52 paid for lights, $4 for sweeping and $5.50 for missions. There were other notations from time to time saying "behind on pastor's salary." In one February report, we note pastor's salary paid in full, referring to the previous year.

The pastor reported in March a Rev. Jim Haymore, a great evangelist, was preaching a revival at Wallburg and might be available to preach one at Abbotts Creek. A committee was asked to follow up on the idea "to see whether his help could be procured." Later in the month word was given that he could and the services were planned to begin the first Sunday in July and continue "through the third Sunday." The very next sentence records a letter being read by the pastor to be sent to all inactive members. The church adopted the letter and it was sent.

On April 14, 1934, the church appointed two members to visit a non-attending member asking him if he would repent of his sin, which was not named, and come back into the church. His refusal to do so was reported, and "the matter was left open until some future conference by vote of the church." Three months later, the matter appears again. The church was informed the wayward one was guilty of drinking and "had served time on the road." The deacons recommended his name be removed from the church roll. The church passed the motion.

Officers for the BYPU (Baptist Young People's Union) were elected at this meeting also. The full slate included Carrick Teague as general director while Cora May Welborn was named assistant director. Cassie Bodenheimer was general secretary and Mary Francis Hayworth, chorister. The pianist was Kathleen Teague. Other leaders were: Adults, Mrs. Roy Hayworth, Senior leader, Miss Velma Teague, intermediate leader, Miss Mattie Teague, with Mary Francis Hayworth serving as the junior leader.

A year and a month had passed since mention was made of the Will of Brother Milton Teague. The church learned that amount was $519.75. The deacons were appointed to look after this. The church voted to record the Will in the minutes, which was carried out in the July 14 minutes. The Will gave specifics for property, real estate, timber and other such possessions. Then we read, "$100...one hundred dollars be given to Friedland Church and the First Baptist Church of Abbotts Creek. One hundred dollars for the upkeep of grave yards." The next paragraph reads this way: "I will that all expenses funeral or other expenses be paid out of my personal estate monies, etc. Any over to be given to churches named above." On December 16, 1934, four more dollars was received from the J. M. Teague Estate from Lawyer Benbow.

Brother Haymore, the evangelist from Atlanta, preached for a two-week revival. We mention the names of those baptized because of the large numbers. Mr. W. L. Lewis, Ina Weavil, Mrs. Harvey Hayworth, Mrs. Frank Spurgeon, John Welborn, Jr., David Wall Welborn, Joseph Hayworth, Dwight Moore, Lee Davis, Clyde Spurgeon, Dorothy Lovelace, Azzie Sexton, Grayson Royal, Ruth Traynham, Henry Traynham, Stanton Bodenheimer, Mrs. Mae Bodenheimer, William Lovelace, Hanale Sexton, and Donald Bodenheimer. Mrs. Jerry Clodfelter was received under watch care pending her letter being sent.

Rent on the plot of land above the cemetery was paid. It amounted to $9.25 and by vote of the church was to be used on the cemetery. This report was given on November 19, 1934. "It was also decided to hold a service on Thanksgiving Day."

In May of 1935, Mattie Teague requested she be relieved of her work as treasurer since she was going away to school. Miss Velma Teague was elected to take her place. In November, the same Mattie Teague was re-elected as treasurer.

On the nineteenth day of the same month, the church had a visiting minister to bring the afternoon message. He was the Rev. Rom Sykes of the Friends Church in High Point. Dinner was served on the grounds.

In August, messengers were appointed to attend the Liberty Baptist Association's meeting at Mills Home Baptist Church. Brother Carrick Teague was appointed to make a one-minute report on what had happened at Abbotts Creek over the past year.

In the past, numerous names were dropped from the church roll because he/she had united with a church "not of like faith and practice." However, we have just mentioned a minister from the Friends Church preached at an afternoon service. Now at the August meeting, the Christian Church in High Point was given permission "of having a picnic on our church grounds on condition that they destroy no property." This should be seen as real mark of acceptance of other denominational groups.

September 15, 1935, Rev. Day preached on the opening day of revival. "Mr. Day preached a series of simple, helpful messages. A great deal of interest was manifested both by the Christians and the non-Christians. Twenty-seven were added to the church: Lucy Siceloff, Blanch Weavil, Mr. W. L. Lewis, Dorothy Bodenhamer, Helen Deal, Dapathana Lewis, Daphne Moore, Elizabeth Hayworth, Kathleen Womble, Pauline Stewart, Dorothy Hayworth, Margaret Garrison, Lucile Hayworth, Mrs. Leona Stone, Jr. Ransome Stone, Cletus Hedgecock, Mrs. Grady Idol, Grady Idol, Blanche Hedgecock, Ivey V. Phillips, Homer Weavil, Randal Bodenheimer, Lucille Proctor, Tom Proctor, Bessie Proctor, James Haynes, and Mrs. Ivey V. Phillips. The above listed group was baptized on September 30, 1935, and given the right hand of fellowship at the end of the morning worship service.

On November 16, of the same year, "A committee of Mr. W. D. Spurgeon, Mr. Ivey Orrell, and Mr. Charlie Bodenheimer were appointed by the pastor to see Mr. Morris in regard to the disposal of the property which he had laid claim to which joins the church property, so that the church would have first chance at it if said property were disposed of. The church voted to not let him connect his plant with the church meter."

The financial report given on this same day has a new item appearing. It is listed as a Hundred Thousand Club to which $6 is shown. Mention was made three months later that the pastor had based his message on a Mr. Huggins' book, *Stewardship*. On that day, February 21, 1936, $12 was listed for this item and later we note $82 had been given. This seems to be in reference to the Southern Baptist Convention's effort to raise one hundred thousand dollars that the church declined to support in early 1933.

During the March meeting, Mr. Charlie Spurgeon informed the church that Mr. W. S. Luck "wanted to preach for Abbotts Creek people some Sunday." The church voted to allow this some second or fourth Sunday. Such Sundays would be the days other than regular worship times. He was given a time, second Sunday in May.

Floyd Teague and "one of the deacons" made a report to the church on April 19, 1936, in regard to the Will of Mr. Charles. He had willed $50 to Abbotts Creek. An attorney for the estate had sent a request asking the church to relinquish its right to this in order for the grandchild of Mr. Charles to use this to continue her education. A committee was appointed "to act on this matter after investigation as they see fit." Mr. Ivey Orrell and John Welborn "made up this committee." At the May 16 meeting, "the church authorized F. Carrick Teague to sign the release to the money of the Will of Mr. Charles." No other information was given, not even a first name of Mr. Charles or the grandchild.

Evidently the Spiritual Committee, though not mentioned in recent years, was still at work. Mr. W. D. Spurgeon reported to the church on June 20, 1936, that one "wished the church to forgive her of her misstep." Surely the committee named the person though it was not recorded. The church voted to grant her request and restore her to full fellowship. At the same meeting, the church was informed that the pastor's salary was behind in the amount of $24.17.

Back in November of 1935, a committee had approached a Mr. Morris about land he had claimed that was adjacent to the church's property. We hear again about this on July 18, 1936: "...A committee was appointed to see Mr. Morris in regard to the lot on which the Morris' factory stands. Mr. Surgeon (W. D.) asked Mr. Morris if the church could purchase the lot. He replied that when he was through with it, he would give it to the church."

The same Mr. Spurgeon reported to the church on September 19, 1936, he had gone to see a member of the church and "she showed penitence." She came and asked the church to forgive her "because she had done wrong and wanted to be forgiven." A motion was made and approved to forgive her and reinstated her in the church. If she had been called before the church, there had been no written account of it and the sin for which she wanted forgiveness was never mentioned. Anyone who knows Baptist business meetings must wonder if there were any discussions or specific questions asked as to the nature of the sin for which forgiveness was requested.

The protracted meeting in September had Rev. E. F. Baker, pastor of the

1933–1949

First Baptist Church of Kernersville, as the speaker. The church had voted to have afternoon services during revival. It is not clear if this was for the entire week or just for the Sunday services. On the opening day of revival, it was reported he "also preached in the afternoon and evening services." Six were baptized as a result of the meeting.

Pastor Mumford offered his resignation as pastor of Abbotts Creek Baptist Church on October 17, 1936. It was to take effect "in a few months." A month later, the church voted to accept his resignation. The next sentence simply states Sanford Hayworth "was re-elected as fireman for the church."

The resigning pastor used the subject "The Constraining Love of Christ" for the January 17, 1937 service. "The pastor gave a few words of admonition, as well as approval for his last sermon."

From all appearances Pastor Mumford was a beloved pastor. We are listing here some of the sermon topic he used and the scriptural basis for them.

Result of Faith in God—Hebrews 11:1-30
The True Disciples Must Have the Sacrificial Spirit—Luke 14:25-35
Christ's Friends—John 15:1-15
Journeys of the Heart—(no scripture listed)
Wayside Ministry—John 9
Christ Building His Unshakable Church—Matthew 16:13-23
The Unknown Companion—John 1:19-33
Judge, Lawgiver, and Savior—Isaiah 33
Moods or Seasons of the Soul—Ephesians 2: 5
When Is Prayer, Prayer?—Luke 23:42

A month after Rev. Munford's last sermon, the church voted to call Rev. V. M. Swaim as a supply pastor." The next meeting, the church voted to limit services to the first and third Sundays while having "a part time pastor." The church finished paying Rev. Munford's salary "thus paying him in full all the church owed him."

In addition to the supply pastor, several ministers had preached during the services. On June 6, 1937, conference was called in order to elect a pastor. "The first item of business was the report of the pulpit committee. The following were nominated for pastor: Rev. T. W. Bray, Rev. Lincoln Fulk, Rev. J. C. Brock, and Rev. R. A. Britt." The vote tally was like this: Bray forty-seven with nineteen against him. Rev. Fulk received thirteen. Rev. Brock had the same number and Rev. R. A. Britt received one vote.

"The Reverend Bray, after some discussion, was declared to be the pastor of Abbotts Creek Baptist Church by W. D. Spurgeon. The church unanimously voted to support Brother Bray even though some voted against him, thus a spirit of cooperation was shown by all." On July 4, Rev. Bray preached his first sermon as pastor of the church. However, it was not until October 3, Rev. and Mrs. Bray actually joined the church.

Rev. and Mrs. Mumford asked for their church letter in June, in order for them to join another church.

The "graveyard committee" was voted authority to purchase two or three acres of the William Pharbee [sic] land.

The October protracted meeting, the first since Rev. Bray became pastor, resulted in nineteen baptisms and two additions by letter. Rev. Bray did the preaching.

On the third Sunday of December 1937, "motion made and carried to change the communion services from third Sunday to first Sunday of each quarter." At the time of this writing, communion is still observed the first Sunday of every quarter.

A committee was appointed at the third Sunday of December along with the pastor to study the by-laws of the church in regard to third Saturday preaching. The church voted 37-1 but the matter was left open for another month "for further study and considerations." Just what needed to be studied or considered as far as by-laws were concerned remained unknown but obviously at least one felt it ought to be done.

A report was given at the January 16, 1938 conference stating, "Proceeds from corn patch on church's land were $3."

W. D. Spurgeon, who voted for Saturday preaching, gave the report from the deacons at this January meeting. "The board of deacons felt it not wise to have Saturday preaching under present conditions." He also stated, "the board of deacons meet every Monday night after the first Sunday of each month." This continues to be the regular meeting time for the deacons to meet. The deacons felt it not wise for the Saturday preaching but no mention is made of the fact the church had previously voted to hold such services.

Months ago, the Hundred Thousand Club was mentioned. At various times, that item continued to show up in the financial reports. For instance, March 20, 1938, twelve dollars was listed and added to the total mission giving which gives confirmation it was for the Southern Baptist Convention's effort to pay the debt mentioned earlier.

A change in clerks took place in June of 1938. Carrick Teague offered his resignation, which was accepted by the church. Clarence Moore was elected to assume the work as clerk.

In October, of the same year, the church voted to begin preaching every

Sunday. The motion carried by one vote, 29-28. Floyd Teague, Walter McCustion, and D. S. Hayworth made up the selected committee to "investigate the possibilities of increasing the pastor's salary to take care of every Sunday preaching." A month later, the committee returned to the church with the report "they thought it wise to let the salary remain as it now is, $800 per year." Then we read "after much meditation and prayer the church decided in conference to go as it has been before having preaching first and third Sunday and that the question of every Sunday preaching be dropped and nothing more said bout it until more of the members were in sympathy with it. The spirit of the meeting was good."

The president of the Woman's Missionary Union reported to the church in December of 1938 "that they are now supporting a mission station in Cuba which costs $5 per month." Two months later, she reported they were now supporting a second mission station in Cuba. That, too, was at the cost of $5 a month. Three new deacons were chosen at this time: Clarence Moore, Robert Palmer and John Spurgeon.

The New Year 1939 began with the Sunday School reporting an average attendance of 208. The spiritual committee is still a functioning group in that Minnie Spurgeon was chosen to replace Minnie Green on the committee since the latter had died.

In March, the church had a motion to adopt a denominational plan that was designed to take care of "our aged or disabled ministers." The September financial report lists $2.67 given toward this cause. The same amount was given the next month as well. It is not stated if this was to help the present pastor as a retirement fund or treated otherwise. Month after month the same amount is shown on the financial statement.

The minutes of May 21, 1939, "We had all day services, third Sunday in May, which is an annual affare [sic] and held a memorial service in honor of our dead." The Reverend L. J. Matthews preached the afternoon service. "There were a number of visiting singers who assisted Brother Carey Davis in the song services."

The church voted in July "to send our pastor to the Baptist World Alliance in Atlanta, Georgia." By the next conference $25 had been contributed toward that cause.

In September, attention was called to the need for repairs on the church building. The trustees were given the responsibility of seeing this work was done. A couple of months later, $123 was listed as having taken care of such cost. If that amount was not collected by the end of the month, the trustees were authorized to borrow funds to pay this with interest.

Routine business was taking time at each conference. This prompted the congregation to make a decision at the November 1939 meeting. "The board of deacons wish to recommend to the church that they feel it's for the best interest of the church that our church defer the reading of church minutes each third Sunday and also treasurer's report and other matters that are more or less a form or record except any business that should be attended at any time." The church adopted this recommendation.

January 1940, "The church voted for the pastor to appoint a committee to investigate the possibility of the church building a parsonage." The committee was to be named later and was at the next conference. Members of the committee were listed as E. F. Mumford, Chairman, Grady Green, Andrew Bodenheimer, Sanford Hayworth, John Welborn, W. D. Spurgeon, and Roy Hayworth.

The minutes of February 4th has recorded it this way: "A committee was appointed by the pastor to assist the WMU in drawing up plans and secure a location for the parsonage. This committee reported W. D. and Charley Spurgeon would sell the church a lot just south of the church property. The church voted to accept the lot. Rev. E. F. Mumford presented the plans adopted by the committee, a six-room house. Church voted to accept the plans. The house was to be built of brick veneer and to cost around nine hundred dollars, not including free labor given." It is of interest to note, a month later a house had been designed and approved by the committee. Even the estimated cost of the building had been determined. The church approved the plans.

The pastor, The Reverend T. W. Bray, offered his resignation as pastor on August 4, 1940 to take effect on November 1. The very next month, church letters were granted to Mr. and Mrs. Bray in order for them to join Rich Fork Baptist Church. The new pulpit committee consisted of D. S. Hayworth, John Welborn, John Phillips, Ray Green, and Carrick Teague. The beloved former pastor, E. F. Mumford was called as supply pastor.

This committee wasted no time with their assignment and search. In March of 1941, Rev. B. A. Mitchell was presented to the church as the prospective pastor. Preaching would be twice a month and a yearly salary was to be $800. Later in the month, the church voted to construct a garage at the parsonage.

The church named a committee in May of 1941 to see about "weekly bulletins for the church." The members of this committee were Robert Palmer, Mrs. Maggie Welborn, and Clarence Moore. The church voted to accept their recommendation and start using church bulletins. Here again,

1933–1949

First parsonage at Abbotts Creek. Photo at right: Rev. and Mrs. Mitchell are pictured with daughter Margaret Ann at front entrance. This porch was covered later. Photo at left shows kitchen in back with Margaret Ann Mitchell in chair on the lawn. Photos donated by Betty Spurgeon Essick. Photos were taken in the early 1940s.

we note a committee appointed and at the same conference their recommendation was accepted.

May 18, 1941 Miss Mary Hedgecock requested her church letter to join the Mills Home Baptist Church in Thomasville. With the interest and emphasis the church always gave to the Baptist Children's Homes, it is not surprising that someone from the church chose to work with the children cared for in the home. Miss Hedgecock did and worked there until her retirement. She had the distinction of being the first person from the church to ever work for any of our Baptist agencies.

The deacons were charged with the decision as to where the money should come from for mowing the grass on the graveyard. At the June conference, the church treasurer had been authorized to pay seven dollars for such mowing. Evidently the question had been raised should the money come from the cemetery fund or the church treasury. The cemetery fund had been started from the Estate of the late Milton Teague.

Previously, the treasurer's report had listed four dollars being paid for sweeping the church but in June of 1941, the amount had been doubled. Other figures show expenditure for YWAs—$2.85; GAs—$.70, and Sunbeams $.15. The light bill for the month was $1.60 and $133.34 paid for pastor's salary. On the same day, Carrick Teague was elected Sunday School director.

In August of that same year, the church voted to purchase three thousand bulletins printed by the press at Mills Home for the cost of nine dollars. Another committee was appointed at the same time and recommended the church have a Daily Vacation Bible School. The committee included Mrs. Daisy Spurgeon, Miss Mattie Teague, and Grady Green. The church accepted the recommendation and for the first time, a Vacation Bible School was conducted.

Four months prior to the Pearl Harbor attack, D. S. Hayworth, Mrs. Daisy Spurgeon, and Robert Palmer served as the nominating committee for Sunday School officers and teachers. The nomination for church officers came from another committee, namely Grady Green, Mrs. Maggie Welborn and John Spurgeon.

The October 1941 conference found the church dealing with the graveyard. The minutes of this conference read, "The board of deacons recommends to the church that we as a church put forth an effort to raise an endowment fund for the upkeep of our graveyard and grounds, to spend only the interest from same at any time. That this money be added to the $747.96 that we now have for the purpose of graveyard upkeep. Grady Idol and Charley Kanoy were elected to serve on the graveyard committee with C. E. Spurgeon, J. L. Green, and Charley Bodenheimer. This committee will have charge of receiving funds and upkeep of graveyard and grounds."

The next conference was held just one week after the attack at Pearl Harbor. This writer grew up hearing two of the most difficult decisions that Baptist churches had faced were dealing with the rotation of deacons in a church and the beginning of a unified budget. I can remember some of the problems with the deacon rotation in my home church in Spartanburg County, South Carolina. The Abbotts Creek minutes written by Clerk Clarence Moore on December 15, 1941 mention no such controversy but the vote suggests it was not unanimous. "A financial plan was presented to the church by our pastor. In this plan we are to put on an every member canvas, set up a budget and have a unified treasure. Church voted twenty-five for the plan and eighteen against."

The committee composed of Rev. B. A. Mitchell, Frank Spurgeon, Carrick Teague, Mattie Teague and John Welborn presented the first unified budget for the church. This took place on Sunday night, December 12, 1941.

Pastor's Salary—$800

Pastoral Help—$90

Building supplies for parsonage and church repairs, bath room chicken house hot water heater—$400

Insurance—$8

Cost of Sunday School—$20
Vacation Bible School—$25
W. M. U. Society, individual supported; flowers for funerals of members of Sunday School—$30
B.T.U. —$25
Church bulletins—$15
Pastor's Retirement Fund—$24
Lights—$8
Christmas program, Library Center books and stencils—$40
Minutes fund—$10
Fuel donated
Sweeping and brooms—$53
Gifts to local poor and unfortunate—$50
Incidentals—$120
Budget —$2003 and
Cooperative Program—$101.

It can be noted the figures do not add up to $2003. In writing these figures, it can be easily understood how one or more could have been left off. Two other notes of interest stand out here. It had been determined in a previous conference to have Vacation Bible School but to this time, a director had not been mentioned. However, the budget projected Bible school as a ministry that would be carried out. We must assume since the church voted for the total items presented, everyone understood another item but it would be interesting to know exactly what the following meant, "building and supplies for parsonage and church repairs bath room chicken house hot water heater $45." It seems there should be a comma or more than one but just where is not clear. No explanation is given to help us understand the part about the "chicken house hot water heater."

It can be noted in this, fifteen dollars had been allowed for church bulletins while earlier nine dollars had been spent for three thousand bulletins. During the conference of March 1942, the church had voted to cancel the contract with the Baptist Children's Homes' print shop and place the bulletin order with the Baptist literature services.

Another major decision was made at the April 1942 conference. The vote was taken to call the present pastor, Rev. B. A. Mitchell "for an indefinite period of time. If the pastor feels that he has been called to move on into another field, he should give the church three months notice. On the other hand, if the church should decide that the present pastor is not best for the spiritual growth of the church, they should give him three months notice."

At the May roll call, the number present had increased to 156 and the number absent reduced to 176. The next month, the Sunday School average attendance for the previous three months was listed as 220. At the same meeting, "Brother C. G. Spurgeon sold to the church for the sum of one dollars one-half acre of land being back of the parsonage." The next financial report showed one dollar was paid to get the deed for the one-half acre of land.

The church accepted the recommendation of the nominating committee on July 19, 1946. Clarence Moore continued to be church clerk with Grady Green serving as treasurer. Cary J. Davis was to serve as pianist and music director. Perry Hayworth was fireman while Blanche Traynham was chosen to sweep the church and be "caretaker." Ushers were Frank Spurgeon, chief; Ray Green, Kermit Green, Howard Dean, Grady Idol and Ivey Bodenheimer. The finance committee included all deacons, plus the Sunday School superintendent Carrick Teague, Training Union Director Henry Traynham, and Woman's Missionary Union President, Mrs. B. A. Mitchell. The next conference mentioned the election of Ray Green as the assistant treasurer.

The minutes of the August conference stated "a nursery will be established here at the church in the near future." A change in policy seems apparent as well in that it was determined to have revival services only at night. Other business matters included the Pastor's salary being raised to one thousand dollars per year.

The teachers for the Sunday School classes were listed as well. The names of some classes tend to stand out in that they had not been mentioned much, if any, in earlier minutes. Mrs. B. A. Mitchell was chosen to teach the "Ever Ready Class." Walter McCustion was listed as teacher for the "Burden Lifter's Class." For the "Buds and Promise Class," Annie Lou Phillips was named teacher. Dorothy Hayworth would assist her. Blanche Traynham was the leader of the "True Blue Class" while Robert Palmer was named teacher for the "Sunray Class."

The cost of the 1942 Vacation Bible School was listed as $25.

The nominating committee recommended to the church at the September business conference teachers for two new classes. J. P. Traynham assisted by Andrew Bodenheimer was to be the teacher for the junior boys. The intermediate boys had Floyd J. Teague as teacher assisted by Mrs. Mable Hayworth. In Training Union, Mrs. Carey Davis was to lead the senior group. Della Davis was assigned to the intermediate group while Aileen Palmer's place was with the junior age.

1933–1949

When the financial report was given for the last three months of 1942, $28 was listed as "Christmas presents for soldiers." The January statement shows $26.69 more for the soldiers. Even wFith Rev. B. A. Mitchell as pastor, the report shows "a gift to former pastor Rev. Mumford $51.50." A ten-dollar gift was stated for the music director, Carey J. Davis.

Appearing for the first recorded time on the financial statement in January 1943, "Treats for Sunday School $20. Other Christmas presents $40."

From time to time, the church had speakers from the outside. In May of 1943, the guest speaker was "a Chinese medical student from Wake Forest Medical College in Winston-Salem." The next financial report reflects a gift of $29 for Edward Chow. We would assume he was the Chinese student.

October 1943, "Plans and by-laws for a memorial association were presented to the church by the graveyard committee and the WMU. Officers of the association were President Daisy Spurgeon, Treasurer Mrs. Eva Hayworth, and Secretary Wilson Hedgecock. Vice President, Carrick Teague, Second Vice President, Mrs. Mary Kanoy, historian, Mrs. Mable Hayworth, and Nina Hayworth, grounds committee Charley Bodenheimer, Charley Kanoy, Charley Surgeon, and Grady Idol." On the membership committee, Miss Mary Frances Hayworth was named. Clarence Moore's name was given for the lunch committee.

For the first time, the cradle role was mentioned with workers named. They were Mildred Bodenheimer, Elva Hedgecock, Hester Idol, Betty Spurgeon, and Margaret Welborn.

In January 1944, the Will of the late Addison Charles left Abbotts Creek Baptist Church the sum of $50. The church voted to add this to the "present endowment fund for the upkeep of the graveyard. As of this date, the fund was $1,243.70. Every expense seems to be listed in the financial report, even fifteen cents for furniture polish. The same report shows "War Relief $100. Christmas presents for the soldiers $24." Mr. Mumford was given a $40 gift as well.

Three new deacons were chosen in March. They were Wilson Hedgecock, Carrick Teague, and Ernest Burton. The Reverend R. R. Jackson of High Point preached their ordination service. The next month, the church voted to discontinue the roll call of members at the annual third Sunday in May meeting. At the same time, the previous three months treasurer's report was given and lists "Honor Roll Board for services men, $33.15."

The Reverend C. B. Atkinson assisted the pastor in the July revival meeting. A large number accepted Christ and were baptized. They were, Raymond Proctor, Doris Traynham, Carol Penn Welborn, Billy Garrison, Betty

Lou Dean, Earl Hayworth, Billie Ann Welborn, Mrs. Ella Hedgecock, Bernice Sells, Perry Bodenheimer, Charles Bodenheimer, Jr., Maxine Hayworth, Charles Edward Palmer, Mrs. Ina Smith, Doris Spainhour, Jay Weavil, Doris Bodenheimer, and Mrs. Ruth Bodenheimer. Later it is mentioned, the visiting minister was paid $111.50.

On June 4, 1944, the church letter for Elizabeth (Beth) Hayworth was granted that she might unite with the Mars Hill Baptist Church. She was the first person from the church to leave with the intent of going into a church-related vocation. That fact is not mentioned in the minutes but the July conference noted a gift of $46 had been given to her. In October, another $5 is listed as having been sent to her. We need to let Beth tell her story and how "family and church members nurtured and encouraged a teen age farm girl who grew up believing that God had a special mission for her and her life." After serving for eight years as Director of the Women's Department of the Baptist World Alliance, she retired. You will find her story at the end of this chapter. Her story mentioned the fact of her ordination, the first female from Abbotts Creek to be ordained.

World War II is not mentioned as such but the honor roll for the military people and the Christmas gift for the soldiers was mentioned frequently. At the July meeting, six dollars was allowed "for the printing a paper to send to our boys who are in the service of our country." A month later, the church felt it necessary "to merge the two young men's classes until after the war." However, the next month this decision was reversed and the two classes would remain as before.

In September, Rev. Mumford was granted a church letter that would allow him to become a member of the Seven Springs Baptist Church in Seven Springs, North Carolina. In June of 1937, Reverend and Mrs. Mumford had asked for their church letter to join another church. With him asking for his church letter alone seem to imply that he had returned to the community and church without his beloved wife who had died. This may explain why on at least two different occasions, a monetary gift had been given to him. A Sunday School report was given at this time meeting showing an average Sunday School attendance for the previous three months was 198.

The church never forgot the men serving in the military. The military was not limited to men but nothing has been mentioned of any females from the church or community serving. The treasurer's report in October, 1944, gave us this statement: "paper for boys who are in the army (meaning other branches of the military as well) $19.50. Names and stars for serv-

1933–1949

ice board $1.95." Later in the report, we noted, "Presents for soldiers $155.08." Before the final line is written, we read "war relief $67." When I arrived as pastor of Abbotts Creek in the fall of 1974, copies of the newsletters that had been sent to the military personnel during their time in service were being copied and mailed to the church family with the weekly newsletter, *The Tie*. The members who had received them while serving away from home were pleased to read them again and it seemed so important to the present church family to be reminded of this. Because of the importance of such material, we include what the first copy was like. This can be found at the end of this chapter.

The church voted in December of 1944 "to discontinue roll call if it is deemed necessary roll will be called on any fifth Sunday business meeting."

Obviously, the promotion of Sunday School members had become an "issue." It was agreed by vote of the church that promotion would become a "recognized policy of our Sunday School throughout." This would take effect on the fourth Sunday of September "and that the class involved in the dispute mentioned not be called upon to observe it till that time but that it be understood that observance will be uniform at that time." At the same conference on the next line, the minutes have recorded, "the church voted to not accept the resignation of Clarence F. Moore as clerk and deacon."

The April 1945 conference heard a plan presented by the pastor for "a new building for the Sunday School. A sympathy vote was taken, 37 for it, no opposition." This conference also heard a report regarding a WMU project. "...They are erecting a bulletin board in front of the church, cost $40. Other material $12. Brother Mitchell will erect the board."

The church was called into conference by the pastor on May 20, 1945 "for the purpose of voting on some additional Sunday School rooms to the church, thirty two voted to do the building which will not be undertaken until after the war when building materials can be more easily gotten. Deacon Ernest Burton was to be campaign chairman, others to be appointed later." Thirty-two voting seems somewhat strange since the report was given a short time earlier that the average attendance in Sunday was 198. The following month, the figures showed $1,947.82 in the building fund. "W. D. Spurgeon will donate five thousand feet of lumber. Brothers Perry and Sanford Hayworth will saw all timber donated for the church building."

The July meeting dealt with the memorial association. D. S. Hayworth, Floyd J. Teague, and Ray Green were appointed to work with the committee of the memorial association and will "recommend to the church whether we have some restrictions on the use of our grave yard are [sic] not. We have always had a free public burring [sic] ground."

A note was made in June of 1945 to received Rev. and Mrs. E. F. Mumford by letter. Two months later, letters were granted in order for them to unite with the Spring Hope Baptist Church. Rev. and Mrs. Mumford had their church letters granted in September of 1937. His last sermon as pastor had been on January 17. When Rev. Bray had resigned effective November 1, 1940, Rev. Mumford was called to return as supply pastor. Then we note in August of 1945, Rev. and Mrs. Mumford were granted letters to move to Spring Hope, North Carolina.

The church clerk would have had no reason to record this and with no church newsletter, there had been no mention of the fact that Mrs. Mumford had died. The church family knew these things. In fact, the Mrs. Mumford the church knew was the second wife of the former pastor. Both had died. Now in August, 1945 we read that the church letters were granted to Rev. and Mrs. Mumford.

The Teague family has allowed us to use this bit of information. Rev. Mumford was alone, having given up two companions to death. Mattie Teague was living alone in her small house in the Teague section of the community. The story has it, one day Rev. Mumford knocked on her door. It seems he immediately stated his intent, "Will you marry me?" No prior dating, no courtship, no time for her to have ever thought of it. Of course, she needed some time to think about such a serious matter. During this thinking process, she sought advice from her brother, Carrick. "What should I do?" His immediate answer was, "Marry him." They were married and moved to Spring Hope where they enjoyed ten or more years happily married before his death. Later, after her death, she was buried at her home church, Abbotts Creek.

Interest in the plans for the Sunday School building continued to be seen. In August, the church voted to have "a preliminary plan drawn for the new building. Brother J. M. Page of Raleigh will draw the plan for $25. Bleu [sic] prints will be drawn later." Four months later, the treasurer's report shows $260 paid for the blueprints.

A month later the church was back in a business meeting with more plans. The committee was composed of Chairman D. S. Hayworth, Floyd J. Teague, J. P. Traynham, Grady Green, Grady Idol, John Welborn, and W. S. Hayworth. "This committee is for the purpose of constructing better equipment for the church. We do hereby authorize these to secure plans and proceed with the construction at any time and in any way they deem wise."

Revival services were conducted in October. Abbotts Creek seemed to always have outstanding ministers preaching for revival services and other special services. For these services, Doctor Ralph Herring from First Baptist Church in Winston-Salem was the speaker. Richard Kanoy, Patty Clinard and Sally Reid made professions of faith and were baptized a short time later. Dr. Herring was paid $150 for his services.

The only matter for a February 1946 business conference had W. D. Spurgeon resigning as chairman of deacons and Floyd J. Teague being named new chairman. Wilson Hedgecock was elected as Secretary-Treasurer for the deacons.

A month later a short conference was called "just before preaching." "Brother C. E. Spurgeon gave to the church 2.58 acres of land to be used as an addition to our building grounds."

In March of 1946, the minutes recorded "the committee who looks after the graveyard made some recommendations to be voted on at a later date. A month later some amendments to the constitution were approved." A note was attached reading, "see the minutes" of the memorial association. Their annual report was given the next month but was not attached to the church minutes.

Over the years the church never seemed reluctant to spend what was necessary for musical instruments or music books. Fifty dollars was reportedly paid out during July, August, and September of this year to send Carey Davis to a "choir director's school."

The budget projected for 1947 called for $8,642 and was approved by the church.

A regular business conference was carried out on the last Sunday of December 1946. "We the Abbotts Creek Baptist Church are claiming and possessing on this day, December 29, 1946 a tract of land adjoining our graveyard. It took the clerk fifteen lines to name all the points defining the exact area of land. The acreage was surveyed back earlier in the year by N. R. Kimery (?). C. H. Bodenheimer paid $12 for the surveying.

The church was informed the insurance on the church property had been increased from $4,000 to $20,000. D. S. Hayworth had been authorized to act as chairman with the trustees to take care of this matter.

In March of 1947, the deacons and spiritual committee recommended to the church certain names be removed from the church roll. Five had joined churches of other denominations. Three had joined other Baptist churches without asking for their letter. For the first mentioned time, the names of three people were dropped because they could not be located.

When the financial balance was listed at the end of 1946, $10.56 was shown "for pins and bars for those who were present every Sunday for Sunday School during last year." Since the pins were given for the first year, it appears this was not the first time for recognizing those with perfect attendance. The bars for additional years were hung below the pins.

A love offering of one hundred dollars was given to Rev. Mitchell "since Mrs. Mitchell had been sick and had an operation." This took place and was recorded in June 1947.

A group was appointed two months later "as a committee in the interest of moving Wake Forest College to Winston-Salem." Members were Wilson Hedgecock, Carrick Teague, and Mrs. W. S. Hayworth.

Two very significant decisions were made at the November conference. "The church voted in conference to go on full time. Our present Pastor B. A. Mitchell was called full time beginning January 1 or as soon as the Wallburg Church can secure a pastor." The two churches had obviously shared a pastor prior to this. "The pastor's salary will be $3,000 per year. " The "church also voted to support a foreign missionary, which will cost $1,200 per year. Three months later, the church authorized the pastor to write the Foreign Mission Board in regards to supporting a foreign missionary.

The first budget with a full time pastor was presented to the church at this November conference. "The budget of $11,460 was rejected by the vote of the church; but later the church voted to try for one month to meet the budget. This month would be the first month full time preaching begins."

Just what was brewing was not clear at this point. D. S. Hayworth resigned as chairman of the building committee and was replaced by Floyd J. Teague. Wilson Hedgecock replaced Mr. Hayworth on the committee. This took place on November 30, 1947. The next conference seemed to be misdated since it is marked November 6. This conference dealt with a recommendation from the building committee. Their recommendations are listed here.

Not to build at this time.
Sell lumber to highest bidder.
Build some steps at the back of present house of worship.
Give W. D. Spurgeon $300 credit for lumber donated.
Give Perry and Sanford Hayworth $140 credit for sawing lumber.
Place money now on hand in Building and Loan Company.
D. S. Hayworth to be on building committee.
Do not slack in our efforts to raise money for the building fund.
The church voted to accept this recommendation.

The first conference in January of 1948 was called at the request of the church treasurer and chairman of the deacons. "The finance committee is asked to meet again and consider and recommend concerning important finance issue." "The board of deacons recommends that due to deficils [sic] in mission gifts for 1947 the one month trial budget on 50% bases be disregarded and that we be responsible to such mission objects as we have otherwise obligated ourselves to until the finance committee can meet and reconstruct our program. Church accepts the recommendation."

On Sunday evening, a week later, the pastor called the church into conference. "The revised budget for 1948, $8,441, was adopted by the church with the exceptions of $3,000 pastor salary and $1,200 to support a foreign missionary. There was some misunderstanding as to whether they have been voted on by the church or not."

With the earlier resignation of Carey Davis as choir director, the new committee recommended Mrs. Johny Hayworth, pianist and the choir director, for the morning services. Shirley Davis would serve in that capacity for the evening services.

The building committee reported in February of 1948 the church had received $838.62 for the lumber. The building fund had a total of $5,330.42.

The church made the decision at this time to give the pastor his "freedom" fifth Sundays. "No preaching morning or evening."

The deacons recommended to the church on March 28 "that our church adopt the rotation system in selecting deacons. This will be voted on the fourth Sunday in April by secret ballot." The church voted to adopt the rotation system. "The plan: the four senior deacons on the board, W. D. Spurgeon, Charley Bodenheimer, Floyd J. Teague and Ivey Orrell will be replaced by D. S. Hayworth, Charley Carmichael, Howard Dean, and Sanford Hayworth elected for a period of three years. Second year and third year deacons will follow same plan. Seniors give way to others voted in. One year must intervene before any retiring deacon is reelected to active service." No mention is made of any negative reaction to the new policy. However, when the present writer arrived as pastor in the fall of 1974, Mr. Orrell was listed as "home bound." The church talk was he had been that way since the church started the rotating system for deacons.

During this time, Brother Carrick Teague was "granted license to preach the gospel. Brother Carrick has felt the call to preach for sometime but due to the feeling of unworthiness has declined to heed the call. But now he wants his church and the world to know that he is willing to do whatsoever God would have him do."

The minutes of May 23, 1948 simply states, "Howard Dean, Bessie Wheeler and John Welborn were named as a committee in regard to the organ." Later in the month the deacons recommended the church take a special collection for Mrs. Flay Royal second Sunday in June to assist in the purchase of a cow."

The very next month, the church voted to "buy an organ, preference a Hammond organ. Cost $2,300. Money not to be taken from church treasury. If we fail to raise the money, we buy no organ. There will be no debt put on the church for this cause."

Clarence Moore resigned as church clerk to take effect at the end of the associational year.

June 13, 1948, "chairman Floyd J. Teague, deacons Ivey Orrell, Charley Bodenheimer, and W. D. Spurgeon are about to retire from the board of deacons. Be it resolved:

That the board of deacons expresses to them their appreciation of a high quality service, that we hold them in highest esteem.

That we ask the Lord's greatest blessing upon each of them as they retire. This request be read to the church in conference and that it be entered in the records of the board."

Treasurer Grady Green offered his resignation to the church at the August 22 meeting. This was to take effect on September 2. This resignation was accepted.

The new church clerk, Robert Palmer, recorded the September conference. It was mentioned that the Sunday School officers and teachers were voted on by secret ballot. This is followed by the statement, "the church received the report of the nominating committee, and those nominated were elected." If secret ballot had been the practice for such elections, it had not been stated as such. If it had been the known ongoing church practice, previous clerks would have seen no reason to state the obvious.

Howard Dean "as chairman of the organ fund reported $460 secured in pledges and $360 in cash, a total of $822."

"The church adopted a resolution to be presented at the Associational meeting, the resolution protested the putting of the new Wake Forest Chapel adjacent to the school of religion only and petitioned that it be given a central location." The 1948 annual of the Liberty Baptist Association does have such a resolution that was passed. However, it was presented from Wallburg Baptist Church to the Association and passed unanimously.

Two months later, in November, "the cemetery committee was given full power to act on matters concerning needs for more burial purposes or any other needs that might arise."

In December, the proposed budget for 1949 was passed by a vote of "32 for 25 against." Two months later, February of 1949, the finance committee called a conference. "This committee made recommendations for reductions in the 1949 budget." No explanation is given as to what was reduced. It is not even stated that the church voted to accept or reject this recommendation. Ernest Burton, chairman of the building fund, reported at the end of the year the total in the fund was $5,504.10. Mr. Burton was referred to as chairman of "the building fund." At the same time, "the board of deacons recommended to the church that the building committee resume their activity." The church voted in favor of this.

Good news is announced at the first conference of 1949. "The trustees have accepted the deed for a piece of land behind the church given by Mr. and Mrs. John Spurgeon, Senior. A motion was made and unanimously carried that a letter of thanks and appreciation be sent them by the clerk." The organ fund continued to increase and by this date totaled $869.21.

The conference on February 27, 1949, had as the discussion the resignation of Rev. B. A. Mitchell as pastor. No mention had been made that the pastor had resigned but "a motion was made and seconded that we not accept the resignation of our pastor. After much discussion, we voted by secret ballot upon this motion. There were fifty-nine votes for the motion. There were thirty-one votes against the motion. The church accepted the pastor's resignation." We do not know what else transpired since the motion that had fifty-nine votes was to not accept the resignation, yet we read the church accepted the resignation.

A meeting toward the end of March showed $5,619.41 in the building fund and $879.21 cash or pledges for the organ fund. The building committee gave no report but the church decided to postpone any building until a new pastor was secured.

An effort was made to secure Dr. Conrad of High Point for supply pastor "whenever a vacuum should occur." A pulpit committee was chosen for the search process. This committee was composed of C. F. Moore, Carrick Teague, Mrs. Mabel Hayworth, Numa Everhart, and Mrs. Daisy Spurgeon." Numa Everhart had become a member of the church two months prior to his selection for the committee. He joined by letter from New Friendship Baptist Church.

The rejection mood seemed to characterize the church at the April 24 meeting. By a majority of vote, the scheduled revival meeting was postponed, and the church "rejected the help previously mentioned" for the revival speaker. The rejected minister's name was not given and the rejection may have been because of the church did not have a pastor at the time. "The church also rejected the recommendation of the board of deacons to secure Dr. Conrad of High Point for supply pastor."

Of seven deacon nominees, four were elected to serve. They were Fletcher Clinard, Cletus Hedgecock, Walter McCuistion, [sic], and Brooks Motsinger.

The deacons had three recommendations concerning the new pastor and the supply pastor that were accepted by vote of the congregation. The supply pastor would be paid "the sum of $10 plus six cents per mile for transportation expense." The new pastor was to be paid $2,500 and the said person would be required to "conduct evening services."

It seemed that the Rev. Mitchell had purchased a hot water heater for his home. The church purchased that from him for $156 and it was to be left at the parsonage. Rev. Mitchell had also constructed a shed at the parsonage and wanted to sell it to the church. This "was considered but the church voted not to purchase." Whether it was left or taken is not stated. The Reverend Mitchell's last service was for the ordination of the newly-elected deacons. At the same May 29, 1949, service, church letters were granted for the Pastor and Mrs. Mitchell allowing them to become members of the Castalia Baptist Church in Castalia, North Carolina.

The pulpit committee was ready for the church to call a Rev. Matthews as pastor. "A motion was made and seconded that this important matter be decided today." The vote was "78 for with 8 against." Mr. Matthew, whose first name is never given, was visited by the committee. He needed time to consider and then declined.

The total membership of the church in July of 1949 was 335. The Vacation Bible School had 131 enrolled, with an average attendance of 124.

"After the preaching service (August 14, 1949), the chairman of the pulpit committee, T. C. Teague, informed the church that Rev. A. R. Snipes was available as a pastor." Rev. Snipes accepted the call to become pastor with eighty-four voting for him and seventeen voting negatively. Rev. and Mrs. Snipes joined the church on August 27.

The organ fund continued to grow, having reached $1,064.24 by September 25 of this year. At the same conference, the church voted to move the regular conference time to Wednesday night rather than on Sunday night. The vote was "unanimous for this." This is a practice still followed by the church.

1933–1949

The October revival meeting resulted in eighteen new converts presenting themselves for baptism and two by letter. They were not named.

The first Wednesday night conference was held on November 23, 1949. At this conference, at the pastor's suggestion, the new members and those to follow would be given a baptismal certificate with their name, the date and the church. The church voted to do so. The above-mentioned new members were baptized at the North Main Street Baptist Church in High Point rather than the local stream. This was the first time a baptism had taken place other than the outdoor pool near the church.

There was $185 in the fund to assist Wake Forest College with the move to Winston-Salem. The church would take another offering for this the first Sunday of the New Year. This offering was reported at the February 1950 conference at $34.30.

The last conference in the forties found the church thanking the deacons "for having purchased a mimeograph machine." The proposed budget for 1950 included $3,500 for the pastor's salary. This motion passed by a majority vote.

Attention

The newsletter was called *Attention* and has this heading: Published monthly by Abbott's Creek Baptist Church for Service Men. Volume 1, Route 1 Kernersville, N.C. December 1943. The editors were mentioned as being Mrs. Roy Hayworth, Mrs. John Spurgeon, Jr., Mrs. Della Moore, Bess Wheeler, and Marie Hayworth. Later, other names were added such as Dot Moore, and Mildred Hedgecock.

The newsletters had two pages dealing with community and church news. The last one was dated September 1945. The first issue started with this note from the editors. "GREETINGS: Hello, and Christmas Greeting to you fellows in the armed forces of our country. FIRST APPEARANCES… ATTENTION makes it appearances today in much the same manner as the groundhog. We did get out and look around a little before we embarked on this venture, and when it was suggested that you might like to hear what goes on around Abbott's Creek…ATTENTION was on its way. You are much in our thoughts and prayers, and we are just as interested in what you're doing as you are in what our doings, so is a line."

A Christmas scripture is given, Luke 2:10-11. This is followed by a prayer and then news about the fall revival in the church for the first ten days of October. Rev. Luther J. Matthews from New Friendship Baptist Church did the preaching and six professions, four of who were baptized Sunday morn-

History, Heritage, and Memories

ing, October 31, Misses Louis Berrier, Bliss Gregory and Mr. and Mrs. Burch Moore. Mrs. Tempie Berrier was received by letter and Mrs. Marie James came on profession of faith but was ill the day of the baptism.

News from the military boys included what is quoted here.

And did we hear that Cpl. William E. Hayworth and his friend Sgt. Harold Filbour spent a few days with his parents recently! William is wearing a badge of recognition of two years efficient service for Uncle Sam.

Sgt. Davis Royal and his wife were reported to have breezed out to "Davistown" November 6th.

We hear that Early Hedgecock felt his way through the dense fog from Portsmouth to his home Friday night, November 6th.

Word has been received that Pvt. Harold Moore has crossed the "Pond" and arrived safely somewhere in Northern Ireland.

Cpl. Wesley Paul Hayworth wrote his "Ma" that he hadn't got hungry enough to eat lizard meat yet. They grow to be four or five feet long down there in the West Indies.

Some of our boys can now see why it takes so many shoes to keep the army going. Cpl. Marion Bodenheimer says the foot work is "something else."

Aviation Cadet Lee W. Davis has been selected by the Classification Board for Pilot Training in the U.S. Army Air Force with headquarters in Santa Ana, California. Good luck to Lee.

Pvt. Ivey S. Smith and Pvt. Willie M. Yokely have recently had discharges from the army. Ivey is now a proud daddy. "It's a boy."

Pvt. Charles W. Davis must be happy too. It's a girl. And Uncle Sam has decided to let him "toot" his horn awhile. Much to his delight, he has been transferred from the Army Air Force to the Army Band.

Maybe a little late but did you know Cpl. David Clyde Bodenheimer did take Lessie Hayworth for better or worse! Yep, September 7. Well, he went back to New Mexico to try to better conditions while Lessie remained here with her parents.

A few others were mentioned but a blur keeps us from reading them.

A small section was devoted to "Sport Flashes." Wallburg won two victories over Hasty in basketball. The scores: boys 25-9 and girls 30-7. Rachel Reece had fourteen points and Ellen Kiger had eight for the girls. Added to this is the notation, Betty Spurgeon played an outstanding game at guard.

! ATTENTION !

Published Monthly by Abbott's Creek Baptist Church for Service Men

VOL 1 ROUTE # 1, KERNERSVILLE, N. C. DEC. 1943 - NO. 1

! Attention !

(G)REETINGS ... Hello, and (Chri)stmas Greetings to you fel(lows) in the armed forces of our (cou)ntry!

(F)IRST APPEARANCE ...

(This) ATTENTION ! ! ! makes its (app)earance today in much the (sam)e manner as the groundhog. (We) did get out and look around a little before we embarked on this venture, and when it was suggested that you might like to hear what goes on around Abbott's (Creek) - - ATTENTION - - was (rea)lly on its way.

(You) are much in our thoughts (and pr)ayers, and we're just as in(tereste)d in what you're doing as (we know) you are in our doings, so (drop u)s a line.

CHRITMAS SCRIPTURE - - - Luke 2:10, 11 - - - "And the Angel said unto them, fear not, for behold, I bring you tidings of great joy, which shall be to all people. For unto you is born this day in the city of David, a Savior, which is Christ the Lord".

A PRAYER ...

In these dark hours of dire need
We lift our hearts above
To Thee, Eternal Father
Of all wisdom, power, and love.
Oh! Living God, defend our souls
Now from despondency,
When doubts would submerge us
May we lean heavily upon Thee:
As our candles of faith go out
Wilt thou light them anew?
And may their flame, through flickering
At times, help us see through
The Myriad clouds that would
Engulf us as little children.
Confiding constantly
In thy great care, and in our
Hearts, may peace abide--
The blessed peace that comes to those
Who keep close to thy side.

FALL REVIVAL

Revival services were held in our church the first ten days in October. Rev. Luther J. Matthews, pastor of the New Friendship Church, did the preaching and we were delighted with the simplicity and power of his messages. There were six professions, four of whom were baptised Sunday Morning, October 31st, Viz. Misses Louis Berrier, Bliss Gregory and Mr. & Mrs. Burch Moore. Mrs. Tempie Berrier was received by letter and Mrs. Marie James come upon profession but was ill the day of the baptism.

History, Heritage, and Memories

Pictured here are Mabel and Roy Hayworth. Mabel was editor of the Attention Picture of Banner of Men in service from the church and community. It had gold stars which represent those who lost their lives during World War II.

Participating in the game were Rachel Reece, Catherine Clinard, Ellen Kiger, Grace Beeson, Larue Henderson, Anna Laura Hayworth, Eudora Traynham, Betty Spurgeon, Dora Mae Walker, Virginia Smith, Louise King, Gladys Swaim, and Marie Beeson.

The boys participating were Johnie Hayworth (leading score with nine points), Dwight Hayworth, Junior Everhart, Howard Craver (six points), Boyce Henderson, Monroe Glascoe, Ronald Willard, Paul Beeson and Clell Spurgeon.

The pastor wrote a letter to the men.

> Dear Boys, I would like to assure you with the first word that all your people are doing well at home. I do not know of serious illness or trouble of any nature in any of our homes, a welcomed report for anyone away from home. You will be glad to know they are well satisfied about you. They have great confidence in the ability of our government to provide for its men. They also believe you to be quite man enough to care for yourself as far as any person could. As far as we know, your sweethearts are still waiting for you too.
>
> The pastor of your church wishes to take this means of expressing a personal word of interest in each of you. We want you

1933–1949

to know that we miss the young men of the church, of whom, there are but few left. There is a definite place in the church for young men, and we want you to know that there will be places of service open to you when you are privileged to return.

We are aware some of you are in danger zones and that others may be at any time. We have a just pride in you fellows who are offering yourselves for the safety of others. You are remembered constantly in our prayers, and petitions are always made for your safety. Thus far, no member of our church and community has come to harm. Who can say but that the prayers made for you have had to do with your safe keeping thus far?

In closing, let me do a little preaching. We are aware that you do not have the same liberties and conveniences that are afforded at home. But let us urge that as far as it is possible, you will make use of every opportunity to cultivate and practice your religious life and experience. Though vice and evil are within easy reach of you at all times. It is possible for you to come through every experience without compromising yourself. I have fullest confidence in the honorable soldier.

Blessings on each of you. Drop us a line and leave your up-to-date address and we will write you a personal word. This was signed by B. A. Mitchell, Pastor.

There were other bits of information concerning the WMU of the church, the Thanksgiving service and The Baptist State Convention that was held in Winston-Salem.

A long list gives us the names of the men from the church and community serving in some areas. We will not list the rank of each one since some are named without rank. Many names seem to be family members or relatives of the church members and from acquaintance of the greater community rather than limited to the church family. The list includes names of the African-Americans from the Clifton Grove community showing the concern of the church for all people. A few names are friends of our community military men.

Marion Bodenheimer, Lee W. Davis, Charles W. Davis, David Clyde Bodenheimer, Paul Craven, Dwight Hayworth, Fred Moore, Elmer James (killed in Europe), Clarence Green, Sgt. Grey, Clay H. Davis, Athel W. Hayworth, Harold E. Moore (wounded), William H. Traynham (wounded in France), Clifton Stewart, Johnny Davis, Orvel Perryman, Lyndon Perryman, Charles W. Green, William M Russ, and Clarence Beeson.

Another page lists Samuel Moore (wounded in Germany), Percy Smith, Grayson Royal (two battle stars), Evan Weavil, Clay Manning, Clyde Green, Felix C. Beck, Charles Johnson, Paul Johnson, George W. Sechrest (air medal Indo-China), Johnie Hayworth, Thomas Moore, Henry Traynham, Paul Motsinger, Evans Weavil, Earlie J. Phillips, Loyde Steward, O'Neal Payne, Norman J. Moore, David Lee Glascoe, and Glenn Welborn.

On our third sheet, we find the names of Homer W. Motsinger, Mack Griffin, Holland Raper, Harold Sexton, John Koltash, Wesley Hedgecock, Lawrence Hauser, David Clayton Phillips, Herman L. Hedgecock, Calvin Orrell, Henry Traynham (wounded in Germany), Worman J. Moore, Charlie M. Griffin, Charles Percy Hedgecock, J. C. Mims, Robert Idol (Silver star), Cleo Curry, Paul Hayworth, Leon Motsinger, and Beauregard Lyda.

The list goes on and these are named: Oren Bodenheimer, Dell Wood, George Traynham, "Lib" Edwards, Wade Idol, John Robert Stokes, Athel Hayworth, Frank Tillman Barnes, Jimmie C. Hines, Staley Idol, Haywood Hyatt, Edwin Hyatt (eight battle stars), Ivan Wood, Weymouth Brooks, G. E. Riggle, Paul Beeson, Joseph A. Hayworth, Wesley Paul Craven (three battle stars, Presidential citation), Robert Paul Payne, Gerald Clodfelter, Charlie Griffin, and Charlie Ines.

We add these names: Sanford L. Hedgecock, Roscoe Evans Weavil, Ralph Green (wounded and later killed, tank, south Pacific), Charles Pierce, Dwight H. Moore, Glen O'Neal Payne, Willie Yokley, Oren L. Bodenheimer, John, Junior, Spurgeon (battle of the Bulge), Stanton William Bodenheimer, Ben Clodfelter, Homer Weavil, Grayson Willard, John R. Davis, Junior, Hubert L. Sells (wounded), Hubert Green, Donald Bodenheimer, Haywood Hyatt, Willie Ciso Curry, Rodney Pilson, Lib E. Edwards, and Bill Kennerly.

The interest and concern from Abbotts Creek continues to stretch to include these: Charles D. Royal, Elmer James (wounded, purple heart, England), Holland J. Raper, John Richard Haworth, Charles G. Willard, Gerald D. Clodfelter, Vance W. Phillips, John R. Davis, Randall F. Manning, William O. Hedgecock, Robert Flynt, Coy Traynham, Walter M. Sechrest, William E. Hyatt, Lindsey Smith, Grady Martin, Howard B. Hyatt, William Hudson, and Junior McGee (wounded, France).

The last page gives us the names of Percy Smith, Harold Sexton, Holland Davis, Numa Everhart, Frank Hayworth, John D. Clodfelter (wounded), J. S. Hedgecock, Weymouth Brooks, Roland V. Weavil, Staley Bodenheimer, Joe Hayworth, Dan Hayworth, G. E. Riggle, Kermit Lyda, Joe Smith, Thomas B. Moore, Clayton Hayworth, James Royal, Clell A.

Spurgeon, and Richard Hayworth (purple heart, Germany).

For any wishing to see the area of service for most of these men or the rank each had achieved, they may be found in the Abbotts Creek Historical Collection at the church.

In one of the earliest issues, a story concerns the community hog killing at the Clarence Moore farm. All in the neighborhood kept up with the weights of the hogs killed. The poundage listed in this issue has Clarence Moore killing 600 pounds of hogs. Charlie Plummer killed 508 pounds. The total poundage killed was 4,646. The neighborhood champion was Dan Hayworth with 518 pounds. This does not explain the way the champion was chosen nor why this poundage earned the recognition when one of the above had more listed in total pounds.

The July issue, volume two, number ten, tells of a baseball team organized by Wilson Hedgecock that included both white and black players. Wilson Hedgecock never had a racial bias and has to be commended for this while segregation was still a common practice. The team was called the Georgetown Wild Cats. The games were played on Saturday afternoon on a field across the road from Clifton Grove Baptist Church. The team members were Breed Traynham, Wilson Hedgecock, Staley Bodenheimer, C. R. Motsinger, Calvin Orrell, Baxter Hayworth, Kenneth Hayworth, Glenn Hilton, B. B. Lyda, J. C. Alcon, Garfield Davis, and Frank Reid.

The best news was reserved for Volume Three, number two, in 1945. This issue states the president had accepted the surrender terms from Japan. A large number of people gathered at the church for a service of prayer and thanksgiving.

Memories of Beth Hayworth Echols

A Letter from Beth Hayworth Echols, former member of Abbott's Creek:

> "Thank you for the privilege of contributing to the history of Abbott's Creek Baptist Church. As you have asked me to do, my story is a personal one, but it will illustrate how family and church members nurtured and encouraged a teen age farm girl who grew up believing that God had a special mission for her and her life.
>
> As I recount many events, each one is permeated with deep appreciation for the church, its missionary emphasis, and its encouragement for one of its own to follow the Lord's call into full time Christian ministry.

It was at Abbott's Creek where I first read aloud the scripture, prayed my first prayer in public, and spoke to the congregation in a Sunday morning worship service about what I understood to be God's call to me for Christian ministry. I owe many debts of gratitude to individuals who influenced me during those years and encouraged me to follow my calling.

As far back as I can remember, my parents, Nina and Sanford Hayworth, took me and my siblings to church. We were all enrolled in the Cradle Roll, attended Sunday School and Sunday evening 'Training Union' activities. I learned to give 'parts' in the Baptist Young People's Union (BYPU), read the Bible daily, and eventually became a director, while still in my teens, of the BYPU.

One of my earliest memories is of my junior class teacher, Miss Minnie Hayworth, looking at me (nearly every Sunday morning), and saying with tears in her eyes, 'Elizabeth, God loves you.' I'm sure she said this to other class members; but the memory is etched in my mind and I took it personally! Aileen Palmer was one of my earliest teachers, and she liked to ask me to read the scripture and to pray aloud. I was nearly always scared of being called on, but I dutifully did her bidding, and am thankful for it now.

When Daisy Spurgeon was the youth leader of the BYPU, she took a group of us teens to Ridgecrest for a week's Training Union event. It was there that I felt God's call on my life and made a public commitment—in a congregation of a few thousand! –to dedicate my life to full time Christian ministry. When we returned home, I was asked to share this decision during the Sunday morning worship hour.

So, on July 25, 1942, I spoke to the congregation of Abbott's Creek Baptist Church, and told them of my decision. To my knowledge, I was the first person (in 'modern' times!) to publicly announce such a call from the Lord and to prepare for training and service. The next January, I entered Mars Hill College and, following graduation and working for two years at the First Baptist Church in Washington, N.C., enrolled in what was then the Woman's Missionary Training School, a part of the Southern Baptist Theological Seminary in Louisville, KY. I graduated from there in 1954.

1933–1949

It was a hardship for my parents to pay college and seminary tuition. But, with the help of various sacrifices on their part, school scholarships and office work, plus a number of financial gifts from the church, I made it!

I remember many times when I was home from college and seminary that Mr. Dan Hayworth would give me a $20 dollar bill, folded up, when he would shake hands with me! He never failed to do this when he saw me. I also recall that Frank Spurgeon and Daisy often slipped dollar bills to me. I don't recall how many checks for $5 I received from the church treasurer, but it must have been a substantial number. These funds helped in ways I can only imagine now.

But, far more important than money, was the encouragement I received from the congregation. They were proud that one of their own wanted to serve the Lord in full time Christian service, and was studying at a seminary. Only God knows the value of the church's nurture, support and encouragement in leading me along the way. I am eternally grateful to many individuals, and to my parents, for helping me widen my horizons and to be of service to the Lord.

An incidental story will be of interest to some members of the church who know Pansy Bodenheimer Moore. When I graduated from the WMU Training School, we were all supposed to wear white. At the time, there was no money for a new outfit, so cousin Pansy lent me a lovely white eyelet embroidered dress to wear on that occasion. With some reluctance, I must admit, the beautiful dress was returned to its owner the next time I came home!

Since those days of training for ministry, my path has taken a number of interesting directions. At one time, I thought of being a foreign missionary. But I was led to believe that my work was to be here at home. Indeed, as things worked out, I found the culmination of my interests and whatever abilities I had, to be in local church and campus ministries, leading ultimately to a worldwide ministry among Baptist women.

Following seminary graduation, I worked in the state student departments of Kentucky and Louisiana Baptists in campus ministries. For the record, the time in Louisiana covered the turbulent 60s, and many of us had to take stands either for or against forced segregation. Without trying to be noble, I took a strong stand against racial segregation and was eventually fired from the Louisiana State Student Department. To be fair to Louisiana Baptists, it was because of pressure from the 'White Citizens Council' that the firing was deemed necessary, and also to protect me from physical harm in certain parts of Louisiana.

My dear parents went to their graves not knowing why their beloved daughter left a job she loved with Louisiana Baptist students to go 'live with friends in Washington, D.C. and to look for another job.' Fortunately for me, 'the briar patch' was the right place for me to widen my horizons and to experience another important aspect of God's calling.

Soon after moving to Washington, I was asked to join the staff of the Baptist Joint Committee on Public Affairs, an organization of several Baptist denominations devoted to studying public policies in light of Christian responsibilities and interests. After a year of journalism and government classes at George Washington University, I became a full fledged Baptist reporter on Capitol Hill, and occasionally the White House. I wrote for Baptist Press, and a number of Baptist periodicals and study materials, specializing in issues that related to poverty and other aspects of human need and Christian responses.

Along the way, I also worked for a congressman; married Robert H. MacClaren (now deceased), a scientist with the National Archives; and served on the staff of Takoma Park Baptist Church, Washington, D.C. In 1979, I was called to be Director of Outreach and Adult Education at McLean Baptist Church, McLean, Virginia, where I worked until November 1987.

While at McLean Baptist, I followed the encouragement of some local Baptist leaders, friends and church members to be ordained to the gospel ministry. This was done, following a long examination on theological views, in 1987. My mother attended the impressive service, along with other family members and a host of friends from other nations and a few from other world religions. I must admit that being ordained did not change my ministry, or any aspect of my commitment. It seemed to put a stamp of approval on what I had been doing throughout my life's calling to Christian service.

In October, 1987, I was installed as director of the Women's

Department of the Baptist World Alliance (BWA). This new challenge seemed to be the culmination of all my interests and experiences. My responsibility was to direct the BWA's work with women, ministering to women leaders on every continent and in most countries. The work included editing a quarterly news magazine and the annual Baptist Women's Day of Prayer program; world conference planning; speaking; and, of course, a lot of travel throughout the world. It was the job of a lifetime for me! I loved it, though I must admit that it was the most challenging—and the hardest—job I have had. However, I felt—on most days!—that God had called me to that ministry.

In 1995, I retired from my work with the BWA, but not from my calling to world ministry in the Name of Christ. As a church member, I am still involved in ministry to internationals and to the work of the BWA Women's Department. A widow since 1986, I married again in 2005, to M. Patton Echols, Jr., a retired attorney, who affirms my ministry, encouraging me regularly, just as scores of people have done throughout my life. It all began when I was just a little farm girl growing up in Abbott's Creek Baptist Church—who realized that God had a calling for her life. "Thanks be to God!"

Officers, 1941: Carrick Teague, Clerk; Grady Green, Treasurer; Carey Davis, Music

GA Coronation, 1940s

Sunday School class of early 1940s

Sunday School class 1940s

1933–1949

Adult ladies Sunday School class 1940s

Adult ladies Sunday School class 1940s

Sunday School class 1940s

History, Heritage, and Memories

Sunday School class 1940s. Pictured with teacher, Mattie Teague

Boys' Sunday School class 1940s

Sunday School classes, 1940s, in front of church

CHAPTER FOURTEEN

The Fifties

The decade of the fifties begin with Mrs. Staley (Patty) Bodenheimer being received as a candidate for baptism coming from Spring Hill United Methodist Church.

This took place on January 1. The year started with the church having a checking account balance of $363.99.

By March, the organ fund had increased to $1,345.15. The cost was reported to be $2,260. "We considered having an old time box party or supper to help secure funds toward an organ. By motion, this was left in the hands of the organ committee to consider."

We keep seeing first-time events taking place. The deacons recommended at the March conference "that we observe youth week in our church April 2-9." At the April business meeting the "youth week deacons recommend to the church that the church adopt a constitution. Also that we adopt a church manual." This two-part motion passed. The youth week trustees "recommended the church sanctuary be painted." This motion did not pass.

With the rotating process of deacons working, the deacons recommended four men to be voted on by the church and left the matter open for a month for consideration and to see if the church had other nominations. Rober Palmer was nominated from the floor and elected along with three of the ones nominated by the deacons, Grady Idol, John Welborn, and Numa Everhart.

The same minutes stated the young people of the church raised sufficient funds and presented the church with a new typewriter. Mrs. Dot Moore was "employed to type the constitution only." She was to be "paid seventy-five cents per hour." The church had accepted the youth week deacons' recommendation to prepare a constitution. No names had been given of those to prepare and present this to the church. However, eleven days later, the constitution was read to the church. After that April 16 date, the action of the church specified amendments could be added or revised.

At the same conference, the church voted to send $45 each month to the Baptist Children's Homes in addition to the "regular Thanksgiving Offering in November." The church has continued to include the children's home in its budget plus the special offering at Thanksgiving.

On May 10, it was decided not to have preaching on the third Sunday evening in May. This practice has been followed and continues to be observed. Some call that Sunday Memorial Day or Homecoming, but many people still call it the third Sunday in May service. Further action of the conference taking place on that day was "a motion was made and seconded that Mrs. Dot Moore make the church bulletins due to the fact that our pastor's time is taken up with other church work."

An organ had been placed on trial in the church. The church voted on May 28 "to retain the organ, also to purchase in the name of the church." Earlier the church had said, "No funds, no organ." It was reported the following month $1,204 had been paid on the organ with a balance to be paid listed at $1,100.

In July the church was dealing with a request for help in building or adding to The North Carolina Baptist Hospital. This matter was tabled for the time being but resurfaced the following month. It was determined that letters would be sent to the entire membership requesting $150 per member for this cause.

Miss Shirley Davis was going away to school leaving no one to play the organ. The church voted for a committee to find an organist "with or without pay." Robert Palmer, W. P. Davis, J. W. Welborn, and Patty Clinard constituted the committee.

The August 9 conference heard the report of the nominating committee. "The committee offered their resignation on motion and seconded. This was accepted by the church." A week later, a motion was made to re-elect those who were presently serving in the various capacities except for the organist who had gone away to school and the Baptist Training Union director.

The Reverend A. R. Snipes offered his resignation as pastor, effective August 20, "letters to be granted November 20th." Rev. Snipes' tenure as pastor was shorter than any previous pastor and continues to be shortest in the history of the church. Over the years, many senior adults have remembered The Reverend Snipes always served communion while wearing white gloves.

The conference held on September 6 heard the resignation of the church treasurer, and Charles Green was elected and accepted this responsibility. "Carey J. Davis was elected as organist and music director of the church."

Ten days later, the deacons were asked by the church to serve as the pulpit committee. One week later, they recommended that Brother B. A. Mitchell be recalled. Just a week after this, the church heard a motion that a 90 percent vote be obtained before a pastor could be called. Voting by secret ballot, Rev. Mitchell did not receive the required percentage. The vote was 77 positive with 43 negative.

The church decided at the first conference in October to pay the supply pastor the same as before, $10 per sermon and six cents a mile for travel. When one came for the trial sermon, he was to be paid $25.

The church considered calling Rev. Luther Morphis as pastor in late November. The vote resulted in "not a sufficient per cent to call him." Two months later, a vote was taken to call Rev. W. A. Walton as pastor. The percentage needed was not met to call him. A month later, the deacons recommended the 90 percent requirement be abolished. The church accepted this recommendation.

A conference was called on January 21, 1951, to consider "revoting" [sic] on Rev. Walton. "There was a request from Mary Frances Motsinger that the pulpit committee go to hear Rev. Joe F. Roach of Hephzibah Baptist Church of Wendell, North Carolina." Evidently the committee did what was requested but during the first conference in February, it was reported Rev. Roach was not available. The church voted on Rev. Walton who was elected. Since percentage did not restrict the call, he was elected with 47 voting for him and 22 against. However, those who voted "no" stood to declare their cooperation. Charlie Carmichael was chairman of the deacons at this time and served as moderator for the business sessions.

The church was called into conference on February 11 to announce Rev. Walton "had accepted the call as pastor and would begin his service March 1, 1951. Forty dollars was to be taken out of the church treasure for moving Rev. Walton and his family from East Spencer to Abbotts Creek." The first conference after the new pastor arrived had the church voting to pay Carey J. Davis $40 a month for his services as choir director and organist. In June of that year, Mr. Davis was paid $25 for playing for Vacation Bible School.

Wilson Hedgecock, Floyd J. Teague, George Sechrest, and C. R. Mabe were elected as the new deacons in June of 1951.

Without any introduction to this matter or without such a topic being discussed in previous meetings, we note the business issue of August 8, 1951: "We, the undersigned members of Abbotts Creek Missionary Baptist Church of [sic]Davison County, North Carolina, we feel that for the best interest of the church, that instead of going on with building an addition to the church that instead we build a baptistery, rest rooms, water fountain and convert the present heating system to oil heat. This resolution was accepted and passed without 'any opposition'." Floyd J. Teague and Wilson Hedgecock were appointed to collect the funds and take the names of the givers.

On Sunday, after the above business matter passed, the church was called into conference and the following action was taken: "Concerning building fund money for baptistery, rest room, water fountains, and converting the present heating system to oil, it will be necessary for each contributor to sign signifying he or she desires to do so."

At an October 10th conference, the report was given that the organ had been paid off and $66.23 was left in the fund. It was also announced during this conference the church would vote on "addition to present building" on Sunday. The building fund had six thousand dollars at this time. The conference was called "concerning addition to the rear of the church. The new building was to be 28 feet by 42 feet with 9-10 rooms for Sunday School." The other parts previously passed were to be included in these plans. A motion was made and passed that the church starts with building the new addition. The pastor, Rev. Walton, was to appoint the needed committees for the work.

The first business for December was information from the building committee. Approximately three thousand dollars was needed to complete the building. Pledges were given and the church pledged to support the cause. Several days later in the same month, the church voted to send fruit cakes to the boys in the military.

With new Sunday School rooms, Wilson Hedgecock (chairman), Daphne Motsinger, Daisy Spurgeon, and Numa Everhart were appointed to, or as the minutes read, "granted the privilege of rearranging the Sunday School" as to which classes would occupy certain rooms.

The first quarter of 1952 ended with the finances looking good. The regular church treasury reported a balance of $897.76. The building fund reported this:

"Building and Loan $6,052.03; Personal receipts $3,136; and Miscellaneous $720. The cost of the building was listed as $5,772.20. Heating and

Baptistry in old church

plumbing was $3,574 and the baptistery $338.62. The estimated free labor was reported to be $1,160. The total cost of the building was $10,884.38. The left-over balance of $223.38 was turned over to the church treasury 'toward the painting of the church.'" At the same time, the Loyal Worker's Sunday School class presented the church with one hundred dollars toward the painting project.

Youth week was observed again with Haywood Hyatt serving as youth pastor. New deacons were elected on June 22, 1952. They were Howard Dean, C. F. Moore, Roy Hayworth, and Haywood Hyatt.

We see another first taking place at the July conference. The church voted for the pastor and six deacons to accept the invitation to attend a deacon's retreat to be held at Fruitland Bible Institute, a Baptist State Convention-owned facility, located near Hendersonville, North Carolina.

In October of the same year, the church voted to discontinue the "Christmas Present Committee." However, the next month a called conference addressed this again. The "church voted to send presents to the boys in military service and also to pay for them out of regular church funds. Kenneth Edwards and Mrs. C. F. Moore were appointed to handle this matter." In November of 1954, the church voted to make the sending of presents to the military personnel a yearly affair at Christmas.

Mr. and Mrs. Grady Idol "donated a piano for the Sunday School." The church voted to have it tuned.

Beginning in May, of 1953, the clerk, with the help of the pastor, was given permission to grant church letters. This practice was reversed by a vote of the church in January of 1957. The minutes carried this notation, "All church letters to be granted will be approved by the church in conference." The next month, deacons were elected to serve for three years. Those elected were Brooks Motsinger, Sanford Hayworth, Cletus Hedgecock, and Kenneth Edwards.

Again, we see the first mention of a new committee. This was recommended by the Sunday School and was called the "Expansion Committee." This may have been what was later called the extension committee, which involved certain ones visiting the homebound and carrying literature into their homes. Committee members were Numa Everhart, Mrs. Mabel Hayworth, Mrs. Dot Clodfelter, and C. F. Moore.

The Vacation Bible School in 1953 had a high attendance of 153 one day. The offering of $25 was sent to the Mills Home, the Baptist Children's Homes in Thomasville. The next year, the report was even better with an enrollment of 177 and average attendance of 162. The mission offering of fifty dollars was sent to the Cherokee Mission Church. By 1955, the enrollment had increased to 185 with an average attendance of 175. Again this year, the offering was sent to the Cherokee Indian mission. The amount was $73.

Numa Everhart resigned as church treasurer in August, and Wilson Hedgecock was elected to serve at the conference a month later. He was elected in September of 1953.

The church voted to purchase books, *Pull of the People*, to be used in a convention-wide emphasis of reaching more people. The Southern Baptist Convention had as a slogan, "A Million More in 54." Nothing more is mentioned about this but it can be assumed the church did the study.

Haywood Hyatt, a deacon of the church, announced his acceptance of the call to become a minister on July 25. At the October conference, the pastor and deacons recommended the church license him to preach. At the April 1955 conference, the church voted to take up an offering for him to pay a semester of college. The need was $125. The offering amounted to $65 but the church voted to take the rest out of the general treasury. In January of 1959, the deacons recommended "that the church pay tuition to finish the school term of H. B. Hyatt (amount $200, passed)."

According to the minutes of the church, during the year 1954, a church nursery began operating. The minutes record the election of Mae Bodenheimer Green and Mildred Bodenheimer as leaders. Doris Hayworth Marion and Pansy Bodenheimer Moore were helpers. We do not have names for

The Fifties

all the children but we know Michael Moore, Lois Beeson, Susan Spurgeon, and Betty Young were a part of the group. Other information confirms a nursery had been in operation for at least six or eight years prior to this time. In fact, twelve years prior to this, the minutes had recorded "a nursery will begin in the future." It does not state that it started but by 1946, Paul and Roxie Beeson had two children, a son and a daughter, being cared for in the nursery. Charles and Evva Smith Spurgeon were also there during this earlier time. Violet Everhart was a nursery worker caring for these and other children. The nursery included her young daughter, Marilyn. Mrs. Beeson remembers her Loyal Workers Sunday School class met at a certain place on the ground floor. Daisy Spurgeon kept the nursery in a section of that oblong room. Apparently, the class saw the need for this and was willing to do what was necessary to care for the children and enable mothers to be in a learning setting at the same time. Factual memories, such as the above, keep reminding us that a church history is more than can be recorded in the conferences of the church.

In November, the deacons and finance committee noted the need for additional Sunday School space. A sketch was shown and discussed or explained. A vote was taken to build additional space. There was no indication of who did the sketch or if the group did it together. The point seems to be there was a need and the church felt it must be met.

The April 13, 1955, conference heard the nomination for four new deacons. The four elected by the church were Wilson Hedgecock, W. G. Jones, W. P. Davis, and Fletcher Clinard. Mr. Jones and Mr. Davis were ordained on June 19, 1955. A month later, George Sechrest was elected as treasurer of the "endowment fund."

The first mention was made of a contribution by the church to a fire department. A $25 donation was given to the Wallburg Fire Department. On July 8, 1959, the same amount was donated to the Horneytown Fire Department. A few rare times when a fire department had to be called, both departments responded.

On January 4, 1956, the church voted to pay for the lights and phone at the parsonage. This was not to be seen as a part of the pastor's salary.

The May conference named the following as deacons to serve for the next three years: Howard Dean, Harry Cline, John Welborn, and C. F. Moore. At the same conference, the Sunday School superintendent, C. F. Moore, made this suggestion: "That the church provide a playground for our boys and girls." The church provided fifty dollars toward clearing the land. A committee was appointed to take care of this. Wilson Hedgecock,

Staley Bodenheimer, and W. G. Jones made up the committee.

Nothing had been mentioned about a building for some months, until the finance committee recommended, at the June 24, 1956, conference, that one thousand dollars be taken from the church treasury to "close in the new building."

At the January 1957 conference, a member of the church addressed the church asking that the deacons be elected from the floor rather than nominated by the deacons, as had been the practice according to the minutes. He then made a motion to select deacons from the floor. The motion received a second made by his wife but was defeated by vote of the church.

In June when new deacons were elected, the deacons had nominated eight with no nominations coming from the floor. The four elected were Grady Idol, Numa Everhart, Charles Carmichael, and Robert Palmer.

Another notation in the minutes had the above mentioned elected in 1958 and the ones elected in 1957 were R. G. Alcon, Sanford Hayworth, C. R. Mabe, and Cletus Hedgecock. Mr. Alcon was ordained on June 23, 1957.

The roll call for the church was heard on July 10 of that year with the minutes noting some corrections were made without information as to what those corrections were. A month later, the projected budget was presented and passed. The total read $9,707, which was $139 less than the previous year.

The choir presented a recommendation to the church that twenty-eight to thirty robes be purchased for the choir members. The cost would be in the range of $450. This recommendation passed and for the first time mentioned in the minutes of the church, the choir members had robes.

The April conference, again, reminds us of the progress being made in services for the community. The North State Telephone Company's desire to buy out the parsonage phone was approved by the church. The company was building a new line to serve the community and would keep up the line. W. T. Hedgecock was authorized to sign over the phone to the company. The church also agreed to purchase two dozen folding chairs that could be used in home prayer meetings or for other needs.

The church elected four new deacons in June. They were Wilson Hedgecock, Fletcher Clinard, Glenn Welborn, and Glaster Jones. Glenn Welborn was ordained later in the month. At the same conference, the names of Haywood, Verta, and Donna Hyatt were removed from the church roll. Rev. Hyatt had accepted the call to serve as a minister in a United Methodist Church.

The church voted on July 8, 1959, to send fifty dollars on September 1 and January 1 to the Liberty Baptist Association to be used on building or buying a home for the associational missionary. This motion passed. The church continued to be involved and supportive of the associational work.

At the September conference Mrs. Annie Lou Phillips was granted a church letter "to unite with the Union Cross mission though the Waughtown Baptist Church of Winston-Salem." The very next month the pastor appointed a committee "to investigate and work with the Pilot Mountain Association with the possibility of starting a mission in or above the Horneytown section across Highway 311."

A personal note is added to the September 26 conferences. It reads, "This terminates my services as church clerk. I was elected September 1, 1948 and served until October 14, 1959." Robert Palmer signed the statement. The church elected Staley Bodenheimer as the new clerk.

The first minutes recorded by the newly-elected clerk show "a rising vote of thanks was given Robert Palmer for his fine service rendered as church clerk." The minutes further state that Staley Bodenheimer was received in the same spirit as the new clerk. Carol Welborn and Numa Everhart were elected as RA leaders for the church. If this mission organization had been active prior to this date, leaders may have been volunteers. None had been listed as having been elected.

The officers for the Memorial Association were listed: Mrs. Carey J. Davis

The vehicle in the forefront belongs to Brooks and Daphne Motsinger. The truck at the far left belongs to Junior Welborn. Note the large trees that formerly stood in the church yard.

president and Elmo Holder vice president. George and Blanche Sechrest were asked to serve as secretary and treasurer. Willie Paul Hedgecock was reelected as cemetery supervisor and Ruth Hedgecock was named historian.

The last conference of the fifties had the church discussing the replacement of the carpet for the church and refurbishing the floor. The motion was made and approved to get this done not to exceed the cost of $1,600. If more money was needed, the matter would be brought back to the church for a decision. Ernest Burton, Howard Dean, and Mrs. Mable Hayworth were appointed to see that this was done.

The choir director is Carey J. Davis. Becky Kearns is pianist. Choir members: First row (left to right) Maxine Hayworth Todd, Marie Hayworth Wright, Nancy Idol, Verta Hyatt, and Ella Marie Leinbach. Second row: Mrs. W. H. Walton, Grace Hayworth, Evie Jones, Marie Hayworth, Ruth Holder Spaugh, Lucille Spurgeon, and Fleta Burton. Third row: Jimmy Hedgecock, Bill Davis, Roy Hayworth, Dave Royal, Richard Carmichael, Numa Everhart, George Sechrest, and Billy Hudson.

CHAPTER FIFTEEN

The Sixties

The decade of the sixties opened with the treasurer's report showing a beginning balance of $3,732.40. The deacons' recommendation to the church that floodlights be placed in the front and on each side of the church was accepted. The second consideration brought by the deacons was to provide a place for the young people to have a choir. The Amen corner was the suggested place. The attendance was low at this conference so a motion was made to postpone this matter until a special meeting could be called at a later date. A positive vote was given by the church when it was presented later and a committee was appointed to take care of providing the place. The committee was composed of Carey David, Roy Hayworth, Grady Idol, Roger Moorefield, Ruth Holder, and Daphne Motsinger. At the March conference, the committee reported they had "decided to let this subject rest as is for a while." If this decision was questioned, such was not recorded.

At the same March meeting, the church was informed the pastor had hired Willie Essick to shovel snow at the church. This was done with the promise that he, the pastor, would pay Mr. Essick if the church did not. The church voted to pay for this service.

Visiting minister Ted Miller led the April revival in 1960. Young men of the church brought devotions prior to the services each evening. Three of the church members led the service. Joe Bryant led the Monday night service with Numa Everhart leading on Tuesday. The pastor concluded the revival services on Wednesday night. Three people were baptized at the end of the revival.

In June, Howard Dean, Harry Cline, James Williams, and Staley Bodenheimer were elected as deacons.

A month later, Clarence Moore, Numa Everhart, Roy Hayworth, Bill Davis, Mrs. Mable Hayworth, and Mrs. Emma Poole were elected to "meet with the Pilot Mountain Baptist Association committee to find out their plans pertaining to the church they are planning to build North of Highway 311 and bring back a report to the church."

The summer Vacation Bible School had 227 enrolled with an average attendance of 211. The minutes of the church mentioned those serving in the Bible school, who were listed in the bulletin earlier, but no names were recorded for the minutes. The offering of $101.65 was designated for community missions.

Numa Everhart had been chosen to serve as chairman of the above-mentioned committee. He gave a report to the church after meeting with the Pilot Mountain committee. "They decided to take a survey in that vicinity to find out how many prospective members there would be." The committee needed to know if the church would approve of this approach. Mrs. Maggie Clinard made the motion to go ahead with the survey. Wilson Hedgecock gave a second and the church approved the motion.

The church voted in October to install a speaker in the nursery. This matter took place before hearing the report concerning the survey. No recommendation was given but Mrs. Ruth Holder suggested the church get someone who has been involved in starting a mission come to help. Rev. Roger Williams was at the November conference to do just that. Associational missionary Ted Williams presented a map of the area where the mission church would be located. After these reports were given, Carey J. Davis made the motion that the church sponsor the project. Mrs. Robert Alcon seconded that motion and the church approved it by a vote of eighty-six for and ten against. "Then eighteen more who did not vote at first voted in favor making it one hundred and four for mission."

The minutes for November 13, 1960, give us this information. "Joe Bryant made the motion that the moderator appoint a committee to help with the mission. Ernest Burton seconded this motion. The church approved. The moderator asked for a little time in appointing this committee. It was announced the church had plans to buy ten and a half acres of land from Carl Cook for $5,000, with five years to build a road. Numa Everhart made the motion that Rev. Walton bring this before the association executive committee for their approval. Roy Bryant seconded this motion. After this motion was passed, the church also approved the moderator's suggestion that we see about purchasing chairs from the Wesley Memorial Church for the mission. It was mentioned there was a piano in the basement not in use. Lucian Gregory made the motion that the piano be moved to the mission. The mission committee to see to this and to see about the chairs." The committee was then listed as Numa Everhart, Charlie Welborn, Catherine Payne, and Robert Palmer.

Two weeks later, the missions committee and the deacons recommended to the church "that we purchase four and a half acres of land from Carl Cook for the mission, price $3,000 plus survey and legal transactions. We also recommend using $2,000 from the church budget." The trustees were given authority to borrow $1,000 to finish paying for the property. Baxter Smith made the motion to do this. Aileen Palmer gave a second and the church approved.

The very next conference the deacons recommended to the church "that the present board of trustees be dismissed due to inactivity." No definition is given for "inactivity." The church accepted this recommendation and decided at the same time to start a rotation of trustees. George Sechrest was elected for five years and served as chairman; Cletus Hedgecock was to serve for four years; Dwight Moore, three years; Sanford Hayworth, two years and Charlie Mabe, for one year.

In January, "it was reported they are having wonderful services at the mission, which started November 20, 1960, in the basement of Mr. and Mrs. Jimmy Welborn."

Shortly after the January conference, the church heard the report the trustees "have purchased the land for our mission." The church was informed that Ethel Motsinger had left one thousand dollars to the church in her will. There were no stipulations as to how the gift was to be used.

The Baptist State Convention's mission department had notified the church of a grant of two thousand dollars for the new mission. Half would be paid on July 1, 1961, and the balance would be paid on December 1, 1961.

In March, the church accepted an offer to purchase a small organ "for use in cottage prayer meetings and services held in homes." This was purchased from Joe Bryant.

The mission committee of the church met with others from the mission at the home of Roy Bryant. The group discussed and prayed as to what direction to follow. A conclusion was made and presented to the church. "We recommend that a worship service be held at 9:45 a.m. and Sunday School at 11:00 a.m. We request the church to ask the pastor to serve with the mission as pastor as he deems advisable not to be interfere or hinder the work at Abbotts Creek. We request also the same privilege be granted to Carey J. Davis for the worship service at 9:45 to 10:45 a.m."

"We recommend the following to be temporarily elected for worship services."

The treasurer was Jimmy Welborn. The clerk was Elizabeth Bryant. Ushers were Roger Payne and Michael Clinard." The Sunday School officers were: Superintendent, Roy Bryant, Secretary, Wayne Welborn, while Grace Davis was to serve as pianist. Joe Bryant was elected to teach the intermediate and young people. Carol Welborn was to teach the primary and juniors. The beginners would have Ruth Vaden as their first teacher. Sara Welborn and Helen Payne would care for the nursery children.

"We further recommend that a building fund be sponsored and supported by the church and the mission and this fund plus the amount on hand be deposited in a saving account for the purpose of a mission church building and related expenses. We also recommend that our mission collection undesignated be channeled into our general church treasury here at Abbotts Creek." Milton Teague made the motion to approve these recommendations. Aileen Palmer gave this a second and the church approved.

At the same meeting, the pastor reported the mission was having an open-air revival on the mission grounds June 5-17, 1961. Hedgecock Lumber Company was donating the lumber for the seats. There would be some expense for lights and other small expenses. "Billy Hudson made the motion we sponsor this all the way. James Williams seconded this and the church approved."

At the June conference in 1961, Abbotts Creek elected George Sechrest, Dwight Moore, Cletus Hedgecock, and Robert Alcon as deacons for the next three years.

The next month, the deacons, trustees, and other men of the church met and discussed the advisability of organizing the mission into a church. The group felt a need to get the feelings and wishes of the mission group. A meeting was held for this purpose. The Reverend Walton led the discussion and gave certain unnamed explanations. "A motion was made and carried to request Abbots Creek Church to organize Abbotts Creek Baptist Mission into a Missionary Baptist Church. A second motion was made to request a continuation of the pastor's services and to contribute to the Abbotts Creek budget ten dollars each week. Included in the same motion, we request any spiritual, physical and financial help, as the church feels led to render. A third motion was made and carried that we request the church to deed the mission church lot to a board of trustees elected by the newly-organized church. Laurence Todd, Jr., made the motion that these requests be granted with the exception of the ten dollars the mission was to pay the church each week." The mission was not to pay anything. Brooks Motsinger seconded the motion and the church approved.

"Wilson Hedgecock made the motion to extend to the mission (the new church) the use of the church, the kitchen, the cemetery or any other benefit they need to use. Also, give the mission the one thousand dollars from the state mission board and the other one thousand when we receive it. We still owe one thousand on the mission lot. And to use the one thousand dollars Mrs. Ethel Motsinger willed the church to pay this." This was seconded and the church approved.

The pastor brought before the church a question of granting church letters individually or as a group to those who were now a part of the newly-organized church. It was decided to give the church letters of the entire group and allow otherS through the month of August to be considered charter members. The Reverend Walton read this note: "The Abbotts Creek Missionary Baptist Church does hereby commend with God's richest blessings all members wishing to become charter member of the newly-organized Hillcrest Missionary Baptist Church." This action was taken in a called conference the sixth day of August 1961.

"A special meeting to constitute the Abbotts Creek mission into a duly organized missionary Baptist church was held on August 6, 1961, 2:30 p.m. at Abbotts Creek Church." Approximately 125 attended this historic occasion. The meeting was opened by the singing of "I Love Thy Kingdom, Lord" and "The Solid Rock." Carey Davis played the organ while the pastor led the singing. The scripture used was from Matthew 16:13-19. Rev. Ted Williams, associational missionary, led a prayer. Rev. Carl Hemphill, pastor of Carolina Memorial Baptist Church in Thomasville, was asked to serve as Moderator and Numa Everhart was the recording secretary. Rev. Hemphill gave some general comments regarding the original mission efforts along the Yadkin River and in the Northern part of Davidson County. "He then recognized the organizing council consisting of Ted Williams, Troy York, A. C. Moody, and himself. The council he said 'is to hear from the mission regarding its organization and its intentions to organize as a full-fledged church.'" Rev. Walton informed the council that a complete record of all meetings and activities "had been compiled and was available for reading. He then recognized Sammy Young, secretary of the mission, who read from the record. The historical data read from the record was very precise with respect to the important decisions, activities, and conferences made and held over the entire period for the mission endeavor." Clerk Staley Bodenheimer expressed his own opinion, for which we can be thankful, by saying this: "It is interesting to record here that the mission set up a $966.80 budget for 1962 and adopted the church covenant, and articles of faith and as well as a fine set of rules and by-laws."

Moderator Hemphill congratulated the mission for the well-kept history of its organization and suggested the council move to approve "the mission as a duly organized Missionary Baptist Church." Rev. Ted Williams made the following motion, "Whereas it appears to us that there is a real need for a Baptist Church in this locality and after much prayer and seeking of divine guidance and much consultation, and after the calling a council to consider the matter, which council has voted that there is a need for such a church, it is resolved and motioned that the Hillcrest Missionary Baptist Church be henceforth recognized as a full-fledged cooperative Baptist church."

The Rev. Walton read a note, "which stated in part the Abbotts Creek Church voted to grant God's rich blessings upon those charter members leaving the Mother church to join the newly-constituted Hillcrest Baptist Church." Sammy Young read the names of forty-two charter members. Others who joined the church during the month of August would also be considered charter members.

At this point, the moderator asked for a motion from the mission (now the new church) that the officers of that church be accepted by the members of the mission that were present. This was done for the benefit of the council. "Rev. Hemphill declared that the mission had now been duly approved by the council and was a full-fledged Missionary Baptist Church being properly constituted." Rev. Walton led the congregation in singing "Must Jesus Bear the Cross Alone." Rev. A. C. Moody, pastor of the Southside Baptist Church in High Point, "brought a thought-provoking and inspirational message concerning 'The Church Jesus Built.'" The speaker pointed out four things that guided the early church he referred to as the "New Testament Baptist Church." Those four things were: "Democratic government, pure in doctrine, simple in worship, and adequate in its ministry." The meeting concluded with the members of the newly-organized congregation standing in front of the church "to receive the right hand of fellowship from the council and everyone present."

Two of the charter members of the Hillcrest Church were deacons at Abbotts Creek. The October conference filled these vacancies by electing Sanford Hayworth to serve for one year and nine months and Ernest Burton to serve nine months. Both would be eligible for reelection since they

THE SIXTIES

Hillcrest Missionary Baptist Church
ROUTE 1, KERNERSVILLE, N. C.
ORGANIZED AUGUST 6, 1961

Praise the Lord, Praise the Lord, Let Earth Hear His Voice,
Praise the Lord, Praise the Lord, Let the People Rejoice
O Come to the Father, Through Jesus the Son,
and Give Him the Glory, Great Things He Hath Done.

Church Officers

Pastor	Robert G. Canipe
Sunday School Superintendent	Harry Cline
Clerk	Gladys Welborn
Treasurer	Mrs. Hilda Brown
Choister	Mrs. Frances Young
Pianist	Mrs. Jean Whitaker
W.M.U. President	Mrs. Louise Canipe

DEACONS

Sammy Young	Ralph Bryant
Ray Whitaker	R. G. Alcon, Chairman
Carroll Penn Welborn	Harry Cline
Glenn Welborn	Charlie Mabe

TRUSTEES

Harry Cline	Weldon Clinard, Chairman
Charlie Mabe	

WE WISH TO ACKNOWLEDGE THE WORK AND PLANNING THAT HAS BEEN EXPENDED IN BRINGING ABOUT THIS BUILDING AND PROVIDING A PERMANENT PLACE OF WORSHIP FOR US. WE THANK ALL THOSE WHO HAVE GIVEN MONEY, TIME AND PRAYER.

BUILDING COMMITTEE

Glenn Welborn, Chairman	Jimmie Welborn
Carl Cook	Ralph Bryant
John W. Welborn, Jr.	Jo Ann Clinard
Ronald W. Welborn	Dorothy McCollum
John Payne	

FINANCE COMMITTEE

Charlie Mabe, Chairman	Elizabeth Bryant
Harry Cline	Weldon Clinard
Charlie Welborn	Gladys Welborn
Cleora Payne	Grace Davis
Ola Clinard	Carroll Welborn

FURNISHINGS COMMITTEE

Mrs. Louise Canipe, Chairman

Mrs. Hilda Brown	Mrs. Ruth Vaden
Architect, Mr. Norman Zimmerman	Builders, Golden and Welborn

The newly-constituted Hillcrest Baptist Church and the bulletin listing the first elected church officers and committees.

were filling the remaining terms of two others.

In December, the pastor read the church covenant and suggested the church adopt the same. The church approved.

The first conference of 1962 took place on January 10. The pastor made a suggestion to the church that church conferences held on Wednesday night be discontinued because of the few people attending. With no comments on this matter, he further suggested that the congregation give some thought to this until a later date.

In April, the Sunday School enrollment was brought to the attention of the church. In October of 1960, 405 members were enrolled. One year later, the enrollment had decreased to 345. By this April conference, the enrollment was listed as 330. The explanation for this decrease was the loss of members who were now a part of the Hillcrest Baptist Church. The average attendance in Sunday School for 1960 was 260 and in 1961, the number was 192.

Doctor Bradley was the visiting minister for the revival services in April

HISTORY, HERITAGE, AND MEMORIES

1962. Four persons were received for baptism. They were Marla Spurgeon, Myra Moore, Karen Everhart, and Sharon Hayworth.

Deacons and trustees who had been nominated in April were elected in June. B. B. Lyda was chosen as trustee. The four deacons elected to serve three years were Numa Everhart, Clarence Moore, Charlie Carmichael, and Robert Palmer.

Vacation Bible School was held in June and reported as "one of the best." No figures were given at this time.

From time to time when the Sunday School report was listed, a few other facts were included. For instance, the quarterly report of July 1962 showed 340 enrolled. The average attendance was 222, twenty-five more per Sunday than the previous quarter. The total offering for the quarter was $2,280.44, an increase of $140.94 over last quarter. A further note is added, "Total gifts per person, 79 cents." This appears to mean weekly contributions.

At the same conference, a recommendation was passed giving the trustees responsibility for all church property, including the buildings.

When the report of the Memorial Association was given, much discussion took place. The details were not given but finally it was decided to put

Philathea Sunday School Class from left to right: Flossie Carmichael, Elsie Motsinger, Mary Swaim, Dorothea Bodenheimer, Doris Sells, Jean Ann Davis, Dot Moore, Pansy Moore, Dot Jordan, Bessie Jordan, Blanche Traynham, Ruth Spurgeon, and Pearl Hayworth.

further discussion off until certain unnamed matters were cleared up.

At the October conference, Rev. Walton offered his resignation as pastor of the church. The request was to add his two weeks of vacation to the end of his pastorate, allowing November 18 to be the date of his final message to the church. Dwight Moore acted as moderator, and the Waltons excused themselves for discussion and a vote. Motion to accept the above was made by George Sechrest, with a second by Clarence Moore. This passed, and the November date was accepted as his last sermon to the church.

Immediately a committee was appointed to select a search committee and report to the church for approval. The committee members chosen to serve in this capacity were Flossie Carmichael, Ruth Hedgecock, Patty Bodenheimer, Numa Everhart, B. B. Lyda, Cletus Hedgecock, Billy Hudson, and Dwight Moore.

Church matters had to go on, and as the conference continued, the Sunday School director reported that a new class was needed in the primary department because the present class had become very large. Betty Essick and Margaret Spurgeon were added as teachers for this new class.

The Reverend Jimmy Hinson accepted the call to be interim pastor and preached his first sermon on December 9, 1962.

A report at the January 1963 conference included this: "Mrs. Ruth Hedgecock gave a report on the work of the WMU. Carey Davis made a little talk on music. James Williams reported on the RAs with twenty two enrolled and an average attendance of fourteen." This was the first recorded report on this mission organization.

Baptismal services were held on January 20, 1963, for Vickie, Cheryl, and Ken Williams, Ray Alcon, Lee Roy Kearns, and Michael Smith.

At the church conference a week later, the church voted to "put in a furnace for heating in the parsonage and to paint the inside as well as put down carpet."

At the January conference, Mr. and Mrs. Robert Alcon requested the transferral of their membership to Hillcrest Baptist Church, which left the church without the extension workers. Later, in the month of January 1963, Pansy Moore and Mary Smith were elected to carry out this ministry.

The Pulpit Search Committee was ready with a recommendation for a pastor, and a special conference was called for March 3, 1963. Chairman Dwight Moore presented the name of Rev. Joe Coltrane for the consideration of the church for pastor. The church gave a strong vote of 152 in favor with seven voting no. Rev. Hinson was to contact the prospective pastor.

Even though there was excitement about a new pastor, other business had to continue and did. Sanford and Nina Hayworth and Mable Hayworth gave up their job as sextons of the church. William and Pearl Hayworth, along with Dwight and Pansy Moore, accepted that job.

With the announcement that the newly-called pastor would arrive on April 14, 1963, it was decided that Rev. Hinson would be the revival speaker for April 7-12. Thirty-six candidates for baptism were received during these services. This continues to be the most people baptized at any one service at the church. The Reverend Hinson baptized the following: Mrs. Laura Clinard, Mrs. Wesley Hayworth, Mrs. John Beeson, Polly Beeson, Becky Motsinger, Bleka Mendenhall, Judy Hayes, Ginger Dills, Janet Jordon, Cynthia Israel, Lynn Hill, Betty Young, Martha Hayes, Jane Craven, Rebecca Israel, Debbie Bodenheimer, Jo Ann Green, Bessie Key, Susan Brown, Monroe Beeson, Wesley Hayworth, Paul Beeson, Vance Hill, Tommy Bodenheimer, Nolan Motsinger, Johnny Hedgecock, Alvin Hayes, Turner Teague, Norman Bodenheimer, Richard Motsinger, Charles H. Davis, Robert Motsinger, Broadus Beeson, Donny Hill, Clifford Butcher, Kenny Moore, Andrew Butcher, and Michael Moore. Debbie Glisson expressed her desire to be baptized and wanted to join the Methodist church in Jamestown. Mr. and Mrs. Monroe Beeson, along with Mr. and Mrs. James Israel, were received under watch care of the church until their letters could be received.

The Reverend Coltrane's first sermon in the church was April 21, 1963.

The publicity card for revival services in April of 1963.

During that service, Douglas Hayworth was received as a candidate for baptism. Lester and Audrey Culler were received under watch care pending the receipt of their church letter from Allen Jay Baptist Church.

The new pastor, presiding at his first conference, was able to hear good reports including the Sunday School. The present enrollment was listed as 377, an increase of 29 over the past few months. The average attendance was 62 more than the previous six months. The same conference named Roxie Beeson as principal for the June Vacation Bible School. J. C. Alcon was elected to serve the remainder of the unexpired term of his father, R. G. Alcon, who had moved his membership, and was thereby the first deacon elected during the pastorate of Rev. Coltrane. A short time later, new deacons were elected to serve for three years. They were Wilson Hedgecock, Ernest Burton, Everett Jordan, Glaster Jones, and John Sulger. Mister Jones was also elected as trustee.

The growing nursery necessitated some changes in the facility used by the small children. James Williams brought to the attention of the church the need to move a partition to give more room for the children. The church approved this request, and the partition was removed.

The first baptismal service by The Reverend Coltrane was held on June 9, 1963. The following were baptized: Joan Culler, Patricia White, Brenda White, Douglas Hayworth, David Mendenhall, and Alonzo Hedgecock. A few weeks later, Mrs. Alonzo Hedgecock joined the church awaiting baptism.

An ordination service was held on July 7 for J. C. Alcon, Everett Jordan, and John Sulger. Rev. Leonard Rollins, director of missions for the Liberty Baptist Association, delivered the ordination sermon.

By October of 1963, Mary Smith and Pansy Moore, extension workers, were visiting in the home of fifteen members. They carried the Sunday School lessons and other materials to those who were homebound. The report noted the same had been mailed to two out of town shut-in members. Mention is also made that the materials were sent "to our fourteen college students and servicemen." A few conferences later, as the report was given, nine college students and five servicemen were named.

Staley Bodenheimer, church clerk, made a motion at the January 1964 conference that the church pay the pastor $50 a month for expenses while he was in college. The church gave 100-percent approval for this.

From time to time, Carey Davis gave information regarding the choir and music. Many times, the minutes stated this "as being interesting remarks."

About that time, Abbotts Creek was one of numerous churches conducting Bible studies called the "January Bible Study." Such studies would last a week and were geared for all ages. The study for 1964 was postponed until February due to weather. Of the eighty enrolled for these studies, sixty-two was the average attendance.

The April 1964 conference showed the usual reports given, and two recommendations were presented to the church and passed. The deacons recommended the church send the pastor to the Southern Baptist Convention meeting in Atlantic City, New Jersey. The second matter passed by the church was that a fund be started to get a new piano for the church. Howard Dean was to lead this committee, which would be made up of those he chose to serve with him. However, Mr. Dean asked the church to select the committee. Glaster Jones and Roxie Beeson were named to assist him.

The pastor asked for secretarial help of four to five hours each week to help with bulletins, letters, and typing. The church heard a motion to this effect and approved it.

During the same conference, the church voted to purchase a slide and film strip projector at a cost of approximately $115. James Williams was appointed to take care of this matter.

The May conference had four deacons elected. They were Staley Bodenheimer, Howard Dean, James Williams, and J. C. Alcon. Brooks Motsinger was elected trustee. Another first took place at this conference as well. Bleka Mendenhall was chosen as librarian for the church. The need for this had been brought from the Women's Missionary Union by Mrs. Blanche Traynham. The library committee consisted of Edith Bodenheimer, Billie Ann Alcon, and Audrey Culler.

A conference was called for July 5, 1964. The nominating committee brought a slate of officers and also a recommendation. The recommendation involved the manner in which general officers were to be elected. In the past, all had been elected at the same time. The motion was this: "We, the nominating committee, recommend that the church be given the opportunity to vote on each officer individually, by ballot. This method of voting would be a source of encouragement to the officers, give a feeling that the church's conviction had been honored and would give the nominating committee a feeling of having done our best job." The committee members were Chairman James Williams, Daphne Motsinger, Edith Bodenheimer, Staley Bodenheimer, and the Rev. Joe Coltrane. All officers presented were elected by the church.

Mr. and Mrs. Tom Dawson were received under the watch care of the church until their letters could be received. Mr. Dawson had been in the community for some months as the groundskeeper for the Willow Creek Country Club. The genuine nature of the church people at Abbotts Creek had a great impact on him during his first visit to the church. Two families invited him home with them for the noon meal. At the time, this was a common practice among the church families. When school was out and his family had arrived, he informed them they could attend church wherever they wanted to go but one requirement was that they had to visit Abbotts Creek at least once. They joined Abbotts Creek soon thereafter.

In 1964, during the third quarter of the church year, the highest attendance for any Sunday was 346. Average attendance for the quarter was 269.

During the fall, the minutes recorded the normal church reports. The Sunday School numbers were announced, several had joined the church by letter or for baptism, the election of workers for the year were elected and messengers were appointed for the Baptist State Convention meeting in Greensboro.

A request came from the Liberty Baptist Association for help in sending the director of missions, Leonard Rollins, to Brazil on a preaching mission. During the discussion of the request for twenty-five dollars from each church, it was decided to double that amount in case some other churches could not do as much. At the same meeting, it was decided "that a partition be built in the back of the basement to provide additional Sunday School classrooms."

Many years earlier, mention had been made that the church support a missionary, but no evidence was ever given that such had taken place. On April 4, 1965, the deacons recommended to the church "that we endeavor to provide one half the annual support of a missionary under appointment by the Southern Baptist Foreign Mission Board. This will amount to $1,000 over and above our gifts through the Cooperative Program and Lottie Moon Christmas offering each year. Jeffrey Traynham made the motion to accept the recommendation. Carey Davis seconded the motion. This carried by a vote of 150 for and 13 against."

The spring revival meeting at the church would not be held this year in order to allow the church to participate in the Central Carolina Crusade scheduled for April 25 through May 9. The vote on this was 110 for and 30 against. On April 11, 1965, the minutes recorded, "Hillcrest Baptist Church and Shady Grove Methodist Church held a joint baptism service here. The Reverend Joe Coltrane administered baptism." No mention had been made, prior to this date that Hillcrest had used the facilities at Abbotts Creek for baptismal service. However, the very next month, it was mentioned that Hillcrest "united with us in this service." We can assume they had done this at other times as well. An announcement was made at this time the piano had been paid in full.

Four new deacons were elected in June. They were Dwight Moore, Lester Culler, Cletus Hedgecock, and Brooks Motsinger. Sanford Hayworth was the named trustee.

Sunday School and Vacation Bible School reports continued to be strong, ranging up to 270 with new members almost every quarter. The extension workers reported each quarter on the visits made and other things done for the shut-ins or homebound. It was not unusual for the two workers to report more than one hundred visits for the quarter. Literature was distributed to the homebound, and at times, assistance was given help to provide medical supplies. General officers continued to be elected by secret ballot.

Various reports had indicated help for a missionary couple, the Negrins, who had served in Cuba. They continued to serve with the refugees in Florida, and mention is often made of financial support being sent to them, assisting with supplies needed for their work.

The March 1, 1966, offering was to be given in its entirety to Hillcrest Baptist Church for their building fund. It was later announced that this offering totaled $567.

Deacons elected in June of 1966 were Wilbur Bowers, Lee Davis, Numa Everhart, and Robert Palmer. Tom Dawson was chosen as trustee. The next month, the church accepted the recommendation of the deacons and trustees to raise the insurance for the church and parsonage from $38,000 to $121,000.

Staley Bodenheimer, church clerk, announced at the January 4, 1967, conference that it had been twenty years, "since the church laid claim to the land between the road and cemetery and made the motion that the trustees go through the proper channels of getting a deed to this land." This was approved by the church.

Deacons elected in June were Everett Jordan, Wilson Hedgecock, Glaster Jones, and Jack Embler. Joe Smith was chosen as the new trustee.

The July conference showed the church dealing with new guidelines for the cemetery. Some land had been given but it was unclear whether there were stipulations. The set of new guidelines was accepted, but some questions still lingered. Motion was made by James Williams to check the deed to find out how the land had been given. Harold Moore amended that to include a map being drawn of the cemetery and a record being made of where persons were buried. The church approved. Two months later, the church heard the report, "there were no strings attached," meaning the church could do with the land as needed.

At the August conference, it was announced by Numa Everhart that "our pastor, Rev. Joe Coltrane, had been granted a full scholarship to Wake Forest Seminary (Southeastern) and made the motion that we permit him to go." Clarence Moore seconded this motion. The church approved.

Another first took place during the year of 1967. Two YWA ladies had earned the right to be crowned as Queens. This was the highest achievement in the organization and required much study and many mission-oriented projects. Myra Moore (Aderholdt) was attended by Miss Cindy Cook and Mister Bernie Smith for her coronation. Miss Lynne Hedgecock and Mister James Bowers were the attendants for Ginger Dills (Amos).

During the first conference in 1968, the church considered participating in an associational-wide crusade planned for July 31–August 11. The church's part of the expense would be $125. This was to take care of preparation for the crusade. Special offerings would be taken each night and given to the evangelist. Some churches benefited from this, but no reference is made as to any type of impact at Abbotts Creek.

Elder V. V. Willard, a highly respected farmer and Primitive Baptist minister of the community, shared his feelings with this writer some years later. His evaluation was that the preacher came to town, preached for several nights, went away with a nice pocketfull of money, and left the churches to the pastors, many of whom were not earning enough to live on. For several years, crusades were well-received by the churches. In August of the same year, the church was informed that funds for the Crusade were short, and the church voted to send another hundred dollars to help with this need.

In the conference of April 3, 1968, the church heard the resignation of both Carey Davis as music director and Jacky Davis as organist. Their resignations were accepted by the church.

Two months later, J. C. Alcon, Staley Bodenheimer, Howard Dean, and James Williams were elected as deacons. Dwight Moore was named as trustee. At this same conference, a committee to secure a music director whose title would be "Minister of Music" was elected. The committee included Pattie Bodenheimer, Wilbur Bowers, Numa Everhart, Mary Smith, and Andrew Spaugh.

Conferences heard reports from the treasurer, Sunday School, extension department, WMU, and others. Some were uniting with the church

Myra Moore (Aderholdt) is attended by Cindy Cook and Bernie Smith.

Ginger Dills (Amos) is attended by Lynne Hedgecock and James Bowers.

and a few were moving membership elsewhere. Love offerings were taken to help those with needs, and food was delivered to different families. The July conference noted the Woman's Missionary Union report that included plans to carry a meal every Sunday throughout the quarter for the Baxter Smith family. Mrs. Smith was bedridden. The church continued to show concern and a willingness to help when that was needed.

At the July conference, attention was given to Minnie A. Spurgeon's will, which had been probated at the clerk of superior court in Davidson County. The will read, "after my debts are all paid, I want one tenth to go through my church, one third of one tenth to the Children's Home at Thomasville, one third of one tenth to home and foreign missions, one third of one tenth to the Memorial Association, if we still have one, if not send it to the Children's Home at Thomasville."

The May 1969 conference showed minutes being taken by Don Livengood, assistant clerk. Pat Dawson was chosen as director of the Vacation Bible School taking place the third week in June to avoid conflict with the Southern Baptist Convention. The second matter of business was a report from the deacons that a new parsonage be built. The minutes noted, "The church accepted this recommendation." A notation is given that quite a bit of discussion took place. In fact, an amendment was made to the motion that a place be given on the ballot for remodeling the present parsonage. This amendment was defeated by a standing vote. Ballots were taken up, and the church voted to build a new parsonage. The count was not listed.

In June, new deacons were elected. They were Bobby Canada, Dwight Moore, Charles Garner, and Hugh Motsinger. Jack Embler offered his resignation as a deacon.

All of these except Dwight Moore were ordained on July 6, 1969. Dr. Olin T. Binkley, president of Southeastern Seminary, delivered the ordination sermon.

The parsonage planning committee was elected at the August 6 meeting but not named. James Williams was to be chairman of this group. A month later, the committee brought this recommendation for the church to consider: "The parsonage planning committee recommended that the church property be surveyed and that the new church parsonage be built on property presently owned by the church, adjacent to the present parsonage. Then upon completion of the new parsonage, the old parsonage shall be sold and or removed." A substitute motion was made to survey the property and plot out the suggested place for the new parsonage and let the church vote on the building site. This motion was defeated by a vote of thirty-seven to twenty-seven. The original motion passed by a vote of forty-eight to seven. Chairman James Williams presented plans for the new parsonage at the November conference. These plans were accepted with no opposition. Later in the month, Cletus Hedgecock, chairman of the building committee, made the motion that Roger Moorefield build the parsonage for cost plus ten percent. This motion passed with no opposition.

The decade of the sixties ended with a December 7 conference that had the normal business reports.

CHAPTER SIXTEEN

The Seventies

The decade of the seventies opened with the announcement that Dr. John Eddins of Southeastern Seminary would be the guest teacher for the January Bible study. Abbotts Creek had never been short of having scholarly teachers and preachers from the outside. Generally, each one expressed gratitude for the opportunity to be able to speak to and worship with the congregation in such a historic church.

The time for church conferences was again brought to a vote by recommendation of the deacons. It was decided for all of them to be held on Wednesday evening. The vote was divided in this regard—79 for, with 54 opposed.

Reports were given by the organizational leaders in Sunday School, Training Union, extension leaders, and the mission organization of RAs and GAs. In the report of the RAs, the leaders were discussing having softball games between the boys and the men of the church. The GA group was carrying out a mission action project by making and sending health kits for immigrants in Florida.

Around this time it came to the attention of the church from the trustees that "Church property was surveyed, one parcel of land we do not have a deed. In order to get this Deed, it will cost $1,000. The trustees decided to leave the deeds as they are."

The need for recreation space for the youth and children was pointed out. A suggestion was made to pave the parking lot and prepare a basketball court along with it. A committee consisting of Charles Garner, Tom Dawson, Kathy Green, and Dwight Moore was assigned to deal with this.

The pastor presented the idea of Family Night on Wednesday evenings. James Williams made a motion, which was seconded by Billie Alcon, to try this. The church approved. The first Family Night was held on July 1, 1970.

At the same conference, Roxie Beeson presented plans for relocating the church library.

Improvements continued to take place. Tom Dawson, chairman of the trustees, brought to the attention of the church plans to carpet the children's department, nursery, fellowship hall, and the front porch and steps. The cost for this was $4,300. The church approved.

No progress report had been given on the building of the new parsonage, but Mr. Dawson asked if the trustees had the power to dispose of the old parsonage or if the matter should be decided by the church. The church gave the trustees permission "to handle this as they saw fit." The building was sold to the Tommy Bodenheimer family, who moved it to a location on Moore Road, did the necessary renovations, and reared their two daughters, Kristy (Mabe) and Nikki (Francis), and their son, Rusty there. Tommy and his wife, Bonnie, continue to live there.

Four new deacons were elected: Numa Everhart, Joe Smith, Wilbur Davis, and Wilbur Bowers. Buddy Handy was the alternate, and Monroe Beeson was chosen as trustee.

The July conference heard a request from Staley Bodenheimer, chairman of the parsonage finance committee. He presented this motion: "that we borrow $5,000 from the Memorial Association and $15,000 from First Federal Savings and Loan." This motion was passed.

The pastor presented an idea to the church to start some type of activity for the youth on Saturday nights. This would be from seven until ten o'clock, with the youth from ninth grade through college asked to attend and to bring a friend. Two volunteer chaperones would be present each night. James Williams made such a motion. Doug Hayworth seconded this. After some discussion, it was decided to try this and see how it worked out until the next conference.

A plaque was presented to Mrs. Laura Moore at the July 1970 conference. It read: "Laura H. Moore: In recognition of her many years of providing the bread for the Lord's Supper Observance in Abbotts Creek Baptist Church, July 1970, by the deacons." When Mrs. Moore was no longer able to prepare the bread, her daughter, Daphne Moore Motsinger, assumed the responsibility and carried it out for the next thirty years. She was recognized by the church on Easter of 2004 and presented a plaque by the deacons of the church.

The above-mentioned activity for youth was called TAT, Teenage Activity Time. Toward the end of the year, it was reported to be going well with possible changes as time goes on. In early January, James Williams and his wife, Betty, consented to be the adult advisors for the group. J. C. and Billie Alcon and several other parents provided additional adult leadership as well. So far as we can determine, this was the first church decision to have an organized program for the youth.

The Reverend James Bolick was guest speaker for the revival services. There were several professions of faith and baptisms following the services.

The Reverend Coltrane, pastor since April 1963, announced his resignation at the end of the service on December 20, 1970. The church voted to accept this as of January 19, 1971.

The deacons were charged with the responsibility of recommending a pulpit search committee at the January 1971 conference. They would also recommend an interim pastor.

For his final services, Rev. Coltrane concluded a series of sermons on the Ten Commandments at the morning service. There were five professions of faith after that service. A love offering was taken for the Coltrane family at the conclusion of the service. "Dreams and Visions" was the topic for his closing message that evening. His ministry was closed with a baptismal service. The following were baptized the last two Sunday evenings he served as pastor: Dianne Dawson, Janet Loggins, Joe, Jeffery, and Jay Craven, Tony Peele, Daniel Hayworth, Kelly Clinard, Randy Kearns, Donald James Moriarty, Kathy Green, Linda Teague, Linda Cook, and Joy Lyda. Two others were listed, George Armstrong and Crystal Taylor, but were not baptized.

Rev. Coltrane was to assume the pastorate at Newport Baptist Church in Newport, North Carolina.

The church moved quickly appointing a pulpit committee in February. Members of the committee were J. C. Alcon, Pat Dawson, Roxie Beeson, Charles Green, H. S. Motsinger, Mary Smith, and Andrew Spaugh. At the same conference and at the request of Ruth Hedgecock, chairman of the flower committee, Mary Smith expressed the desire of the committee to have fresh flowers in the sanctuary each Sunday. The WMU announced a single rose bud would be placed in the sanctuary on the arrival of new babies of the membership.

The efficient church clerk, Pearl Hayworth, had learned with evidence that fifteen people were members of other churches and had not requested their church letters. Her motion was to remove those names from the church roll. The church approved this and the names were removed.

Open house for the new parsonage had been held on August 16, 1970. The total and itemized cost was recorded in the minutes prior to the April

THE SEVENTIES

Open house for the new parsonage was held on August 16, 1970.

1971 conference and included the 10 percent above cost that the contractor, Roger Moorefield, was paid. The cost was listed as $36,672.16. Donated work amounted to at least $603 with some amounts not included.

The importance of the youth in the church was constantly in the minds of the congregation. A youth rally was held in Fayetteville, North Carolina in April. The church accepted the recommendation of the deacons to pay for the motel and travel expense for the youth of the church to attend this rally.

In the same conference, April 7, 1971, an announcement was made that a called conference would be held on a Sunday morning to vote on the recommended pastor.

J. C. Alcon gave a "progress" report from the pulpit committee. The subject concerned paying the moving expense of the new pastor. The church approved this plan. At the June conference, obviously the committee had learned the pay scale of the church was low, and a motion was made and accepted to increase the pastor's salary of $110 per week by $15. The committee chairman, J. C. Alcon, had talked with the prospective pastor and made a motion to amend the previous salary decision. "This motion asked for a yearly figure of $7,260 for salary and travel." Of this total, $1,200 would be considered for travel. This would amount to a $910 increase in the overall budget. This motion carried.

The church heard Rev. Charles Tanner on July 4, 1971. His sermon topic was, "20th Century Disciples," with the scripture taken from Luke 14:25-35. Two hundred seventeen members voted, with 213 in favor and four voting negatively. This information was given to Rev. Tanner, who agreed to accept. The Tanner family moved to Abbotts Creek, with his work beginning on August 16, 1971.

The names of those elected as deacons and the trustee were omitted from the minutes.

Two motions were brought to the attention of the church on September 8, 1971. The first concerned a new church directory. The second one concerned the purchase of a typewriter and mimeograph machine. This would also involve preparing the small room outside the pastor's study for this equipment. The estimated cost would be $800. Both recommendations passed.

The trustees were asked to deal with a recommendation to place partitions in sections at the rear of the sanctuary, which would allow mothers with small children to care for their children and attend worship at the same time. It was decided by vote of the church to enclose only one side.

The new pastor preached the fall revival, October 10–17, 1971.

The music committee, chaired by Numa Everhart, recommended that the church call Perry Dull as minister of music on January 12, 1972. He would be responsible for men's, youth, and junior choirs, plus the sanctuary choir. His responsibility would also include Easter and Christmas or other special-event music. If families asked, he would be involved with music for funeral services as well. The pay would be $55 per week with $25 extra for the weeks of revival.

Several motions were presented to the church by the deaconship at this conference.

1. A committee to be appointed to draw up a new constitution for the church.

2. In lieu of a fall revival, a World Mission Conference would take place. This was part of an association-wide effort.

3. The third motion concerned the church securing a youth core worker for the summer, which would be done through the student department of the North Carolina Baptist Convention.

4. A vote was taken to begin locking the church doors between the services. These motions were presented separately, and all passed.

Locking the church became necessary when a member of the congregation found someone sleeping on the back pew (and it was not even during a preaching service). It had become obvious that people were entering the church and using the kitchen facilities.

A decision was obviously made at some time to start a weekly newsletter called *The Tie*. Volume I, Number 2 was dated January 28, 1972. This *Tie* listed those who had a perfect attendance in Sunday School during 1971. They were Grady Green, 8 years; Baxter Smith and Mrs. Whittington with an unknown number of years; Patricia Todd, 8 years; Debra Sulger, 6 years; Dawn Sulger, 4 years; Kim Alcon, 3 years; Diane Sulger and Jennifer Alcon, both at one year. Kathy Green was secretary and a few newsletters later, thanks were expressed to Dot Canada and Roxie Beeson for assisting the secretary and pastor in getting the newsletter ready for mailing.

The deacons presented other recommendations in February. The first one concerned securing a bus for church use at a cost not to exceed $3,000. There seemed to have been lots of good stories about the bus. Most of the time, a mechanic had to be among the passengers. Some recall the time when the bus filled with passengers was on the way to Charlotte for a Billy Graham Crusade. The bus broke down. Drivers for the bus included Fred Peele and Don Livengood, both with mechanical skills. It took their effort to get the bus started again and on to their destination.

Perry Dull was called to be minister of music on January 12, 1972.

The second recommendation concerned support for the chaplain at the High Point hospital. The church voted to contribute one hundred dollars annually. In addition to these motions, the Music Committee recommended Mrs. Becky Bell be employed to lead the youth choir. The pay would be thirteen dollars for each rehearsal and for each time they sang in the church, which was to be every other Sunday evening.

Dr. Eual Lawson was the guest minister during the March revival. Dr. Lawson was with the Evangelism Department of the Home Mission Board.

The church voted on May 10, 1972, to secure workman's compensation for all employees of the church. The deacons had brought this recommendation to the church. It was announced at the same meeting that the church had purchased a fireproof box for the safekeeping of church records.

An announcement was made at the June business session concerning the will of Ray W. Teague. George Sechrest reported the late Mr. Teague

History, Heritage, and Memories

The first copy of the church newsletter was dated October 8, 1971.

The Seventies

Covered wagon driven by Tom Dawson and used on Heritage Day 1972.

Rev. Charles Tanner

had left $2,000 for the Memorial Association.

Vacation Bible School was conducted June 12-26, 1972 with average attendance of 154. Seventeen children and youth made public their salvation experience. Eight of these united with the church the following Sunday.

The mission group, having left the anti-mission group, organized the Missionary church on July 4, 1832. One hundred and forty years later, the congregation celebrated by dressing as nearly as possible as their forefathers had dressed. The worship attendance was 261 for the morning service. Old songs were used in worship, and lunch was served with families sitting on blankets sharing their meal together. The pastor's scripture was

Pictured at the Old Fashioned Day are: from left Laura Moore, Joe Smith, Kay Green, Numa Everhart, Brooks Montsinger, Grady Green, and Rayford Hayes.

Mary Garrison, Mary Jane Kanoy, Aileen Palmer, and Norma Dills in 1972.

taken from Joshua 4 with the sermon topic, "What Mean These Stones."

The church considered a recommendation to study the need for a recreational area, tennis, and basketball courts with a location suggested. James Williams, Joe Smith, Tom Dawson, and Wilbur Bowers formed the committee for this study.

Deacons elected in September were J. C. Alcon, Brooks Motsinger, John Hedgecock, and George Sechrest. Bobby Canada was the elected trustee.

Another study group was named in October. This, too, was recommended by the deacons of the church. This study was "relative to opening a kindergarten." Pat Kanoy, Dot Canada, Evva Spurgeon, Betty Williams, Ruth Spurgeon, Maxine Todd, and Ginger Amos made up this study committee.

For some time, a Constitution-By-Laws committee had been at work. They presented for a revised constitution to the church at the October conference. Much discussion took place with some additions being made. The vote of the church was to accept the revised constitution with twenty three positive votes and thirteen voting against it.

The December 1, 1972, issue of *The Tie* expressed thanks to Kathy Green for "the fine job she has done as our church secretary." Her resignation was to be effective the next week.

The church presented a live nativity scene each night from December 17-24, 1972. Rain caused the program to be canceled one evening. This was well accepted by the community. The December 22 issue of *The Tie* showed an insert of the scene. Various members were portrayed acting out the part of the shepherds, wise men, and the other nativity characters. Those who played Joseph and Mary were listed as: Sunday—Joe and Mary Smith; Monday—Everett and Bessie Jordan; Tuesday—J. C. and Billie Alcon; Wednesday—Richard and Pat Kanoy; Thursday—Tom and Pat Dawson, Friday—the pastor and Mrs. Tanner; Saturday—Staley and Patty Bodenheimer; Sunday—Brooks and Daphne Motsinger.

The very first newsletter in 1973, thanked the congregational members who had prepared the props or participated in the scenes. Thanks was expressed to those who allowed their animals to be used. More than one hundred people had been involved in the presentation and more than 900 cars passed the scene. By this time, Mrs. Richard Kanoy was listed as secretary and had typed *The Tie*.

The Recreation Committee reported they were considering the area in the woods near the west end of the church property for the play area. There was no vote involved.

This was spelled out a bit more at the next conference with an explanation the area to be cleared would be 120x120 feet. The cost of the project, which was accepted by the church, would be $2,000.

The deaconship brought a recommendation to purchase a large screen, 12x12 feet, for use in the sanctuary. The cost would be $206 and would blend with the present furnishing. The church voted to accept this recommendation.

Earlier in the Extension Department's report, college students, service personnel, shut-ins and other homebound members had been included. In several of the newsletters, short thank-you notes were included from some of the college students.

J. C. Alcon, deacon chairman, brought a recommendation from the deacons that a youth worker be employed for eight or nine weeks in the summer. The worker would be Stewart Stokes. The church accepted this recommendation.

The March revival was lead by the Rev. Calhoun Johnson, missionary to Chile, South America. On the Wednesday night of this revival, Charles Garner announced to the church he had felt God's call for the ministry and asked for the moral support and prayers of the church family. His wife, Marilyn Everhart Garner, was reared in the church. At the April conference, James Williams, Vicki Hilton, Matthew Dunn, Mrs. Robert Palmer, and John Hedgecock were elected to administer a fund that would help with financial support for the Garner family while he was in school. At the September conference, the church accepted the recommendation of the deacons to license Charles Garner to the gospel ministry. At the November conference, church letters were granted to the Garners allowing them to unite with the Floyd Baptist Church near Denton where he would serve as pastor.

Support for a member preparing for ministry was not forgotten. The April 20, 1973, conference reported the establishment of the Charles Garner fund. Any person desiring to help support the family during the educational preparation for the future minister could contribute through this fund. James Williams was to chair the committee. Two hundred and forty letters were sent to the membership asking for monthly help.

The deacons recommended to the church that the minutes of the church be placed on microfilm at Wake Forest University. They would be placed in the Baptist historical section at the Wake Forest library. This significant vote took place at the April 1973. The minutes from the Primitive church were done at the same time. For a number of years, these minutes were the only ones in the Wake Forest collection that included both sides of a division.

Joe Smith, chairman of the recreation committee, brought a recommendation to the church requesting that asphalt paving be put on the recreational area rather than leaving the sand rock base. This would cost $2,200. The church approved this recommendation at the July 1973 conference.

The first mention of a separate junior church service was given in June. The youth worker, Steward Stokes, initiated and led this effort. He and his helpers, for the first Sunday, reported thirty-two children attending.

Perry Dull invited the junior choir to his home, in Kernersville, for an overnight camp out. The children played games and took a long nature walk through the pasture and by the stream. The next day they visited an elderly couple as their mission project.

About the same time, Patricia Todd was commended in the church newsletter for her 4H honors. She was part of the first-place team from Davidson County in horse judging in Dallas, Texas.

New deacons were elected in August. They were Dwight Moore, Richard Kanoy, Donald Livengood, and Bobby Canada. The new chairman would be John Sulger.

Glaster Jones was the trustee selected. The ordination service for Donald Livengood and Richard Kanoy was held on November 4, 1973.

The church voted at the September conference to install private telephone lines for the parsonage and the church. An extension line would be added to the secretary's office at the church. At the same conference, the deacons recommended that the church hire a youth worker for weekends during the winter. The very next conference, October, Joel P. Jenkins, Junior, was recommended to the church and called by the church to become that weekend youth worker. He would travel from Southeastern Seminary and be paid $75 per week which would include his travel. He would arrive on Saturday and return on Sunday night. The length of his call was left open. He was to be in charge of "youth outreach, Saturday night program, youth Bible study and related activities."

At this time, 30 families were required to make a quorum for a business conference. Reminders had been issued and pleas made for this. However, at the October 19, 1973, conference, phone calls had to be made and after a thirty-minute wait, there were enough people to transact the business.

A statewide vote for liquor by the drink was to be held in November. Several issues of *The Tie* and numerous announcements in the Sunday bulletins kept this before the people urging all voters to cast a ballot against this.

Brooks Motsinger, chairman of the trustees, bought a recommendation to the church during the November conference. The trustees had met with the deacons prior to presenting a motion to the church that "the church buys 4.49 acres of land from the Spurgeon heirs which joins the church property in back, at the price of $4,000 per acre and the total of $17,960. Terms cash in 90 days." After a long discussion, a vote was taken by secret ballot. Eighty-one voted in favor of this with 19 opposing. The nominating committee was asked to appoint a ways and means committee to study how this would be financed.

During the first conference of 1974, deacon chairman John Sulger brought a recommendation from the deacons that an offering be taken at the door after each communion service and used as a benevolent offering for local needs. The church voted in favor of this motion. Brooks Motsinger reported at the same conference the church now had the deed for the newly-purchased land.

The church heard from Laurence, Todd, Jr., chairman of the ways and means committee, a recommendation for the payment of the land. He asked the church to use the savings account of $7,966.22 to pay off the balance due on the parsonage. The remainder of the account would go toward the purchase of the land. In addition, the church was asked to borrow

$15,000 from First Federal Building and Loan Association of High Point against the parsonage to complete payment on the newly-purchased land.

At the close of the morning service, on February 24, 1974, Pastor Charles L. Tanner read to the church his letter of resignation listing March 24 as his last service at Abbotts Creek. He informed the church that a week earlier he had accepted the call to become pastor of First Baptist Church in Garner, North Carolina. Rev. Tanner had served Abbotts Creek since August 16, 1971.

Joel Jenkins had served well as youth worker at the church. However, a fuel crisis was making it difficult to find gasoline for traveling. Sometimes long lines would be seen at service stations. The youth worker cited that the difficulties of finding gasoline on the weekends made it impossible for him to continue his work at Abbotts Creek.

At the March conference, the deacons brought the names of the pulpit committee to the church. They were Lee Davis, Wilbur Bowers, Bobby Canada, Maxine Todd, Pat Kanoy, and Daphne Motsinger. Bobby Canada was chairman of this group. John Sulger, Wilson Hedgecock, Charles Green, and Dwight Moore would serve on the committee to secure an interim pastor. Rev. Charles Hodges, employed by the Children's Homes in Thomasville, would serve as the interim. In following the guidelines of the Homes, he was allowed to preach for four Sunday and to be away the next. He would be available for crisis ministry unless on assignment pertaining to his work at the Homes.

In April, a benevolence committee was formed to assist local needs as such became evident. An offering would be taken at the door after each communion for this need. The committee assigned to look after this was make up of John and Betty Sulger, Bobby and Dorothy Canada, and George and Blanche Sechrest.

The March 26, 1974, newsletter asked the church to remember the pulpit committee in prayer. They were "traveling this Sunday to hear a prospect."

About the middle of May, Stewart Stokes, former Youth Director, took a group of youth to Ridgecrest for a weekend conference. Youth attending were Debbie Dawson, Terri Peele, Mary Jane and Keith Kanoy, and James Bowers.

The May conference concerned the Rev. Aubrey McClellan leading revival services. The following month, the church dealt with the need of a new piano in one of the departments, but the church decided to get a new piano for the sanctuary and use the sanctuary piano in the department. The July conference heard a motion to spend $190 to get material for robes for the youth choir. Motion was made also to pay for two couples going with the youth choir to Boone.

Sometime earlier the church had purchased a bus that was, by the August conference, giving much trouble. Charles Green asked to be replaced on the bus committee by Don Livengood, a mechanic, who knew more about the needs of the bus. This was accepted by the church.

Debra Sulger was recognized in the July 26 newsletter for being the "territorial winner for the electric congress" and won a television set. She would, as the state winner in 4H long-term records, attend the national convention in Chicago and did so later in the year.

A called conference in August was for the purpose of electing deacons and a trustee. William Hayworth was the trustee named. Wilbur Bowers, Lee Davis, Tom Marsh, and Laurence Todd were the deacons elected and *The Tie* added "in a very close election."

The older Acteens were planning ahead. The National Acteens Convention was planned June 25-29, 1975, in Memphis, Tennessee. They were beginning fund-raising projects to care for the needed expense.

The youth choir had practiced long and hard and had opportunities to sing in some nearby churches. They were also able to travel to Starnes Cove Baptist Church, near Asheville, N.C., for a weekend. The Starnes Cove Church provided a picnic on Saturday for the youth and allowed the choir members to stay in the homes of the members for the night. The youth choir was in charge of the Sunday morning worship service.

The pulpit committee called a conference on September 8, 1974, for the purpose of presenting a prospective pastor, Roy Cantrell, to the church. Rev. Cantrell had served for four years with the Home Mission Board and the North Carolina Baptist Convention as pastor of the Cherokee Baptist Church, Cherokee, North Carolina, and director of the Day Care at the church. In addition to the chairman, Bobby Canada, the committee included: Maxine Todd, Pat Kanoy, Daphne Motsinger, Wilbur Bowers, and Lee Davis. The group had decided they would hear a prospective pastor twice before giving the church a recommendation. One trip had been made to Cherokee and part of the family had visited the community, looked over the church and parsonage. The invitation to become pastor had been made but the second trip to Cherokee was still to come. Two of the committee members were unable to make this trip, but spouses for two other members traveled with the group.

On the eve of September 8, the pastor's family and the families of the search committee had a meal together in a local restaurant. In addition, the families of the outgoing chairman of deacons, John Sulger, and incoming chairman, Dwight Moore, were included.

After Rev. Cantrell's sermon using Matthew 16:13-18, as the scripture, Bobby Canada, chairman of the pulpit committee, entertained a motion "that the above be voted on as our pastor." The vote was taken by secret ballot with 232 voting. The vote was 226—in favor with 6 negative votes. The church was informed that Rev. Cantrell would accept the call and begin his ministry on October 6, 1974. At that October service, he and his wife, Linda, and son, Christopher, united with the church by letter from the Cherokee Baptist Church. Their daughter, Beth, was only four at the time. Sons David and Chet had remained in Cherokee because of commitments with the Sylva-Webster High School band. They joined the church by letter a week later.

First group of Acteens from the church to attend a National Acteen Convention are pictured rom left: Lynn Smith Parnell, leader; Phyllis Peele, Mary Jane Kanoy Coble, Terri Peele Andrews, Donna Moore, and Kathy Green Cline. Photo by Acteen leader, Jean Brookie.

Over the next few weeks, several joined the church. Leroy and Becky Kearns joined by statement while Henry and Betty Rose Alcon joined by letter. Both couples had moved back to the community and were previously members of the church. Brian Smith, Kenneth Smith, and Lori and Debra Hedgecock came for baptism. Rodney Rickard and Mrs. Kenneth Smith came by letter. Angellee Dunn and James Allred also came as candidates for baptism. Pamela Smith came on profession of faith. Pamela had an illness that caused her arms and body to be constantly moving. In order for her to be baptized, she was placed in a small chair and carried into the water. Dwight Moore and Brooks Motsinger assisted the pastor in the baptismal experience.

On the same day, the church had called the new minister, the evening service was unusual. *The Tie* tells us of that on September 8, 1974, the evening service was, "a candlelight service." A violent electrical storm had caused the lights to go out and candles were used for the service. The junior choir sang and Rev. Charles Hodges delivered the message.

Some firsts were taking place for the new pastor. Laurence, Todd, Jr., was the first to be ordained as a deacon after the pastor arrived. A few weeks later, funerals were held on Saturday for Mrs. Grace Spainhour and Sunday for Mrs. Maggie Welborn. Former pastors, Charles Tanner assisted with one while Rev. Joe Coltrane helped with the other.

Sunday after Christmas, Student Night at Christmas was held. Several college students took part in this service. They were Lynn Canada and Kim Alcon from University of North Carolina at Greensboro. Having a part of the service also was Joanne Green from Wake Forest. Lynn Smith and Jill Jordan from Appalachian State University participated. From Western Carolina University, three took parts, David and Jerry Bowers and Janet Jordan. Catawba Tech was represented by Doug Hayworth and Michael Moore. Jamie Spurgeon, who was attending and participated, represented Guilford Tech. From Davidson County Community College, Debra Sulger, Pam Crouch, and Randy Kearns assisted in this worship service.

A new ministry was set to be launched in January of 1975. A cassette player had been used to record the worship services and carried to some of the homebound members. Soon five or six cassettes were in use to record the services. The deacons recommended to the church that a duplicator be purchased in order to make this ministry more effective. The church approved this at a cost in the range of $1,300. James Williams was responsible for the purchase of this machine. By late spring, the church had fifteen tape players in the homes of the shut-ins.

The children's choir had grown to the point that a new ministry needed to be created. Perry Dull continued to work with the children's choir, ages 4-6. Linda Cantrell directed and Linda Sprinkle played the piano for the junior choir, grades, 2-6. The younger choir started with twelve children present.

In March, a group from Waterfalls Baptist Church in Cherokee came to lead our worship services. They arrived a bit late but the choir sang and Rev. Johnny Driver, a minister and member of the church, brought the message. The Abbotts Creek congregation seemed pleased to have the Native American group leading the worship service. A covered dish meal allowed the people to mingle and talk with the visitors.

The church continued to be strongly involved in work of the Liberty Baptist Association. At the April 1975 conference, the church voted to give

Pictured here are children from the 1974 Christmas Program, including: Shepherds: Dale Essick, Shane Sells; Wisemen: Scott Hedgecock, Brian Motsinger, Ken Fowler; Joseph: Jason Hedgecock; Mary: Jennifer Alcon; and the Angels include: Beth Kearns, Zane Sells, Beth Cantrell, Amy Hutchens, Christi Cook, and Shane Loggins.

one hundred dollars toward the cost of the director of missions, Leonard Rollins, going to the Baptist World Alliance in Stockholm, Sweden. The spring revival was lead by Rev. Roy Smith who later became the general secretary of the North Carolina Baptist State Convention.

The Acteens were busy with fund raisers preparing for their trip to the National Acteens Convention in Memphis. The first Acteens from Abbotts Creek to attend such a convention were Lynn Smith, Mary Jane Kanoy, Donna Moore, Kathy Green, and Terri Peele. Leaders were Phyllis Peele and Jean Brookie. This was a tremendous experience for the Acteens and leaders. One of their side trips was a visit to Graceland, the home of the late Elvis Presley.

For a number of years, the Acteens, RAs, and GAs helped promote missions by carrying out a Walk-A-Thon. Those participating enlisted sponsors with the money going for home missions. It was a big event for the church family. The mission groups were there to walk but dozens of others walked, some pushing baby carriages making it a family affair. While this was going on, other adults were at the church cooking hamburgers and hot dogs on the grill for a cookout. Matthew Dunn drove his truck along with the walkers providing water when that was needed. This took place for a number of years with a special recognition given on Sunday night at the end of the walk and meal. Trophies were given to the boy and girl in the different age groups who raised the most money for the mission emphasis.

In the spring and summer, the RA boys participated in the state track meet at Gardner-Webb College with leaders Jimmy Kennedy and Larry Sprinkle along with Linda Cantrell and Don Livengood. Generally there were several others making the trip as well. During this time, the youth choir traveled to several nearby churches to sing. Kathy Price was the youth worker for the summer.

In August, Pat Kanoy resigned as secretary because of the illness of her husband, Richard. Georgette Bullard was named temporary secretary for a short period of time but was soon named secretary. She continued to serve for several months.

The church voted, in September, to increase the number of deacons by one each time the church received thirty-four new members. The number would decrease one if the membership dropped by the same number. Some years later, the church voted to cut off the number of deacons at eighteen.

September was also the month for new deacons and a trustee to be elected. Those elected were Numa Everhart, Hugh Motsinger, John Sulger, Joe Smith, and Robert Palmer. J. C. Alcon was chosen as trustee.

John Hedgecock representing the Baptist Men's organization of the church recommended to the church that a picnic shelter be constructed. The recommendation called for a 24x60 foot shelter to be built. The initial cost would be approximately one thousand dollars. Much of this cost was actually provided by Baxter Smith, in memory of his late wife, Sue. During the time this was being done, Mary Willie Orrell, a homebound member, collected $130 from friends and family members who did not attend Abbotts Creek, but wanted to help with the shelter.

Conferences continue to include reports from the various organizations of the church, such as library, youth, treasurer's report, WMU, Sunday School, trustees, and others. Some letters were granted while still others were uniting with the church from time to time.

Revival services were held with Rev. D. W. Cooper, from Dillon, South Carolina, the visiting minister. Rev. Cooper was serving as the Cantrell's last pastor prior to Rev. Cantrell's first pastorate. Several new members joined the church during this time. On November 9, 1975, Mrs. Mae Canipe

This is picture of Walk-A-Thon, 1977, with the old bus in the background.

joined the church by letter from a church in Weldon, N. C. James Atkins joined by letter and his wife, Blanche, joined by statement. Mr. Atkins had been attending for several Sundays but she was present for the first time. During the invitational hymn, he presented himself for membership. While the pastor was talking with him, she came up talking a mile a minute explaining he had heart problems and was hard of hearing and had other ailments. Finally, the pastor was able to share with the congregation that Mr.

RA Track Team: Darrin Spurgeon, Dale Wall, Arlyn Wall, Timmy Spurgeon, and Michael Gann; Back row: Judy Wall and Seth Moore.

THE SEVENTIES

Track Meet with Tim Spurgeon, ready to run, with leader/coach Linda Cantrell. Other members also pictured in the background.

Atkins wanted to join the church. The church voted to accept him. She said, "Well, I just as well join too." The church accepted her for membership as well. This became a family that the RAs of the church ministered to greatly during Mr. Atkins' illness. Some of their Wednesday night programs were at the Atkins' home. When death came to him, the RAs carried his casket, the first such experience for most of them.

The neighboring church, Clifton Grove, was dealing with some financial problems meeting the payment for their building. Abbotts Creek members took a special collection to help with this need. A thank you note was received but one of their leaders, Coy Traynham, came to the deacon's meeting to thank the group in person saying a letter was not enough.

The year 1976 started off with the church voting to participate with the churches of Davidson County for an E. J. Daniels Crusade which was scheduled for later in the spring. At the same conference, a Bicentennial Committee was appointed. Named to the committee were Lee and Charles Davis, Pearl Hayworth, Roxie Beeson, named chair person, and Vicki Hilton. Shortly, the names of others were given: Kim Alcon, Pat Dawson, Art Hedgecock, Jamie Spurgeon, Dwight Moore, Daphne Motsinger, and Georgette Bullard.

A called conference was held on February 4, 1976, to consider a recommendation from the deacons and trustees. Two acres of land joining the back side of the church property were for sale with the church having first choice to purchase. Laurence Todd, Jr., chairman of deacons, presented the recommendation "that we consider purchasing this land at the price of $6,500 to be paid in two payments, $3,800 now, and the remaining $2,700 in the next two weeks. The money was to come from the church treasury." More that one thousand dollars of the latter payment had been pledged already. The vote, which was by secret ballot, was fifty-six in favor, with five voting no.

Rarely would February have five Sundays but this was a year for that. Sunday School attendance had been stressed with the church trying to make this rare occasion something to remember. For the five Sundays, the average attendance was 259.

For several weeks, *The Tie* included a short biographical sketch of a deacon and listed the families on his family ministry's deacon list.

Fun night was planned with the church renting the Ledford Middle School's gym for basketball games. The youth of the church challenged the adults for some competition. The men played against the male youth and the women against the female youth. The charge for this was twenty-five cents to pay for the rental of the facilities.

Eddie Hilton and Kenny Moore took the RA boys for a weekend camping trip to Fontana, in Western North Carolina. Plans were to attend services at one of the Native American churches in Cherokee. However, heavy rains caused everyone and everything to be soaked and the campers arrived

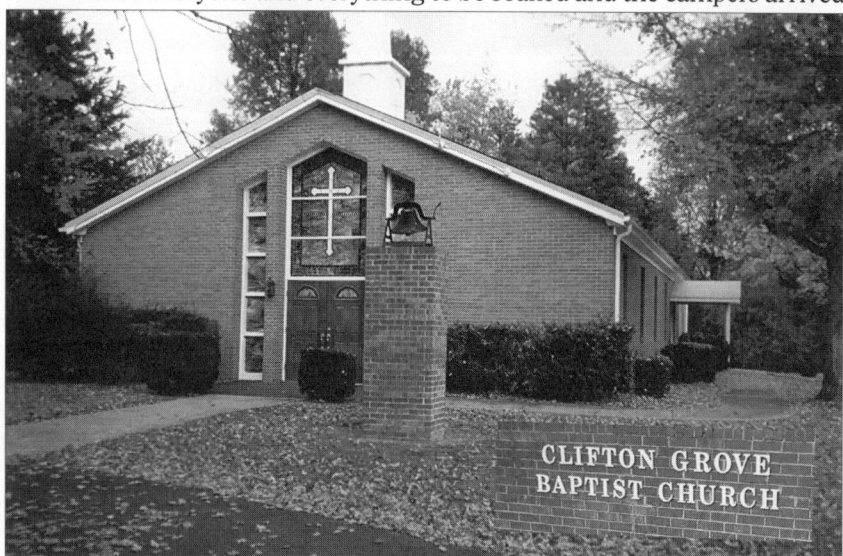

The Clifton Grove Baptist Church featured here is part of the Abbotts Creek Community.

home by the time the Sunday morning services were over at Abbotts Creek.

In May, the church participated in an E. J. Daniels Crusade sponsored by the churches in Davidson County.

The church voted for Debbie Jones to be the youth worker for the summer of 1976. This vote was taken on May 23. Miss Jones, a public school teacher in High Point, would be at Abbotts Creek for five weeks.

The church was a part of the celebration of the nation's bicentennial and planned activities to celebrate the history of the church as well. In fact, a Saturday service was planned. Old hymns were sung and Jeff Traynham gave some of his memories of the earlier days in the life of the church. Church clerk, Pearl Hayworth, and assistant clerk, Betty Jo Motsinger, called the roll of members with 135 present out of a total members ship of 523. The Rules of Decorum were read by deacon chairman, Laurence, Todd, Jr.. Art Hedgecock read some parts of the old history. The pastor's sermon was entitled "A Foundation for Dreams of Tomorrow." After the two-hour service, the congregation went to the picnic shelter for lunch and then to the fellowship hall to observe a display of articles from the earlier days of the church.

On Sunday, July 4, 1976, the choir presented a musical, "I Love America." This was written especially for the bicentennial celebration and many churches used this as part of their activities of remembering. Soloists were Betty Craven, Crystal Chewning, Perry Dull, Michelle Luck, and Velecia Everhart. Becky Bell directed the choir assisted by Cheryl Rickard playing the piano. The church clerk summarized by saying, "This was enjoyed by a filled church including a good number of visitors."

Back in April, the church was informed the parsonage had been paid off except what was owed to the Memorial Association. The church immediately voted to pay the association what had been borrowed.

The Memorial Day services had Rev. T. E. Robinette as speaker. He was serving as pastor of Enon Baptist Church, in Salisbury. He had performed the wedding ceremony of the pastor and Linda back in 1956, in Waynesville, North Carolina.

Another special event occurred when a former member, Jacky Davis, brought the choir he directed at First Baptist Church, in Madison to lead an evening service. The Cantata presented was "Behold the Lamb" which had been written by his father, Carey J. Davis. Both Carey and Jacky Davis had grown up in Abbotts Creek and both were heavily involved in the musical emphasis of the church.

Sometime during the year, the Young Believers Sunday School class was

Pictured here is the choir on July 4, 1976.

started. This was designed for young married couples not enrolled in Sunday School. This seemed to have been the first class in the church where husbands and wives could be together. This class was started and first held in the living room of the parsonage with Linda Cantrell teaching the first few Sundays. This class continued to grow in numbers and with excitement. After a few years, the younger couples getting married wanted to create a new class and did. Some years later, the same thing happened again.

The proposed budget was presented in September for the 1976-77 years by Chairman Wilson Hedgecock. It was amended to include $150 for Christmas treats and $100 each for the men and women's softball teams. Other reports were given at this and all other conferences. This included a thorough Sunday School report, enrollment, average attendance, visitors, and the amount of offering that had been collected throughout the Sunday School classes.

New deacons and a trustee were elected at the called conference in September.

Deacons were J. C. Alcon, John Hedgecock, Kay Green, George Sechrest, and James Williams. Paul Kearns was selected as the new trustee. An ordination service for Kay Green was held on September 26, 1976.

Revival services were held October 17-22, 1976, with Rev. Tom Jones from First Baptist Church, in Travelers Rest, South Carolina, as the guest speaker.

The Davis families were noted for their musical contributions to the ministries of Abbotts Creek Church. Pictured here is the late Charles W. Davis, father of the late Carey J. Davis, who is pictured at right.

On December 12, 1976, Jerome Hayworth was accepted into the church in absentia. His health prevented him from being present. A service had been held in his home the previous day with his five children and other family members present. Earlier the pastor had visited him in his workshop where Mr. Hayworth had made a profession of faith while sitting at his workbench and asked for church membership. This is the first time the minutes had recorded the church having accepted someone in absentia. However, Mr. Hayworth asked for this because he remembered many years earlier, one had became a part of the church in this manner.

Throughout the years, the church had acquired bits of land, some purchased, and some donated. Trustee, Brooks Motsinger had worked with diligence to get the proper deeds for all properties. He reported to the church on January 5, 1977, "Now the church has deeds to cover all the church property. These have been signed and recorded. After a period of seven years, a deed can be made to cover the entire church property on one valid deed."

The church voted at the same conference to purchase 250 new hymnals. Memorial stickers would be placed in front of the hymnal for those who purchased one in memory or in honor of a person. By the July conference, 181 of the 250 had been donated. Guy Messer, the pastor's father-in-law died in June. Mrs. Messer asked for anyone who wished to give a memorial to donate toward the purchase of the new hymnals. Several books were donated in his memory. At the same business meeting, with a pressing need for a dependable machine to makes copies of the newsletters and bulletins, J. C. Alcon made a motion that we spend $910 to purchase a new A. B. Dick Mimeograph machine.

Jacky Davis

The church voted at the April conference to donate five hundred dollars to the Liberty Baptist Association to help in securing 2.77 acres of land for an associational office. J. C. Alcon had been a part of the associational committee to find the property and then became a part of the building committee. The church contributed $500 toward this project.

The memorial services were held the third Sunday in May, with former member, Rev. Joe Bryant, bringing the message. Two months later, the Baptist Men purchased some outdoor play equipment for the children's playground.

The RAs would not give up on a camping trip to Cherokee. They left on Friday with the intention of returning on Sunday. As in their previous trip, rain came in strong portions and they returned on Saturday evening. Leaders Don Livengood and Charles Jordan had endured the rain with the boys.

Music director, Perry Dull offered his resignation on August 28, effective September 25, 1977. His letter of resignation was read to the church on September 7, 1977.

At the same September conference, a new budget was accepted and a motion made to pay off the remaining debt to the Memorial Association. Though nothing had been mentioned in a business meeting about this debt, some had reasoned the church's decision to borrow from the association earlier would mean that the church would make no effort to repay it since the church owned all of it anyway.

The annual election of deacons took place on September 11, 1977. Mike Beavers, Art Hedgecock, Glaster Jones, Brooks Motsinger, and Donald Livengood were elected. Deacon Tom Marsh had moved from the community and was replaced on the deacon board by Charles Green. The first two mentioned were ordained on October 2. Staley Bodenheimer was selected as the new trustee.

The church referred to Charles and Bonnie Wiggs as "our missionaries." During each of their furloughs home, one or both would speak at the church. This usually took place as soon as they were home and just prior to their return to Korea. At the October 1977 conference, Georgette Bullard, president of the Women Missionary Union, presented the desire of the missionary group for the church to pay the expense of Mrs. Wiggs to accompany her daughter, Debbie, to Wake Forest for the beginning of her college career in the fall of 1978. A motion was made and carried to do this. A few months later, long-time member Perry Hayworth died. His widow, Mary, requested in lieu of flowers, contributions be made to help Mrs. Wiggs make the trip with her daughter. Several memorials were given in keeping with her request.

It had long been a practice for the deacons to present Bibles to children going into the first grade class for Sunday School. Some years, names were listed but not always. In the fall of 1977, a Bible was presented to each of the following first graders: Denice Bullard, Kim Lewis, Jodi Spurgeon, Tonia Wheeler, Kanette Smith, Sharon Gann, Arlan Wall, Markus Tucker, Julie Green, Eric Wilson, Jim Snyder, and Timmy Spurgeon.

The need for a music director prompted the deacons to recommend Mrs. Becky Bell as interim music director. Her duties were spelled out to include the youth choir as well as the adult choir, choir practices, prayer meeting, special music for services including revival, and for funerals. Mrs. Bell served in this capacity until February 19, 1978.

The church hosted the fall session of the Liberty Baptist Association's meeting. The meal part was catered with the excellent cooks of the church providing the cakes and pies. The church was always a great host for such meetings.

In 1974, when the Cantrells came to the church, David, Chet, and Chris had become members by letter. During the revival services of October 1977, Beth, the pastor and Linda's daughter, joined the church on profession of faith. The Reverend James Herron, from First Baptist Church in Hudson, was the visiting minister.

The Christmas Cantata was presented at the morning hour of worship on Christmas day. It was entitled "His Love Reaching" by Bill and Gloria Gaither.

From the time Charles Garner left the church, to attend college in preparation for the ministry, each financial statement showed the amount sent to the Garners for the quarter and listed the balance in the fund. Hugh Motsinger, chairman of deacons, brought a recommendation from the deacons at the January 4, 1978, conference that the church present Charles with a set of commentaries upon his graduation from college. This motion passed.

At the same conference, the church accepted the deacon recommendation to participate in a World Mission Conference sponsored by the Liberty Association. Each church would be asked to care for a missionary during the week and also contribute $125 to the association for additional expense.

Up to this time, the church was not air conditioned. However, someone gave a gift in memory of a loved one and listed it as "air condition fund." This opened the door for more gifts. Questions had been asked about how such a fund started. Since this is being written almost thirty years later, the writer can reveal the secret that has never been told. Edith Bodenheimer made that first contribution. The deacons responded to this question trying to explain how it began without knowing who made the first contribution. The deacons had discussed this and informed the church it would be treated as any other fund. The trustees were checking into the cost for air conditioning in the church.

At the February conference, a committee was appointed to begin the search for a new music director. The committee members were George Sechrest, Georgette Bullard, Kathy Green, Mike Beavers, and Charles Davis.

The spring revival, in 1978, had Dr. Victor Glass as visiting minister. Dr. Glass was the uncle of Linda Cantrell and worked with National Baptists through the Home Mission Board in Atlanta, Georgia.

The financial statement presented to the church on April 5, 1978, gives insight as to the funds for the church. The church balance was $16,252. The other funds listed were: Charles Garner fund—$330, benevolence fund, minus—$218; softball fund—$567; air conditioner fund—$496; and the Bonnie Wiggs fund—$855.

With the recent purchase of extra land, the Baptist Men brought to the attention of the church a suggested use for part of it. Lee Roy Kearns presented on chalkboard a drawing with a layout for a suggested soft ball field. This would be placed as far back on the property as possible. Two motions were presented, first, that the church approve such a project. The vote was carried by show of hands with two negative votes. The second motion was for the church to pay up to $2,500 to have the necessary grading done. This passed by a 26 to 6 vote.

The music committee had met with the deacons to discuss a possible staff member. They had found someone willing to come and work full time with music and youth. Since the music committee had been asked to secure a music director, at the May 10, 1978, conference, the deacons presented to the church a recommendation to call a music and youth worker at a salary not to exceed $7,500. This was accepted by the church without opposition.

Once this vote was taken, the music committee recommended David Clemmens to become a staff member with responsibilities both with music and youth. David had worked in a similar capacity at Southside Church in Thomasville for the past three years. He and his wife Debbie began their work at Abbotts Creek, on June 1, 1978.

At a summer meeting, the senior adults decided to collect recipes and prepare a cookbook. This project was immediately underway with an additional request for recipes for diabetics. This brought a strong response and the book was well received when completed. The pastor served as advisor for this project which was really carried out primarily by Evva Spurgeon and Pansy Moore. The first Abbotts Creek cookbook was published in 1981.

The Bonnie Wiggs fund had grown to $1,514 by July. She and her daughter came from Korea to Wake Forest in late August where Debbie enrolled as a freshman. In the September 10, 1978, issue of the church newsletter, Bonnie has a note thanking the church family for helping her be with their daughter as she enrolled in college. She was preparing to return to Korea after being in North Carolina for two weeks.

About the same time, the church voted to send five hundred dollars for the new office building for the Liberty Baptist Association. The same amount would also be included the church's budget for the next church year.

On a hot July night, the deaconship recommended in conference that we air condition the sanctuary and do further study for the remaining facilities. As pastor, I knew there were strong feelings both ways about this and I always determined to be pastor for all people regardless of how they felt about any church issue. For the first and only time, I asked my family members not to contribute to the discussion concerning this. My wife did not participate but to my surprise our eight-year-old daughter held her hand and wanted to speak. She was a member and I recognized her. Her statement was, "We have heat to keep us warm in the winter, why can't we have air to keep us cool in the summer?"

Prices were presented; a twenty-ton unit would cost $8,375. This did not include the cost of additional insulation from ten to twelve inches. Much discussion was given to this matter. When the vote was taken, sixty-five voted to air condition the church with twenty-six voting no. A committee was appointed to raise the necessary funds for this. Betty Craven, Tom Dawson, and Glaster Jones were given this responsibility.

Sixteen people were baptized on August 6, 1978. They were Kim Stratton, Annette Everhart, Jennifer Alcon, Denise Bullard, Bonnie Smith, John and Dorothy Allred, Carrie Tucker, Kristy Bodenheimer, Bonnie Bodenheimer, Dianne Sulger, Cherrie Hedgecock, Kirk Clinard, Amy and Lori Hutchens, and Wayne Stratton, Jr.

A called conference on September 6, 1978, allowed the church to elect a new group of deacons. Staley Bodenheimer, Bobby Canada, Lee Davis, Sanford Hayworth, Laurence Todd, Jr., and Charles Jordan were elected. All had previously served except Charles, who was ordained on October 15. Tom Dawson was chosen as trustee.

The mission organizations were strong and very active. The RA group was led by Linda Cantrell, Don Livengood, Charles Jordan, Wayne Bullard, and perhaps others. The deacons recommended to the church that camping equipment be purchased at a cost of $825. This was to serve for the mission groups of both boys and girls. The church, always supportive of their youth, accepted this recommendation.

Evva Spurgeon who was serving as church secretary part-time informed the church of a calendar being prepared that would include the anniversaries and birthday of each person. Time and again, we see first things taking place in the church and many of these "firsts" are still being carried out in the church, including the birthday and anniversary calendars.

Rev. Hugh Biggers, pastor of Liberty Baptist Church, Thomasville was the revival speaker for the April 1979 revival. Rev. and Mrs. George Dowd had moved to the community from Martin, Georgia. They united with the church in absentia because he was serving as interim pastor in Archdale and not able to be present.

It was mentioned earlier about the windows being broken at the Primitive Baptist Church. We include here the letter sent to Abbotts Creek since it had been so rare to have any connections. "Dear Rev. Cantrell, The members of Abbotts Creek Primitive Baptist Church would like to thank you for your quick action in stopping the vandals who were wrecking our church. We feel the Lord blessed us to have a kind and helpful friend like you. We pray He will be with you and bless you always." Signed, the members of Abbotts Creek Primitive Church.

Several matters were considered during the April conference. The clerk was given the support of the church to send church letters for those who had joined another church without the church vote. Any request in question would be brought to the church for discussion. With the Southern Baptist Convention stressing bold missions, the church responded by voting to support another missionary at the cost of $2,000 per year. This continued for some period of time. One missionary couple the church supported resigned due to some health reasons. A second couple retired after a few years of support. A vote was taken to send $500 to the Christian Action League to help in the fight against liquor by the drink in North Carolina.

A community event that perhaps would never make church minutes was a beautiful sight to see. Willie Paul Hedgecock had been ill and unable to get his farm work started. On a Saturday morning, several GAs and their leaders were heading to a special meeting in Thomasville. Men and women of the church were cleaning the yard and church facilities. While this was going on, fifteen or sixteen tractors were plowing the field for Mr. Hedgecock, getting his land ready for his tobacco and other crops. This was a community-wide project that probably got started with the area farmers gathering around the community store.

The April 22, 1979, *The Tie* informed the church the air conditioning units had been installed and were ready for use.

The speaker for the May Memorial Day service was Kenneth Edwards, a former member. Mr. Edwards had found it necessary to retire because of his disability. He had informed the pastor and the church of his call to preach. He expressed appreciation for the support he and his wife had felt while they lived here and were part of the church family. The next week's newsletter stated, "He did a commendable job as our afternoon speaker."

The church had been giving the pastor two weeks of vacation each year. In July 1979, motion was made to add an additional week. This was passed with an amendment added, "To include present pastor only."

Earlier in this history, we had mentioned Jerome Hayworth joining the church though unable to attend. In July of 1979, Mrs. Minnie Smith was presented for membership. She had attended the church for years having membership elsewhere. In a wheelchair now, she was unable to be baptized and was accepted by the church for membership.

Danny Gann was ordained as a deacon on August 12, 1979, replacing Sanford Hayworth who had died. A month later, new deacons were elected. They were Numa Everhart, Hugh Motsinger, Robert Palmer, John Sulger, and Ronald Young. Ronald was ordained on September 30. Roger Hedgecock was selected as trustee.

Wilson Hedgecock had served as church treasurer for twenty-six years. His wife, Ruth, had taken a major role assisting him during this tenure. On September 30, the church family surprised Mr. and Mrs. Hedgecock with flowers placed in the sanctuary in their honor and a special recognition during the morning hour of worship. They were presented an engraved tray in appreciation and in recognition of their faithful ministry. A fellowship meal was held at the Horneytown Fire Department in their honor. The couple asked to be relieved of their duty in this role. Hugh and Betty Jo Motsinger were elected to serve in this capacity.

Ruth and Wilson Hedgecock

A proposal was presented for the church to have a pictorial directory made. The church agreed to this. It was also recommended at this time that a building fund be established. Future church action would determine when and what type structure will be considered. It came before the church, "because the deacons see a need to establish a fund with this name."

The church participated in a World Mission Conference with five missionaries speaking on different nights. The congregation was always very receptive to missionary speakers and this time was no exception.

Abbott's Creek Primitive Baptist Church

The Seventies

Lee Hedgecock leads the way as the community farmers plow the field of Willie Paul Hedgecock.

CHAPTER SEVENTEEN

The Eighties

The first Sunday in January of 1980, Chris Motsinger united with the church. Mrs. Motsinger had previously been a member of a neighboring church. The first three months of the year, three others joined the church by letter and two by statement. Eighteen joined by baptism. The last Sunday evening in January, the congregation welcomed missionary Archie Jones from Chile as the speaker.

During the February conference, Deacon Chairman Don Livengood brought a two-part recommendation from the deacons in printed form. The first part of the motion was to employ an additional youth worker for the summer. The pay would be $75 per week plus mileage. The second part was to employ Chet Cantrell to be the youth worker. The church accepted this recommendation.

At the March conference, J. C. Alcon, chairman of the trustees, brought to the attention of the church the need to expand the seating capacity of the choir. This would require some renovation at a cost of $1,500-$1,600. After the motion and second, the church voted to accept this and moved ahead with the needed addition.

After consulting with a representative from the Baptist State Convention, the trustees came back to the church at the April conference with some suggested changes. These changes were accepted by the church and about $500 was added to the price of the needed renovation. As the conference continued, Steve Johnson had offered the church a gift of an organ. The church accepted this gift with the understanding that the cost for installation would be about $300. The trustees added another recommendation: that we install a fiberglass lining in the present baptismal pool at a cost of $2,000. This recommendation was accepted.

The youth of the church stayed busy with weekly meetings. Added to their regular activities, the church rented the gym at Ledford Middle School for Saturday night events—mainly basketball for different ages.

A recommendation came from the deacons that we pay the Charles Wiggs family $2,000 for a five-month period when they would be in North Carolina for Mrs. Wiggs to complete her college work. It seems this stay would have been longer than the mission board would have allowed as far as support was concerned. By this time, the church felt the Wiggs family was a vital part of Abbotts Creek. The church received an invitation to attend her graduation exercises on August 2, 1980, at Campbell College.

The church had included in the budget funds to assist the Wiggs daughter, Debbie, with spending money while she was a student at Wake Forest. The church did the same for the other two daughters, Lisa and Toni, as they became college age. Debbie's thank you note in *The Tie* in August of 1980, pictures so clearly the heart of the people of Abbotts Creek. It is included here.

> Dear Abbotts Creek Church,
>
> The longer I am away from my childhood home in Korea, the more my heart feels at home in America. Likewise, the more I visit and worship in your church, the more a part of it I feel. My family has been closely associated with your church for fifteen years, but not until I began attending while I've been at Wake Forest have the dear members of this fellowship become dear to me. Sincerely, you express God's love in your words and actions, and in the providing of a monetary gift which most certainly eases the great financial weight of tuition costs and room and board. I know that God's Spirit is working in your fellowship because of the manner in which you give this gift. Truly, only His Spirit can teach us about and provide us with this kind of selfless giving.
>
> I count it a privilege to be a part of Abbotts Creek. Our Lord is honored by the love in action in your church; truly this action is the expression of the love which He shares with you.

As the conference continued, the trustees' recommended new carpets be installed in the sanctuary at the cost of $1,800. Two more recommendations were presented and accepted by the church: construction of a backstop at the softball field at a cost of $1,034 and sealer to be applied on the tennis court, at a cost of $650.

In April, Rev. George Williamson was the visiting minister for the revival service. Rev. Williamson, a retired minister, had been called to the First Baptist Church in Thomasville as interim pastor but later accepted the request of the church to become pastor. During the revival service, ten persons were received as candidates for baptism and two by letter.

Several matters were handled at the July 1980 conference. The cost for a grave plot in the cemetery was raised from $250 to $750. The church voted to send the pastor's wife, Linda, to a minister's wives retreat at Camp Caraway for three days at the end of the month. At the request of Hillcrest Baptist Church, Abbotts Creek voted to send representatives to their homecoming the first Sunday in August. Those sent were Robert Palmer, Danny Gann, Art Hedgecock, and Numa Everhart.

Deacon election in September resulted in the following being selected: Kay Green, David Mendenhall, Wayne Bullard, Dwight Moore, and the father-son combination of James and Jamie Williams. Jamie and David were ordained on October 26. Roxie Beeson was elected as a trustee. She was the first female to serve as a trustee.

The church voted in October to purchase new choir robes. Dwight Moore presented this to the church explaining the robes would cost $53.11 each and choir members would purchase their own stoles at $10.20 each. The motion was amended by Kara Dean to let the church purchase the stoles also. The amendment was passed as did the motion. The church also voted to purchase fifty-one metal chairs for use in the fellowship hall "when we have the funds."

Many events and activities in the church were never discussed or voted on in the church conferences, therefore, would not be in the minutes that have been used for this history. The church's weekly newsletter, *The Tie*, added numerous other events in the life of the church. During the year, the Pioneer RA Chapter was recognized by the Brotherhood Department of the state convention for being an honor chapter, the highest honor given to a chapter. Linda Cantrell, Don Livengood, Steve Wallace, and Charles Jordan were leaders of this group. In April of that year, Dwight Moore was congratulated for having taken care of the heating of the water for baptisms during the past twenty years. During this time, more than two hundred and fifty people had been baptized. This covered the span of ministry by Joe Coltrane, Charles Tanner, and five years of the present pastor.

Cindy Cook was congratulated in the church's newsletter in late June of the year for having competed in the Miss North Carolina contest. She was named fourth runner up in the event.

The Eighties

Pew cushions had been discussed by many in the congregation. During the first conference of 1981, a recommendation came from the deacons for this to be decided by a vote of the church. The recommended stipulations stated first, if the church voted to do this, that it include starting a fund to pay for the pew covers. Secondly, cushions were not to be attached to the pew for fear of damage. Third, a committee was to be appointed to oversee choosing the color of the cushions, raising funds, and selecting a contractor. Fourth, none of this was to be done until sufficient funds had been secured. Later in the year, at the October conference, a decision was made that the trustees would serve as the committee for oversight.

The church had a strong youth program and many outstanding youth. For the summer of 1981, the deacons recommended that Tony Peele be employed as summer youth worker. The church accepted this recommendation. Articles in *The Tie* reminded the church family of the number of youth being assigned summer work in churches or summer camps. Jerry Earnhardt and Tebin McDowell were assigned to work as counselors at Camp Caraway, the state RA Camp. Kirk Stanley's assignment was working in the camp canteen. Guy Hutchinson would work as a counselor-in-training. David Cantrell had been selected to be youth worker in the Aulander Baptist Church near Ahoskie, North Carolina. Chet Cantrell's assignment was First Baptist Church, Wadesboro. In support of these young men, the church allowed each of them to bring the evening messages on Sunday night for part of the summer. Also, during the summer, two students from Barbados Baptist College visited the church. They were Osbert James from Grenada and a young lady whose first name was Dan from Trinidad. They were working at the summer camps for RAs and GAs.

When the new proposed budget was presented, a motion was made that we send six and one half percent of our cooperative giving to Wake Forest University. The college was no longer included in the dispensing of funds through the North Carolina Baptist State Convention. This was the second year for the church to include this and it had to be voted on each year according to a previous church vote. This continued for several years.

Deacons elected at the September conference were Don Livengood, Mike Beavers, Art Hedgecock, Kenny Moore, and George Sechrest. Laura Clinard was chosen to serve as trustee.

On the third Sunday in May, during the lunch at the picnic shelter, there was more talk about a cookbook with favorite recipes from the excellent cooks of the church. This idea seemed to spread quickly and recipes were collected. A special effort was made to include recipes for diabetics.

Picnic Shelter

Through the work of Evva Spurgeon and Pansy Moore with help from her husband, Dwight, and the pastor, the idea became reality. The church's first cookbook was published in 1981.

A scholarship fund was established by vote of the church on January 6, 1982, for persons entering a church-related vocation. This was to be done with $1,500 that had been given in memory of Ida Hammer (August 1892—July 1980) by her daughters. Their request was for the funds to be used for something of a permanent nature. A committee was to establish guidelines and oversee this matter.

Roger Hedgecock brought a recommendation from the trustees that included clearing additional land in the cemetery area for grave use. The second matter concerned the guttering for the church. The cost would be in the $1,500 to $1,800 range. Both recommendations were accepted by the church.

A conference was called in February of 1982 to discuss the purchase of choir chairs at the same time cushions for the pews were purchased. The pew cushion fund had a surplus of funds which could be used for the chair project. The church accepted the recommendation, which came from the trustees. The hope was that this work could be done before the third Sunday in May, and it was completed prior to that date.

At the April conference, the deacons brought a recommendation to the church to send the pastor on an evangelistic mission trip to Southern Chile. Missionaries Bill and Connie Andrews along with Archie and Caroline Jones had requested a team of 15 to 18 ministers from North Carolina to assist them in revival services in several churches in their district of work. This was to be in October of 1982. The cost would be about $2,000. The church accepted this recommendation. The pastor preached in a small church in a very poor village in Paillaco. Robert Bates, a missionary in Chile from North Carolina, was the interpreter. The streets were dirt with no parking spaces at the church. None were needed since no one had automobiles. The pastor of the church had no formal education and learned to read by reading the Bible. Missionaries from all over Chile came to assist the North Carolina pastors as interpreters. The church had no heat and no hymnals. The music was written on a large writing tablet and the pages were turned as needed. Guitars were used but the people sang with excitement. The pastor and one layman taught the adult Sunday School class and together purchased a book to use. During the week, 14 persons became Christians including the adult step-son of the pastor. The Foreign Mission Board owned the property and had a parsonage next door. With the seasons reversed, families had gardens started and farmers were plowing their grounds for the planting season. Oxen were used for some of the farming. The entire effort resulted in more than 600 professions of faith. The missionaries felt the effort gave the churches a boost of more than a dozen years. Money for the pastor to go on this mission trip came from every group in the church including: the mission groups, the Baptist Men, and the softball team, and some money was used that had been left in a fund for the Saturday night activities of some years earlier. That group, all adults by now, agreed to use the remaining money in their fund to assist the pastor with this trip.

About this time the Liberty Baptist Association was involved in partnership with St. Albans, West Virginia. The Baptist men of Abbotts Creek voted to take the lead in this effort. Several members of Abbotts Creek traveled to St. Albans giving their time to help build the church. This was part of a statewide effort between the North Carolina Baptist State Convention and our counterpart in West Virginia. Numerous churches in the Liberty Baptist Association sent money or work teams thus saving the new church thousands of dollars.

For one mission trip for Vacation Bible School and prospect visitation, 29 youth and adults went to St. Albans. The youth had prepared for this effort but had not forgotten to have some fun with it. Some of them had prepared a sign to attach to the rear of the loaded fifteen-passenger van without the adults leaders being aware of it. The sign read, "Just Married."

HISTORY, HERITAGE, AND MEMORIES

While this partnership was taking place, Chris Cantrell and Jeff Hutcherson went with another church to Capon Bridge, West Virginia. James Williams carried a group to Louisburg, West Virginia, working on a church there. Months later, when these churches were ready for use, letters came with invitations to be present. Several from the church went to be a part of such celebrations. In the summer of 1982, the youth from Abbotts Creek worked in churches or camps at various places. Guy Hutcherson went to Bermuda on a work trip. Donna Rudd and Karen Robarge were counselors at Camp Munda Vista. Tony Peele and Chris Cantrell worked at Camp Caraway. Chet Cantrell worked with migrants in Eastern Maryland.

The pastor was not the first to go on a mission trip. J. C. Alcon was invited to be a part of a construction team going to Tok, Alaska. J. C., an electrician, had the skill to assist and was a part of a group forming a mission team from a church in Greensboro.

One hundred and fifty years had passed since the group moved across the road and the name "missionary" was attached to the church's name. Plans had been made in advance and the church had a chance to celebrate again. Dr. Keith Parks, president of the Southern Baptist Convention's Foreign Mission Board (now International Mission Board), was the guest speaker for

Rev. Cantrell is greeted by Pat Dawson, while Dr. Keith Parks, president of the Foreign Mission Board (now International Mission Board), is waiting to be greeted by Jamie Hartsook, May 23, 1982.

THE EIGHTIES

the May 23 morning service. As one would expect, the church was challenged in her mission effort.

On July 4, Sunday School was conducted like the olden days. Men gathered in one class with the females in a separate class for adults. People were encouraged to dress as nearly as possible as had been the custom years earlier. Dwight Moore taught the men and Roxie Beeson taught the women. Rick Motsinger taught the youth while Vicki Halker taught grades one through six. Dr. Cecil Ray, the general secretary of the North Carolina Baptist State Convention, was the speaker for the eleven o'clock service. Lunch was served covered-dish style. An afternoon service consisted of a drama that was been written by the pastor. The pastor's wife directed the drama, depicting the beginning of the church in 1756, and the factors that led to the division in 1832. A covered wagon pulled by two horses was available for those who wished to take an afternoon ride.

Dr. Cecil Ray, general secretary/treasurer of the North Carolina Baptist State Convention, is seen here with Rev. Cantrell on July 4, 1982.

Three days later, participants at the church conference, discussed paving the church parking lot. An opinion poll had been taken and showed that it was favored two to one. Much discussion took place before a vote was taken. Thirty-five voted to pave the parking lot and twenty-six voted against that motion. The trustees were to oversee the work. The church was beginning to lose some of its rural appearance.

New deacons elected in September were Laurence, Todd, Jr., Michael Christian, Charles Jordan, Harry Craven, and Rodney Rickard. Rick Motsinger was the newly-elected trustee.

Before students could enter seminary or divinity school, the church had to give approval. At the October 6 conference, the deacons recommended that the church give approval for David and Chet Cantrell to attend seminary for the 1983 term. David was entering Harvard Divinity School and Chet was to enroll at Southeastern Seminary.

At the Baptist State Convention in November, Molly Millis Hedgecock was elected as a trustee for Mars Hill College. This was another first for Abbotts Creek, having a member as a trustee of one of our Baptist colleges.

Abbotts Creek Church never backed off from helping youth. Earlier in our research, we have noted help for two ministers in school, plus their pastor. There was some help for Beth Hayworth in college and in the Mission Training School as well. In December of 1982, another investment was made. Chet Cantrell was one of nine young college students invited by the Brotherhood Department of North Carolina to go to the Island of Barbados to work on a building at Barbados Baptist College, owned and operated by the Southern Baptist Foreign Mission Board. The church accepted the deacons' recommendation and paid for him to go. The work actually consisted of making what had been a goat barn into living space for a couple who were about to attend college there. Later, the couple who lived there first, Wayne and Shanti Rowbottom and their son, Levi counted Abbotts Creek their home away from home while he was attending Wingate University and Southeastern Seminary. Wayne was later ordained at Abbotts Creek Church. Barbados Baptist College trained young ministers from many of the Caribbean Islands to go back to their island nation and preach.

Mention had been made of the involvement of the church family in the construction of a Baptist church at St. Albans, West Virginia. Liberty Baptist Association's partnership with the church could not stop at this point. The church needed $5,000 to get the building ready for use. The association agreed to raise the money but the church needed it immediately. J. C. Alcon, representing the Baptist Men of Abbotts Creek, made a motion that we allow the association to borrow the needed amount from our Memorial (burial) Association. This motion passed and the money was sent. In a short time, the other churches collected their share of the money and the Baptist men were able to repay the funds to the Memorial Association with interest. The dedication service for Riverwood Baptist Church in St. Albans was the first Sunday in May of 1983.

In March of 1983, the church voted to assist J. C. Alcon with a mission trip to Costa Rica to work on a church building. With limited time and the great need, the team of workers stayed on the job for long hours in the day.

In the April conference, Roger Hedgecock, chairman of the trustees, informed the church that the cost for paving the parking lot, removing stumps, doing the brick work, and grading and landscaping would be around $50,000.

Several from the church had been helping with Vacation Bible School at our neighboring church, Clifton Grove, for the past few years. However, in

The Eighties

June of 1983, the children and workers from Clifton Grove were invited to be a part of the Bible school at Abbotts Creek. Fourteen children and one worker, Margaret Traynham, attended and for the first time, the church had an integrated Bible School. This plan continued for a few years until Clifton Grove selected another pastor who wanted the church people to carry out their own school.

Chris Cantrell had been selected to serve as a page at the North Carolina Baptist State Convention meeting, in November of 1982. He was chosen as one of ten Royal Ambassadors from the churches of the Southern Baptist Convention to serve at the June 1983 convention meeting in Pittsburg, Pa. This was another first for the church.

The deacons announced July 6, 1983, that "We hold a special called conference for the purpose of voting if we should enter into a building program. Motion made and carried.

This conference concluded the term of Pearl Hayworth, as church clerk. She had served for the past thirteen years."

The minutes of the next conference were kept by the newly-elected clerk, Kathy Green. There were eighty-five families of the church represented at this conference. The minutes of the called conference recorded this: "Chairman of the deacons, Kay Green, brings a recommendation from the deacons that we enter into a building program. A further recommendation is, a planning committee for the church be appointed. An architect be secured and work with this committee to project what we will propose to build. This would be brought back for church vote at a preannounced time. Motion brought by Wayne Bullard and seconded by Rodney Rickard. James Williams was named chairman of the planning committee." A motion was made to vote by secret ballot but this motion did not pass. The vote was by show of hands and carried.

The church newsletter in August carried information about the church's softball team. The world tournament was to be held in Cincinnati, Ohio, on Labor Day weekend. The team had qualified to enter. The team was made up of regular attendees of the church. It was never a "come one Sunday a month" to be eligible to play. This team coached by C. R. Motsinger and Bobby Canada had two deacons and one trustee in addition to other elected workers in the church as players.

Lee Roy Kearns has relayed information to us about its beginning. He and Monroe Beeson organized the team in 1959. Over the years, the church team was always strong and very competitive. C. R. Motsinger has been manager of the team since 1961. In 1993, the team playing in class D, won the North Carolina USSSA State Championship. In 2000, the team played in class A and earned the world USSSA title.

The youth activities attracted a large number of church youth plus others from the larger community. One attraction was called "Fifth Quarter" which was held at the church after the home football games of our local high schools.

The church elected new deacons in September. They were J. C. Alcon and son, Carl, Bob Best, Lee Davis, H. S. Motsinger, John Sulger, and Ronnie Young. This was the first time seven had been elected bringing the total to eighteen. Staley Bodenheimer was chosen as trustee. Bob Best and Carl Alcon were ordained on October 16, 1983.

Pearl Hayworth is seen here with her husband, William.

After the conference minutes were recorded, the clerk adds this: "Chet Cantrell, a student at Southeastern Seminary, has been called as pastor of Lick Creek Baptist Church."

Lick Creek was a part of the Liberty Baptist Association and located in the southern part of Davidson County. The deacons recommended that Chet be ordained by the church. This service took place on January 1, 1984. Kathy Green, church clerk, presented the Bible to Chet, on behalf of the church.

On the last Sunday in January, the visiting speaker for the morning was Missionary Wayne Dunn from Barbados Baptist College, on the Island of Barbados. He gave special thanks for the church sending workers there to do building and repairs that the college did not have funds to do. In addition to the workers who had been there, the deacons of the church, present and former, had taken on a project of paying the tuition for one who could not afford it. The student helped was Pam Scheem. When Rodney Rickard was there working, he attended Pam's home church on Sunday. They had no building. The congregation met under a large tree.

A recommendation was brought to the church by John Sulger on behalf of the nominating committee. The planning committee for the new construction would include Kelly Clinard, Edith Bodenheimer, Kay Green, Daphne Motsinger, Becky Sink, Laurence Todd, and the pastor. Also on the committee were the chairmen of deacons, Kenny Moore, and the chairman of the trustees, Roger Hedgecock. This recommendation included whomever the deacons and trustees had as chairperson. As the committee began meeting, Kelly Clinard was elected as chairman with Becky Sink serving as secretary.

Revival services were held in March and were led by Rev. Franklin Myers, pastor of Sabbath Home Baptist Church at Holden Beach, N.C.

C. R. Motsinger has been manager of the men's softball team since 1961. He is seen here as third base coach. Mike Motsinger is the runner on third base.

A recommendation came from the deacons to the church in April to pay the plane expense for J. C. Alcon to go on a mission trip to Columbia, South America. Because of his knowledge of electrical work, J. C. was needed for a particular project and traveled with a group he had worked with prior to this trip.

During the summer of 1984, Laurence Todd, III, served on the staff at the North Carolina Assembly at Fort Caswell. He was the first youth from Abbotts Creek to serve at the Baptist assembly. Also during the summer, the church's newsletter offered congratulations to Cindy Cook for entering the Miss North Carolina competition and being selected as third runner up.

The church continued to offer some help to Toni Wiggs with extra funds for her college education. The Abbotts Creek congregation was always looking for ways to help where help seemed to be needed. In the spring of this year, heavy storms did much damage in the eastern part of the state. The church voted to send $1,000 to Red Springs Baptist Church to assist some families whose homes had been damaged or destroyed. Others had donated also and by the time the Red Springs pastor wrote a thank-you note to the church, the amount had exceeded $2,000.

The interest of the church in missions and mission trips continued to increase. The deacons recommended to the church that we put $5,200 in the 1984-85 budget for the purpose of helping those who could and were willing to represent the church on mission trips. This had been discussed in the deacon's meeting and the pastor had challenged the church to do this in the preceding Sunday's sermon. The committee to care for this would be the pastor, and directors of WMU and the Baptist Men. The church approved this plan.

Deacons elected in September 1984 were Staley Bodenheimer, Wayne Bullard, Kay Green, David Mendenhall, Dwight Moore, and Robert Palmer. Rodney Rickard was elected to serve as trustee.

Evva Spurgeon had served as part-time church secretary since October of 1980. She was the first to do most of the work at the church. The deacons recommended to the church that she be allowed to attend the North Carolina Southern Baptist Secretaries Seminar at Camp Caraway with the church paying her expenses.

The last newsletter of the year had a reminder that Michael Gann was in Costa Rica on a mission work trip with other RA Pioneers from North Carolina.

In January of 1985, the deacons brought to the attention of the church the desire of the Foreign Mission Board to again assist Southern Chile in an area-wide revival. The pastor had been invited to return as one of the preachers. The church voted to approve this. For this assignment, the pastor went to the La Union Baptist Church. This church was in the small town of La Union and had just finished a new building. The La Union church was one of the few churches in all of Southern Chile with a seminary-trained pastor. He had just finished seminary and had been pastor only a few weeks. Southern Baptist missionaries made up the faculty at the seminary. The church had been without a pastor for eleven years. Laymen had alternated preaching at the services. An impressive fact about this church was while without a pastor, they had established five missions. The result of this revival effort was similar to previous one mentioned. The work of Chilean Baptists had been greatly enhanced.

The missionary couple whom the church had sponsored in Israel was no longer with the Foreign Mission Board, so the church chose Bobby and Peggy Compton as the new missionary couple to support. Bobby was from North Carolina and Peggy was from South Carolina. J. C. Alcon and Michael Gann had met them while on the earlier-mentioned mission trip to Costa Rica.

North Carolina Baptists had entered a partnership with the country of Togo, West Africa. The association had voted to send Leonard Rollins, our director of missions, to preach. The church voted to support this with $100.

Rev. Rollins was the first minister to go with this project. Gene Smith from the Reeds Baptist Church of the Liberty Association accompanied him. Other persons had gone but their purpose had been to dig wells and assist in building a bridge over a stream that separated the country during the raining season.

At the same conference, the church voted to be a part of a world mission conference planned for the Liberty Association. This conference would bring different missionaries to the church enabling the congregation to learn about missions in various parts of the world.

With the growing interest in mission trips, the pastor had inquired of the Foreign Mission Board about possibilities. The missionaries from the Island country of Grenada needed five teams of four each to assist with Vacation Bible School in four churches and one mission on the island. The pastor contacted the mission board asking for one of these churches but was asked by the coordinator of the project to take the challenge of getting teams for all five needs. With this in mind, the deacons recommended to the church that a fund be established to help care for this since it would be more than our budgeted funds. This motion carried.

There seemed to be great interest in this effort. Some questioned the church giving money for people to "go on vacation." However, volunteers were willing to go and the money came in to support the effort. The trip was planned for August. The scheduled time for travel had been such that no one could say it was vacation. Unable to get a direct flight, the group left on Friday flying to Barbados where they spent the night at Barbados Baptist College. This was the same college where members of Abbotts Creek had been and worked. Chet Cantrell went first, and then Rodney Rickard and Chris Cantrell had been on work projects as well. James Williams, Rodney, and his son, Jeremy, made up yet another team working at the college. Missionary Wayne Dunn, who had cared for the work teams earlier, took care of all plans for the traveling mission group that evening. After a short night of sleep, the group left Barbados, early on Saturday morning, flying on to Grenada. After settling in their motel, the group met with the local pastors and missionaries. Osbert James, who had worked at Camp Caraway and visited Abbotts Creek, was one of the pastors.

Others teams were to go later but with this being the first for the church, we will mention the team members. There were five teams of four persons. Wayne and Georgette Bullard along with Charles and Debbie Goad were assigned to work in Emmanuel Baptist Church. The pastor along with Carrie Tucker, Betty Williams, and Vicki Halker worked at Grand Anse Baptist

Church. Tammy Livengood and Lorie Hedgecock joined Bessie Blackwell from Center Hill Baptist Church in Lexington and Barbara Foster from Summerville Baptist Church in Denton working at Grand Backlet Baptist Church. David Clemmens, Keith Curlee were paired with Carl and Sonya Alcon to work at the mission in a community called Grand Roy. They worked with missionaries Mike and Robin Eberhardt. Cheryl Rickard and Evva Spurgeon worked with Patty Shoener from Rich Fork Baptist Church and Doris Yates from Wallburg Baptist Church at the St. George's Baptist Church where Rev. Osbert James was the pastor. With extra volunteers, Daphne Motsinger, Matthew Dunn, Debra Sulger, and Chris Cantrell went to the Island of Jamaica for Vacation Bible School. Debbie Thomas, from Wallburg Baptist Church, was a part of their team. The missionaries from Jamaica and Grenada reported that each team did an excellent job. One purpose of such an effort was to train the local leaders how to do their own VBS which they did the next year. The group at Grand Roy finished their Bible School on Friday night. The team left early Saturday for their return home with the people saying "you did not even have time to see our beautiful island," which was true. Trips after this were planned to avoid such a tight schedule allowing some time to see some of the sights and experience bits of the local customs.

The spring brought much recognition to the youth of the church. Their accomplishments were listed in the church newsletter from week to week. Beth Cantrell was recognized for serving as a page in the North Carolina General Assembly for one week. Darren Spurgeon was selected to serve on the State RA executive committee joining Michael Gann who was beginning his second year of serving. Brad Kearns was a state winner for his paper and project with horses and was awarded a scholarship of $1,000 for college and a chance to go to the national convention. The shooting team at Ledford High School had won the state championship in Hunters Safety Shooting Tournament. Brian Motsinger and Ken Fowler from the church were members of this team. Annette Everhart was declared the recipient of a $500 scholarship to attend Davidson County Community College. Carrie Tucker was elected as president of the student body at Ledford High School. Several of the youth had achieved honors for their athletic achievements at the school.

As the summer approached, Toni Wiggs, a student at Wake Forest, gave the church an opportunity to assist her in financing a mission trip to the Philippines for part of the summer. The church had responded with some helpful assistance.

The church newsletter recognized Rayford and Dorothy Hayes who were able to see Pete Rose break Ty Cobb's record for the most hits in baseball history, while visiting their son in Ohio.

The RAs planned a mission trip to Union Baptist Church near Louisville, West Virginia. James Williams guided the youth and adults in carrying out building projects. The group consisted of Timmy and Darren Spurgeon, Sonni Wheeler, Wayne Stratton, Don, Marty and Tammy Livengood, Linda Cantrell, Danny, Mary, Lee, Michael and Sharron Gann, Mike Shillinglaw, Steve Wallace, Marcus Tucker, and Charles Goad.

Earlier in the spring, The Reverend John Pace, pastor of Reeds Baptist Church, had preached revival services for the church. Rev. Robert Clegg, a building consultant for the Baptist State Convention, had discussed a "Together We Build" program with the church about financing a building program.

A conference was called on July 14, 1985, to vote on a recommendation from the planning committee. Chairman Kelly Clinard brought the recommendation that we enter the second phase of our building efforts. It was further recommended that we establish a finance committee for raising funds for the intended construction. Architect Vernon Lewis of Burlington was introduced to the congregation and explained the drawings. Kelly reported the architectural estimate was $574,660 plus $86,494 for the parking lot. The total estimate was $661,154. This recommendation passed by a majority standing vote. At the next conference, Kenny Moore was elected as chairman of the fund raising committee and the name of the planning committee was changed to building committee.

New deacons elected in September were Kenny Moore, Charles Goad, Kelly Clinard, Don Livengood, and George Sechrest. Eddie Hilton was chosen as trustee.

David Clemmens, for several years the church's music and youth director, had accepted a call to South Elm Street Baptist Church in Greensboro. He and his wife Debbie moved their church letter in September. During his tenure, the youth program at Abbotts Creek had been strong. Retreats, mission trips, and weekly meetings had led to a stable, strong, and active program, and ministry for the youth.

While the church was heavily involved with plans for additional space, nothing else seemed to be lagging. The extension workers made sure the homebound were not being neglected by making regular visits. Sunday School attendance was good and the giving pattern of the congregation was strong. New carpets were being laid at the parsonage.

The October conference reported Kenny Moore bringing a recommendation for the church to enter the "Challenge to Build" program. He explained the cost to the church, four dollars per resident family plus cost for travel and needs of the consultant, and the needed printed material. The church agreed by vote to pay for a banquet in March that had been recommended by leaders experienced in working with building projects. Many questioned the expense of a banquet when the money was needed for building. Yet all seemed to leave the banquet with the feeling it had been the right thing to do and was a good kick off for raising the needed cost. It was agreed at a later conference that the cost of the above amounting to $6,000 be paid out of the general fund.

Job descriptions had been recommended by the appropriate committee for both youth and music directors. This was brought by Carl Alcon, chairman of the search committee, for both positions.

The committee recommended Ben Rowe to become the church's minister of youth and education. The vote held on February 16, 1986, concluded with 192 in favor, and 17 voting no. He was to be part-time until his graduation from seminary in May. Ben was ordained by his home church, West Hickory Baptist Church, shortly after his graduation.

A couple of months later, the church learned about a student from Nigeria who had graduated from seminary but did not have funds to return to his country to preach. The church voted to pay the $700 plane fare. The church heard from him later with a thank you note and update. He was back home teaching young ministers in seminary.

With overwhelming financial needs facing the church, the deacons still recommended that $1,000 be sent to Rich Fork Baptist Church. Their church facilities had been destroyed by fire. The Abbotts Creek congregation supported this 100 percent.

The church newsletter gives us numerous other decisions and activities. The children's sermon was added as a part of the morning worship service. The children remained in the congregation until the children's story and then went to children's church. Ann Joyce, from High Point and a recent graduate of Wingate College (now University) with a major in music, was called as interim minister of music. Michael Gann served in June, 1986 as a page at the Southern Baptist Convention in Atlanta.

Other things were taking place involving the church family. The pastor along with Matthew Dunn and Wayne Bullard made a trip to Grenada helping with evangelistic visitation and revival preaching. Shawn Pope traveled to Seattle, Washington, for a mission trip. Chris Cantrell served on the staff at Caswell for the summer. The Baptist Men of the church sponsored a work trip to Caswell helping to prepare the grounds for the summer camps. James Crocker of Boiling Springs, S.C. assisted in revival services in March.

The church had led out in bringing Osbert and Margaret James from Grenada allowing him to attend Wingate College (now University). The couple was scheduled to arrive in the summer of 1987. The 'Challenge To Build" program was getting off the ground with Charles Davis serving as chairman of the promotion committee. Those assisting him with getting materials ready and mailed were Vicki Hilton, Rick Motsinger, Donnie and Beth Welborne, Gene Craven, Patty Spurgeon, Mary Gann, Tammy and Marty Livengood, and Diane Sulger.

The youth had spent a weekend at Ridgecrest and the report was described as, "this will probably be the most exciting time some of our youth will ever experience."

A letter from missionaries Charles and Bonnie Wiggs, serving in Korea, reminded the congregation of the church's support for them twenty-one of their twenty-six years in Korea. They kept us informed about their daughters whom the church had assisted while they were students at Wake Forest. Debbie was serving as a missionary journeyman in Japan. Toni was working on the staff at Calvary Baptist Church, in Winston-Salem. Lisa was still a student at Wake Forest.

The pastor preached the associational sermon at the annual meeting and was elected moderator. He had served for two years, as vice moderator. He was the first person from Abbotts Creek to serve as moderator since lay-

The children's sermon became a vital part of the worship service.

man Joseph Spurgeon had served back in 1854. The last pastor at Abbotts Creek to deliver the associational sermon was W. H. Walton, in 1961.

Deacons elected in the fall of 1986 were George Dowd, Ricky Embler, Numa Everhart, Charles Jordan, Laurence Todd, James Williams, and Will Wright. Matthew Dunn was elected trustee.

Carl Alcon from the search committee brought a recommendation before the church that Ann Joyce, presently serving as interim, be named minister of music for the church. This recommendation passed by a 68-11 vote.

The year 1986 ended with Darren Spurgeon and Wayne Stratton serving in Trujillo, Peru, South America for a two-week work trip. They were part of a team composed of older RAs from churches across the state.

The ministry of the church never seemed to slow even with the building demands and the heavy financial challenge. A youth team from Mars Hill College led in a weekend youth revival. Rev. Ron Wilkerson, pastor of East Grimes Street Baptist Church in High Point, spoke for the Home Mission emphasis in March. He was the first African-American to preach in the church.

In March of 1987, the deacons received a letter from Rev. Amrit Bridgetat, chairman of the Trinidad and Tobago Baptist Association, asking the church to ordain Wayne Rowbottom. The deacons recommended that the church proceed with this request. Wayne and his wife, Shanti, and their son, Levi, had been in the church numerous times while attending college and seminary. They had made their home at Abbotts Creeks with the Wayne and Georgette Bullard family.

A month later, the deacons recommended that an estate check from Mattie Teague Mumford in the amount of $2,000 be divided with half going to the building fund and half going to the scholarship fund. The church accepted this motion.

The Annuity Board of the Southern Baptist Convention had devised a new and better retirement plan for ministers. The recommendation was made to the church by the deacons that we enter the new plan with the church paying 10 percent of the pastor's salary and the pastor paying five percent. This was to start at the beginning of 1988. The church accepted this recommendation at the July conference.

At the previous conference, the church voted to elect a personnel committee for the first time. The church voted on guidelines the committee was to follow. This took place in April of 1987.

Reports were always given during the church's business meetings. At

THE EIGHTIES

Missionaries Charles and Bonnie Wiggs pictured with their children, (l-r) Toni, Lisa, and Debbie.

the July conference, Mary Smith and Pansy Moore reported for the extension department. Forty eight visits had been made to the homebound. This was a normal number of visits each quarter. The elderly members who had served so well in the past were never forgotten. Mary and Pansy had been doing this for twenty years.

Darrel Bunce, pastor of Coggins Memorial Baptist Church, in Lexington, led the church in revival services in the spring. Brian Motsinger was selected as the Outstanding Senior, at Ledford High School graduation. His brother, Kevin, earned the same honor a couple of years later. Mary Smith was chosen as the WMU "Lady of the Year" and was honored at the associational WMU annual session. Dr. Leon Smith, vice president of the North Carolina Baptist State Convention, was guest speaker for the memorial services in May. A thank you note came from Lisa Wiggs for assisting her while she was at Wake Forest. She had graduated in June.

The youth continued to receive honors for their work in RAs, GAs, Acteens, and for their achievements in school. Brian Motsinger and Ken Fowler were members of the Hunting Safety Shooting team at Ledford High School, which won first place in state competition. Lee Shackleford and Kevin Motsinger were on the junior high shooting team. Osbert and

Margaret James arrived from Grenada on June 24. They remained at the pastor's home for a few days before going on to Wingate where the churches of the association had provided furniture for their apartment.

A funeral pall was given to the church in memory of Mildred Bodenheimer. This was given by her husband, Ivey, and their son, Tommy (and Bonnie Bodenheimer), and their daughter, Peggy (and her husband, Walter) King, and Philip Jones.

The Foreign Mission Board had given the church an opportunity to conduct Vacation Bible School on the tiny Island of Nevis in the Leeward Islands. Wayne and Georgette Bullard prepared and led the team. To get to Nevis, the team had to fly to the island country of St. Kitts and go by boat the short distance to the island where they would conduct Bible school and fall in love with new friends.

A group served on a work trip in New York. J. C. Alcon and Dean McGuire were needed electricians working on a church while Timmy Spurgeon, Kirby Johnson, and Michael Gann helped to construct the Metro Baptist Association's building.

Michael and Robin Eberhart, missionaries from Grenada, visited the church in August and led the congregation in worship. They spent some time thanking the church for sending help for their struggling churches in Grenada.

Another highlight of the year was the recognition of Tonia Wheeler for her achievements in Acteens. She was on the North Carolina Acteens Advisory Panel for 1987-88. With this honor came the opportunity to serve on the program held in Greensboro, North Carolina, for missionary appointment which took place in March of 1998. Tonia would also have the honor of serving as a page at the national WMU Convention and the Southern Baptist Convention in 1989 in Las Vegas, Nevada.

Beth Hayworth McClaren was congratulated in one of the October issues of the church newsletter. The country girl and pride of Abbotts Creek had been selected to serve as the executive director of the Women's Department, of the Baptist World Alliance.

An invitation from the Foreign Mission Board came asking the church to plan for and conduct a Vacation Bible School in Antigua, in July of 1988. The church had learned by now if there were willing workers, there were places for service. The Foreign Mission Board had learned of the willingness of the church family to participate and was giving requests before the church could ask for them.

A partnership of North Carolina Baptists and South America brought an

THE EIGHTIES

Tonia Wheeler Dyer is pictured (with her sister Kara) at the Southern Baptist Convention in Las Vegas, Nevada, where she served as page. She was a member of the Acteens' National Advisory.

invitation to the Liberty Baptist Association to send volunteers. Liberty Baptist assumed the partnership with the state of Sao Paulo with a particular invitation to the city of Sao Jose de Rio Preto. The pastor along with Matthew Dunn helped to make up an associational team.

Deacons elected in the fall of 1987 were Carl Alcon, Harry Craven, Lee Davis, Hugh Motsinger, John Sulger, and Ronnie Young. George Sechrest was the trustee named.

The resignation of Angie Dunn, as organist was announced at the September conference.

The building committee presented a recommendation for the church in January of 1988.

It was: 1. that we employ Vernon Lewis as architect, 2. that we employ Southern Design and Construction Consultants to manage construction, 3. to proceed with renovation and new construction already voted on by the church, 4. for construction to begin in the first half of 1988. Southern Design's guarantee to stay within one percent of the projected cost may have been a reason they were chosen to build the new facility. They were able to do this by meeting with the Building Committee each week. If material they planned to use was not suitable to the committee, changes were made but cost added to their estimate thus allowing them to stay with their estimate even with it changing every week.

Kenny Moore, of the Building Finance committee, announced we would need to borrow $600,000 and interest would be 10 percent. Monthly payments for twenty years would be $5,787.51. Further information was given saying that the past giving offerings were more than the required payments.

After much discussion, the church accepted the recommendation by a secret ballot vote of 220 positive with 15 voting no.

The church had been giving annual support through the Foreign Mission Board for Bob and Peggy Compton. They had now been assigned to work in the Richmond office for the board and were no longer in Costa Rica. The church voted to adopt and support Mike and Robin Eberhardt, missionaries to Grenada.

With the heavy demands the building emphasis was placing on the church, the congregation knew other things must go on as well. Trustees recommended at the January conference that the church purchase a new typewriter and a Canon copy machine at the cost of almost $5,000. At the same conference, the church voted to allow a one-time love offering for those planning on a Vacation Bible School mission trip during the summer.

Beth Echols

A February 28, 1989, called conference had to do with the specific details of borrowing money the church had previously agreed to borrow. Rather than a twenty-year loan, the monthly payment for a fifteen-year loan from Wachovia would be $6,449.56. Several questions were answered to the satisfaction of the congregation. By the April conference, the treasurer announced that bills were coming in and being paid from the building fund account. The first mentioned payment was made on April 1, 1989.

In the July conference, the chairman of the personnel committee recommended the secretary be paid for one week of vacation and for any time when she was away on official church business.

A called conference was held on August 18, 1988, with the deacons' recommendation that the pastor be allowed to accept an invitation to participate in an evangelistic crusade in Brazil, South America. The trip was scheduled for September 29 through October 10. There were six ministers from the Liberty Association going and several laymen including Matthew Dunn from Abbotts Creek. Such evangelistic efforts seemed to have been of great benefit to the work of Southern Baptist missionaries and this one was no exception. The missionaries always reported that with the new converts, there were possibilities for starting new churches. This crusade was held in Rio Preto, in the northern section of the state of Sao Paulo.

The congregation did not sit waiting to see what was to happen next. Wayne Bullard was chosen to serve on the General Board of the Baptist State Convention. A Back Yard Bible study took place for the children in the neighborhood at the home of Bobby and Dorothy Canada. In addition to Mrs. Canada, Pam Ford, Norma Dills, and Mary Smith assisted. Henrietta Wheeler and Kim Frank and some Acteens did the same in a housing development. Several news items came of interest to the congregation. Beth Hayworth McClaren had been ordained to the ministry by her church in McLean, Virginia. Margaret James began studies at Anson Community College. Tonia Wheeler was notified she had been chosen as one of the Acteens' Top Teens from across the Southern Baptist Convention.

In the spring graduations, the church had 23 graduating from the high schools and three from college. Saturday night recreation at Ledford Middle School gave the youth and children chances to play basketball and participate in other activities.

Vacation Bible School mission teams went to the Islands of Nevis, conducting two Bible schools there and one in Antigua. The three schools had a combined average attendance of 962 with 124 professions of faith.

The ground breaking for the new building took place on April 24. A scoop pan owned by Marion Bodenheimer was used by him and Staley Bodenheimer to remove the first bit of earth for the new facility. This pan had been used by the two helping their fathers when they were young boys as the basement under the old sanctuary was dug. Back when the basement was dug the first time, Clifton Stewart remembers the teams and scoop pans of C. H. Teague, Milton Teague, and Moses F. T. Teague were also used.

Wayne Rowbottom graduated from Southeastern Seminary. The church assisted him and his family as they returned to Trinidad for him to begin ministering as the only trained Baptist minister on the Island.

On September 14, 1988, Kathy Green completed her tenure as church clerk and Sharyn Craven assumed that role.

Hugh Motsinger, church treasurer, reported at the August 12, 1988, conference that grading of the parking lot had begun and funds previously in the "Parking Lot Fund" were now transferred to the construction account.

Church leaders from Abbotts Creek had been very influential in leading the association to bring Osbert James and his wife Margaret to Wingate

College (now University) in order for him to earn his college and later his seminary degree. The couple arrived on June 24, 1987. The WMU and Baptist Men of the churches in Liberty Association worked together to pay for them to return to their home in Grenada for Christmas vacation.

The Acteens of the church were making plans to attend the National Acteens Convention in Texas.

Evva Spurgeon resigned as church secretary, after serving the church almost eight years, to begin work at the Baptist Children's Homes of North Carolina. Her resignation created the need for a committee to find a new secretary. Numa Everhart, George Sechrest, Patty Spurgeon, Nancy Best, and Kathy Green were elected to carry out this responsibility. Patty Spurgeon reported she was unable to serve and was replaced on the committee by Sandy Jordan.

The intent of the church was to add new educational space and renovate the present sanctuary including the nursery area behind the sanctuary. Years earlier at a funeral, the church was filled to capacity, including the balcony. Those seated in the balcony heard some type of noise and from that time, the floor of the balcony seemed to sag. The renovation attempt was to lift the balcony by inserting strong beams from the basement. The county building codes required that any renovation above a certain cost involve the county inspector. As bidding estimates were sought for the renovation, the committee was told the damage was in the rafter area and beams underneath would not correct the problem. It was suggested by more than one inspector that the cheaper way would be to tear the building down and rebuild. The committee was not ready for this. An engineering firm from Greensboro was employed to give their recommendation without any information the committee had been given. Their recommendation was the same, citing the age of the building and the fact that in trying to correct the problem, the entire roof would have to be removed. Questions were raised about the strength of walls once that was done and they were left standing.

The members of the building committee were having a hard time dealing with this. By this time, the construction workers on the educational wing were going to the community store for snacks and talking saying they were going to have to tear down the church building. All sorts of rumors were spreading. The committee was having trouble digesting what they were facing. A very influential member, Joe Smith, asked a contractor friend to give his opinion. This friend agreed with the engineers which helped in-

THE EIGHTIES

Marion and Staley Bodenheimer are seen with the scoop used for the groundbreaking. This is the same pan used for the basement of the church built in 1928. Pulling the rope are (1) Kenny Moore, Kelly Clinard, Laurence Todd, Jr., and Vernon Lewis, architects. Right side of the rope, Roy Cantrell, Leonard Rollins, and Ben Rowe.

fluence several people that building a new sanctuary was a sad fact the congregation had to face.

There was no doubt; tension was building in the church. To tear down the beloved sanctuary where parents and children had grown up, been baptized, married, and family members' funerals had been held was not easily accepted. Committee members had time to gradually face reality, but for most of the congregation, the store talk and then having to hear it from the committee was too sudden and too harsh to accept.

However, on February 12, the building committee brought a proposal to the church to amend the original building program plans. The following recommendation was presented to the church. "After considering the opinions and advice of our construction management team, Architect Bud Evans, and Freeman and Associates Engineers concerning the present condition of our sanctuary, the building committee is in complete agreement that spending more building fund money on our existing sanctuary and nursery structure would not be in the best interest of the church family. Renovations and repairs would prove too costly for the functional life of the completed structure. Therefore, to avoid additional costs associated with ending and restarting construction, increased material costs and increased contracting fees, it is the decision of the Building Committee to make the following proposal:

That the present building program and plans be amended to delete the renovations to our existing sanctuary and nursery areas and to proceed immediately to design and construct a new sanctuary/fellowship hall to replace the renovation plans." This proposal was presented by Chairman Kelly Clinard. Two hundred twenty-five voted by secret ballot. Of these, 188 were in favor of the motion, with 37 opposed. The pastor encouraged the people even with different visions by saying we can still be of one spirit and support the vote of the majority of the church family.

Evva Spurgeon, church secretary

At the April 12, 1989, conference, it was announced Tonia Wheeler would be a page at the national WMU conference and at the Southern Baptist Convention in Las Vegas, Nevada. Tonia had earned numerous honors for her work in Acteens. Earlier, she had served as a page at the North Carolina State Convention and at the annual state WMU conference. Darrell, Henrietta, and Kara Wheeler planned to attend the convention in support of Tonia and were elected to be messengers at the Southern Baptist Convention.

Dr. Hoke Coon, pastor of First Baptist Church in Lexington, was the visiting speaker for the spring revival. On Friday, April 14, 1989, construction workers had somehow hit a gas line and a strong aroma could be detected throughout the building on Sunday morning. As Sunday School was taking place, the local fire department was called with the request that they not use the siren. Soon the fire truck arrived with sirens blasting. The building had to be evacuated with no morning service. Evening services were held.

Mary Smith pointed out that the April 12, 1989, conference might be the last one in the old sanctuary. She wanted to express this for future generations. "We want future generations to know that this decision was made with much soul searching, agonizing, and prayer. It was a difficult one to make. If you are called upon to make such a decision, as you will be, know that your ancestors also faced difficult decisions. As long as you people are in prayer, harmony, and unity you can do all things for the glory of God and his kingdom."

The architect sent drawings for the new proposal in early April. May 14, 1989, was designated as a time for the building committee to explain the details. The committee wanted everyone to understand as much about the building plans as committee members did.

A letter arrived at the church, dated May 25, 1989, from the Davidson County Inspection Department. The letter stated many structural problems existed involving the sanctuary and the structure immediately behind the sanctuary. The balcony was deemed unsafe for use. A further statement says, "Due to the increasing decline in structural safety of the sanctuary, the Inspection Department deems the sanctuary unsafe for occupancy." It further recommended the balcony should not be occupied until structural repairs could be made to bring the building up to North Carolina building code. "Any further occupancy of this building would be the liability of Abbotts Creek Baptist Church."

Kelly Clinard brought a proposal from the building committee: "As soon as a preliminary study for a sanctuary/fellowship hall complex is approved by the church that we proceed immediately to obtain financing and take the necessary measures to begin and complete construction as soon as possible." It was also decided at this conference that we adopt a plan calling for the sanctuary to be 48 feet wide. The vote for the above was 144 yes and 38 voting no.

A conference had been called Sunday morning June 4, 1989, for the purpose of nominating deacons. An added notation from the conference read like this: "John (Sulger) stated Trustees deem it necessary that this will be the last service in this sanctuary. Next Saturday, will be moving day into new educational building. Next Sunday, we will start two morning services at nine and eleven with seating for approximately 120." Open house was planned for Saturday afternoon from three until eight. Moving into the new facility took place on Friday night with help from volunteers. The new classrooms were used for the first time on June 11, 1989.

The sanctuary was demolished in three days.

Thanks were expressed in the newsletter to Henrietta Wheeler and Kim Frank for helping to make it possible for the Acteens to attend the National Acteens Convention in San Antonio. In addition to the leaders, the Acteens attending were Denise Bullard, Ashley and Christy Cline, Christy Craven,

History, Heritage, and Memories

Sharron Gann, Alicia Halker, Stacy Kiger, Tracy Spurgeon, Katie Tucker, Tonia Wheeler, Sherri Young and Christy Wright.

All organizational reports were good at the July 19, 1989, conference. The treasurer's report showed $78,018 as total contributions for the quarter. Charles Davis gave a good Sunday School report as did Matthew Dunn for the Baptist Men. The men had built a wheelchair ramp for an elderly lady in High Point. The WMU reported purchasing a dress for a marshal at Ledford High School. Roxie Beeson stated workers were needed for the library. Mary Smith reported almost thirty visits by the extension workers. Ben Rowe gave information about a senior adult cookout. In the midst of all the physical changes taking place involving the building, the ministry of the church continued to be very strong.

Other things taking place during this time included Wayne, Georgette, Denise Bullard, and Sandra Johnson going to St. Eustacius for a mission Vacation Bible School. The missionary requesting the team had also arranged for them to spend the night in St. Maarten. It was soon evident that the purpose in spending the night there was to allow the missionary to show them where he was requesting them to bring a teaching team the next year, 1990.

During the year of 1989, Kirby Johnson traveled to Brazil for a building

The sign in front of the church brought sadness, but indicated the necessary decision of the church to enter Phase Two of the building efforts.

project. Tracy Spurgeon was selected as one of six Acteens across the state to serve on the North Carolina Acteens Advisory Board. She served at various WMU functions in the state. Carl Alcon was elected as chairman of deacons for the church. He was the youngest ever selected for this honor and responsibility. Beth Kearns was chosen as the 1989 North Carolina Quarter Horse Association Queen and competed in the national competition in Columbus, Ohio. The August 21 *The Tie* expressed appreciation to Staley Bodenheimer, Larry Essick, and William Hayworth for planting the greenery around the new educational facilities.

Rev. Chet and Michelle Cantrell were appointed by the Home Mission Board in October to serve in East St. Louis, Illinois, with inner-city children. Tammy Livengood and Lorie Hedgecock, representing the church and the family, attended the appointment service in Atlanta. The Cantrell family was unable to attend due to heart bypass surgery for Chet's father.

John Sulger reported that the deacons wanted the church to investigate the feasibility of becoming incorporated. The State Convention was urging churches to consider such. This would require bylaws, a president, vice president, and a treasurer. This matter was presented as a motion which the church voted to accept. Aileen Palmer made a motion for the first conference held in the new facility to be adjourned.

The next month at a called conference, Jimmy and Patty Spurgeon were elected to serve as joint assistant treasurers.

September had new deacons being elected. They were Bobby Canada, Don Livengood, George Sechrest, Dwight Moore, J. C. Alcon, David Mendenhall, and Kay Green. James Williams was elected trustee.

The September 25 newsletter recorded a statement by Kelly Clinard, chairman of the building committee, which spoke volumes about the congregation working together. He said, "I have been told by persons outside Abbotts Creek of their admiration for our ability to weather this building project. Times like these can often weaken or even separate churches. We can take pride in our strength and steadfastness in seeing this project through."

With the congregation gathering for different worship services, a church-wide fellowship was planned for Ledford High School. This was a welcomed opportunity for the entire congregation to be together.

As a follow up for the evangelistic effort in South America, the Liberty Baptist Association had been challenged to raise $4,000 to purchase land for a church to be built. The deacons recommended $500 toward this. The congregation quickly contributed the requested amount.

Demolition of the old church.

Senior Ladies Sunday School Class Late 1980s: Back row: left to right: George Sechrest–teacher, Dwight Moore - teacher, Elva Hedgecock, and Mary Kanoy Middle Row: Nellie Gann, Mae Canipe, Dorothy Patterson, Vivian Dills, Kara Dean, Maggie Clinard, Front row: Reba Weeks, Fleta Burton, Mary Hedgecock, Evie Jones, Flossie Carmichael, and Ruth Jones.

THE EIGHTIES

The church family always enjoyed a meal in fellowship hall.

Helping Hands Sunday School Class Late 1980s: Back row: left to right: Pansy Moore, Betty Sulger, Linda Cantrell, Betty Craven, Mary Smith, Dot Canada, and Betty Rose Alcon; Front row: Pauline Hedgecock, Lois Hill, Daphne Motsinger, Bessie Jordan, Maxine Todd, Grace Green, and Billie Ann Alcon.

History, Heritage, and Memories

Dan Hayworth Sunday School Class Late 1980s: Back row: left to right: Jr. Welborn, Reitzel Hedgecock, John Sulger, Middle Row: B. B. Lyda, Charles Mann, Everett Jordan, Joe Smith, Rev. George Dowd, Front row: Rayford Hayes, Bobby Canada, Charles Green, Numa Everhart, Wilson Hedgecock, and Harry Craven.

CHAPTER EIGHTEEN

The Nineties

The first conference of 1990 was recorded by Carma Ann Robertson, assistant clerk. During this period of time, the senior adults were having their gatherings at the Horneytown Fire Department. The activities of the church did not seem to slow down though alternate arrangements had to be made often. Mission organizations, extension workers, Sunday School classes, and other organizations were all busy carrying on their ministries.

The pastor reported that the noted church historian, Walter Shurden from Mercer University in Macon, had requested the microfilms of the church minutes. These minutes were (and are) significant for research relative to early Baptist life.

The newsletter dated the middle of January informed the church that the building committee had been to Statesville to "inspect the progress made on matching our old window glass and designing the window behind the pulpit. Matching of the glass was satisfactory and complete. The design of the new window was nearing completion, but not until changes requested by the committee are made and approved." This note from the building committee was given by Kelly Clinard.

Phase One of the building plans was for the educational building. This was the intent at the outset of the project. However, the sanctuary problems necessitated Phase Two. Money was borrowed and the church voted to enter the bond program to finance the new sanctuary. By this time, the church had been in the building program for a few years and had received over $650,000. This amount included what was in the building and parking lot funds already. The church collections and gifts for the building fund had averaged $2,241.86 per week for the previous two years.

More money was needed immediately to continue with Phase Two. A short term loan of $125,000 was secured from First Federal Savings and Loan. The church entered the bond program with the intent of selling $550,000 bonds. This was to be used to pay the Savings and Loan Company and the balance to complete the sanctuary. To cover this, the weekly giving must increase by $549.51. This information was given to the church family in the January 15, 1990, *The Tie*. At this time, Sunday School attendance for the past three months was reported at 267 in December, 286 in January, and as of early February 326. During this time, Abbotts Creek Church joined with the Wallburg Baptist Church for baptismal services.

Denise Bullard and Dale Marshall were the first to wed in the new facility, April 7, 1990. They are pictured here with the officiating ministers, Rev. George Dowd (grandfather of the bride) and Rev. Roy Cantrell.

In the midst of pressing building needs, Ledford students brought information to the church that a fellow student with Cystic Fibrosis needed help in going to France with his French Club. The need was for a $400 deposit which was paid by the Young Willing Workers Class. The WMU ladies gave $100. In addition to this amount, almost $800 had been pledged to help.

On April 7, 1990, Dale and Denise Bullard Marshall were married in the parlor of the educational building, as the first couple to be married in the new facility. The parlor and all hallways around it continued to be used for worship while the sanctuary was being constructed.

At the June conference, prayer was requested by Rev. Ben Rowe for the youth group going on a mission trip to work with the inner city children and youth at the Christian Activity Center in East St. Louis. Rev. Rowe also made a motion that a committee be appointed to study the feasibility of starting family night suppers on Wednesday nights. This recommendation passed.

Patty Weavil Koontz was elected to serve as part-time secretary at the church in June of 1990.

The brick masons for the new educational facility had left chunks of ce-

THE NINETIES

ment scattered over the newly-placed brick. It looked very unattractive and cheap. On behalf of the trustees, James Williams made a motion that we pay $3,900 to have the brick cleaned. This would be paid from the $4,000 that had been retained for the job. This motion passed quickly.

The mission-minded Abbotts Creek Church did not allow the building demands to prohibit mission projects. In July, Wayne and Georgette Bullard, Denise Marshall, Tim Garner, Sandra Johnson, Lorie Hedgecock and Evva Spurgeon traveled to the Island of St. Maarten to conduct Vacation Bible School. Before they returned, Ben Rowe, John Sulger, David Johnson, Tracy Spurgeon, Katie Tucker, Stacy Kiger, and Brad Best left for East Saint Louis, Illinois, to work with inner-city children attending camp.

The Acteens Activators carried out their mission project in Cherokee, North Carolina. The girls, Tracy Spurgeon, Alicia Halker, and Christy Cline, with their leaders, Evva Spurgeon, Betty Jo Motsinger, and Henrietta Wheeler worked there for six days. Tonia Wheeler worked at Camp Mundo Vista, GA Camp, for the summer. Beth Cantrell was youth worker at Calvary Baptist Church in Reidsville, N. C. Kirby Johnson was a part of the North Carolina partnership with Sao Paulo, Brazil. He helped in building a church at Rio Preto.

It had been a troublesome decision to remove the old church building even when it was obvious it had to be done. This seemed to have made other decisions more difficult. In an earlier survey of members, regarding their wishes for the new facility, easy access to the entrances were frequently mentioned. Evidently, opinions were expressed that prompted the building committee to recommend to the church in September of 1990 that the front entrance be completed as the architect had designed. That would have a driveway with a curb and sidewalk beside the driveway, making easy access into the building. Some feelings were that the slope toward the entrance would make it difficult for the elderly to move from the parking area to the entrance. Steps were mentioned and it was pointed out if more than two steps were used, hand rails would be required. After much discussion, the vote was taken by ballot. The result showed 106 in favor of the original drawing, with 70 opposing.

The church was to elect six deacons in September. There was a tie which meant seven men received enough votes to be elected. Carl Alcon speaking for the deacons recommended to the church that all seven be allowed to serve. Those elected were Staley Bodenheimer, George Dowd, Charles Green, Rayford Hayes, John Hedgecock, Eddie Hilton, and Laurence, Todd, Jr.. Roger Hedgecock was elected trustee.

These following minutes were the first to be recorded by the newly-elected clerk, Joni Smith.

A ministry among the migrants in the area was taking place by the Liberty Baptist Association. Brenda Emmons from Cedar Lodge Baptist Church was the associational leader, and Abbotts Creek was the location for the Sunday afternoon worship service. The WMU report included how the church's mission groups had taken their weekly turn to assist with the food for the group after the services were over. This ministry actually went on at the church for several years.

The October 1 newsletter gave tribute to Marion Bodenheimer who had served as general secretary for the Sunday School from 1957 before asking to be relieved of the job as of September 30, 1990. Two weeks later, Jennifer Alcon was congratulated for having been chosen as a marshall at University of North Carolina at Greensboro.

The opening day service in the new sanctuary was on October 14. The sermon topic was "What Means These Stones?" Over four hundred worshippers were in attendance. The dedication service was held on October 28 with Rev. Leonard Rollins, director of missions for the association, bringing the message. The chairman of deacons, Dwight Moore, gave the call to worship. Kelly Clinard, chairman of the building committee, led in the dedication of the building. vice-chairman of the deacons, Bobby Canada, led the dedication for the baptistery and musical instruments. The dedication of the pulpit and the altar table was led by chairman of the building finance committee, Kenny Moore. This was also the beginning of revival services. In addition to Rev. Rollins, guest speakers were Rev. Dr. Brooks Hunt, Rev. Dr. Joe Coltrane, Rev. Charles Tanner, and the pastor.

The following day, new members were mentioned in *The Tie*. They were Andrew Paul and Gary Arnold, profession of faith and for baptism. Scott Ford came from another denomination and asked for baptism and membership. Larry and Laura Arnold along with Tony and Barbara Hyde joined the church by letter. The newsletter states, "Andrew Paul was the first person to join the church in the new Sanctuary."

The reported attendance for that opening day was 319 for Sunday School and 411 plus 19 in the nursery for the hour of worship. Several ladies from Wallburg Baptist Church attended the children in the junior church and the babies in the nursery to allow all of the Abbotts Creek family to worship together for this special service.

At the close of the October 28, 1990, service, Rev. Ben Rowe read his resignation to the congregation. He was to assume his new ministry at Lake-

The Nineties

view Baptist Church in Hickory, North Carolina, on November 18, 1990.

Eddie Hilton and Rayford Hayes were the first deacons ordained in the new church.

The first Christmas musical program in the new sanctuary was presented by the adult and youth choirs. The newsletter announced the attendance for this service in this manner: "Can you believe we had 573 (this is not a misprint-573) for morning worship?" Special thanks were expressed to Ann Joyce, Kim Moss, and Pam Ford for the directing and playing the instruments. A note of thanks was given to Angela Clinard for directing the drama part of the presentation.

Andrew Paul (age 11) was the first person to join the church in the new sanctuary.

A Sunday night service, on February 2, 1991, was led by the Koinonia Circle of the church. The candlelight service called the congregation to remember the military personnel in the Middle East. A candle was lit by a family member of each military person in our community now serving in the war zone.

The proposed budget for the year 1990–1991 was not presented until a called conference on February 13, 1991. No mention was made as to why it had not been done in the previous fall as normal. At one of the fall meetings of the deaconship, the chairman of the finance committee spoke to the deacons on behalf of the committee. The essence of his comments was that the finance committee did not feel comfortable recommending a salary of any amount for any present staff member. At that time, Ben Rowe, Ann Joyce, and the pastor (who also is the present writer) composed the staff. There was total silence. No one voiced an opinion. The staff had not received as much as a cost of living increase over the past several years. After some time of silence, the meeting moved on to other matters. When the budget was presented, again without any increases, a motion was made and passed to vote by secret ballot. The ballot vote had 58 for and 33 opposed.

Memorial Day services on May 19, 1991, had Rev. Gary Myers of Oak Hill Baptist Church in Thomasville as the guest speaker.

The veterans of the church were honored in a special service on July 14, 1991. The speaker for the morning service was Lt. Col. David Hatcher. A covered dish meal followed the service. From at least World War II days, and perhaps earlier, the church had always given special consideration to the military personnel and veterans.

The North Carolina Baptist Men had (and still have) a Medical-Dental van that is available for mission needs across the state. The Liberty Baptist Association sponsored the van on a Sunday afternoon in late July. The van was located at Abbotts Creek with many volunteers assisting the doctors and dentists who gave their services. Over thirty migrants working for the area farmers in the tobacco fields received medical and dental assistances during the afternoon. The associational leaders were excited about such a ministry as well as the Abbotts Creek Church family.

Ann Joyce, director of music

The proposed budget for 1991-92 came before the church for a vote in August of 1991. Again secret ballot was called for and the proposed budget, still with no cost of living increases, passed by a 49-44 vote.

New deacons were elected in September. They were Ronnie Young, Jeff Craven, Charles Jordan, Hugh Motsinger, and John Sulger. Zane Hedgecock was chosen as the new trustee. Jeff was ordained on October 10, 1991.

The Reverend Clovis Martinoff from Rio Preto, Brazil delivered the evening message at the church on September 22, 1991. Matthew Dunn and the Abbotts Creek pastor had served as part of an associational mission team in Rio Preto earlier. Pastor Martinoff had coordinated the mission partnership between the Liberty Association and the Rio Preto Association.

For a number of years, the church had helped to support two missionary families and sent financial assistances to them through the Foreign Mission Board. The Charles Wiggs family had been supported by the church for twenty or more years. The Carson Brissons had been the second missionary family the church supported. Once they were no longer with the mission board, the church chose Mike, Robin, and David Eberhardt from Grenada as the second missionary family to support. After they retired from serving in Grenada, the church selected the Larry Phillips family. The church voted to support this family on October 16, 1991.

The October 28 newsletter gave recognition to Mary Smith and Pansy Moore for having led the Extension Department for twenty-five years. During these years, they have visited the homebound members giving literature, information concerning the church, and having prayer with them. The pastor in his regular visitation ministry always heard how much the elderly appreciated this ministry and looked forward to their visits.

The first wedding to take place in the new sanctuary was Sandra Jean Houston and Laurence H. Todd, III on October 27, 1991. The wedding was planned to take place earlier but the sanctuary was not completed. The couple, anxious to be married, chose to wait and be married in the sanctuary where they would worship for years to come.

With Osbert and Margaret James preparing for their return to Grenada after completing his college and seminary training, the mission teams that had first gone to Grenada and Jamaica proposed that Abbotts Creek try to raise enough money to purchase their plane fare back to Grenada. The association was actually paying for the tickets but the amount raised from Abbotts Creek could help them get reestablished in Grenada. Abbotts Creek had been the most supportive church in the association during their time here.

Sandra Jean Houston and Laurence H. Todd, III were the first to be wed in the new sanctuary, October 27, 1991.

For the very first time, a Christmas dinner was planned for December 8, 1991. Money had been given to purchase the turkeys and various ladies had agreed to do the cooking. Families brought the vegetables, drinks, bread, and desserts. This was the beginning of what became an annual affair and was attended by 350.

Early in 1992, guidelines were prepared, presented, and adopted by the church for the use of church facilities. A study group was chosen to propose a job description for an associate pastor. The members were Pat Dawson, Leroy Kearns, Michael Gann, Jeff Jordan, Laura Arnold, and Debra Paul. The three-page guidelines were later presented to the church and adopted.

The trustees had approved an idea by April of 1992 for the Young Married Couples Class to create a playground in the woods near the softball field. Sonya Alcon reported plans were to clean out the wooded area, place swing sets, and picnic tables and leave leave the area as natural as possible.

Much discussion concerned securing an associate pastor. Questions were raised as to exactly what was needed, and could the church afford it at this time? Much discussion took place. A motion was made to appoint a search committee but after more discussion the motion was tabled until a later date.

The speaker for the Memorial Day service in May 1992 was the Rev. Haywood Hyatt. A former member of Abbotts Creek, he was now a retired Methodist minister.

Joann Chestnutt was employed as secretary working twenty hours per week.

Jack Rose, a member of English Road Baptist Church in High Point, was attending John Wesley College, also in High Point. One requirement was to serve as an intern in a church. He contacted Abbotts Creek about such a possibility. Deacon chairman, Laurence Todd, Jr., presented this to the church at a called conference on May 20, 1992. The intern work required twenty to thirty hours a week for ten weeks. The church accepted the recommendation of the deacons to allow Mr. Rose to carry out his intern requirement at Abbotts Creek.

The church celebrated 160 years of being called the Missionary Baptist Church on July 4, 1992. Emphasis had been put on trying to make a large contribution toward the building fund. Zane Hedgecock had used his artistic ability and made a replica of the church building which stood prior to 1928. He had used the descriptions several of the older members had shared. As individuals saw it they seemed to remember something else allowing him to include those aspects as well. The miniature church was constructed with a small opening in the roof allowing the congregation to make the special offering for the day through that opening. The congregation "seemed astonished," according to the minutes, when the total offering was announced as $30,725.75. The church was informed a payment of this magnitude would save about the same amount of interest as the payment itself.

In a called conference August 26, 1992, the proposed budget for the 1992–1993 was presented and after some discussion passed by a vote of 67 to 14. At the same conference, a job description was presented for an associate pastor. This was to replace the job descriptions of minister of youth and minister of education. Laurence Todd, Jr., brought a recommendation from the deacons that Jack Rose be employed as associate pastor interim for August and September with remunerations of $1,500 per month. The church accepted this recommendation.

Upon the recommendation of the deacons, the church voted on August 30 to call Mr. Rose as associate pastor beginning on October 1, 1992. The church voted 209 in favor of this with 15 voting against the motion.

The Nineties

The church newsletter dated August 17, 1992, gave information regarding Barri Hilton. Barri had been accepted by the Southern Baptist Home Mission Board to work for a school term with the Baptist Student Union director at the University of Washington in Seattle.

Seven deacons were elected on September 13, 1992. They were Harry Craven, Richard Cockrum, Keith Curlee, Charles Davis, Danny Gann, Zane Hedgecock, and James Williams. Zane and Keith were ordained on October 18. Staley Bodenheimer was selected as trustee.

The first Saturday in October, the pastor and his wife, Linda, invited the senior adults to the back yard of the parsonage for a cookout. A larger than expected number attended and it was immediately evident more space was needed for such an outstanding group. Over the next few years, the cookout took place at the church's picnic shelter. By the second year, the new staff member, Jack Rose and his wife, Patsy, assisted the pastor's family with this social event.

The general officers and other leaders had been elected for the 1992-1993 church year. The name of those elected had been distributed to the congregation but not listed in the church minutes and no mention made of any changes. However, the October minutes were recorded by the new church clerk, Evva Spurgeon, who continues to serve in that capacity fifteen years later.

Dwight and Pansy Moore always kept a running record of membership and other interesting happenings concerning the church. At the end of the associational year, August 31, 1992, their records indicated the church membership had reached seven hundred.

At the October Liberty Baptist Association meeting, the director of missions announced his retirement at the end of the current year. The associational meetings took place at Wallburg and Abbotts Creek Baptist churches.

The Sunday evening worship for November 15, 1992, was not held at the church thereby allowing the church family to attend the ordination service for Jack Rose which took place at the English Road Baptist Church in High Point. Two weeks later, the evening services were canceled to allow those who wished to do so to attend the First Baptist Church in Lexington, honoring The Reverend Leonard and Polly Rollins upon their retirement.

The church secretary, Patty Koontz, had been seeking full-time employment. When a job came open for her, she had to take the work immediately. Wanda Stone agreed to do the secretarial work on a temporary basis.

The first conference in January of the New Year, 1993, heard the various reports and three recommendations from the deacons. One was to allow the personnel committee to receive applications for a part-time church secretary. The other two concerned cushions for the church pews. A vote to determine interest in the cushions was 35 to 9. The second which also passed was to authorize the trustees to begin to gather adequate information concerning color, price, and method of payment and bring the information with a recommendation back to the church for disposition on the matter.

Joann Chestnutt

On January 17, 1993, baptismal services were held for Molly Sink, Louise Schlotfeldt, Erin Bennett, and Mike Smith. This was the first times robes had been used that were purchased for that purpose. Mrs. Schlotfeldt had donated baptismal robes in memory of her late husband, Oz, for the minister and the ladies being baptized.

Having meals on Wednesday night had been discussed for some time. It was decided to start serving meals on a trial basis for two months. A minimum charge was selected to cover the cost of the meal only. Dinner would precede the missions and choir activities and prayer service.

Congratulations were given in the January 17, 1993, edition of the church newsletter for Alan Young. He had been notified by the Brotherhood Department of the Southern Baptist Convention that a drawing he had sent in two years earlier had been selected for the RA *Lad Magazine*. Debra Paul was his leader and had encouraged him to send it for consideration.

Several from the church went to Florida becoming a part of the North Carolina Baptist Men's project to help repair or rebuild homes that had been destroyed or damaged by the recent hurricane, Andrew. Those participating in the work project were James and Betty Williams, Danny and Mary Gann, Patty Bodenheimer, Eddie and Barri Hilton, John Payne, and Lorie Hedgecock.

The information above shows some interest in pew cushions. Art Hedgecock and James Williams were prepared to share their research including the cost for such a project, as the congregation had requested at a previous conference. Much discussion followed at the April conference. More than twenty people raised questions or expressed their feelings during the question and discussion time. Only two expressed the advantage of having them installed. The question was called for and the vote showed 44 against the installation of the cushions and 18 voting to proceed with cushions.

For the first time, the third Sunday in May Memorial service was scheduled during the morning worship service rather than in an afternoon service. Goals were set for Sunday attendance at 400 and a goal of $25,000 which would be used to pay on the principal of the building debt. There were 303 for Sunday School and 390 for the worship service. The announced amount contributed for the building debt was $21,549.

Maxine Todd's death occurred on May 19, 1993. The Easter Cantata had been dedicated to her. She had learned the music but was unable to attend. She had been a long-time choir member and Sunday School teacher and was a part of the 1974 pulpit search committee. Shortly after her death, the family found a note written to the church which said, "Thank you very much for all the many ways you remembered me during my illness. I especially am grateful for you who have been faithful in praying for me. Love in Christ, Maxine Todd."

As the reports were given for the July 14, 1993, conference, the financial report included designated gifts to the youth ($2,248.74) and senior adults ($2,204.13). The giver was anonymous. It was also reported at this conference a group of eight people went to Supply, North Carolina, to help in building a church.

The Davidson County Board of Elections requested to use the church fellowship hall as the fall voting precinct. That request was granted with the understanding all signs would be removed immediately after the voting.

The church hosted the Medical-Dental Van on Sunday August 16, 1993, sponsored by the Liberty Association. Many of the Hispanics working in the area were able to receive these services which were rendered by volunteers.

The memorial committee learned on August 22 that much vandalism was done to the stones in the cemetery. Eighteen stones were turned over but none broken. No clues were left. More damage had been done in the cemetery of the Primitive Church.

The church approved a recommendation from the deacons to send the church secretary to Caraway for the North Carolina Southern Baptist Secretaries' conference. Joann Chestnutt had been secretary for the church for a few months.

A matter was mentioned as a recommendation to be considered at the October business conference. It had two parts, whether to allow women to serve as deacons and if divorced men should be allowed to serve in that capacity.

The church treasurers had their names withdrawn, after being nominated, for the 1993–1994 church year. Since a change was being made, the deacons brought this to the church: "The Deaconship has looked into bonding, auditing the church financial records, making church treasurer and the Finance Committee separate positions, instituting a counting committee and other changes pertaining to the church treasurer." There had never been questions concerning the manner in which this work had been done, but with no personalities involved, if a study was to be made, now would be the time. A committee was chosen, the study made, and the recommendation was to continue the job as before, a tribute to those who had served previously. This took place on August 18, 1993.

Deacons elected in September, were: Carl Alcon, Bob Best, Don Livengood, Dwight Moore, George Sechrest, and Albert Sink, with Doug Paul as the alternate. Lewis Peacock was chosen as trustee. An ordination service for Albert Sink was held on October 17, 1993.

Albert and Becky Sink were chosen as the new treasurers for the church. They, along with the other general offices, were elected by secret ballot as the constitution called for though it had not been followed in recent years. All had previously been voted on by show of hands.

Hugh and Betty Jo Motsinger had served as treasurers for the past thirteen years. During their time of serving, the church had various funds, regular, building, parking lot, scholarship, and others that required skilled bookkeeping. This was also the time the church had borrowed money, sold bonds, and had special gifts in addition to the regular church collections. They had to collect, count, and disperse more than a million dollars during the building process of the church for that project alone.

It was announced on October 10, 1993, two rocking chairs were presented to the nursery in honor of Betty Williams and Violet Everhart for their many years as workers in the nursery.

In early December of 1993, Charles E. Hayworth, Jr., expressed interest in donating money to the church for the purchase of an organ in memory of his father, Charles E. Hayworth, Sr. This gift would come from the Charles E. and Pauline Hayworth Foundation and would be $6,000 a year for ten years. The two stipulations were: first, the money plus any interest accumulated would be used to purchase an organ. In the second place, a plaque would be placed on the organ with the inscription that it was in honor of his father who was a member of Abbotts Creek from 1901 until his death in 1928. Mr. Hayworth was in the hospital at this time, and died on January 2, 1994.

Early in 1994, the church was able to accept changes in the constitution that were required mostly by the fact of the church becoming incorporated. There were some other wording changes as well.

During the month of January of 1994, volunteers saved the church hundreds of dollars by painting the class and assembly rooms. Windows were caulked and bathrooms cleaned. Workers on this project were Grace Green, Patty Bodenheimer, Zane Hedgecock, Betty and James Williams, Bobby Canada, Lewis Peacock, Doris Sells, and Wilbur Bowers. Mary Smith contributed by serving the group a meal. During the same month, the trustees asked James Williams to work with Tony Craven to prepare signs for each class room. Most classes were willing to pay for their own sign, and other contributions made it possible to accomplish this without affecting the church budget.

Ann Joyce leading the congregational singing

James and Betty Williams purchased material for, made, and installed a "Post Office" outside the church office.

The parsonage required a new roof. The church voted to do this including adding a new ridge vent for the attic. The cost would be three to four thousand dollars.

The February newsletter carried information about a new study, "Experiencing God, Knowing and Doing the Will of God." Much publicity had been given to this in Baptist materials. Fifteen elected leaders began meeting with the pastor for this study on Sunday evening during the time for worship. We felt this study should be evaluated by the leaders before jumping into it on a church-wide basis. Rev. Rose led the evening worship services. This was a highly profitable study and prompted the need for others to experience what the "trial group" had learned. The same study was given for several years with Pat Dawson leading the groups once or twice a year. This first study led to other studies given during the evening hour of worship and taught by various leaders.

Steve Martin, pastor of Churchland Baptist Church near Lexington, was the speaker for the spring revival services.

During the spring of 1994, a new Hispanic church was under construction near Union Cross. Abbotts Creek organized a work team to assist in some of the framing of this building.

On April 22, 1994, tragedy came to the church family with the news that Lynn Canada was in the Baptist Hospital helicopter that crashed in Tazewell County, Virginia with no survivors. The pilot and crew of nurses were going on an emergency trip to pick up a patient before returning to Baptist Hospital in Winston–Salem.

A few days later, long-time faithful member Aileen Palmer did not show up for prayer service nor call anyone to ask for help in getting to church. Her absence was very unusual and noticeable. Deacon Charles Jordan and others went to her home and could see her on the floor. They had to break in and called for ambulance help. Abbotts Creek Church had been made strong by such dependable members. Her absence from one service caused friends to be alarmed enough to check to see if there was trouble. Oddly enough, about two months later, Mr. Jordan sustained a broken leg at work with North State Telephone Company. The day before his discharge at the hospital, he suffered a heart attack caused by a blood clot and subsequently died. A day later, Clyde Bodenheimer died. The church family reached out to these grieving families giving support during their time of greatest need.

During the July conference, Lewis Peacock, director of the Baptist Men's group of the church, reported that four men had accepted the challenge of going to the Ukraine to work on a church building. This was part of a partnership between the Ukraine Baptist Convention and the North Carolina Baptist Men. Those going in addition to Lewis would be Jack Rose, Danny Gann, and James Williams. The proposed trip was set for August. The Baptist Men began fundraising projects. The group learned of their work assignment. The Ukrainian government had turned an old church building built in 1536 by Lutherans over to the Baptist group with the understanding that it would be restored for use. The men from Abbotts Creek would start the restoration process. Dr. Luther Copeland, former missionary to Japan and teacher of missions at Southeastern Seminary, led in the installation service for this group on July 31, 1994.

Information was shared indicating that six or eight cars were required to transport the youth for any event away from the church. It was pointed out that the church needed to look seriously into some type of transportation such as a bus or van.

A motion was made from the floor that the church appoint a committee to consider the cost and feasibility of having a prayer garden between the sanctuary and the educational building.

It was also recommended that the trustees carry out some plans for additions to the playground area that would include a volleyball court and a

The Nineties

Hugh and Betty Jo Motsinger served the church for thirteen years, as treasurers.

small building to care for the playground materials or equipment, such as balls, bats, and nets.

New deacons were elected on September 11, 1994. Because of a tie among some, seven were elected. They were John Hedgecock, Rayford Hayes, Laurence Todd, Tony Craven, Ricky DeLappe, Michael Gann, and Patrick Moss. The latter four were ordained on October 30. Numa Everhart was chosen as the new trustee.

In late September, a group from the church formed a team and traveled to Blackwolf, West Virginia, to do repairs on a small Baptist church. Materials for the team to do the needed work had to be purchased as well. Contributions were accepted to help with this project. With the volunteer labor and contributions from Abbotts Creek, the Blackwolf Baptist Church had a new look.

Discussion had gone on for sometime about the non-attending members of the church whose locations were unknown. The church made the decision to try contacting each of these people and inquire about their desire to retain membership. About one hundred cards were mailed. Five responded saying they were members of another church. Nine requested that their names be removed. This left many not responding at all. From 1974, through 1998, 102 names were erased from the membership roll. Of course, some of those would have been of persons joining a church of another denomination where acknowledgements were made but letters not granted.

The church celebrated the twentieth anniversary of the pastor and his family at the morning worship service on October 9, 1994. The pastor had no hint that anything was going on behind his back. The secretary had given the pastor a copy of the church's newsletter with no mention of the service. She then included the announcement for everyone else to see. The prepared sermon was not used because others had been asked to speak. In their comments, they included the work of the pastor and his wife, Linda. She had been a vital part of the ministry working with the children and youth music from time to time, and led in the development of a very strong

RA mission program for the boys. A covered dish lunch was enjoyed in the fellowship hall after the service. For the worship service, 418 people were present.

The conference on the following Wednesday, heard a recommendation from the deacons asking the nominating committee to select a committee to study the need for a before and after school program. It would serve to minister to families who needed help with the children while parents were working. The committee was asked to investigate the need and to bring a recommendation regarding this back to the church.

A called conference took place on December 21, 1994, considering a recommendation from the deacons regarding a prayer garden that had been discussed some months earlier. "The deacons recommended to the church that a fund be established to build a prayer garden. ..." As time passed, large contributions were made in memory of the late Lynn Canada. Many other contributions were made in memory of or in honor of loved ones. At the same conference, a committee was presented to work out details and bring a recommendation back to the church for an after school care ministry. The initial interest showed the need for after school care, with little interest being expressed for preschool care. Members of the committee were Danny and Sharon Gann, Carol Settles, Sonya Alcon, Barbara Hyde, and Terri Hunter.

Betty Williams and Violet Everhart, long-time nursery workers are seen here with Taylor Gann and Emma Smith.

The first three months of 1995 were exciting times for the church family. The average attendance in Sunday School was January–307; February–336; and March–329. Becky Sink, treasurer, reported that the church was in the best financial shape seen in a long time. She kept the church informed as to progress being made on the bank loan and the bond payments encouraging the church to continue the giving pattern and paying off these debts earlier than scheduled.

The first two church newsletters in March gave information about the Home Mission study which was generally well attended since it was given at the prayer meeting or Sunday evening time of worship. The March 6, 1995, issue included an invitation to attend the twentieth anniversary of the church in St. Albans, West Virginia. Many of our people, including the youth group, had helped in building the facility there. The next week, the church received a certificate of appreciation for the assistance several of our men and women had given to the newly-constructed church building there. The same newsletter spoke of the invitation that had been received for a return work trip to the Ukraine.

The spring revival took place the last of March with Pastor Ken Evans from Fork Baptist Church in Davie County as the speaker. The Sunday evening service was held at the Ledford High School stadium. This was because the youth and many adults had been involved in a Walk-A-Thon for home missions during the afternoon and enjoyed a cookout before the service.

At the evening service on March 27, 1995, Veteran Rayford Hayes shared some of his military experiences. He served as a prisoner of war in a German prison camp for one hundred days. This was the first time he had been able to bring himself to share his story. In his testimony, he shared that he often wondered why he had been picked up and given medical treatment after being wounded, while others beside him were left to die. He shared his answer for that. A few days after he had been able to return to his home in Wilkes County, he was walking around looking at the old home place. He heard a noise in the barn and noted a door was open that usually was not. After slipping up close to investigate, he said, "I saw my Daddy down on his knees thanking God for bringing his boy home from prison." The former POW emphatically said, "That's why I got home."

The minutes of the April conference heard a recommendation from the after school committee. It was projected that such a program would begin with the 1995–1996 school year. A committee was to be formed to secure a director and workers, develop the policies, provide an ongoing evaluation, and keep the church informed with periodic reports.

The trustees brought a motion to the church to accept the plans for a prayer garden after the money was collected. Jennifer Blevins gave the committee's report passing out the drawn plans and projected cost. Since $9,660 would be needed, the committee's motion was to wait until that amount was on hand to begin. This motion passed.

At the same conference, Zane Hedgecock brought a recommendation from the trustees that the church accept the offer of Sandy Jordan to erect a flag pole in the church yard, near the General Green monument, in memory of her late husband, Charles. The United States and Christian flags could be used on the new pole.

The new Baptist Hymnals were dedicated and used for the first time on April 26, 1995. Charles Storey, from the North Carolina Baptist Convention's Music Department, was present to talk about the new hymnals and to lead in an all-music worship service.

Jack Rose, Danny Gann, James Williams, and Lewis Peacock made up a work team in the Ukraine.

A called conference on May 3, 1995, heard a report from the nominating committee. On their behalf, Laurence, Todd, Jr., made the motion to name the following for the after school program committee: Sonya Alcon, Barbara Hyde, Sharon Gann, Carol Settles, Danny Gann, and Jack Rose.

A recommendation from the church council was that any profits from the Wednesday night meals be used to support the future mission trip back to the Ukraine.

Carol Settles was recommended by the after school program committee to be director of the after school ministry. This motion passed. Much discussion had centered on just how the ministry would operate. Some investigaton took place and the committee learned of two plans that were used in other places. One plan would have the church collecting funds, buying all supplies including daily snacks for the children, and paying other bills. The other option was to secure the director with the church allowing the space to be used as a ministry free of cost for the ministry. The director would then be responsible for the total cost and the financial risk involved. This was the approach the church chose to take. The ministry would start at no cost to the church.

The pastor's paragraph in the May 22, 1995 issue of the church's newsletter reported that more than one hundred members had now completed the study, "Experiencing God."

July 12, 1995, was the normal date for the quarterly conference. The deacons recommended that a fund be started to purchase a van for church use and the finance committee be asked to include a line item in future budgets for the upkeep of the vehicle.

Alicia Young had been employed to assist Rev. Rose with the summer program for the children's ministry.

The church secretary had been attending a yearly conference for church secretaries at one of our Baptist assemblies. It was decided at this July conference rather than voting on this every year, a line item be included in future budgets to provide for this.

Osbert and Margaret James had been sponsored by the Liberty Baptist Association to secure his college and theological training before returning to Grenada where he would be serving as pastor. He was pastor of the St. George's Baptist Church and was working at a full-time job. The deacons proposed that the church use what had been in the line item of the budget supporting a second missionary to help with Osbert's support allowing him to serve as full-time pastor. One hundred dollars per month would be sent to him for this purpose. This motion was passed by the church body.

On July 27, 1995, Jack and Patsy Rose, Danny and Mary Gann, and Lewis and Frances Peacock left for a two-week work trip to the Ukraine. Their assignment was helping with further renovation on the same building as had the earlier team.

Early in September, of 1995, the new after school ministry began. Fifteen children were signed up for every afternoon, two were to attend four days, one three days, and four would be attending only one day during the week. There were snacks for the children, time for homework, and play time. The newsletter stated, "What a valuable way to see our facilities being used meeting the needs of parents from our church and several who are not from our fellowship." One non-member parent said, "Because of Abbotts Creek's reputation, I knew it would be a good program."

The called conference on September 17, 1995, was for the purpose of electing deacons. Those elected were Scott Ford, Tony Hyde, Hugh Motsinger, Jimmy Stilley, John Sulger, and Ronnie Young. Scott Ford and Jimmy Stilley were ordained on October 3, 1995, and Tony Hyde, later in November. Matthew Dunn was named trustee.

As a continuing part of the mission outreach of the Baptist Men, one hundred dollars was sent each month to assist Wayne and Shanti Rowbottom from Trinidad during their time here for college and seminary. With them back in their own country, it was decided the support should continue for some time while they were getting reestablished in their ministry.

Replacing the heat pump at the parsonage was presented for church consideration at a called conference on December 20, 1995. The cost would be $1,908.16 and carry a year's guarantee. This motion passed.

The first conference in 1996 was held on January 3. The purpose of this conference was to hear a recommendation from the transportation committee concerning the purchase of a new van. Chairman James Williams brought the motion before the congregation. The 1995, fifteen-passenger Dodge van was brought to the church a couple of weeks earlier allowing anyone who wished to see it. The cost would be $18,000. Much discussion pro and con took place before the vote to purchase the vehicle. At the same time, guidelines for use of the van were passed as well.

The regular quarterly church conference was held two weeks later with numerous organizational reports being given. Assistant Pastor Jack Rose had received a request from the North Carolina Baptist State Convention to be one of a few making a trip to the Ukraine to help map out strategy for the remaining time of the North Carolina-Ukraine partnership. The deacons, viewing this as a great honor, recommended the church allow him to go. The church accepted this with a strong positive vote.

Another recommendation was made, and passed, to establish a mission fund allowing contributions to be given to assist volunteers who wished to be a part of church-approved mission trip. A mission interest survey had been taken trying to see which mission projects to pursue. The most interest was expressed in trying to do more local missions. East St. Louis and Grenada were the other two mentioned most.

A motion came from the trustees to have a sound system installed. The cost of this would be $10,749.30. Four wireless hearing aids would be purchased for use in certain wired locations in the sanctuary for those with such needs. The church voted to accept the recommendation. Just after the church voted to make this purchase, a fine Christian family outside Abbotts Creek Church expressed an interest in paying for it. They pledged to contribute one thousand dollars for ten months. This was to be done anonymously in honor of Charles, Vicki, and Amanda Davis.

The spring revival started on April 14, 1996, with Rev. Morris Hollifield, retired minister and former pastor of Jersey Baptist Church, as the visiting minister.

One of the May newsletters mentioned that a water fountain had been installed in the prayer garden. Dorothy, Bobby, and Dot Canada and Tanner Ford along with Wilbur and Marie Bowers kept the garden looking lovely. As time moved on, the garden was used as a lovely setting for outside weddings. From time to time, it has been used as the scene for pictures by high school juniors and seniors dressed for the proms.

The summer was a busy one for the Abbotts Creek congregation. Eleven members from the church were preparing to go to Grenada for a Vacation Bible School. Leaving on July 27, 1996, were Ashley Hedgecock, Joann

Chestnutt, Alicia Young, Katie Tucker, Guy Halton, Patsy Rose, Leslie Rose, Patty Bodenheimer, Bobbie Burris, Betsy Leach, and group leader Evva Spurgeon. The work trip to Grenada included: James Williams, Patrick Moss, Junior Sink, and the pastor participating as part of the team from Liberty Association going to make pews for the St. George's Baptist Church. Twenty-two pews were made during the week. The church's pastor, Osbert James, sent this note to Abbotts Creek, "You will never fully understand or capture the euphonic in the hearts and faces of our people when they walked into the church on Sunday morning; it was glorious."

The work team going to the Christian Activity Center in East St. Louis from June 22-30, 1996, was made up of Betty and James Williams, Linda Cantrell, Grace Green, Patty Bodenheimer, Carl Alcon, Ben Settles, Ben Cline, David and Heather Crews, Allen Young, and Jamie Settles. The Associational Vacation Bible School team going to East St. Louis included Lou Schlotfeldt and Mollie Sink.

Lewis Peacock, trustee chairman, informed the church that the trustees were working on a fire alarm system with bids ranging from $2,000 to $4,000. The church did not vote on this until a called conference in September. The fire protection system accepted by the church had a price tag of $5,280.

A recommendation was brought to the church by the church council to hire someone to cook for the continuation of Wednesday night meals with volunteer teams doing the clean up. This motion passed by show of hands.

Back in April, Jack Rose had informed the church family a letter from the Ukraine announced the dedication of the renovated church would be held in August of 1996 rather than January of 1997. He recounted how two years earlier four members had gone to help renovate the 465-year-old building in the city of Livi. These four had been invited back to help with the dedication of the building. On July 22, James Williams, Jack Rose, Danny Gann, and Lewis Peacock left to go to Livi for the dedication of the building. They arrived in time to assist another church at Radiviliv. The North Carolina partnership office allowed the group to carry extra funds to assist as the needs were known. The church at Radiviliv hoped to have chandeliers for their new sanctuary. The group of four decided to "borrow" from the extra funds and pay the thousand dollars needed for this project knowing they would need to repay it. After they came back to Abbotts Creek, the church was able to collect sufficient funds for the payment. The chandeliers hang there now because of the gifts from Abbotts Creek.

In September, Doris Crews and Sue Young agreed to cook for the

Wednesday night meals. Cleanup teams needed to assist or the meals would be discontinued. This system worked for several years adding to the ministry of the church.

Sonya Alcon gave a report of the after school care ministry that just celebrated the first anniversary. As chairman of the committee, she had observed closely and gave this report. "The word has spread that our program is about more than just child care, it is committed to sharing God's love by teaching acceptable behavior, promoting Christian values and offering a home church to those who need one.... The program has also benefited several of our local high school and college students by allowing them to work part time while attending school."

Deacons elected in September were David Chestnutt, Charles Davis, George Dowd, Danny Gann, Mike Motsinger, and James Williams with Joe Craven as alternate. George Sechrest was elected trustee.

At the close of 1996, there were twenty-nine children enrolled in the after school program. In addition to the director Carol Settles, the staff includes Jamie and Ben Settles, Angela Jilcott, John Gwaltney, Melissa Essick, Scott and Alicia Young, and Gretchen Saintsing.

There were several reports given and a few matters requiring a vote presented during the first conference in 1997. The nominating committee was asked to select a music committee to assist in music decisions. At the same time, revised guidelines were given for the use of the church van. It was also reported that several men and women from the church would be going to Camp Mundo Vista, at nearby Asheboro, to help prepare the camp for summer campers.

The church was honored to have Mrs. Donice Harrod, the state president of WMU, to speak on February 2, 1997. One month later, Beth Hayworth MacClaren spoke to the church family about the work of Baptists around the world. Beth grew up in the church and community and has always been a proud product of Abbotts Creek Church. At this time, she was serving as director of the Women's Division of the Baptist World Alliance.

A called conference for March 5, 1997, allowed the deacons to present a wedding policy for the church's consideration. Immediately, questions were asked. One of the first asked was, "How many women were on that committee?" There were numerous other questions asked and opinions expressed before the church rejected the recommendation and accepted an amendment to send it back and have it redone. Eleven opposed the amendment while thirty-six approved thus sending it back for some reworking. In fact, the regular conference in April suggested a wedding policy committee be selected and made up of four women and four men, two of whom would be deacons.

The second motion for the night had to do with a policy concerning the use of church facilities. Some amendments were added before being approved by the church.

The purchase of an enclosed trailer for use with the van was brought before the church by the chairman of the transportation committee, Michael Rinehardt. The size of the trailer would be 6x8 feet. The cost would be $1,490. This motion was accepted by the church.

Dr. Ray Howell, pastor of First Baptist Church in Lexington, was the revival speaker for April 22-May 1, 1997.

Deaths saddened the church family in late April. Leon Rudd died on April 21, 1997. Two days later, Harry Hood died. The death of Clete Hedgecock occurred the next day, April 24.

The trustees and personnel committee jointly brought before the church a job description for the sexton and custodian. This took place on May 7, 1997. Two weeks later, the personnel committee presented a revised job description for the committee on which they were serving. The church accepted both recommendations.

In the June 3, 1997, issue of the church newsletter, the congregation learned Alicia Young had been employed to work at the Reeds Baptist Church for the summer. The ordination of Joe Craven as a deacon took place on June 29, 1997.

The spring and early summer were filled with projects to raise money for the mission teams for the summer. East St. Louis, Grenada, and New Windsor, New York, mission teams were named in the church's outreach efforts.

A donation to the building fund was given in memory of Harry Hood, Junior, and Harry Hood, Senior, by Edith Hood. This was listed in the financial reports on June 22, 1997. Mrs. Hood tried to give this without any fanfare and did not even want her name mentioned. Actually, she had made several sizeable contributions previously.

The regular quarterly conference was held on July 16, 1997. Reports were given and accepted. Three days later, eleven youth and six adults left for New Windsor, New York, for a work trip. They were George, Lori, and Christi Blake, Danny and Mary Gann, Shannon Tuttle, Amber Martin, Nathan Cockrum, David Crews, Allen Young, T. Dawson, Nicholas Paul, Andrew Cassels, Chip Jordan, and Jack Rose.

On Sunday, July 28, 1997, there were twenty-seven people absent from the church services because they were on their way back from a mission trip (New York) or on their way to a mission trip (Grenada). Those on the Grenada trip were Georgette Bullard, Craig Burris, Linda Cockrum, Betsy Leach, Dale and Denise Marshall, Andrea McGuire, Evva Spurgeon, and Scott and Alicia Young. Also in attendance were three more workers from the after school program and from the Shady Grove United Methodist Church. They were Lesha Hedgecock, Suzanne Johnson, and Elizabeth Koch. Such trips would not have been possible without the total support of the mission-minded people of the church.

In August, the church council expressed concern about the cost of the newsletter being mailed each week. A suggestion was made to do one newsletter a month rather than every week. There were immediate reactions to this. Much of this came from those attending on a regular basis but the greater cry came from the homebound. There were 145 responses. Of that number, 102 expressed the desire for a weekly newsletter. That immediately eliminated talk of a once-a-month newsletter.

The September conference resulted in new deacons and a trustee being elected. Only seven men allowed their names to be considered for deacon election. The church, in a called conference prior to the election, voted to allow names presented that represented only one more than would be elected. The constitution required more than one. At the conference for the election, the trustee chosen was Bobby Canada. Carl Alcon, Roger Hamby, Dale Marshall, Mike Rinehardt, Albert Sink, and Wayne Wilson were elected as deacons. Wayne, Roger, and Dale were ordained on October 19, 1997.

For the senior adult cookout given by the Cantrell and Rose families, there were seventy-five in attendance. J. C. Alcon, Wilbur Bowers and Gerald Smith demonstrated carving wood products. Billie Alcon was busy demonstrating how to make baskets.

When the proposed budget was presented for the 1997-98 year, the finance committee allowed pay for some added hours for the church secretary which has been requested by the personnel committee. The secretary would now be working thirty-five hours each week.

The minutes of the October 1, 1997, called conference, gave information concerning the extension workers, Pansy Moore and Mary Smith. They have served in this capacity for thirty-one years making hundreds of visits over the years. They had no records of their first four years of visiting. Since 1976, the two made 2,860 visits. During these years, they visited 133 different shut-ins in twenty-two different nursing homes. Pansy writes, "We have been caught in snow storms, hail and rainstorms." There had been four months during these years they were unable to make their regular visits.

The Nineties

At the regular conference on October 14, 1997, the treasurer pointed out that expenditures for the past year had been $30,000 less than what had been allowed in the budget. At this time, the trustees presented two motions concerning the church's sound system. The first motion was to put the present sanctuary sound equipment in the fellowship hall. The second was to accept a bid to install a new system in the sanctuary. The costs for installation would be $1,601 in the fellowship hall and $2,044 for the purchase of and the installation for the new one in the sanctuary.

The November 24, 1997, newsletter informed the congregation of the retirement of missionaries Charles and Bonnie Wiggs from Korea. Upon their return to North Carolina, plans were for them to leave for a short mission term in Bosnia. They led the worship service on December 7, 1997.

The pastor and his wife, Linda, along with Patty Bodenheimer and Grace Green were in Israel at the time of the first church conference in January of 1998. Rev. Jack Rose presided at the business meeting. The reports were given and after some questions or discussions, all were accepted by the church.

The church heard the information given by Lewis Peacock, trustee chairman.

Someone wished to donate gas logs for the parsonage, but the church would assume the responsibility for the lease of the tank and for the gas to be used. The congregation accepted this gift.

The deacons recommended that the church allow the Girl Scouts of the community the use of the building on Tuesday evening. Betty Essick brought a request from the Davidson County Board of Elections for the use of the fellowship hall for the 1998 spring (May 5) and fall (November 3) voting place. Six members of the church were working at the polls at this time and could assure the proper care of the building. This, too, was accepted by the church.

Abbotts Creek Church was the first church in this part of the state to carry out a mission "In-As-Much" community project. Mike Rinehardt and Evva Spurgeon led the way in this mission effort. The pastor had read about such taking place in churches in Fayetteville and the one in the Town of Elon College and presented the idea to the church council and deacons.

Nine projects were carried out. A clean-up team directed by Linda Cantrell picked up trash on the roadside from the church up Abbotts Creek Church Road and down Mock Road. Peter Howard picked up the bags of trash and hauled a few truck loads to the dump. Several were involved in painting Mrs. Norman's house on Barney Road with Matthew Dunn leading the team. Jack Rose with several youth and adults prepared a meal at church for the workers and fixed meals for the homeless shelter in High Point. James Williams led a group repairing a garage door at the home of Evie Jones. Don Livengood and Lee Gann with mostly RA boys took care of the home and yard of Don's elderly mother in High Point. Mary Gann worked with the GAs of the church making cookies and delivering them to five fire departments in the larger community. They were given to the men and women on duty for the day. Carol Settles led some of the Acteens in taking care of the children of parents who were working at the other jobs. Betty Williams and Violet Everhart, with some additional help, cared for the children young enough to be in the nursery. This was discussed as early as February, but took place in late May, with more than one hundred people involved.

The April reports were given to the church at conference. The WMU had six women attending a Mission Extravaganza at Ridgecrest recently. The report was given by Evva Spurgeon. Matthew Dunn reporting for the Baptist Men shared with the church that ten men and women of the church had been part of an associational team working at Fort Caswell a couple of weeks earlier. Jimmy Stilley did some much-needed electrical work and had to return for additional work. The church raised enough money to put a roof on a church in Blackwolf, West Virginia. The minutes listed James Williams, Jack Rose, Hugh and Betty Jo Motsinger, Mike Rinehardt, and "others will be going to Blackwolf on April 24-25, 1998, to put the roof on."

The pastor's paragraph, in the April 20, 1998, newsletter, announced that the Cantrells were building a house in the community meaning they would continue to make their home in the Abbotts Creek community after retirement.

The Encouragers Sunday School class reported that they were working with the trustees to erect two church signs at the front entrances of the church. This was brought to the attention of the congregation by Tony Craven, Jimmy Stilley, and Michael Gann.

The new extension department workers, Betty Rose Alcon and Billie Ann Alcon, gave a report of their activity during the previous quarter. It was immediately obvious that the shut-ins would not be neglected by the new leaders.

A conference was called on May 10, 1998, and heard a recommendation from the finance committee. Chairperson Becky Sink made a motion to increase line item 444 from $4,000 to $5,240 to allow the choir to purchase thirty-five new choir robes. This motion passed.

The Nineties

The messengers from Abbotts Creek were present at Center Hill Baptist Church in Lexington for a called meeting of Liberty Baptist Association. The purpose of this session was to (and did) terminate the services of the association's director of missions.

The trustees recommended and the church accepted a bid from a cleaning service to be responsible for cleaning the church facilities. This was the first time outside help had been employed.

On July 12, 1998, as pastor, I announced my intent to retire at the end of October. This was done in sermon form rather than just reading it in the form of a letter. Since October 1, 1974, it had been a great honor being able to say, "I am a part of Abbotts Creek Baptist Church." I mentioned in the following newsletter, "I could hope the time will come when I will be able to be as supportive of my pastor as our retired minister George Dowd has been to me. What I have learned about a retired pastor in the church, George has taught me."

A couple of weeks later, Scott Ford addressed the church family by way of the newsletter. He discussed a time to recognize or honor the Cantrells, a love offering to be taken, a separate hospitality committee to plan some type farewell gathering, and what steps to take to secure an interim. He outlined the plan to be followed as directed by the constitution.

On July 19, 1998, eleven youth and chaperones left for Blackwolf, West Virginia, to participate in a mission effort leading Vacation Bible School.

The trustees recommended the church authorize Duncan's piano service to completely rebuild and refurbish the Steinway piano for the price of $7,626.44. The trustees were not finished with their recommendations. Additional septic tank lines at the church were required by the Davidson County Health Department. The church agreed to pay the $2,800 to complete this work. George and Lori Blake, members of the church and owners of the Blake's Locksmith Company, were authorized to change all outside locks for the church and provide keys as needed.

Scott Ford, deacon chairman, brought a deacon recommendation that a committee be selected to assist the Hospitality Committee in preparation for an honor celebration for the retiring pastor. The names of the committee chosen were not listed in the newsletter or minutes. An effort was made to recount those who served but the list was not conclusive. Included on this committee were Faye Curry, Kim Frank, Linda O'Connor, Molly Hedgecock, Peter Howard, Craig Burris, and Lorie Hamby.

Much discussion over the years concerned allowing women to be nominated for the position of deacons in the church. The conference

Vacation Bible School

called for September 23, 1998, was to deal with this issue. The church constitution stated deacons shall come from the membership without specifying male members. The constitution further states, "The deacons shall be elected from among those members who have proven themselves to have spiritual qualifications according to 1 Timothy 3, and Titus 1. The selection process allowed every member to nominate two persons. The deacons would then count the number of nominations each person had received and the top ones would be presented to the church equal to two more than were to be elected. Every year, the names of some outstanding ladies were listed. Sometime that person(s) would have more nominations than some of the males who were later elected by the church. But the long-standing practice had been to present only the names of male members, despite what the constitution allowed.

At this conference, two matters were presented for discussion. This sensitive issue brought more people to church than had ever attended a Wednesday night conference. There were people present who never attended any services except Sunday morning worship, not even revival services. This was a matter of great importance and people expressed heartfelt convictions.

One ballot stated in effect to follow the same practice that has always been used of electing only male members. Of 148 ballots casts, 45 percent voted yes. The second ballot was to support electing deacons "regardless of gender or previous marriage." This motion received 51.3 percent. Three ballots were turned in without being marked. The deacons had announced that in order to change the previous practice there must be a two-thirds majority. Since this percentage was not received, the election of deacons would continue to follow the previous practice of the church.

Vacation Bible School

The Interim Pastor Search Committee was announced at another called conference on September 30, 1998. Three of these would be deacons: Mike Rinehardt, Hugh Motsinger, and Joe Craven. The other four were Vicki Hilton, Becky Sink, Marshall Settles, and Matthew Dunn.

Missions were still a high priority for Abbotts Creek. Betsy Leach was to join Evelyn Reece from Cedar Lodge Baptist Church and travel to South Africa on October 6, 1998, on a mission trip. A couple of days earlier, Missionary Jimmy Joseph from Grenada was the speaker for an evening service. He discussed how the money that had been sent to Grenada was helping in starting a church building in an area of the island where there was no church.

Until this time, the church had used computers that family members had donated after purchasing a more updated one. This changed as of the September 30, 1998, conference. The trustees brought a motion to the church that the church purchase three Gateway computers plus a laser printer and a Brother 1997 fax machine. The motion was amended to purchase only two now and the third when needed, probably when a new pastor was on the field. The church accepted this amended motion and conference adjourned.

Vacation Bible School

Vacation Bible School

The church had learned that Rev. Osbert James was no longer a pastor in Grenada. However, money had been listed in the budget for the year. A storm had devastated the small Island of Nevis, a place where mission teams from the church had conducted Vacation Bible Schools in the past. The Finance Committee recommended to the church this money be sent to help purchase materials for the people from Nevis who had gone to Montserrat as refugees. The motion carried.

Reports were given at the October conference and accepted by the church. Carl Alcon, the newly-elected chairman of deacons, announced a called conference for October 21, 1998, to nominate deacons. Deacons would then be elected on November 15 or 22. The motion also included allowing the diaconate to operate with only twelve until the new ones were elected. This was acceptable to the church.

It was mentioned earlier how the study "Experiencing God" led to other studies. One such study was called "Thine is The Kingdom." Those who participated in this study were not satisfied doing nothing about what they had learned and felt. The class presented the idea to the church to begin a Labor of Love ministry. The idea was to assist person or families with need. Contacts were made with the Social Services Department, of both Davidson and Guilford counties. The church officially voted on this during this October conference. The need for this may have been underestimated at the outset but the ministry has been helpful to many families each month.

The service on October 25, 1998, was the last service for the retiring pastor. The congregation greeted the entire Cantrell Family at the front door of the church. The last one to pass through the line did so right at 2:00 p.m.

The previous evening a meal, paid for from the church's budget, had been served. The fellowship hall was filled with people. The Cantrell children were all present, David and Teresa from California, Chet and Michelle from Illinois, Chris from Greensboro, and Beth and David from Burlington. Each of them had been asked to make some comments and did. Tony Hyde served as the master of ceremonies.

Special music was provided by the Creekside Quartet, Tony Hyde, Craig Burris, Tony Craven, and Patrick Moss. They were accompanied by Kim Moss. They sang four songs. Other special music was provided by Sandi Todd, David Clemens, former music and youth director at the church, and Ann Joyce, present music director. Lorie Hamby did a flute solo.

Individuals from previous pastorates were present. Henry and Adel Homes from Mount Olivet Baptist Church, near Franklinton, North Carolina, brought some remembrance of the Cantrell's first pastorate. Hugh and Nancy Doss were present from Swepsonville Baptist Church, Graham, North Carolina. No one was present from Mayo, South Carolina, or Cherokee Baptist Church in Cherokee, North Carolina. Additional comments were made by Director of Missions Leonard Rollins and Ben Rowe, former youth and educational leader. Long-time friends of the pastor's family, Bill Morrow and Morris Hollifield, added their comments as well. Former church secretary Evva Spurgeon and the present secretary Joann Chestnutt gave an inside view of working with the pastor.

Dwight and Pansy Moore maintain personal records of the happenings at the church. Dwight had recorded some interesting information that was passed on to the retired minister some time later. The church membership on October 1974 was 466. The membership on October 25, 1998, numbered 755. Between those two dates, 363 had been baptized; 265 had joined the church by letter, and 73 by statement. In addition to those names erased, 129 members had died, and 182 had moved their church letter elsewhere.

Good reports continued to be heard at Abbotts Creek. The church was informed that some of the youth had helped in a Vacation Bible School at Hasty Baptist Church in Thomasville and in a church in West Virginia. In the report concerning senior adults, it was pointed out that the church had 135 senior adults, 40 of whom were widows.

The November 22, 1998, conference was led by Carl Alcon as moderator. Deacons elected at this time were Tony Craven, Ricky DeLappe, John Hedgecock, Zane Hedgecock, Patrick Moss, and Laurence Todd, Jr., with Rayford Hayes as alternate. Sonya Alcon was selected as trustee.

Rev. Jack Rose was moderator for a called conference, the last conference in 1998. The Finance Committee needed to redistribute some money from the pastor's salary item to care for the guest speakers who would fill the pulpit for some time. At the same time, the church adopted a proposed personnel policies manual.

Pictured here left to right: Pansy Moore, Mary Hayworth, and Mary Smith.

Pictured from left are Chet Cantrell, his wife Michelle Cantrell and Beth Cantrell.

These lovely young ladies served at the retirement dinner. Front row: Leader-Denise Marshall, Leann Chestnutt, Ashley Delappe, and Leader-Alicia Young; Back row: Nicole Hutchens, Ashley Ford, Christi Blake, Jenilee Moss, Amanda Davis, and Brittany Miller.

Chris and Chet Cantrell (back to building) are greeting those leaving after the service.

Pictured from right to left on the front pew are, David Cantrell, his wife Teresa O'Rourke, and David Counts.

CHAPTER NINETEEN

The Transitional Period

Chairman of deacons, Carl Alcon, presided at the last conference in 1998 on December 30. The Interim Search Committee had requested a called conference. A request came in the form of a motion to have Dr. Dave Odom from the North Carolina Baptist Hospital Pastoral Care Department to use the Sunday School time, on January 10, 1999, to explain the Intentional Interim Program. He would then bring the eleven o'clock message. The church would decide by vote the next Sunday if an Intentional Interim was the way the church wished to go. If approved, the search committee would review a list of qualified candidates and recommend a person to the church. On January 17, 1999, the church voted to accept the Intentional Interim Program by a vote of 182 as opposed to 44 negative votes. The church would be informed as soon as the committee had time to go through the process they felt necessary. The committee members were Becky Sink, Matthew Dunn, Marshall Settles, Joe Craven, Vicki Hilton, Mike Rinehardt, and Hugh Motsinger.

The following worship leaders were announced for the next several Sundays: The Reverend Jack Rose and Rev. R. N. Hardin one Sunday each and The Reverend Leonard Rollins for two morning services.

The first conference of 1999 heard the normal reports by organizational leaders. The new ministry, Labor of Love, reported that fifteen people had gone to the North Lexington Baptist Church to learn more about how to carry out the ministry. Already needed supplies had been given such as a filing cabinet, clothes, a freezer, and a refrigerator. Application authorizing the purchase of food from the Winston-Salem Food Bank was made. The ministry was on the verge of beginning.

Bobby Canada informed the church that someone wanted to donate a large sum of money for the prayer garden. He made the motion to open the prayer garden fund to allow this to be given and to purchase a sprinkler to

The Transitional Period

keep the "garden green and beautiful." Of course, the motion passed.

In early February, plans were being made by Betsy Leach for a return trip to South Africa. The church was carrying out fund-raising projects to assist with this. About the same time, Matthew Dunn, Patrick Moss, and Craig Burris had become a part of an associational work team also going to South Africa. Such mission teams and trips were made possible by the congregation working together to provide the means for each one to go.

The Interim Search Committee's recommendation was presented by Hugh Motsinger, chairman of the committee. Hugh "made the motion that we take a vote on an Intentional Interim Pastor, Rev. Lee Stocks and his wife Doris." The vote was 246 in favor of this recommendation with 9 opposed. The chairman announced Rev. Stocks would be at work the next day which would be March 1, 1999. A week later, The Intentional Interim Ministry Covenant was signed by Rev. Stocks and on behalf of the church by Carl Alcon. This covenant gave some of the expectations of the pastor and the church. A group called the Transitional Team would work closely with the pastor. The term of service for the Intentional Interim Pastor would be one year. This could be extended with the consent of both parties.

Sunday morning, March 21, 1999, Ann Joyce, minister of music since the summer of 1986, announced her resignation effective on July 11, 1999. It was later written in full and included in the newsletter. She had plans to be married in the summer and would move to Vermont with her husband, Clive Reed.

On the last Sunday in March, the church would have opportunity to nominate individuals who would serve as members of the Transitional Team. The nominating committee would then add five names to bring the total to fifteen. Members of this team were Lorie Hamby, Pat Dawson, Patrick Moss, Benji Frank, Hugh Motsinger, Zane Hedgecock, Carl Alcon, Bobbie Burris, Evva Spurgeon, Vicki Hilton, John Hedgecock, Matthew Dunn, Marshall Settles, Jimmy Stilley, and Scott Young.

Revival services were planned for April 15-19, 1999, with Rev. Calvin Knight as the visiting speaker.

The community mission project, Operation In-As-Much, took place on May 1, 1999. More than eighty people joined together to make a difference in the lives of community families. Storm windows were put in, painting was done, a house had a new roof put on, windows were washed, and trash along the road was picked up and carried away. Some work took place around the church such as mulching, trimming hedges, and other needed tasks. Several people worked in the kitchen preparing food for the workers

Memorial Day, Left to Right: Rev. Jimmy and Margaret Hinson, Rev. Lee and Doris Stocks, Rev. Jack and Patsy Rose, Rev. Chuck and Marilyn Garner, and Rev. Roy and Linda Cantrell

and for 45 homeless people in High Point. Marty Livengood kept the smaller children in the nursery allowing parents to work on other projects. Evva Spurgeon was the leader of the total project.

The work team left for South Africa on May 6 and returned on May 20, 1999. Russell Fox representing the Church Council brought a recommendation on May 26, 1999, that a mission project be adopted to send a work team to Nevis to construct a home for one whose home had been destroyed in a recent storm. The church would raise the $15,000 needed to purchase the material and enough to send the team of workers. After discussion, the motion passed. Later, on July 28, 1999, Pat and Parnell Ficklin, from Nevis, brought the morning message.

Other matters pertaining to background checks on future employees were also adopted during this conference.

A town meeting was called for June 20, 1999, as a part of the transitional team's purpose. Members of the congregation were able to share hopes and dreams for the church. Such information would be fed back to the Transitional Team for their discussion and consideration. If recommendations came from this process, the church would deal with each one. Topics were discussed such as appreciations for certain people and things, disappointments, suggested changes, missions, organizational issues, ministry, and many other matters. It gave the people a chance to say "this is what I like," "this is what I don't like," "this is what I would like to see changed." This gave the interim pastor and the Transitional Team ideas to discuss. Among other topics, the unsettled issue of female deacons or divorced persons serving in that role was discussed.

The Transitional Period

It was also decided to secure an interim music director until the church decided what the future program of the church would need. A conference was called on July 28, 1999, to deal with a recommendation from the interim music director search committee. Bobby Canada made the presentation. The request was to call an interim music director with the understanding he (she) be allowed to work twenty hours per week with the pay stated as $15 per hour. This motion passed and it was announced that he would be present with the choir on Wednesday and "do his trial Sunday on the 8th (August, 1999)."

The Rev. David Clemens, who had previously served as music and youth director of the church, was recommended and elected by a positive vote of 226 with 26 opposing.

August had been declared to be "Heritage Month." Among other things taking place, Vicki Hilton, Benji Frank, and Zane Hedgecock planned and carried out a reenactment of an 1899 service for the congregation. A history room was arranged with special memorabilia from the past on display.

Carl Alcon presided at the called business conference on his birthday, August 25, 1999. Officers for the new years were presented by Patrick Moss and accepted by the church. The first mention of "volunteer bond redemption of $20,000 with a $25,000 interest total, calling for $45,000" was given by the church treasurer, Becky Sink. This motion passed.

Several times a month, the newsletter carried information about the money being raised to build a house on the thirty-six-square-mile Island of Nevis. By August 22, 1999, almost $14,000 had been collected. Announcement was made for a group meeting to be held to determine who the builders would be.

Deacons were elected on September 12, 1999. They were J. C. Alcon, Scott Ford, Ronnie Young, Hugh Motsinger, Don Myers, and Joe Craven. Jimmy Stilley was selected as the new trustee.

A second town meeting was scheduled for mid-September. Members were encouraged to say in small groups what they liked or disliked "about past/present ministerial staff." "What has disappointed you most about past and present ministers and church staff?" The idea was to help determine qualities the congregation would like to see in future staff members.

When the new budget was presented, it was pointed out the secretary's pay was increased by 24 percent. The committee explained this was to help bring the pay up to what church secretaries were being paid. The church had lagged behind for years in this area.

Nine men went, in early October, to Mount Holly Baptist Church near

Choir on Sunday morning of Heritage Day 1999

Burgaw, North Carolina to work with homes of flood victims. In some homes, they removed insulation and paneling and whatever else was necessary tearing out the interior so new materials could be used to repair the homes. During their days there, they worked on four different houses. The group consisted of Lee and Danny Gann, Bobby Alcon, James Williams, Wayne Bullard, Lee Nooe, John Hedgecock, George Blake, and Tom Schultz.

The October 11, 1999, newsletter informed the members of the church's first website.

On October 13, 1999, Evva Spurgeon representing the Church Council brought a recommendation for the church to pay plane fare and other related expenses for the work team going to Nevis to build the house mentioned earlier in the minutes.

A November 3, 1999, called conference heard Bobby Canada bring a recommendation from the trustees to plant a Weeping Cherry Tree near the flagpole. The tree was given in memory of the late Dwight Moore by friends of his son, Michael. Michael planted the tree and a monument was placed at the base. The dedica-

Pictured on Heritage Day, 1999, is Seth Moore, now deceased.

The Transitional Period

tion of the tree was held after the morning worship service on November 28, 1999. With the congregation gathered around the tree, Zane Hedgecock made remarks about Dwight's life and numerous contributions he had made to the life and history of Abbotts Creek Church. Laurence Todd, chairman of deacons, read the inscription on the monument before Rev. Jack Rose led the dedication prayer.

At the Baptist State Convention in November, Abbotts Creek was recognized as one of the top ten churches in North Carolina for state mission contributions in 1998. This was in the size category for the church and for total dollars given. The newsletter states, "we ranked number two in the 300-499 Sunday School enrollment, giving for North Carolina Missions Offering for the total dollars given, and for the per member giving."

The church voted on December 1, the last conference in 1999, to purchase a second van for the church. This motion passed by a vote of 49 with 15 opposing.

The decade of the nineties ended with a work team going back to the eastern part of the state to work with disaster relief needed after so many homes were damaged or destroyed by the previous flooding conditions. Their

Heritage Old Fashion Day, 1999, Vicki Hilton, Zane Hedgecock, and Evva Spurgeon

Rev. Lee Stocks dipping homemade ice cream, Heritage Day 1999.

journey took the team members to the First Baptist Church in Tarboro where they lodged and received their work assignment. Team members were James and Jamie Williams, Wayne Bullard, Lee Nooe, George, Lori and Christy Blake, J. C. and Bobby Alcon, Lewis Peacock, John Hedgecock, Chris Halker, Dean McGuire, and Tom Schultz.

The new millennium (2000) opened with the church having been active in four different centuries. The January 10, 2000, newsletter gave the following report concerning the work team's efforts to rebuild the home for the John Bellot family in Nevis: "John and his wife have both been working on the Island of Nevis after they lost their home due to volcanic action on Montserrat. Mrs. Bellot lost her job (in Nevis) when the hotel where she was working was destroyed by Hurricane Lenny. The Bellots have three children, the youngest of which was born during the holidays (Christmas)." The conference of January 12, 2000, showed in the financial report that the plane fares had been paid for the people on the Nevis work assignment. It was also announced that Dr. Tom Lolley, state missionary to Western North Carolina, would be present to discuss the gender and marital status of prospective deacons.

The after school program reported an enrollment of sixty-five children and most of those attending were full time. The report added, "There are seven workers included the director, Carol Settles."

The deacons brought a recommendation for the covenant between Lee and Doris Stocks and the church to be extended to the time it takes to secure a pastor. It was mentioned that a large contribution had been donated for the Prayer Garden but the amount was not stated. The January financial report shows a balance of $23,000 in the prayer garden fund. Other reports were also given.

A called conference February 9, 2000, heard a report from the "T" Team. This committee of five would be recommended by the nominating committee, which would include at least one trustee. The task of the committee was outlined to study the church property "reviewing available building areas on our current church property and their feasibility." That committee was elected on March 22, 2000, and was composed of Tony Fowler, Zane Hedgecock, Peter Howard, Jim Stilley, and Mike Motsinger.

Other matters pertaining to background checks on future employees were also adopted during this conference.

The pastor gave a report in the February 21, 2000 issue of *The Tie* concerning the associate pastor being enrolled in the clinical pastoral educational program conducted by the Department of Chaplaincy and Pastoral

THE TRANSITIONAL PERIOD

Education at Wake Forest University Baptist Medical Center. This study had been approved by the church. The course would take place February 21 -May 9, 2000. Rev. Rose would do the clinical part of the study with the Abbotts Creek Church family.

Laurence Todd, Jr. presided at the called conference for March 1, 2000. The Board of Election of Davidson County had requested the use of the fellowship hall for the community voting place in May and again in November. The church approved this request.

The "T" team did a church survey regarding membership profile. Eighty-three people responded in this study. The information revealed 38.6 percent of the membership was sixty-five years old or older. Another 18.1 percent had ages ranging from fifty-five through sixty-four. About 26 percent fell in the age range of forty-five or under. Sixty-eight percent of those mentioned had attended Abbotts Creek for twenty or more years.

The March 13, 2000, newsletter included information from the after school care committee. The committee had been dealing with the questions raised in the town meeting concerning the ministry of the after school care. "Should the after school day care pay to use the church facilities?" The committee responded to the question in this way. "We would like to inform the church family that the after school care ministry had been giving financially to the church since its inception. Starting in the school year of

The Nevis work team is pictured in front of the house they built: Jimmy Stilley (kneeling) (from left front row) Betty and James Williams, Georgette and Wayne Bullard, Frances Peacock; (back row) Matthew Dunn and Lewis Peacock

1995–1996, $24,450 has been given to date. Of that, $7,225 was given during the 1999 calendar year alone."

The Rev. Tom Stocks, pastor of Rosalind Hills Church, in Roanoke, Virginia was the visiting evangelist for revival services May 7-May 10, 2000. He is the son of Lee and Doris Stocks.

The quarterly conference in April reported a very strong cash position. The finance committee announced that calls would be made for volunteer bonds for 2003, 2004, and 2005. Bonds totaling $50,000 could have been paid but only $9,000 was paid.

Pastor Stocks brought the recommendation from the church council projecting busy days for the summer. First, the church would conduct a Vacation Bible School in Arnoldsburg, West Virginia. The second plan was to send a mission team to Honduras to build houses for the victims of Hurricane Mitch. The third project included the youth from the church leading a Bible school in West Virginia.

The conference was busy with numerous reports. One report came from the deacons concerning the search committee for a new pastor. Those nominated were Russell Fox, John Hedgecock, Hugh Motsinger, Crystal Myers, Evva Spurgeon, Kandi Stilley, and Laurence Todd. When a question came up about why no youth were members of the committee, Charles Davis made a motion that someone between the age of eighteen and twenty-five be added. This entire motion passed. Sherry Byrd was added to the committee on June 14, 2000.

Mrs. Edith Hood had been generous in her gifts to the church. Earlier, she had donated money for the prayer garden. At this conference, J. C. Alcon reported money had been given to pave the upper driveway of the cemetery. There would also be enough to do other clean up work. The kindness and generosity of Mrs. Hood was seen again.

Mike Motsinger representing the Nominating Committee made the motion to accept the printed job descriptions for the various committees of the church.

Called conferences seemed to be the order of the day showing various committees carrying out the business of the church. June 9, 2000, was such a conference. The trustees recommended the purchase of a duplicator copy machine for the Media Center at the cost of $2,522.80. Three tapes could be duplicated at one time.

The trustee presented another recommendation. "The trustees recommend that we accept a triangle parcel of land given by Abbotts Creek Primitive Church with the understanding that we help them find their property lines, and give them a small parcel that is on state right of way on their side in order to have a straight line between the two churches. Abbotts Creek Missionary Baptist Church would bear all expenses of lawyer fees for change and expenses the surveyor might have." Mike Motsinger, a member of the church, had agreed to do the surveying.

The trustees further recommended that the church accept a gift of land from Larry and Libby Essick. This land is "a wedge shape parcel of land approximately 35 feet wide on Abbotts Creek Church Road running north 180 feet to metal pipe." All three motions passed.

The called conference on June 14, 2000, heard the report from the transportation committee with prices for two different vans with 25,000 miles or less on each. Much discussion took place with questions being asked. A motion was made to purchase a new van but failed to pass by a 17-22 vote. More discussion was heard and then a motion to pursue a van with a center aisle was made. Finally, the committee was asked to investigate a new or used van and bring a recommendation back to the church for disposition.

The quarterly conference on July 12, 2000, had eighteen reports called for and most had reports to give verbally or in printed form. At this very meeting time, the youth were in West Virginia on a mission trip. Eleven days later, the group going to Honduras was commissioned with Rev. Mike Ester, associational missionary, as the speaker.

A letter was attached to the business reports regarding the after school care program. The church continued to be blessed with one of it most successful ministries. A parent wrote, "Abbotts Creek has been a blessing to many of us.... Quality day cares are extremely limited to say the least.... To have the peace of mind that our children are being taken care of in a safe nurturing Christian environment is worth more than you will ever know. Since starting to Abbotts Creek after school care my son has begun praying every night, leading prayers at meals and has asked if maybe we should start back to church."

The day of August 23, 2000, found the church in a called conference. A motion was made for the church to pay for the evening meal for the Liberty Baptist Association's meeting to be held at the church in October. The second matter involved the transportation committee with Craig Burris and Bobby Canada bringing the motion and information. Their recommendation was for the church to secure a mini-bus rather than a van at the total cost of $49,910 plus tax, title fee, and tags. This motion passed with 60 in favor and one opposed.

One week passed before another conference was called. Hugh Motsinger brought to the attention of the church, on behalf of the Pastoral Search Committee, a compensation package for a prospective pastor. This was given in a way to help the church see the difference in the actual income the pastor would receive and what the cost would be for the church. For instance, health insurance, retirement, car expense, and other such benefits that would not be pocket money for the pastor but a cost to the church were included in the report.

The first church newsletter of September 2000 quoted an article first used in the "Sustaining the Miracle" newsletter published by Wake Forest Baptist Medical Center. It concerned the late Harry Hood, Jr., who had been a member of Abbotts Creek Church. Harry had lived with disabilities and had numerous operations over his life's span. Harry expressed his appreciation for what Dr. Gary Poehlin had meant to him over the years doing several surgeries. He made a sizeable contribution to Dr. Poehlin's research in orthopedic surgery. According to the article, Harry's mother, Edith Hood, added to that gift with almost $200,000 in Harry's memory. There is a plaque in the Medical Center's CompRehab Plaza mentioning the Hood Research Fund.

In September, a trustee and deacons were elected. Deacons were Frank Hedgecock, David Chestnutt, Wayne Bullard, Billy Hutchens, Andy Chappell, and Evan Myers. Tom Schultz was chosen to serve as trustee.

On September 20, 2000, a conference was called to present the proposed budget for the New Year. The budget with some slight modifications passed. The teachers and other officers and committees for the church were elected at this time as well. A missions committee was appointed to "research and discuss mission opportunities" that might be presented by the association, state, or mission boards where church members could be involved.

Numerous reports were given at the quarterly conference on October 11, 2000. The after school care program had been discussed from various angles. Some felt a business was being operated within the church while paying no rent as such. From time to time when the report of this ministry was given to the church, it was mentioned that a contribution was made to the church by the director which was more than a tithe of the profit earned. A committee had studied this ministry thoroughly before bringing a recommendation back to the church allowing it to operate as it had in the past.

By the first conference in 2001, January 17, Patrick Moss was chairman of deacons and presiding. Numerous reports were given, some as printed while others were given with explanations. Among the reports given, David Essick shared the ministry of the Labor of Love saying, "We are giving away 1500 to 2000 pounds of food a month." Pat Dawson shared that the attorneys dealing with the Charles Hayworth estate have informed the church, "That we need to purchase the new organ this year." A listed committee included the names of Pam DeLappe, Pam Ford, Christy Fox, Kim Moss, Charles Davis, and Sonya Alcon. They were asked to deal with this matter.

The first newsletter of the new year shared several helping activities carried on by the church. Sue Young and The Rev. Jack Rose were assisted by Nicholas Paul, Zach Ritchie, Charles Myers, Austin Craven, Kelly Baker, Ben Cline, Allen Young, Nathan Cockrum, and Christopher Meredith in feeding hot lunches to two hundred homeless men and women in High Point plus sharing gift bags with them. Zach Ritchie, T. Dawson, Allen Young, and John Hedgecock removed leaves from the yard of Don and Marty Livengood. Ashley DeLappe, Christi Blake, Patsy, and The Rev. Jack Rose traveled to Blackwolf, West Virginia, and delivered stuffed stockings for the children of the Blackwolf Church. Christmas for these Abbotts Creek people was indeed a time of sharing.

The very next newsletter carried a thank-you note from Dale Marshall who had just returned from a medical mission trip to Jamaica. He, along with three other team members, provided "a free doctor's clinic" in an area that had been without any medical help since a similar team had left three months earlier.

It was announced that the new bus should be delivered by March 1, 2001. The chairman of the pastor search committee asked the church to increase the proposed salary for the prospective pastor by 10 percent in order to bring the pay up to what their prospects were being paid already. All the above matters were passed.

The trustees brought a recommendation for consideration regarding upgrading the sound system for the church. The motion presented was amended by Lorie Hamby to include two small speakers in the hall entrances enabling the choir members to hear as they entered the sanctuary. The total cost of this upgrading with the amendment was almost $13,000, which the church accepted.

The land search committee brought a drawing for the congregation showing the layout of the church property. "This committee presented a drawing of the Abbotts Creek site plan and the study they had done in checking to see how much land would perk and where buildings could be built on the existing land that we have. Abbotts Creek owns eighteen and one-half acres and is able to use only eleven or twelve acres of land." This committee was composed of three builders, Tony Fowler, Jimmy Stilley, Zane Hedgecock, a licensed surveyor, Mike Motsinger, and an engineer, Peter Howard.

The prayer service on February 7, 2001, was lead by Dale Marshall. Dale shared his recent medical mission trip to Jamaica.

On March 18, 2001, on behalf of the search committee, Hugh Motsinger brought to the attention of the church a letter signed by each member of the search committee recommending Rev. Mark O. Hollar to become pastor of the church. The Rev. Hollar had served as pastor of Baptist Home Church in North Wilkesboro, North Carolina for the past ten years. He and his wife, Anita, have two children, Laura Nicole, and Rebekah Emily. He graduated from Appalachian State University and in 1985 graduated from Southeastern Seminary at Wake Forest, North Carolina. His excellent credentials were included on two pages plus the schedule of events for calling him as pastor. There would be time to study the resume and ask the committee questions. The committee planned for a "floating reception in the fellowship hall to give everyone an opportunity to meet the prospective new pastor and his family." The next day, April 1, 2001, he would share information about himself and then bring the morning message. The vote would be taken and the church informed of the count. If called, the new minister would begin his work on June 1, 2001.

In the called conference on April 1, 2001, Hugh Motsinger spoke on behalf of the search committee and served as moderator. Three hundred nineteen ballots were turned in with 305 voting to call Rev. Hollar as pastor with 14 negative vote or 95.6 percent.

The regular quarterly conference for the church was held on April 11, 2001, with Patrick Moss serving as moderator. Pastor Lee Stocks brought the recommendation from the Missions Committee asking the church to support seven mission trips that had been projected for the year. These would involve more members in more trips than any previous year. The church would take care of 30 percent of the cost of those going. A medical support team would serve in a girl's camp in Alaska leaving on July 10, 2001. Betsy Leach and Christy Blake were the two for this assignment. The next day, a construction team left. Their destination was Alaska also.

The church responded to a request from South Africa for a Sunday School and evangelistic team. Some would serve in the need for a disaster relief team going to Grifton, North Carolina, and El Salvador. During the second week in July several adults and youth went to West Virginia for Bible School. The church provided part of a larger team going to the Ukraine.

The minutes included a small booklet detailing the work of the Transitional Team over the past several months. This concluded with high praise for Lee and Doris Stocks for their superb leadership. The team "expressed that the strength of Lee and Doris Stocks has been wonderful, and the knowledge they brought before our church was in the value of teamwork. They opened eyes, gave new visions and began supervision of staff, which included updated staff evaluations. They taught many to be leaders and they are compassionate and showed understanding. They were both encouragers." Rev. and Mrs. Stocks had made a valuable contribution to the church and fell in love with the community to the extent they decided to build their home in the community. In addition to the Stocks and Cantrell families, former pastor Dr. Joe Coltrane and his wife Zemma have built their home and live in the Abbotts Creek community.

The April 9, 2001, newsletter of the church contains Rev. Stocks' notice of the end of their ministry at Abbotts Creek. The morning service of April 22, 2001, would be their final service. The church held a celebration service and gathered in the fellowship hall for a pot luck lunch that day.

The following week, *The Tie* outlined the speakers for the worship service throughout the month until the new pastor arrived. These services were led by Rev. Jack Rose and Rev. David Clemens. At the evening service of April 22, 2001, someone from Moore's Music Company was present to demonstrate the new organ which the church had on "trial." The same newsletter spelled out the dual role of the co-treasurers, Becky Sink, and Jennifer Blevins. Becky would have the responsibility of the cash receipts and deposits detailing any special matters relating to gifts or designations. Jennifer would take care of the check writing, paying bills, and maintaining and reconciling the bank accounts. Other responsibilities were spelled out in detail.

In the last newsletter in April, the new pastor shared by letter his excitement about being called to serve at Abbotts Creek. The Hollar family began the process of saying their goodbyes and making plans to become a part of the Abbotts Creek family.

In early May, Joann Chestnutt announced her resignation at secretary at the church, a position she had held for eight years. Joann had been a tireless worker very dedicated to her task and to the church. A love offering was taken on May 27 and June 3, 2001, for her in appreciation of her contributions to the work of the church.

The personnel committee reported to the church their recommendation to secure an interim secretary allowing the new pastor to arrive and have input as to who the full time secretary would be. Their report added that the church would continue to use the term interim minister of music allowing Rev. Hollar to evaluate the need and give a recommendation to the committee. The committee continued to study the need for an additional staff member to expand the youth and children's ministry.

The church was informed of a $5,000 gift for the building fund from the estate of the late John Welborn, Jr.

The International Mission Board had received the money the church had sent for the Baptist work in Grenada back in November of 2000. However, the money did not get to its intended destination until much later. In fact, the May 14, 2001, newsletter included a note from Jimmy Joseph, Missionary in Grenada stating such. His letter explained it was being used to purchase blocks for a new church building in a poor community on the East Coast of the Island.

Alaska Mission Team: (front row) James & Betty Williams, Betty Jo & Hugh Motsinger; (second row) Lewis and Francis Peacock, Evva Spurgeon; (third row:) John Hedgecock & Dean McGuire; (fourth row) Wayne Bullard, Tony Fowler, & Mathew Dunn; (back row:) Charlie Davis, Benji & Jonathan Frank, Carl Alcon, and J. C. Alcon

CHAPTER TWENTY

June 2001–August 2006

The new pastor began his preaching ministry on June 3, 2001. A "Pastor-Church Covenant" was signed by the pastor, the chairman of deacons, Patrick Moss, and the pastor search committee, namely, Hugh Motsinger, Evva Spurgeon, Kandi Stilley, Sherry Byrd, John Hedgecock, Russell Fox, Laurence Todd, Jr., and Crystal Myers. The covenant was broken down into several headings. 1. The pastor's expectation of the church. 2. The church's expectation of its pastor. 3. The pastor's obligation to his church. 4. The church's obligation to its pastor. 5. Matters of mutual Agreement. 6. Annual salary compensation. 7. Church ministry related expenses. 8. Annual time arrangement.

The new pastor arrived at Abbotts Creek at a very exciting time. Almost immediately the youth headed to Caswell for youth week. Vacation Bible School also took place in June. How impressive it was to have the dedicated faculty make up of many public school teachers plus other highly talented and qualified persons carrying out Bible school for a total enrollment of 328.

The first conference the new pastor moderated was a short called conference for the nomination of deacons. This took place on Sunday morning, June 24, 2001. His first quarterly conference was held on July 11, 2001. Many of the reports for this conference were typed and handed out including the minutes of the previous quarterly conference and any called ones since the middle of April. Minutes of this conference were recorded by assistant clerk, Donna Tucker.

Among the other reports given, David Essick, on behalf of the Labor of Love ministry, reported twenty or thirty families were being served each month. The extension workers reported fifty-four visits during the previous quarter. Betty Rose and Billie Ann Alcon had stayed busy carrying out this ministry.

It was reported that an additional youth worker was on board for the summer. He was Drew Rorex. Plans were given for some future happenings among the youth and senior adults. Drew kept the church informed of the activities in the weekly newsletter.

In the pastor's comments in the July 9, 2001, newsletter, he reported on the commissioning service for forty-three persons who were committed to summer mission trips.

On July 21, 2001, a team left for West Virginia working in an area heavily damaged by flooded conditions. It was a sad situation as the team members viewed the community which was already poverty stricken. For two weeks, the church had a place designated to collect relief items. Food products were needed along with household supplies and personal hygiene items. Thirty-four people were a part of this cleanup group.

A called conference took place on July 25. On behalf of the nominating committee, Pat Dawson presented the general officers plus teachers and committees for the 2001–2002 year.

The newsletter for August 20, 2001, informed the church family that Keith Gallimore would serve the remaining term as a trustee replacing Jimmy Stilley, whose workload prohibited him from serving. The trustees encouraged anyone to become a part of the team helping around the church if they had extra time saying that there would be small jobs to do. "Your help would be appreciated."

The next called conference was held on September 5, 2001. The church needed to approve the Congregational Profile to be presented to the association and elect messengers to attend the meetings. It was announced at this time that Donald Myers had been chosen as chairman of the deaconship for the year 2001–2002. A notation was included in the minutes stating the church was in need of a minister to care for the youth and children. Additional information would be coming regarding this.

The church voted for deacons on September 9, 2001, and elected Carl Alcon, Tony Hyde, Rick Robertson, Bob Best, Mike Motsinger, Jamie Williams, with Michael Gann named as an alternate. John Hedgecock was chosen as trustee. At this same conference, David Clemens offered his resignation as interim minister of music. His letter of resignation was given to the clerk for inclusion in the minutes. Vicki Davis, the church-elected assistant music director, assumed the role of directing the choir and leading congregational singing. She had served in this capacity for a number of years.

The tragedy of the terrorists on 9-11-01, and the two buildings at the Trade Center, brought the church together at Abbotts Creek that evening.

JUNE 2001–AUGUST 2006

It was announced that the church doors would be open from 6:00 a.m. until 6:00 p.m. over the next several days for any who wished to stop by to pray. At the time of the terrorists' attack, Betsy Leach and Kim Moss were attempting to leave South Africa after completing their medical mission assignment. Their return was delayed for a short time.

A committee searching for a minister to students was ready to present a prospective leader. They recommend David and Ellen Mills to the church including a letter of introduction. A timetable was given for meeting the couple with September 29, 2001, as the time for voting. If elected, he would begin work on October 13, 2001.

Rev. David Clemens, minister of music

The proposed budget for 2001–2002 was presented at a conference called for that purpose on September 19, 2001. After much discussion and questions, the budget passed as presented. The needed amount to meet the budget was $9,070 each week. It was announced that Wayne Bullard "and a group of eight" would be traveling to West Virginia on Thursday working on a home for a disabled veteran. Rev. Russ Dixon from Elkin was announced as the visiting minister for the revival service scheduled to begin October 28, 2001. "Jamie Williams who had just returned from South Africa on a mission trip closed in prayer."

Seven days later, a conference was called asking the church to approve a recommendation from the deacons regarding a search committee to access the need for and to proceed in securing a minister for youth and children. This motion passed.

The church met for its regular quarterly conference. The normal reports were given. The deacons presented the names of Wayne Bullard, Vickie Davis, Sonya Alcon, Tarinda Chappell, Tony Hyde, Crystal Myers, and Perry Griffin, to serve as search committee for a youth/children's worker. Ricky DeLappe was chosen as an alternate. The committee was also asked to look into the music needs of the church and find a full-time or part-time staff member for this position.

The personnel committee recommended that Linda Russell be named church secretary thus having the term "interim" removed. This was to be retroactive to October 1, 2001, as far as benefits were concerned.

The second recommendation from the personnel committee concerned the continued employment for Drew Rorex as minister of youth and children. His compensation would come from the budgeted item for this position. This, too, would be retroactive back to the first of the month.

The church was informed at this meeting that the previous cleaning service was no longer under contract by the church. Sonya Alcon and Andrea Valero had assumed this responsibility.

Mrs. Linda Russell, church secretary

On December 5, 2001, the church was called into conference and heard a recommendation from the staff search committee. First, it was spelled out that the Rev. Jack Rose was now minister for senior adults. Tony Hyde made a motion getting the affirmation from the church to look for a full time youth/children worker and a part-time minister of music. After this motion passed, Mike Rinehardt representing the finance committee made a motion to add a line item in the budget including $500 to cover expense of the search committee.

The New Year, 2002, opens with the first conference being held on January 16. The treasurer's report was given showing the church was strong financially. Some explanation was given to clarify any line item that might have raised a question. To show the thoroughness of the treasurer's report, sixteen typewritten pages were used. This included the amount of every check and the cause for which it was written. Numerous other reports were given keeping the church informed about the many organizations at work in the church. The after school care report showed sixty-eight children enrolled full time in this caring ministry. As their mission project for Christmas, the children brought canned goods for the Labor of Love ministry. A total of 542 cans were brought.

The finance committee, represented by Jennifer Blevins, brought six recommendations for consideration. The salary for the pastor was increased by 2.6 per cent. The associate pastor would be reimbursed for mileage at the acceptable IRS standard. The instrumentalists playing the piano or organ for funerals would be reimbursed by the church. Five hundred dollars was added for "kitchen supplies." This was an increase for the total budget by

$4,878. All of this was approved by the church. In addition, the church voted to secure a commercial bankcard with a maximum line of credit of $10,000. The pastor, associate pastor, and church secretary would each have a card with a certain limit. In addition, Evva Spurgeon, for the Labor of Love ministry would carry a card. Purchasing food for the Wednesday night meals would mean Sue Young would have the last card secured. Of course, these five cards would only be used for the ministry of the church.

Several of the reports were given in printed form for the congregation and to be included in the church's minutes.

Two weeks passed before the church was called into conference with a two-fold purpose. The finance committee recommended the church call all remaining bonds before maturity. The total call would be $149,000. Some of the payment would be from the church's capital reserve fund and the other ($100,000) from the Edith Hood contribution to the church. It was later learned Mrs. Hood's Estate had specified the money was to be used for scholarships for college students therefore could not be used for any other purpose.

The pastor and Wayne Bullard gave the recommendation from the church council regarding mission trips for the year. These projects would be in keeping with suggestions from the State Convention or the Liberty Association. Individuals or teams would be going to Honduras, Alaska, West Virginia, and New York. The church would support each participant up to 50 percent of the cost. The pastor would lead the group to New York in July. Betsy Leach was to serve as leader for the Alaska group to work in a camp also in July. Jack Rose planned to lead the workers to Honduras. Backyard Bible schools would be held at various places in the local community.

It seemed conferences were called often to deal with matters that should not be delayed. Again in February 2002, two matters needed the attention of the church. One was to state the bond call had been canceled. A report to the church would come later.

The second matter was a question-and-answer time concerning a new minister of music. The committee searching for a minister of music was made up of Perry Griffin, Vicki Davis, Tony Hyde, Sonya Alcon, Tarinda Chappell, Ricky Delappe, Crystal Myers, and with Wayne Bullard as an alternate. This committee unanimously recommended the church extend a call to Mrs. Rebecca Barnes for part-time work. This part-time position would amount to twenty hours per week. This information was given to the church on March 13, 2002. One week later, the conference was called to vote on her. Her credentials were outstanding and the church voted with 278 positive and four negative. Mrs. Barnes began her work on March 18, 2002.

April 28-May 1, 2002, Missionary Lee Ray Green was the visiting Evangelist for revival service. He and his family were serving as Southern Baptist missionaries in Tanzania and were on furlough.

The April 29, 2002, newsletter offers congratulations to the Bible Drill team from the church. The state winners for the youth were Brooke Anthony, Laura Hollar, and Christina McGuire. Laura had received the highest score allowing her to participate later in the finalist drill. The children's Bible Drill state winners were Brianna Anthony, Amber Chappell, Kyle DeLappe, Anna Hayworth, Rebekah Hollar, Radford Hyde, Rebecca Moss, Tyler Myers, and Cody Williams. Rebekah Hollar had been a state winner for three years.

The May 6, 2002, newsletter served as a reminder of the achievement of the youth and young adults in the church. Ten were graduating from five different high schools and seven had completed requirements for their college degree from five different colleges.

An announcement was made on May 22, 2002, at a called conference that youth worker Drew Rorex would end his service the last Sunday of May in order to enroll at the college division of Southeastern Seminary.

Anita Hollar was elected to lead the children and preteens ministry for up to twenty hours each week during the summer months only.

A staff search committee along with the youth and children's council brought a request to the church to name a preteen council to oversee a specific ministry involving the current and rising fifth and sixth graders. The children's council was composed of Lori Idol, Anita Hollar, Tracy Gann, Sherri Byrd, Debbie Anthony, Lorie Hamby, and Angie Essick. The recommendation for the preteen council includes Sonya Alcon, Crystal Myers, Dawn Williams, Anita Hollar, Barbara Hyde, and Tarinda Chappell. The church body accepted the recommendation.

Forty-three families were represented at the called conference on June 19, 2002. Two recommendations were given. First, a research scholarship committee was nominated for the Edith Hood gift to the church. The church had learned the estate designated the money for scholarship for the youth of the church. Gaye Anderson was to chair this committee made up of Jennifer Blevins, Molly Hedgecock, Bobby Canada, Andy Chappell, Charlie Davis, and Sandy Jordan. The preteen council ministry team mentioned above was voted on at this meeting.

At this conference, the prayer list for the evening included the names of

Walter and Dot Dills who were serving on a work mission project in Alaska for the summer. Matthew Dunn was serving there for the summer as well. This Abbotts Creek trio would be working with various mission groups traveling to Nikiski, Alaska, and building the parsonage for the North Kenia Baptist Church. Jenilee Moss was serving on the staff at Caswell for the summer. Jenilee was the first female youth from the church to serve on the Caswell staff.

A week passed before another called conference. The business matter involved financial resources included for the staff search committee. The line item in the budget for the ministry for children was increased to meet the expected need. At the time the pastor was called to the church, he and the church had agreed on a covenant that stated the church was to pay utilities for one year and then an appropriate amount based on the past twelve months expenses would be added to the pastor's benefit package, at which time he would assume payment for the utilities. This agreement was confirmed by the vote of the church. The church approved the extra funds necessary to cover the trash pickup for the parsonage. All of the above matters were approved with thirty-five families represented. The church also approved paying the "tenant insurance" for the contents in the pastor's home.

Four days later, Sunday June 30, 2001, the church was in conference again for the purpose of allowing members twelve years and older to nominate two male members of the church for deacons. From this, a list would be prepared and those with the highest number of those nominated would be presented to the church for the election of the required number.

Reports were heard from the various organizational leaders during the quarterly conference held on July 17, 2002. Bobbi Burris gave the Labor of Love ministry report saying forty families had been served caring for the needs of 117 family members. Betty Jo Motsinger reported 429 persons had been enrolled in the church's Vacation Bible School and the backyard Bible schools. This was the highest number ever to attend Vacation Bible School at Abbotts Creek. The extension department reported sisters Betty Rose and Billie Ann Alcon had visited with forty-five of the homebound members.

By the July conference, the pastor and his wife, Anita, gave the report for the children, preteens and youth. Mrs. Hollar was working with this group for the summer.

Tony Craven brought a recommendation on behalf of the playground committee. The recommended equipment cost would be $25,000 of which $16,000 had been raised and was on hand. A committee would be selected to work with the trustees in caring for this ministry. The church voted to accept this proposal.

The North Carolina Baptist Men's Dental and Medical Van was at Abbotts Creek on August 11, 2002. This gave migrant workers a chance for free medical service provided by nurses, doctors and dentists who had volunteered their time and skills.

At the business meeting on August 21, 2002, committees and teachers were elecated for the 2002–2003 church year.

The main business on September 8, 2002, was the election of six deacons and a trustee. Deacons elected were Ricky DeLappe, John Hedgecock, Zane Hedgecock, Patrick Moss, Lee Nooe, and Scott Young. Hugh Motsinger was chosen as trustee.

September 18, 2002, the proposed budget for the church year 2002-2003 was presented to the church. The five-page itemized listed budget was an increase of three per cent over the previous year. In dollar amounts, it was $14,183.75 more. In addition to the five-page proposal, there was an eight-page "Glossary of Budget Line Items." This gave an explanation of each line item and the party responsible to the church for the expenditures. The congregation was informed that the church debt would be paid off by September 15, 2002.

Other matters for consideration at the conference were the approval of the church letter to be sent to the Liberty Baptist Association's office and the election of committees and teachers for the approaching church year that had been added since the August 21, 2002, vote.

The building project for the church began in 1987. The minutes of a conference called on September 29, 2002, record this. "This was a Sunday set aside for sharing the history of the church and for burning the note that began as a debt of $1,000,000, for a church that was prayed for and built and paid for this day." In addition to the note burning, the church voted to call David Mills as minister to students, ages two through college youth. There were 259 votes in favor of calling them and there were 4 votes against.

Following the note burning, there was a lunch at church. After the meal, Dale and Angie Essick offered a ride on the wagon pulled by their horse. Amanda Moss gave carriage rides while Ronnie Young provided rode in his old car, a 1929 Model A.

The fourth quarterly conference for the year was held on October 16, 2002. Numerous reports were given, some verbally, and others were printed. These reports were accepted by the church. There were no recommendations from any group requiring a vote.

JUNE 2001–AUGUST 2006

In addition to the four regularly quarterly conferences, the church had been called into conference nine times during the year before the one held on November 13, 2002. Two matters came to the attention of the church on this date. A wedding policy was presented for consideration and accepted by the church. The second matter was a requirement of Southeastern Baptist Theological Seminary assuring the school that David Mills was an active member of the church.

An added notice was included in the bulletin for the evening. The Acteens of the church were making plans to attend the National Acteens Convention in Nashville, Tennessee, in July of 2003. They were now in the process of raising funds to assist with this. One way would be preparing another cookbook with recipes from church families or friends.

Note burning

Pictured here is Amanda Moss with a horse and carriage on Old Fashion Day.

History, Heritage, and Memories

Old Fashion Day 2002, with Ronnie Young in his old car

Choir on Old Fashion Day

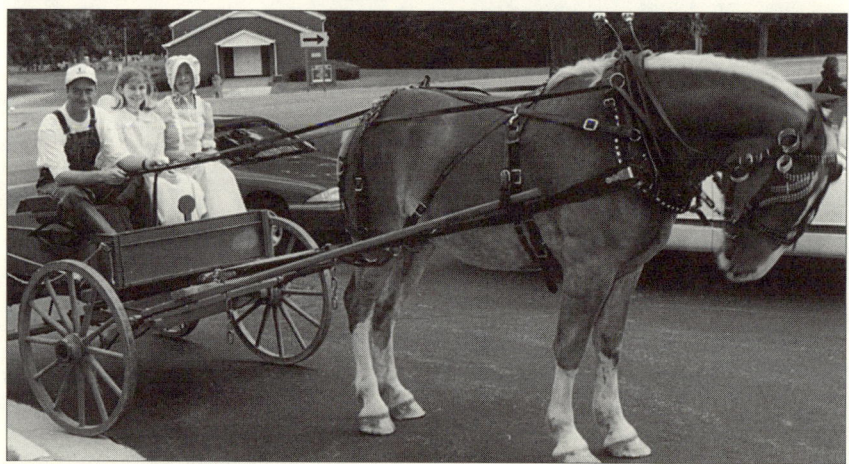
Dale Essick's horse and wagon on Old Fashion Day, 2002

JUNE 2001–AUGUST 2006

Congregation, Old Fashion Day, 2002

Old Fashion Day 2002: Evva Spurgeon holding Megan Gann, Jack Rose, Doris and Rev. Lee Stocks, Danny Gann, and Rev. Mark Hollar

Old Fashion Day 2002: left to right: Charles Spurgeon, Danny, Michael, Megan and Tracy Gann, Evva Spurgeon, Taylor and Mary Gann, and Ronnie's old car in the background.

The church newsletter dated November 11, 2002, had a short note worth quoting. "Words fail us to adequately thank you for your warm heartedness and hospitality. Inviting us to preach and share in your church listening so intently and genuinely praising us appears to be the hallmark of your spiritual/social behavior. Thank you for the delicious meals. As we prepare for our Centenary next year when I will be President, we covet your fervent prayers." This was signed by Noah Moses Israel and Raji, Vice President Association of South Africa, Box 93, Maidstone 4380, South Africa. This couple from South Africa shared that they had spent the night with Fred and Betsy Leach, which was the first time they had ever stayed in the home of a white family. They were in the United States because of his leadership role in Baptist life in South Africa.

Dewey Linnville is pictured here with his wife, Hazel (now deceased).

The Labor of Love ministry reported in early December, some of the ways people in need were helped. Seventy-nine families were assisted on December 2. This involved a total of 272 people. Thirty-eight people assisted in this ministry on this particular night.

The Baptist Men's group assisted with funds for some of the farm laborers who had gone back to Mexico. Their homes had been destroyed by a devastating storm. There was government help for some but when it was learned that family members were in the Unites States working, those distributing funds thought those families needed no help. One of the farm helpers employed by John and Scott Hedgecock sent a letter explaining their plight and asking for assistance. The Baptist Men were able to send $1,500. The Abbotts Creek Church family was never shy in helping persons in need.

Craig Burris, chairperson for the personal committee, announced in the December 16 newsletter that Rebecca Barnes had submitted her resignation as minister of music effective December 30, 2002. Mrs. Barnes began her work at the church on March 18, 2002.

The prayer needs for the church family were listed as the first concerns at the opening conference in 2003. Some members were scheduled for surgery; and sympathy was expressed for several families where death had occurred. On this cold night, January 15, 2003, the opportunities for ministry were listed. The financial report was the first of many given to the church family. The deacons recommended the nominating committee name a search committee for a minister of music.

The church council along with the mission committee jointly recommended projected mission projects for 2003. Missions projects would be to Alaska, Honduras, New York, and the Appalachian Mountain Region. Other matters included some discussion relating to the Edith Hood Scholarship money. One hundred thousand dollars had been given and $150,000 more was expected at some future date. It was also announced that a pager system had been installed in the nursery enabling mothers who needed to be called to the nursery to do so with less interruption during the time of worship. Some office and media center equipment was also being updated.

Dewey Linville was recognized in the March 3, 2003, issue of the church newsletter. Dewey had perfect attendance in Sunday School for forty-four years. He recounts after becoming a Christian, he started attending Sunday School. On one occasion, he had just been released from the hospital on Saturday but his Sunday School class went to his home on Sunday and had their class. The same thing happened later when his wife died early on Sunday morning. His Abbotts Creek class went to his home for their Bible study.

The church council asked for a called conference on March 12, 2003, to consider a time for Sunday evening studies to begin. A series called "Home Improvement" was beginning. The decision was to combine the evening worship with the study. All would start in the sanctuary for a short period of time and then go to the chosen classes. Those not attending a class would remain for the sanctuary service.

The second called conference for 2003 took place on April 2. The nominating committee recommended and the church elected a music director/minister of music committee. Members were Debbie Anthony, Dawn Williams, Gary Dobbins, Christy Fox, Betty Alcon, Patrick Moss, and Tony Craven. Robbie Bryant was chosen as an alternate.

The second of four regularly scheduled quarterly conferences was held on April 16, 2003. Following the procedures of the past, prayer concerns were given prior to the reading of the minutes. The first report heard was always the financial report. Jennifer Blevins gave this report with needed explanations. By this time, the extension department had added a new worker, Barbara Lewis. Mrs. Lewis and Betty and Billie Alcon had made forty-five visits to the homebound during the previous quarter. Lisa Hedgecock gave the Media Center report indicating the center had been open a total of twenty-two hours during the quarter.

Ten thousand dollars was added to the line item for the trustees to carry out some of the needed projects for the church. This would include a new sidewalk in front of the sanctuary.

The Rev. Stuart White, pastor of First Baptist Church, Whitmel, North Carolina, was the guest speaker for revival service held May 18-21, 1993.

The church needed to give attention to a couple of matters and did so at a called conference on June 25, 2003. Drew Rorex was now serving as a youth worker in a church near Rocky Mount but still held membership at Abbotts Creeks. The church was asked to verify his membership was in good standing and to forward that information to the seminary he was attending. The second matter spelled out the cost of mission trips and the part the church would pay. The New York mission would cost $9,165 for the fifteen people going with the church paying one half the cost. The West Virginia mission effort, involving eleven people, would be $1,000. The church would pay $500. The amount to be paid by the church for the eight members going to Honduras would be $4,375 still one half of the total cost. The budgeted amount was sufficient to take care of this. In addition to these, a group of RAs from the church were scheduled to do campground ministry at Raccoon Holler Campground near Glendale Springs, North Carolina, on July 11 and 12.

The quarterly conference took place on July 16, 2003. The normal reports were given. Joni Smith gave recommendations for general officers, which were accepted by the church. Bobbi Burris reported the Labor of Love ministry helped 155 people at their last serving.

During the conference, a motion was made from the floor to call for another Town Meeting similar to the ones held earlier during the transitional period. The motion included having the same two questions as had been considered before. 1.) Name three things you most appreciate about Abbotts Creek and 2.) Name three things you are most disappointed about at Abbotts Creek. Some questions were raised and discussion given before the motion passed by the vote of 27-7. With fifty-three families represented at this conference, it seems obvious some members expressed no opinion.

The new cookbooks had been completed and orders were being taken. This was a project to assist the Acteens with future plans for the National Acteens Convention. Beth King and Alicia Young served as the Acteens leaders. The GAs of the church had been busy as well. Their mission project was collecting items for the High Point Women's Shelter.

J. C. Alcon, chairman of the Memorial Association, reported that dirt had been given to allow the church to level up some land at the back side of the cemetery lot that would make it useable in future years. The cost for moving 100 loads of dirt for this fill-in would cost almost $49,000. This would be paid for by the Memorial Association and was made possible because Edith Hood had given $40,000 for the association to use for upkeep.

Other workers and committees were elected at a called conference on August 29, 2003. Another matter brought to the attention of the church came from the church council. The subject concerned Wednesday night meals. For a number of years, Sue Young and Doris Crews had prepared meals for Wednesday night prior to the mission activities, choir rehearsals, and prayer service. Because of a change in jobs, the Crews family had moved away. Molly Hedgecock joined Sue in the meal preparation during the school term. More than 100 persons were generally present and family and friends spent happy times together. By this time, Sue and Molly had given up the Wednesday night cooking. The church council and others were trying to restore the ministry of the Wednesday night meals. John Sulger and Zane Hedgecock had agreed to the cooking role for an unspecified time. The minutes state, "After much concern of menus, serving teams, clean-up teams, cost of meals, and the way our past cooks were treated (no explanation), a count was taken for the motion made by the council." The motion passed by a close vote of 27-23. However, a motion was made since the count was so close to send the need back to the church council for more consideration. The motion passed and the council still had work to do.

History, Heritage, and Memories

Following the guidelines listed in the constitution, deacons were elected at the called conference on September 14, 2003. The six elected had previously served, therefore, there was no need for an ordination service. J. C. Alcon, Bobby Canada, Tony Craven, Charles Davis, Scott Ford, and Ronnie Young were elected with Hugh Motsinger as an alternate. Bob Best was elected trustee.

About this time, a new video ministry was started. Steve Gibson volunteered to prepare a video of the church worship services for distribution for those unable to attend the services. Those who desired to receive such a video would contact their family deacon.

Ten days later, after the September 14 business meeting, the church was in conference again. The church profile needed to be approved by the church before it was sent to the Liberty Baptist Association. The church clerk also brought a recommendation from the church council asking the church to proceed with Wednesday night meals by securing paid help for preparing the food and using volunteer help for cleaning up. Finally, after many questions and much discussion, the church approved this recommendation.

At the same meeting, the projected budget for the years 2003–2004 was approved after some explanation, discussion, and questions. The weekly need to meet the budget would be $8,999.

Three days prior to this conference, the town meeting was held. Six typed pages were included in the minutes of the church under the title, "What we are most disappointed/concerned about at Abbotts Creek." Many good features of the church were mentioned and other feelings bordering on harshness were likewise given. There was nothing in the minutes or the church newsletter to show any conclusions reached. It seemed to result in a "get it off my chest" time.

The last quarterly conference for 2003 was held on October 15. Reports were given in the usual fashion. Jennifer Blevins gave any needed explanation with question in reference to the budget. George Sechrest reported some of the projects carried out by the Baptist Men. They had sponsored a group of RA Challengers for a resort ministry mission trip. Some of the men had gone to Grifton, North Carolina, to help repair flood-damaged homes. They had provided money for concrete blocks the Honduras mission team would use in building a church.

The trustee recommended the purchase of a copier for the church office. The church voted to give authority for the trustees to purchase the needed equipment.

The fall revival services were held October 26-29. Rev. Charles Gardner, pastor of Southgate Baptist Church in Thomasville and a former member of Abbotts Creek, was the visiting minister.

The last newsletter of the year mentioned the estate gift of $14,253.91 left to the church by the late Doris Sells. Doris had been a long-time faithful member of the church. Her plans were to move into an independent living facility at the Presbyterian Homes on Saturday. She died earlier that morning in her own home.

The first business meeting of 2004 took place on January 14. Prayer concerns were given before the minutes were read and approved. The treasurer's report was given which showed the church in good financial standing. Fifteen pages were needed to include the full report. An account was given for every check written including date, amount, and line item. Most reports did not include recommendations. However, the music staff search committee asked the church to change the working hours for the minister of music to thirty hours rather than twenty each week. A survey had been conducted with 64 percent of the people wanting the position to be full-time while 32 percent wanted half-time. The recommendation was a compromise based on the survey.

A town meeting had taken place back in the fall. The deacons had identified a plan of action to address the topics discussed. However, the topics were not listed.

1. What action do we need to take addressing the need for better communications?

2. Determine church identity, including theological, worship style, accepted leadership style and history and what part it should play in our direction.

3. How do we develop a process whereby members can express their concern?

4. How do we develop a trust that leadership will lead appropriately?

5. Identify what is confidential in deacon's meetings and what should be or could be shared with the members.

6. Relay to church members the responsibility of all committees and the responsibility of the church members to those elected committees.

The church council continued to look for a solution for the Wednesday night meal. A decision was made for a trial period of six weeks with Chef Scott for simplified meals. Forty-nine families were present for this conference and the motion passed by a five-vote margin, 17 favoring and 12 opposed.

The pastor's remarks in *The Tie* mentioned an annoying problem with which several people had to deal. "For two weeks now anyone who stops by during the day will probably get a visit from a crazy cardinal. He unabashedly lunges at any car's side mirror and commences to fight with the bird he sees in the mirror. All of the staff have tried parking in different spaces. Yet the cardinal always 'gets his car.' Does anyone out there know how to stop our state bird from destroying a mirror or a paint job?"

The main topic for consideration at the February 4, 2004, called conference concerned the job description for a minister of music. The church approved the printed job description after expectations, hours of work, and salary were thoroughly explained.

Another conference was called March 3, 2004, to project the mission opportunities for the church. A church construction team had plans to travel to Palmer, Alaska, in August. Walter and Dot Dills served as the coordinators for the project on this site from May 14-September 7, 2004. Matthew Dunn spent the summer assisting those volunteer workers with various duties. A church repair group and a Bible teaching team was needed for the Philippine Islands. This team would do some much-needed work on the church attended by Andrea Valero's family. Andrea was a faithful teacher and choir member of Abbotts Creek. A construction and Vacation Bible School team was scheduled to be in Spruce Pines, North Carolina from July 17-23. A Vacation Bible School team had plans to be in West Virginia a week earlier. The cost of those mission efforts was almost $4,000 more than the budget had allowed. Money from various projects covered the balance.

Debra Paul was congratulated in the March 29, 2004, newsletter for being honored as the Middle School Teacher of the year in Region Five which included Davidson County.

The second quarterly conference of the year took place on April 14, 2004. The reading of the minutes was approved by the forty-seven families represented. Numerous reports were given which required no action by the church. The finance committee presented a motion to care for an increase in insurance premium and rearranged the salary and benefit for the minister of students. A new job description for the associate pastor was accepted. The new guidelines allowed him to focus heavily on the senior adult population. The trustee report included several necessary small type jobs that had been completed.

The Rev. Gary Jennings led revival services at the church April 18-21, 2004. Rev. Jennings had served as pastor at East Taylorsville Baptist Church in Taylorsville, North Carolina for many years. The revival theme was "Finding My Purpose."

A letter dated April 19, 2004, from Carol Settles was addressed to Pastor Mark Hollar and Scott Young, chairperson of the after school committee. This letter announced her retirement as director of the after school ministry. This appeared to be ample time for the church to work toward the continuation of the ministry. The after school committee bought two recommendations to the church at a called conference on May 19, 2004. The committee had studied three unnamed scenarios for the future of the program. The first recommendation was that the program be concluded on May 26, 2004, the date of retirement for Mrs. Settles. This would bring to a close one of the most effective ministries ever carried out by the church. The second recommendation asked for a new committee to be formed to study future possibilities of the same type ministry. Many people did not want the ministry to cease, but the first recommendation passed as presented. Appreciation for the ministry and the director was expressed.

Rev. Ben Rowe, former minister of youth and education at the church, delivered the message for the third Sunday in May services, May 17, 2004.

Three recommendations claimed the attention of the business meeting called for June 2, 2004. The first concerned painting the hallways and fellowship hall. Donald Smith was the low bidder for this and was awarded the job because of the bid plus the high quality of his work. The second concerned replacing the carpets in the same areas. The steeple was in great need of care which necessitated the third motion. That motion was "to clean the steeple and treat with Dur-A-Shield." The motion passed and prayer services continued.

The first three recipients of the Edith Hood Scholarship given by the church were Zach Ritchie, Charles Myers, and Ty Moore. Zach Ritchie was to attend Wilkes Community College where he planned to play baseball. Charles and Ty would enroll at High Point University and University of North Carolina at Wilmington, respectively. Each scholarship was valued at $1,000.

The third quarterly conference of the year took place on July 14, 2004. At the time of this meeting, the Vacation Bible School mission group was in West Virginia. Twenty-four organizational reports were given; many in printed form, and showed strong ministries were taking place. The finances of the church were on solid footing. General officers were presented to and accepted by the church.

The music staff search committee was ready to present a candidate after searching for fifteen months. Aaron Moore was presented to the church as

Memorial Day speaker Rev. Ben Rowe and family are pictured with Rev. Mark Hollar at a meal after the service.

prospective "music ministry director." Aaron graduated from Gardner-Webb University with a degree in Arts in Music Composition. He and his wife, Ellen, were the parents of one son, Elliott Oliver. The church voted to accept him for this position on July 25, 2004.

The trustees had done their homework concerning pew cushions for the church. The Sunday School class of which the late Doris Sells had been a

Ty Moore

Scholarship recipients Charles Myers(left); and Zach Richie (right).

member had been given the opportunity to suggest to the deacons and trustees how the estate money should be used. The class made their suggestion and as a result, the trustees recommended cushions be installed for the sanctuary and pulpit pews. The description and cost were listed on an informational sheet. The motion passed.

The trustees further recommended the church subscribe to DSL Internet Services. This, too, was approved.

On Sunday following this conference, another called conference was called to allow the church to nominate deacons.

The resignation of David Mills was announced on August 22, 2004, with David reading his letter of resignation to the congregation. There was no written statement given for the minutes and no mention of this was made in the newsletter.

Thirty families were present at the called conference on September 1. Sunday School teachers were elected for the 2004–2005 church year. Additional teachers were elected on September 22. The congregational profile prepared for the association was presented and approved. The proposed budget for the year 2004–2005 was presented and accepted. The adopted budget called for a weekly amount of $9,593.

New deacons selected on September 12, 2004, were: Robbie Bryant, Wayne Bullard, Andy Chappell, Billy Hutchens, Jeff Jordan, and Hugh Motsinger. Tony Fowler was elected as trustee. Jeff Jordan was ordained on October 16, 2004.

The acceptance of the minutes in printed form from the previous conference opened the fourth quarterly conference for the year on October 13, 2004. As in the past, numerous reports were given. Zane Hedgecock, chairman of the deacons, presented a recommendation for consideration regarding a video ministry for the church. The church approved $5,000 for equipment and installation sufficient to duplicate ten DVDs at one time. The committee made up of Scott Ford, Michael Gann, Charles Davis, and Steve Gibson was selected to care for this ministry.

The church accepted a trustee recommendation for Tar Heel Paving Company to do the needed work for the parking lot. This included repairing cracks, repainting the parking lines, and applying two coats of sealer for the entire area.

The October 18, 2004, church newsletter recognized Rick Motsinger who had just been inducted into the Davidson County Sports Hall of Fame two days earlier. Several years earlier, Rick had played college baseball. He had been drafted and played minor league ball before an injury forced his retirement. A couple of weeks later, the newsletter congratulated Madison Hedgecock, son of Art and Louallen, for being chosen to play football in the Hula Bowl in Maui, Hawaii. He was chosen from among college seniors nationally.

The Labor of Love ministry reported serving ninety families on December 20, 2004. Two hundred and sixty people made up these families.

The first conference of 2005 was held on January 12. Normal proceedings took place. Some reports were printed while others were given verbally. After giving the treasurer's report, Carl Alcon made some comments informing the church that offerings for the previous quarter were $10,000 less than the same quarter a year earlier.

A committee working on refurbishing the parlor asked the church for $7,000 to carry out plans for the parlor including a sofa, love seat, chair, ottoman, and other accessories. A hutch was included in this to display historical items. Other work would be included as well.

The trustees recommended painting the sanctuary at a cost of $2,300.

The mission projects for the year were projected by the church council. Possibilities were expressed for trips to Cuba and Wyoming.

The Edith Hood Estate had left $29,000 for the Prayer Garden and its upkeep. The committee represented by Bobby Canada had two recommendations both of which were approved by the church at the February 9, 2004, conference. The motions were to provide lights for the garden and to purchase an archway for the entrance. These projects added to the beauty of the area.

The church continued trying to restore the Wednesday night meals. It appeared everyone was trying together to make this work. The March 30, 2005, conference was called to deal with the subject. Cooking teams and clean-up teams had volunteered. One cooking team included Lewis and Francis Peacock, Bobby and Dot Canada and Robbie Bryant. Zane and Carol Hedgecock made up team two. They had help from Molly Hedgecock and Evva Spurgeon and several other women who assisted in serving the meal. Team three consisted of Ron and Becky Rogers and David and Carolyn McBrayer. The fourth team was listed as Acteens. The following were listed to make up seven clean up teams: Lee and Susan Nooe, Sherri Gilbert, Anita Hollar, Tarinda Chappell, Crystal Myers, Debra Paul, Dawn Hutchens, John Sulger, Hope Hundley, Rick and Leslie Frances, Camie and Nancy Best, and Sara Moore. The Acteens were listed as a separate team. The RAs had accepted the responsibility to clean up the fellowship hall each week, arrange the tables, chairs and vacuum the eating area. Matthew Dunn was assigned

Prayer Garden

Prayer Garden

the job of collecting the money for the meal. Each team was to contact Rev. Jack Rose about needed items for the preparation of meals. In addition to serving at the church, extra meals would be prepared and carried to some of the homebound or those who had been recently discharged from the hospital.

Sandi Todd was presented to the church as interim children's director during the quarterly conference on Wednesday, April 13, 2005. The minister of students search committee brought this recommendation. The church accepted her as the interim worker with the children for a period of thirteen weeks. It was announced that Aaron Moore would continue to work with the youth during the summer months in addition to his work with the church's music ministry.

Other reports were given showing many activities involving the entire church family were taking place. The missions committee presented an ambitious schedule of summer mission opportunities. Work trips were scheduled for Wyoming, Eastern and Western North Carolina, and to the

Christian Activity Center in East St. Louis, Illinois. Vacation Bible School teams were heading to West Virginia and Vermont.

During March, April, and May, two major projects were carried out to assist the Tsunami victims. Both were in response to the Franklin Graham ministry of Samaritan's Purse. Bicycles were collected and sent to a designated location. The other project consisted of sending shoe boxes filled with needed items, T shirts, underclothes, toothbrushes and other items for personal use. Candy and gum could also be included. The church collected over one hundred boxes for this mission. Earlier in one of the shoe box projects, Betty Craven had included her name and address. It was a couple of years later when she received a thank you note from the one who had received the box. The note indicated the little girl had to wait until she learned enough English to write.

The April 25, 2005, newsletter announced the winners of the State Bible Drill competition. Rebekah Hollar was the high scorer for the youth. Amber Chappell and Kyle DeLappe tied for second place. Other winners were Radford Hyde, Jackson Crickenberger, Dustin Hale, and Anna Hayworth. Winners in the children's competition were Jarred Nooe and Matthew Hutchens. Christina McGuire was the winner of the speaker's tournament.

The community mission effort, Operation-In-As-Much, was scheduled for May 14, 2005. Projects included doing extensive yard work for a family and replacing the floor in the home of one of the widowed ladies of the church. Another group washed the windows and did needed yard work for an elderly member. A group with nursing skills carried out their ministry by doing blood pressure checks near a grocery store in High Point. There were forty-five people involved in these various ministries.

The Rev. Jimmy Hinson was the speaker for the Memorial Day service the third Sunday in May. Rev. Hinson had served as interim pastor prior to the beginning of Rev. Coltrane's ministry.

The nomination of deacons required a called conference on June 26, 2005.

Madison Hedgecock was offered congratulations in the July 18, 2005. issue of *The Tie*. He had been drafted by the St. Louis Rams of the National Football League and had signed a three-year contract.

Hurricane Katrina had devastated the Gulf Coast and opportunities to minister were abundant. The North Carolina Baptist Men were asking churches to gather boxes of food items that would be distributed to needy families or individuals in the area of destruction. Suggested items costing about fifty dollars were recommended to fill each box that would be sent and distributed. Before this was even announced, Jimmy Todd, a businessman and member of the church, had already sent a trailer load of water and other goods. Jimmy was acquainted with many of the people of the area because of his connections in purchasing seafood products from the businesses there.

Robert Brasington, Richard Coffey, Jerry LaPoint, Don Myers, Evan Myers, and Bud Welch were elected as deacons on September 11, 2005. Dale Marshall and Michael Gann were named as the first two alternates. Sonya Alcon was elected as trustee.

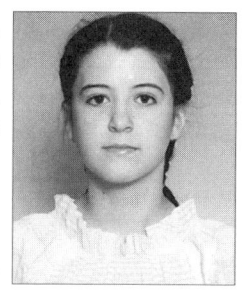

Child received shoebox from Shoebox Ministry and Betty Craven received a letter from her two years later.

Rev. Ben Rowe from Lakeview Baptist Church in Hickory was the visiting minister for revival services held on October 9-12, 2005.

The first African-American family to become members of Abbotts Creek in recent times joined October 10, 2005. During the time of the interim pastorate of Rev. Lee Stocks, an African-American male had indicated his desire to join but did not follow through on that and was no longer attending. Abbotts Creek, among other churches in the Liberty Baptist Association, had African-American members before and after the slaves were freed, though Abbotts Creek had not in recent years. The new family included Kisha Davis, T'Keyah Morris, Isaiah Moore, John Davis II, and Elijah Davis. The family was introduced to the church through the Labor of Love ministry.

The October quarterly conference was held on the 19th of the month. Thirty-three committees were called on for reports. Some were given verbally but most in printed form. Fourteen committees had no report to give at this time. One week later, a conference was called to approve a job description for the minister of students and youth. At the same time, an announcement was made by the search committee regarding a person to fill the position. That person was Scott Reid.

The church voted to call Scott on Sunday morning, October 30, 2005. Sandi Todd was named director of children and preschool ministries at the same time. Scott Reid received 270 positive votes with only eleven against the recommendation. Sandy received 250 out of the possible 270 votes cast. Sandi and her husband, Laurence III, had been active members of the church for a number of years. Scott and his wife, Stephanie, came to Abbotts Creek after being a part of the ministry of Christ Wesleyan Church near Union Cross and began their ministry at Abbotts Creek in November of 2005.

The year ended with the Labor of Love Ministry serving sixty-nine families with family members totaling 226 people. Toys were given to the children allowing families to have added blessings at Christmas. Twenty-one people had assisted these families.

The year of celebration for 250 years of history found the church meeting for the first conference of the New Year with thirty-five families represented. This took place on January 14, 2006. The normal reports were given and accepted by the church. The history committee announced plans for the church to celebrate 250 years of ministry in September. Eight mission projects were announced for the years. A VBS was scheduled for West Virginia and East St. Louis. Construction teams were scheduled to go to Clermont, Wyoming, East St. Louis, Honduras, Cuba, and Gulfport, Mississippi. Plans were also in the works to go to Eastern North Carolina.

Aaron Moore offered his resignation on February 11, 2006. He had endeared himself to the church family with his musical leadership and his work with the youth. His plans were to enter business with his brother that would require his family moving near Charlotte. His resignation was effective April 17, 2006.

Plans were announced in February to reproduce the cookbook that had first been printed in 1981. The recipes were to be the same but the cover different.

The history committee held their first meeting on February 5, 2006, to begin working on the church's first history book.

A March 1, 2006, conference was called to deal with the revision for the general scholarship fund left to the church from the Edith Hood Estate. The previous requirements were such that few, if any, could qualify. For instance, the applicant would have had to keep a log of church activities over the last two years. After much discussion, the chairman of the committee, Michael Rinehardt, withdrew the motion stating changes would be made and brought back to the church at an announced date. This was done on March 22, 2006. Whatever revisions were made, the church accepted. The church had deposited $250,000 from the estate with the North Carolina Baptist Foundation. The interest was to be used for scholarship help for the youth of the church.

After the reports were heard at the quarterly conference on April 12, 2006, Bobby Canada, representing the transportation committee, made a motion that the church purchase a fifteen-passenger used van with 20,500 miles and an extended warranty. After discussion and questions, the motion was accepted by the church.

Evan Myers, chairman of the personnel committee, presented Kim Moss as the interim music director. She was requested to serve until a permanent replacement was named. The church accepted this recommendation.

The conference called for June 25, 2006, was for the purpose of allowing each member of the congregation, twelve years old and older, to nominate two deacons. The list would be compiled and the church would follow the normal procedure for the election.

The church's regular quarterly conference was held on July 12, 2006. Reports shared with the congregation the activities that were taking place by the various committees of the church. Carl Alcon gave a report on the financial status of the church. The offering had been slightly lower than the budget required leaving the checking balance and the general fund balance less than the previous quarter. The Labor of Love ministry had served ninety-two families which included 183 people.

The missions committee reported one had gone on a preaching mission to Brazil and a team had helped to restore a home in Grifton, North Carolina. The trustee chairman, Hugh Motsinger, presented this: "the trustees recommend that the church contract with North State Communications to replace our outdated (phone) system with a new Nortel Network Business Communications Manager

Zane, Lisa, Daniel, and Caroline Hedgecock

History Committee: (back row) Sue Foust, Libby Essick, Roy Cantrell, Betty Craven (front row) Pearl Hayworth, Evva Spurgeon, and Doris Loggins

(BCM) at a cost of $4,435 plus tax." The church voted to accept this.

Charles Davis made the motion to accept the newly-revised constitution. Some matters were omitted while others added. The most noted change was "To assure the church is aware of upcoming recommendations, any individual or committee desiring to make a recommendation or motion to the church concerning old or new business in a conference will present the recommendation or motion in writing within a minimum of two weeks prior to a conference, to the church office. Any recommendation or motion that does not meet the two-week minimum notification period will not be acted on at that particular conference." Heretofore, the two-week notice had applied only to a called conference.

The North Carolina Baptist Men's medical and dental van visited the church on August 13, 2006.

Teachers and committee members were elected at the called conference on August 30, 2006. Three hundred names were included to serve in various capacities.

The roots of Abbotts Creek have been traced back to 1756. September 2006, was planned as the month of celebration. These plans were announced for the month on August 30, 2006. The minutes had this recorded:

Our 250th Celebration Sundays

September 3, "In The Beginning" Drama Re-enactment 1756. The speaker for the morning service was John Woodard, director of the North Carolina Baptist Historical Collection at Wake Forest University. The evening service was listed as "History Lessons from the Past."

September 10th, "The Split 1832." Dr. Tony Cartledge, editor of the *Biblical Recorder*, was the guest speaker. "Old fashion prayer service" was listed for the evening service.

September 17, "The War Effort 1781." Representatives from Sandy Creek Baptist Church were present for this service. At 5:00 p.m. that evening, there was a reenactment of the Revolutionary War concluding the services for the day.

CHAPTER TWENTY-ONE

The Woman's Missionary Union of Abbott's Creek

Abbotts Creek, like an endless number of other Baptist churches, would not be what the church has become today had it not been for a strong Woman's Missionary Union (WMU). The history of the WMU at Abbotts Creek dates back to 1920. This was only thirty-two years after thirty-two delegates met in Richmond, Virginia, and organized the WMU—an auxiliary to the Southern Baptist Convention.

Mrs. Dan (Eva) Hayworth was the first president listed in the Abbotts Creek records. Nine members enrolled as the first members. In addition to Mrs. Hayworth and to this date, at least eighteen Christian women have served as presidents. Many of them served more than one term.

The WMU has been a strong working mission organization since its beginning. In 1934, a Sunbeam Band (now Mission Friends) was organized followed by Girls Auxiliary five years later. In 1941, the YWA (now Acteens) group was started.

Mrs. N. R. Teague served during 1932–1935. At her death, she left $500 in her will for missions through the church. Mission giving by the church was always encouraged by those who studied the needs and opportunities for Christian women and men to be involved in carrying out the Great Commission of Jesus throughout the world.

The women of this organization have made significant contributions in carrying out responsibilities in leadership in all areas of church life. For instance, the WMU was instrumental in drawing plans for the first parsonage built by the church. They helped draw up guidelines for the Memorial Association dealing with the cemetery. The first bulletin board in front of the church was paid for by the WMU. In reading the minutes of the church, time and again, the WMU made financial contribution to various needs of the church or causes the church supported. Members have ministered to numerous grieving families by serving a meal at the church or in the home when death had occurred. One WMU member would be responsible for notifying a particular circle responsible for the meal.

This organization helped to support two missionaries in Cuba for several years starting in 1938. After Missionaries Mr. and Mrs. Negrin retired from mission work in Cuba, the WMU helped them as they served the Hispanic-speaking group in Florida. The Abbotts Creek mission organizations sent Bibles and boxes of other things helpful for their work. These dedicated women have led out in seeing that the church adopted missionaries to support in an ongoing way as part of the missionary outreach. The supported missionaries are mentioned earlier in the book. The church always looked forward to having these individuals or couples visit and speak in the church while they were on furlough.

We have select notes from a speech given by Mrs. Victoria Richardson Teague at what is believed to have been an associational meeting in 1932. In that address, she spelled out what she was helping to accomplish at Abbotts Creek by saying, "the society not only prays for the spread of God's Kingdom but it also studies the various missionary fields and thus teaches its members how God's work is prospering.

WMU Leaders at Abbotts Creek

	Year(s)
Mrs. N. R. Teague	1921
Mrs. D. S. Hayworth	1924
Minnie Hayworth	1925–1927
Mattie Teague	1928-29
Nina Hayworth	1930
Mary Hayworth	1931
Mrs. N.R. Teague	1932-35
Miss Mattie Teague	1936
Miss Minnie Hayworth	1937–38
Blanche Traynham	1939
Daisy Spurgeon	1940–41
Mrs. B.A. Mitchell	1942–43
Daisy Spurgeon	1944–47

Ethel Teague	1948–49
Ruth Hedgecock	1950
Ruth Holder	1951
Ruth Hedgecock	1952
Mable Hayworth	1953–54
Ruth Hedgecock	1955
Margaret Cline	1956
Mable Hayworth	1957–61
Blanche Traynham	1962–64
Mary Smith	1965–6
Blanche Traynham	1967
Mary Smith	1968–69
Zemma Coltrane	1970
Mary Smith	1971–74
Vicki Hilton	1975
Georgette Bullard	1976–77
Kathy Green	1978
Evva Spurgeon	1979
Pat Dawson	1980–81
Betty Jo Motsinger	1982
Pat Dawson	1983
Evva Spurgeon	1984–85
Debbie Goad	1986
Evva Spurgeon	1987
Mary Gann	1988
Evva Spurgeon	1988–91
Donna Tucker	1992–93
Betty Jo Motsinger	1994
Mary Gann	1995–2004
Donna Tucker	2005–06

This information was provided by Pansy Moore and Evva Spurgeon.

CHAPTER TWENTY-TWO

Ordained Ministers from Abbotts Creek and Ministers Licensed

Daniel Marshall was the first minister ordained at Abbotts Creek in 1756.

Ashley Swaim was ordained in August of 1819.

Carrick Teague was licensed to preach by the church on March 28, 1948.

Haywood Hyatt was licensed to preach by the church in October 1954. The minutes of June 1959 reported his family had united with a Methodist Church where he had been called to serve as pastor.

Charles (Chuck) Garner was licensed to preach by Abbotts Creek Baptist Church in September 1973. He was ordained to the ministry by the Kingswood Baptist Church, in Columbia, South Carolina, on August 12, 1979.

Chet Cantrell was ordained to preach by Abbotts Creek Baptist Church on January 1, 1984. He was serving as pastor of Lick Creek Baptist Church near Denton, North Carolina, at the time and came at the request of Lick Creek.

Ben Rowe was called to serve as minister of youth and education at Abbotts Creek in the spring of 1986. Shortly after his graduation from Southeastern Seminary in May of that year, he was ordained by his home church, West Hickory Baptist Church, in Hickory, N. C.

Wayne Rowbottom was ordained by Abbotts Creek Church on April 26, 1987. His ordination came as a request from the Trinidad and Tobago Baptist Association in Port of Spain, Trinidad. The request from Trinidad was written by Rev. Amrit Bridgelal.

Beth Hayworth MacClaren Echols, who grew up in the Abbotts Creek church and community, was ordained to the ministry by the McLean Baptist Church, McLean, Virginia.

David Clemens served as minister of youth and music at Abbotts Creek for a long period of time. He was called to South Elm Street Baptist Church to serve. That church ordained David to the gospel ministry on November 11, 1990.

Jack Rose was called to serve as associate pastor at Abbotts Creek on October 1, 1992. He was ordained for the ministry at English Road Baptist Church in High Point on November 15, 1992.

Beth Cantrell-Counts received her ordination by the First Reformed United Church of Christ in Burlington, N.C. Her ordination took place on May 23, 1999.

Keith Curlee was elected as a deacon on September 13, 1992. His ordination as a deacon took place on October 18, 1992. He and his wife Paige and their children moved from Abbotts Creek to Green Street Baptist Church. At the time of this writing, they are serving as missionaries with the International Mission Board somewhere in the Near East.

Epilogue

At the request of the history committee, Pastor Mark Holler has shared with us some of the highlights of the ministries of the church since his arrival as pastor six years ago, in June of 2001. Many good and exciting things have taken place, with several "firsts."

There has been a great emphasis on Bible Buddies, Bible Drills, and Speakers' Tournaments. Starting in January of 2002, over sixty children and youth have been involved in memorizing Bible verses and learning where key verses can be found easily. Speeches have been prepared and delivered on the state level as well as in the church and the association. In competition, several of these youth have been named state winners.

Vacation Bible School has always been strong at Abbotts Creek. However, the number of children and youth attending over the past few years has exceeded any previous year. It continues to be the "church's best evangelistic outreach" according to the pastor. In 2003, the VBS at the church, backyard Bible studies and mission groups leading VBS elsewhere had 614 enrolled. Average attendance over the past seven years has been 394 for the children and workers.

The challenger of Jesus in the Great Commission is taken seriously by the leadership of the church. From June 2001, until the time of this writing (November 2007), more than 300 people have united with the church as new Christians being baptized or being accepted in the church by letter or statement. This has given the church a net increase of membership from 770 to 913. Learning classes are provided for children on a regular basis.

"Prayer at the Pole" has been successful stressed at four to six of the area schools with "as many as 450 students at one of the schools." The leadership and church have "taken seriously the need to 'put prayer back into schools.'"

The youth ministry at the church seems to have exploded over the past two years under the leadership of Scott Reid. In 2007, over 100 youth and chaperones attended Caswell, the Baptist Retreat and Conference Center, near Southport, North Carolina.

The church family keeps following the challenge of missions. Needs are made known and volunteers are ready to go with strong support from the church both financially and prayerfully. In the two-year span of 2006-2007, 217 were involved in mission groups. Some were part of more than one of the high number of trips sponsored by the church. It is exciting when church members can go to some destination for the first time to serve the Lord by doing hands-on mission work.

The mission motif of Abbotts Creek Missionary Baptist Church keeps enlarging with plans already in the making for 2008.

Memories of Our Past History

The History Committee invited the senior members of the church to share some of their memories of growing up as a part of the Abbotts Creek Church. This section includes the memories of those who responded and some memories of the History Committee.

Staley Bodenheimer
May 16, 1917–March 15, 2007

The first time I remember being in church, I got restless and Mother gave me a book to look at. When I turned through the pages a few times, I said, "Momma, this book ain't got no pictures in it."

When they started building the new church, the members did a lot of work on it. When I was nine years old, I drove a team of mules to scoop out the basement and Marion Bodenheimer also had a team of mules scooping it out. For the building, part of the members furnished the logs. They were taken to Uncle Perry and Uncle Sanford Hayworth's sawmill where they were made into lumber. I don't remember too much about who built the church except I know that members worked on it. The pastor, Rev. Mumford, also worked on it and he was doing something in the sanctuary at the second window from the balcony on the right hand side. Something broke and he fell. The sub-floor was finished and it burst two or three of the sub-floor boards when he fell. I'm not sure, but I think he broke his hip. I know he went to the hospital.

Miss Minnie Hayworth taught our first Sunday School class. When our names were called, instead of saying "here" she had us repeat a Bible verse.

At first the church had four deacons to serve for a lifetime. I don't remember when they changed to rotating. The first time I was nominated for deacon, all the names were written on a black board that was up on the platform at the pulpit. As the names were called out, a mark was placed beside the names.

There was a tract of land (no man's land) between the cemetery and the Primitive Baptist Church. We put in a claim for it and if no one claimed it for nine years, we could get a deed for it. When the nine years were up, the church sent Clarence Moore, Tom Dawson, Uncle Sanford Hayworth, Rev.

Joe Coltrane, and me to get a deed for it. The association lawyer said they would have to sell it to someone and they would sell it back to the church to get a deed. The church sold it to me for $1 I think, and I sold it back to the church and we got a deed for the land.

The deacons were all men back then. They were Christians and they were deacons. Back then the church fellowship was great and the love was great in the church. Up until I had to quit attending regularly, the church was a friendly, loving church.

This was written February 17, 2007, and Staley died March 15, 2007.

Betty Craven

If I were to tell you what Abbotts Creek Missionary Baptist Church meant to me, I would have to say it has played a large part in molding my life. I was born into this church seventy-five years ago. I have been so fortunate that I had parents and grandparents and even great-grandparents who worshipped God here as well as my husband, our children, and me.

We were a group of sinners saved by grace. I have always felt God working in my church. I saw people praying and caring about each other. Any differences that may have occurred, they worked them out.

I could tell you many memories of the happenings through the years. Our finest hours were during World War II. We were on our knees praying. I was just a young girl but the scene of grown men praying on their knees is still so vivid.

Our dress code has changed through the years as times changed. Our church has adapted well though. When I was young, women always wore dresses and hats and gloves on Sunday morning. We are not as formal with our dress or with our services as we were in the past. We have changed our lifestyle somewhat but we have never changed our beliefs in God the Father, Son, and Holy Spirit.

Abbotts Creek has grown a great deal in my lifetime. It is hard for some of the older people to change to the way of a larger church but with God directing us we will grow even greater in His plan for us. We have had some hard times in recent years but God has brought us through. My prayer for the future is we will let God be the center of our church and we will always do His will, not our own.

Charles Davis
Taken from an interview in 1976

Charles Davis was born in 1895. He remembers being told when the church divided in 1832; the missionary group went across the road and built a brush arbor. He does not remember how long this was in use before a one-room building was constructed. "That was the old building when I first can remember it." Rev. Spellman was the first preacher he remembers but does not remember if he was the pastor or speaking for a service. The preachers used to spend the night at the Davis' house. His father was a music teacher. "Dad was a member and great one to shout."

Mr. Davis had a part in construction of the church including digging the basement and remembers a Preacher Purdle (?). It was said he could not read but he would talk about the scripture and say I know it is in here somewhere but he could never find what he was going to read. He must have been close to ninety years old when, "I remember this old man preached this young girl's funeral and he preached an hour and everybody bout froze and he preached and his nose kept getting redder and redder and that tickled a lot of people." Mr. Davis remembers most of the people were Primitive Baptist but he had heard his mother say they used to go to church and rather than having Sunday School, they would study from the old blue back speller. His granddaddy Teague went with the missionary group when they "pulled out." In his granddaddy Davis' will, he had it written his children would lead the singing like he did at the Primitive church if it was the Lord's will." All of them led the singing but my Daddy.

At Thanksgiving, the people would take up money for the Children's Home in Thomasville. They would load up a wagon of vegetables and take them to Thomasville.

"People didn't have too much money. I remember a fellow died.... Ivey Orrell's daddy was secretary and he said I don't know what we are going to do. The man who died gave a dollar every month and that was the most of anybody in the church."

Speaking of revival meeting, "They always had visiting preachers who stayed a week or two. They used to have some real old timey preachers who were really good. The colored preacher used to come down there. The black people sat in the back. One old lady who always shouted at their church, she'd holler when the preacher got to preaching, kind of a holler, squeal.' That person was Crissie Traynham, married to Preacher Traynham. The preacher in Georgetown had been a slave.

"Granddaddy Teague had a girl slave. He got her when she was four years old. He hauled salt from down in the country and someone owed him money and could not pay. He gave Granddaddy the girl to pay the debt of $400. She lived here and went to church and was a member and is buried over there. She died when she was 27, Ann Teague buried in our church down in the corner. There are a lot of colored people buried there. They were always buried there until they built the new church, then they didn't come anymore."

He remembers his Grandmother Davis living with them and talking about the split and the fact that the people didn't think the small minority would amount to anything. They thought it would "last a little bit and fall through."

Mrs. Victoria Teague, Carrick Teague's mother, was the first teacher Mr. Davis remembers. He remembered Minnie Hayworth and Uncle Jeffrey (Jeff Traynham's Daddy) taught the old class, until he could not hear well enough to continue teaching.

"Preacher Hilliard was a good old fellow. He wasn't too well educated but he was a good preacher." Preacher Carrick was the most educated of the ministers remembered by Mr. Davis. "He was really a smart lawyer, had a real practice. (Some) People did not like him because he had no pets. ...He knew the law and everything but he was just like an old farmer around town." Mr. Davis remembers most preachers did not preach until they were older and they were expected to preach loud. "If you didn't preach loud, you weren't a good preacher."

After the split in the church, his father was the only one in his family to go with the missionary group. Early after the split some of those who split off would still attend the Primitive services. His grandmother did not remember any of the Primitive people attending any services with the missionary group.

In talking about people waiting until they were older to join the church or to preach, Mr. Davis said, "I never knew of but one young boy, John Roe Davis, to join the church. Everybody thought he was going crazy because he was the only young person ever to join."

Kara Motsinger Dean—July 5, 1908–2006

I am not sure when our family of Mostingers came across the road from the Primitive Baptist Church. Our church records state in the minutes dated June 1834 that Hulda Motsinger, my great-grandmother, joined the fellowship. She and my great-grandfather are buried across the street with a slave named Absalom at their feet. My grandfather and grandmother, Moses M. and Mary Jane Hedgecock Motsinger, raised their family in the Abbott's Creek Church. In fact, there are several of their descendants here today. My parents were William Frank and Carrie Elizabeth Hines Motsinger. They chose to raise their family in this church as did five of us girls. My daughter and her husband, my three grandsons and their families, and my two great-grandchildren are regular attenders here.

I can remember when Dad would hitch up the surrey and the wagon to bring us to church. Mama and Dad had nine kids so the surrey wouldn't hold us all. We would carry our lunch and whatever was needed for the trip for all the kids. We really had to huddle up in cold weather because it was a long drive. We lived where Johnson Street in High Point is now. They have taken the creek that ran through our place and made it part of Oak Hollow Lake. We would really have to get up early to get all the kids ready and pack our provisions for church. Sometimes some of us children would spend Saturday night with the Spurgeon's if the meeting lasted all weekend. We would have more fun! Other big families would invite us for a "stop-over" at their house sometimes. We would spread out lunch on a sheet on the ground and eat as a family.

I remember how Uncle Willie Spurgeon used to pray in church. He would always go up to the altar at the front of the church and kneel when he prayed. He would talk real slow and every sentence would start with "Our Heavenly Father." Our church has always been a praying church and as I think back over the past I think of how different people would pray. And the music, Carey Davis meant so much to this church. He could really play a piano. In fact, the whole Davis clan has contributed a great deal to the music of this church. Our church has always been known for its good music.

I joined this church when I was about eight or ten years old. Miss Minnie Hayworth was my teacher. She would talk to you about the Lord and be sure you knew how important it was to have Him as your Saviour. All of us joined while we were fairly young. I know one thing; I've been here all my life. Discipline was strict. You didn't talk or laugh in church and you better not go to sleep unless you were very young. Church was not something we were asked if we wanted to go to or not. Church was something we did.

Through the years different trials have come up in the church. At these times you would hear people say, "that will surely split the church open." You know, through Christians working together with common sense and reasoning we would always come through theses trials and be stronger for it.

In my eighty-four years (her age at the time), I have been through many happy times as well as a few sad ones. When we lost our son we thought we couldn't go on but our Christian friends and our faith in God pulled us through. Almost twenty years ago my husband passed away. That left a void that can never be filled. He was always so active and really loved his Christian friends here. He was a big tease and everybody loved it. He really loved this church.

There have been so many people that made this church strong that have passed on but they left a legacy that can be felt in the strength of our church today. Many of our younger people have never heard of them. You take Mr. Dan Hayworth and Clarence Moore. When they prayed, you knew they were talking to God. We really had memorable prayer meetings. Like the summer the crops were dying from lack of water. We had a special prayer meeting to pray for rain. Mr. Dan Hayworth brought his umbrella to prayer meeting and he was sincere in bringing it. I remember in his prayer he told the Lord if he could see fit to give him a good crop he would share it with others. There was right much hail in the storm that night, yes; it rained a good rain before midnight. Mr. Dan's crops were saved and he shared his corn and wheat that year with others less fortunate.

I guess we were never closer as a church than during hard times. My brother-in-law was a teacher of a class of twenty young men December 7, 1941. Soon, there was only one or two left in the class because they had all gone to war. Oh! How this church prayed. We saw every one of them return home safely. Clell Spurgeon was missing in action for a while. We met over at John Spurgeon's house and had a heartfelt prayer meeting. He was soon reported safe. Many of these men have been strong leaders in our church and are here today with their families.

I remember that once we outgrew the old church we built the new one. We hated to see it torn down although it was just a square box with a room on the side of it. There were many memories left there but I have recently seen what was the new church then be torn down to make room for our present new church. You see my friends; it is not the buildings that make the church, it is the love of God and the faith of the people. Remember, my friends, these are the days that are the memories of tomorrow. ...So, live them well.

Libby Essick

As a member of the History Committee, I have heard and read many great stories about the people of Abbotts Creek Church. This church has a very rich history in the community.

I was introduced to my new church in 1988. My husband's family has had a long tradition with Abbotts Creek Church. I came to love the church as much as Larry did and the congregation made me feel very comfortable. I have made lasting friendships over the years. In 1998 Larry and I joined the church and were baptized by Mr. Cantrell. We regularly walk to church on Sunday mornings. If you do not see us along the roadside walking, just look for us on the back row. I am proud to be a part in such a wonderful church.

Violet Everhart
August 27, 1925

My daddy, Charlie Bodenheimer, and my momma, Cleta Bodenheimer, took me to Abbotts Creek when I was a baby. They loved Abbotts Creek and Papa wanted peace. I was thirteen years old and during revival, I gave my life to Jesus and was baptized in the pool. The Reverend T. W. Bray was our pastor.

Rev. B. A. Mitchell was our next pastor and he married Numa and me. I worked in the nursery for forty years and more. I had the opening assembly for children and sang the song entitled "9:45" every morning. I had Sunbeams every other Sunday. I loved my church, Abbotts Creek. I sang in the choir when Mr. Carey Davis was our leader. My birthday is August 27, 1925. I'm getting old, 81 years. I worked in Vacation Bible School and brought several children with me. (Violet always brought a carload of her neighborhood children even when her own children were grown and away from home.)

When I was growing up, Mr. Hilliard would walk and Momma had a big dinner he would eat with us and trot us on his lap and sing "Good News Going to Canaan." Even in the hot summer, he would wear his bow tie and long-back coat. Those were good memories. We miss church so much (health reasons).

Sue Foust

We rode to church in a green 1939 Chevrolet. Barney Road was a dusty mess that rode like a washboard. It was always fun to go over the narrow one-lane Abbotts Creek Bridge.

Mom would tell us the story about the night the headlights went off on the Chevy just as she was about to cross the bridge. When the lights came on, she was in a dangerous place headed down toward the water.

I can remember after church was over on Sunday morning, the men would stand in front and talk, and talk, and talk. Of course, Nancy (my sister) and I wanted to go home to have lunch so we could play.

The 1940s and 50s were fun times at Abbotts Creek Missionary Baptist Church.

Grady Green
Taken From an Interview in 1976

Mr. Green talked about his father sawing the wood for the old church. His father died in 1895, which means the sawing took place in the late 1880s or early 1890s. Near the crossing of the Abbotts Creek Church and the old Willow Creek Roads, there was a Post Office, feed mill, flour mill, and a sawmill. It was called the Orinoco sawmill. The community men sawed the logs and brought them to be made into lumber.

He recalled that he and Andrew Bodenheimer did a lot of work toward building the first parsonage along with help from Johnny Welborn. Much of the timber for the building was donated but the two of them sawed and planed the lumber. The church people liked it but the church had never needed one before because the "preachers live here and yonder."

Mr. Green never finished what he started to say about the need for a parsonage because it would not sound too good. It seems to have concerned a pastor and rent problems.

He remembered the church had a wood cutting in order to have wood to burn for the winter. He tells of Clarence Moore getting up before daylight and starting the fire so the people could worship in a warm building. Lester Green decided one day to give Clarence fifty cents for doing that. Mr. Moore resisted but it seems from time to time, some of the fellows insisted for him to take a little in appreciation for what he was doing.

He remembered "one of the worse problems." He never mentioned the problem or the personalities but it seems an open meeting was held on Sunday evening. "There were accusations and so on." He did not take his wife because he thought the meeting should not have taken place and it was too cold to get his wife out of the house. When he got home, she asked how the meeting went. He said, "Well, we buried the hatchet but we left the handle up."

"I told different ones of them that I had been in a lot of meetings but that was the roughest meeting I'd ever been a part of in my life. ...Nobody called nobody a liar, but they did say that's a lie. In other words, you'd say something and somebody else would pick it up, that's a lie. ...Right there in the open meeting."

Part of the argument seems to have gone on outside, but on Sunday morning, the pastor resigned without preaching. The church paid him for three months even though he did not preach during this time. It seemed he moved in the night. Mr. Green attended Sunday School forty-two straight years without missing.

Pearl Hayworth

My first memories of Abbotts Creek Missionary Baptist Church are of visiting with my late husband's cousins, Marie and Elizabeth Hayworth, and attending church with them in the mid-1940s. On my first visit I remember Miss Minnie Hayworth left where she was seated some rows from where we were seated and asked me if I was a Christian. I learned in later years what this lovely lady had meant to Abbotts Creek. It was some years later that I married one of the Hayworth cousins. In December of 1959, I joined Abbotts Creek Church. William had attended Abbotts Creek with his family since he was a small child. I remember him recalling when the first brick church was built in the late 1920s, and he helped move the brick to the brick masons who were laying them. At that time he was about ten or eleven years old.

One of my memories of Abbotts Creek is listening to Lucian Gregory's beautiful prayers. I am sure these prayers were enjoyed by many of our membership.

We have always had those who were faithful to help in the choir and they have meant a lot to me. During the years I have been and am still a member of the Welcome Circle and a member of a Sunday School class. I served as the Church Clerk for some 13 years. I was the first female in the church's history to serve in this office. There have been many ladies who have served since. I worked with the Bible school for a number of years and worked with the Primary and Beginner departments.

Working with the History Committee has been quite a challenge for all of us, and a learning experience also. We owe a lot of thanks to Rev. Roy Cantrell for all of his help. His knowledge of the early background history has added much to the content of the book.

Elva Motsinger Hedgecock

My first remembrance of Abbotts Creek was in the old church. All in one room built in a T shape.

When I went to Sunday School, Miss Mattie Teague was the teacher. We went on the third Sunday of May, and had dinner on the ground. We took a tablecloth or white sheet and put it on the ground for our food. I remember the big black ants crawling on the cloth. Other memories were the outhouse down behind the old Primitive Baptist Church. It was a long way to go. We had to go on the road at the left of the Primitive Church to the spring to get water or walk to Arthur Hedgecock's well.

In my childhood, we went to church in the carriage. Later Dad bought a 1928 Model T Ford. In bad wet weather the road was real bad. It took a lot of grinding to get up the hills we had to travel.

The first Pastor I remember was Mr. J. M. Hilliard. I remember him coming and having meals with us and he always wore a long back coat and pants with a white shirt.

Sometime passed before we built a new church. Later an addition was added. We had a well with a hand pump and the outhouse was behind the church. Later, they put restrooms in the church.

Wilson Hedgecock

Wilson Hedgecock has been a part of numerous committees and held many positions in the church. He and his wife, Ruth, have served strategic roles in the life and ministry of the church. Memories here give us more of an update of their beginnings in the church. He was born in 1920, two years before Ruth's birth. She grew up Primitive Baptist. His father died when he was eight years old. He and his mother moved to live with his grandmother. The grandmother was a member of Shady Grove United Methodist Church. The families divided their church time. They went to Shady Grove one Sunday and Abbotts Creek the next.

Wilson and Ruth were married in 1939 and shortly after their marriage, they both joined Abbotts Creek Church and perhaps neither of them could have envisioned how their lives would help shape the future events of the church or the lives of those who would be blessed by their ministries. Wilson was elected to serve as a deacon when he was twenty-three or twenty-four years old.

Without doubt, Wilson's friendship and working relationship with Coy Traynham, Sr., allowed the Clifton Grove and Abbotts Creek communities to have a respectable relationship with each other as integration was worked out.

Ruth was always the first one to carry food to a home when a death had occurred. She also served as chairperson of the committee to see that adequate food was always taken to the home where death had occurred.

The church honored them on September 30, 1979, for having served as church treasurers for twenty-six years.

Memories from Carlye Bodenheimer Kearns

I was asked to contribute to our church's history. First, let me say that my roots go back to my ancestors who were instrumental in the founding of Abbotts Creek Church. My Grandparents, Hattie & Andrew Bodenheimer, (who raised me), brought me to church as an infant and I have attended Abbotts Creek ever since. They were Bible-believing, God-fearing Christians who did not compromise their beliefs for anything or anybody. Despite evil forces, which have taken away some of our religious freedoms, & others who are trying to take away even more, I still believe and try to live by these basic truths that were instilled in me as a child.

I remember our church as a holy, sacred place where upon entering one could feel peace, tranquility and a reverence for God. It had a lot of wood inside which gave it a feeling of warmth. Some years after it was built an artist painted a gold trim above the wainscoting, making the beauty even more noticeable. There were large oak chairs on the pulpit—a large one in the center and a smaller one on either side. These were for ministers to sit in when they weren't preaching. I wish we could still have them there. When the baptistry was added, an artist was employed to paint a mural on the wall behind it that looked like what I imagined the River Jordan to be. This made it very impressive. The ladies of our church made drapes to hang in front of it, which were closed when not in use. My aunt, Mary Willie Orrell, was one of the ones that helped with this.

There was a big furnace in the downstairs part of the church, which was an assembly room that heated the church. It was a wood burning stove with a wood shed behind the church. Some of the older men would get wood and start the fire before services began on Sunday mornings. Upon entering this assembly room, there were wooden benches on the left in alcove where the older men's Sunday School class was held. Directly opposite was a space used for the older ladies Sunday School class and as a choir room when needed. There were Sunday School rooms along both sides of the walls. There was also a dais in the center front downstairs that was used as a pulpit when needed. As a small child I was shy and did not want to go into my class, so I went with my Granddad in his. There was an older gentleman, Mr. John Welborn, in his class who would give me chewing gum sometimes. As I grew older, I was in Miss Minnie Hayworth's class, which was the last room on the left. All the boys and girls were in her class at one time or another. We all loved her. When she went to join her Savior, I went to the visitation and started to cry. It was if she spoke to me and said, "Don't cry for me." I knew that this was exactly what she would have said if she could have spoken!

Homecoming or Memorial Day was third Sunday in May as it is now. The men would put boards on sawbucks behind and to the left of the church, under our big shade trees, to form tables. All our ladies would load them down with food. It was a day we looked forward to. People who were former members would come back home to see and fellowship with everyone. After a big meal we would return to the sanctuary and listen to a lot of good singing. Someone would always call the roll of all the members in the afternoon. In those days there were no modern conveniences so our "restrooms" were wooden structures behind the church in a little patch of woods.

Back in 1928, when our previous church was built, two members of my family, Andy Bodenheimer and Ivey Orrell, did a lot of the work in building this church. For this reason our family particularly hated to see this structure come down. This was a very impressive and beautiful building. When the first parsonage was built, my granddad did a lot of work on this too. I remember riding with him in our mule drawn wagon to do this work.

When I was small, my granddad walked to church at times (although I've been told he was one of the first in the community to own a "T" Model vehicle). One Sunday morning there was snow on the ground when he and I walked to church. He told me to walk in his footsteps, which I did. We took some shortcuts through woods and behind what is presently Wilson Hedgecock's house and Chester Spurgeon's house, crossed the road (Mock), and cut across the corner to the present Abbotts Creek Church Road.

The first minister I remember was Rev. Joseph Marcellus Hilliard. In fact, he had been minister for several years. He was a tall man with white hair and a bushy white mustache. He was pleasant looking always wore black, with a long black coat and wide-brimmed black hat. After his death that hat was given by his family to my granddad, which he proudly wore until his death. I've often wished I had kept that hat so that my husband, Paul, could have worn it when we celebrated our church's anniversaries. Mr. Hilliard (we always called our minister "Mr.") would walk down (present) Mock Road, around (present) Willie Bodenheimer Road, up (present) North Clodfelter Road (that was before roads in this area were named), forming a circle and visiting everyone along the way. One time he spent the night at our house and while my grandmother was cooking breakfast the next morning, he sat by the fireplace in the kitchen singing. He carried an overnight black bag and always had a supply of peppermint lozenges to give to the children. (My uncle Marion Marcellus Bodenheimer was named after him).

We had another pastor, Rev. Thomas W. Bray, when I was a child that my family thought a lot of. Because of this, I decided that if I ever had a son I would name him after Mr. Bray. Our oldest son's (Randy) middle name is Thomas. Mr. Bray had one son about my age, his name was Tommy. One night we sat in church together (with my family) and we tore up paper (don't know where we got it!) during the service. After the service, Mom (my grandmother) made me pick up the pieces. I don't think this was fair, I thought he should have helped me!

When I was saved, most of the girls had made a profession of faith during revival the summer before; however, I was not ready so I waited until the following year during revival when I was thirteen. Rev. B. A. Mitchell was our pastor then. He kept waiting to baptize me thinking that he would have some more candidates. When no one else professed, I had the distinction of being baptized by myself! This was done in the original outdoor pool in the woods. It was in the fall and I rode home in the rumble seat of my step-dad's "A" model. Had it not been the occasion it was, I would probably have a cold. The trend was, as now, to be baptized in white. My grandmother made little sacks out of flour sacks and put washers in them. They were pinned to the bottom of my dress to keep it in the water. When my cousin, Haarala Shelton, was baptized our aunt, Mary Willie Orrell, made Haarala's dress from one of her son's (Calvin) white Navy uniforms.

When I was sixteen, Peggy, Lyda, and I taught a Vacation Bible School class and one boy was very disruptive. One day Mr. Mitchell stood outside the window to see how he was behaving. (It didn't help!) I also sang in the choir for a short time when I was young.

Our present windows were also used in our previous church. We really had no need for air conditioning (which did not exist then) but on hot days the lower section and very top section of the windows were opened. There was a long reed with a hook on the end to open the top ones. This was usually done by one of the older men. The one I remember doing it was Sanford Hayworth. If this did not provide enough air, we had wicker fans and/or cardboard ones provided by local funeral homes with religious pictures on them. I remember after the service on Sunday mornings people would stand around outside visiting and fellowshipping. My granddad particularly enjoyed this and was always one of the last to leave. We miss a lot by not following this tradition today.

As already stated, my granddad was a deeply religious man. When our house burned early Sunday morning, September 1, 1946, he started getting ready to go to church at the usual time. He wore the only things he was able to save from the fire, bib overall's and rubber boots. Someone in the family asked if he was actually going to church and his reply was, "Of course." We all need more faith like that today.

Doris Bodenheimer Loggins

As a child, I did not realize just how poor I was. We always had plenty to eat, a place to sleep and hard working parents. That is more than a lot of children can say today.

In the summer time, we did not have any shoes so I came to Abbotts Creek Missionary Baptist Church barefooted. I can remember the cool concrete floor and how it felt on my feet.

Everyone would meet for assembly in the basement. You did not have a choice as you do now. The Sunday School rooms were along each side of the assembly room.

As a child, I remember Miss Minnie Hayworth as a kind, but very strict woman. We did not have Sunday School books like we have today. Each Sunday you would get a card about the size of a penny post card with your next Sunday's memory verses printed on them. I do not know when we began using books.

You also knew everyone in church by name because you grew up with them. Now you are seeing new faces that you can't put a name to but the attendance has not increased that much. With the increase in population you would think we would be busting at the seams but there are a lot of empty seats each Sunday.

As far as behavior in church, there was no getting up running to bathrooms (of course they were outdoors) or talking or laughing. If the look of your father and mother did not put the fear in you, then a good pinch would do the trick most of the time. Thank goodness, I never went the limit that I had to be taken out of church. And there was no way that any child was seen walking on the pews. (Goodness, I must be getting old, things sure have changed).

I for one cannot carry a tune in a bucket, but I can hear my mother singing alto to those good old gospel songs and it makes tears come to my eyes.

Abbotts Creek has always had the name missionary in it as far as I can remember. In 1938–1940, Abbotts Creek Missionary Baptist Church and Pastor Bray helped my oldest sister, Beatrice, enter into the Baptist Hospital where she had part of a lung removed due to bronchiectasis. Without that help from Abbotts Creek Church, my family would not have been able to get her any help. That made me feel that Home Missions was a part that everyone can do. Beatrice died in 1955 but to this day as I ride up Main Street and down Marshall Street in Winston-Salem, I think of what part Abbotts Creek Missionary Baptist Church had in extending her life to the age of 32 instead of her dying as a teenager.

I was baptized in the 1940s in the old out-door pool that was filled with water from a spring. It may have been summertime, but my teeth were chattering as if it were the dead of winter.

As I think of Abbotts Creek Missionary Baptist Church, our silent missionaries come to my mind: Ruth Hedgcock, Nina, Mable and Mary Hayworth, Minnie Smith, Daisy Spurgeon, Mae and Cleta Bodenheimer, Maggie Welborn, and Betty Williams. I am sure there are others as there are today people helping people as they see the need in the church and the community. They don't need a picture in print or a pat on the back for what they do because they a have the joy in their hearts for doing God's work.

Shirley Davis McLellan

My Family lived in Charlotte. When my Grandmother became ill, Daddy moved us back to his original home. I was 5 years old. My mother immediately joined Abbotts Creek. My Dad was already a member and I began to attend every Sunday. Rev. T. W. Bray was the pastor and Miss Mattie Teague who later became Mrs. E. F. Mumford was my Sunday School teacher. She was a School teacher and a very good Christian and therefore was a great Sunday School teacher. Next I moved up to the Junior Department and Miss Minnie Hayworth was my Sunday School teacher. Everyone knows that Miss Minnie saw to it that you brought your Bible and studied your Sunday School lesson every week. Mrs. Aileen Palmer became my next teacher and was my teacher until I left the church to go to college. She was a devout Christian and taught us faithfully for many years. She was our GA counselor and our YWA counselor. She always kept up with us. Soon Rev. B. A. Mitchell came as our pastor and we had Vacation Bible School that summer. He brought in a teacher from down East where he had been before his coming to Abbotts Creek. Little did I know that years later I would marry this teacher's brother and he would become a minister. During Mr. Mitchell's tenure, I became a Christian. Mr. Mitchell would work you in BTU and Bible school or wherever you would express an interest. I served as principal of Vacation Bible School for three or four years. During this time, I decided to do Christian work full time. I prepared myself for music ministry in the churches. Between Rev. Mitchell and Rev. A. R. Snipes, Dr. J. T. McRae and his wife Jane Carroll McRae came and preached for several Sundays. They were missionaries in Gaza and he was at Baptist Hospital preparing to return to the mission field. She wrote many study course books for the WMU. The McRaes were a great influence on my life. After Mr. Snipes left, Mr. Luther Morphis came and preached for us. I was convinced then that I was supposed to do some church work. I went off to college and began to further my music career.

I knew Mr. Walton and came to hear him occasionally but I went to work as a minister of music at a church in Asheboro. My parents made sure I met and learned something about Rev. Jimmy Hinson, Rev. Joe Coltrane, Rev. Charles Tanner, and Rev. Roy Cantrell. I did not attend during their tenure because I had married a minister and we served several churches in North Carolina. After my husband's retirement, we moved our membership to Abbotts Creek and Rev. Mark Hollar welcomed us to the church. It seemed I was coming home once again. This church gave me my beginning in Christian service and prepared me for work in churches as a professional and as a minister's wife. My recollection of my youth at this church makes me proud to be a member here, although I am still serving in the music ministry at another church. Rev. Hollar preached on Sunday, when I was at Abbotts Creek that we should use our talents for Christ daily. I shall play the organ and direct choirs as long as I am able. All of this writing says to me that Abbotts Creek is and always has been a mission-minded church. Let's keep it that way!

Pansy Moore

I have been a member of Abbotts Creek Church for almost seventy years, and attended all my life, with the exception of being in Louisiana when my husband, Dwight Moore, was in the Air Force stationed at Barksdale Field.

When arriving at church, we could almost identify who was there by the vehicles in the churchyard, as back in those days families drove the same ones for several years. Families also came together in one vehicle as many only had one way of traveling. I remember until 1954 everyone attending Sunday School met in the fellowship hall for a short devotion before going to our classes. I also remember everyone got a brown paper bag with nuts, fruits, and candy for Christmas.

Some of my childhood memories were my mother telling me if I needed to go to the toilet (which was a small building outside) to go between Sunday School and preaching, as there were very few people going in and out during morning worship services. Morning worship was a very sacred service in those days. There was no hand clapping or other noises to distract from the reverence of worship. I loved singing the old hymns. People being saved and the ordinance of the Lord's Supper were a special part of a service. I also remember Rev. J. M. Hilliard, a former pastor. I can just see him walking up the hill to my home after visiting other members. Rev. Hilliard always wore a top black hat, a frock tail coat suit and carried a black bag. I was very young then, but I remember he always had candy mints in his bag that he gave us children, which made us very happy, because in those days, we had very little candy. Oh, what fond memories!

I was baptized in 1937, in the outside pool with nineteen others. I remember my mother sewed rocks in the hem of the dress I wore for the baptizing. This outside pool was used until 1952 when one was built inside the church. When I was eighteen years of age, I began helping in Bible school and taught for many years, until one of my pupils said, "My teacher runs funny." When I heard this, I realized I should let younger folks take my place.

Sunday School picnics were a highlight of every summer. In those days many of the members were farmers and would take the day off to go to the picnics. Some of the places I remember us going were Hanging Rock, Morrow Mountain, Moore Springs, Reynolds Park and others. My mother made me a bathing suit to wear when we would go swimming at the picnics. I remember one of my favorites had navy blue and white flowers. Oh, what fun we had!

I remember our church revivals would last for two weeks and Abbotts Creek Church was filled with members, neighbors and community friends. Our pastor and the visiting minister were invited to a different member's home each time to eat and what a meal my mother always cooked when they came to our home.

Dwight Moore and I were married in Abbotts Creek Church, on October 28, 1950. The church was filled with family members, friends, and neighbors. I cherish those memories and have all the names of the guests in my bride's book and love to read and reminisce about each person.

Dwight and I were very active in church and didn't miss many services. I taught, led the singing, and was secretary in the beginners-primary department many years. I was also Sunbeam leader for several years and served on different committees.

Dwight was ordained a deacon in 1961, and was elected chairman at his first deacon's meeting. He also served as a trustee, Sunday School director, and teacher, and sang in the choir and was elected to other positions and on many committees over the years. Dwight loved Abbotts Creek Church and recorded much of its history, of which I treasure having in my home. He faithfully served the church as long as his health permitted and he passed away on June 21, 1999.

What a joy it was to us when our daughter, Myra, was baptized on April 25, 1962, and our son, Michael, was baptized April 14, 1963. Dwight was baptized August 5, 1934, and I followed on October 31, 1937.

I remember pastors serving Abbotts Creek Church: E. F. Mumford, 1923–1937; Tom Bray, 1937–1940; B. A. Mitchell, 1941–1949; A. R. Snipes, 1949–1950; W. H. Walton, 1951–1962; Joe Coltrane, 1963–1971; Charles Tanner, 1971–1974; Roy Cantrell, 1974–1998. Jack Rose served as associate pastor, 1992–2006; Lee Stocks was interim 1999–2001. Mark Hollar became pastor in 2001. I am grateful to my parents, Willie and Emma Hayworth Bodenheimer, and to Dwight's parents, Clarence and Laura Hammer Moore, for taking us to Abbotts Creek Missionary Baptist Church. These special memories are dear to my heart.

Daphne Moore Motsinger

My first memories of Abbotts Creek are in the building built in 1835. There were no special rooms for Sunday School classes, just a section set aside for each class. One year at Christmas, there was a large Christmas tree and Santa Clause came. Dan Hayworth furnished the treat bags given which had an apple, orange, candy and nuts. Clarence Moore brought the treat in the wagon pulled by the old mule he had at that time. Santa Clause was Gil Traynham, who worked at the Hayworth's.

I remember riding to church in the buggy pulled by the mule, Mandy. Daddy didn't own an automobile. Later, we rode with the Hayworths, who had that Nash auto that had three sections of seats. One time when it snowed, we were going on the sled. When we all got on it, the runners came off so we went on the sled that they put plows on. When we started having BYPU, Mary Frances drove the Nash and went through the area picking up teenagers. The old oak tree has been here since when the white church was here (1845). (This was written in February of 2007).

Mary Willie Orrell
January 7, 1904–April 30, 1981
Taken from an interview with her in 1976

We had a small organ and had to peddle the little peddles all the time we played. We had kerosene lamps all along the wall to light the church when we had our "big meetings" or "protracted meetings."

Rev. J. M. Hilliard was the first preacher I remember. He would spend the night with us. He always wore a long frock tailed coat and always carried pecans and lozenges candies for us little folks.

Rev. Thomas Carrick came next and had a horse and buggy and would have to have $150 a year rather than $100 like Rev. Hilliard.

Rev. E. F. Mumford came next and stayed several years. He was a Bible teacher and taught at Liberty Piedmont Institute at Wallburg. He served as the contractor of the building (which was removed for construction of the present facilities).

Revered Bray served as the next pastor. He helped with building the first parsonage but left before living in it.

Rev. B. A. Mitchell came next. He helped to keep up the telephones and was a very friendly person. He had a blue print made to add Sunday School rooms across the back of the church but the church voted not to do that.

Mary Willie adds, "Rev. Henry Walton came and he helped build the present Sunday School rooms (this was written in 1976)."

R. A. Snipes came as the next pastor but did not remain as pastor long. He would wore white gloves when serving communion.

She named pastors Joe Coltrane and Charles Tanner.

I remember walking with my sister, Era, to church. We walked barefooted though the woods. Later, we drove a buggy pulled by a mule. "Later, Papa got a Surry with two seats and we all went."

Mary Willie's first Sunday School teacher was Miss Flora Banks Traynham. "We had little cards with memory verses on them" and they were to be memorized. "We all gave a penny for collection."

"The first baptizing I remember was above the Curry Road Bridge. We all went in the Surry and Papa's horses would not cross the bridge so he tied them to a tree." She remembers her grandmother saying she was baptized in the creek when six-inch icicles were hanging on the bridge.

Evva Spurgeon

I am honored to be a part of the History Committee as I feel I have a rich history with Abbott's Creek. The first pastor I can remember was W. H. Walton. Mrs. Walton was a wonderful Sunday School and Vacation Bible School teacher and caring person to everyone she and W. H. came in contact with.

One of my first remembrances of the church was the boiler that was in the basement of the church where you first came in from the cold to warm. Sometimes it seemed dark in there, but you always had people standing around waiting to talk with you. I miss having that important spot in the church we are in today. No one stands around and talks to each other anymore.

I am told my mother took me to Abbotts Creek when I was two weeks old. I do remember walking to church and sometimes different people would come along and pick up my family while we were walking and I sure was glad they did.

I remember Violet Everhart in the nursery singing the song "9:45, I'll be at Sunday School at 9:45," and "This Little Light of Mine," and "Jesus Loves Me." Oh! What happy times we had when we were young and had those wonderful teachers like, Violet Everhart, Doris Sells, Mary Smith, Mrs. Walton, Laura Clinard, Aileen Palmer, and Mary Francis Motsinger. Another thing I remember was when a young lady got married, she was given a white Bible by her YWA leaders, and this was a big deal with candlelight ceremony. My YWA leaders were Laura Clinard and Aileen Palmer and I was given my white Bible at the home of Laura Clinard.

They didn't have all the different classes for Sunday School that they have now. They had one class for ladies from high school to forty years old and when I got married at the age of eighteen, I had to be in the same class with my older sisters. I worked for Abbott's Creek for 10 years as the part-time paid secretary with no benefits. I worked under Roy Cantrell and became a friend more than a secretary.

Pastors during my time at the church: W. H. Walton (Jimmy Hinson, Leonard Rollins served as interim pastors), Joe Coltrane, Charles Tanner, Roy Cantrell, Ben Rowe (minister of youth and education), associate pastor Jack Rose, Lee Stock (interim pastor), Mike Ester (preached several times), and Mark Hollar. Abbott's Creek has changed over the years with the coming of the different pastors, but God's word has always been spoken at the church and I am thankful for that.

Charles and I were married on July 7, 1965, at Abbotts Creek.

Memories of Robert Teague

A couple of things stand out in Robert Teague's memory of growing up in Abbotts Creek Church. Robert fondly remembers BYPU, this Sunday evening Training Union had good materials for youth to study in church. But he remembers most the "socials" that were encouraged for age groups. On Sunday nights and during these monthly "socials," the young people would get together. Boys could bring their girlfriends and the girls could invite their boyfriends as well. So much of the community activities centered on the church and this gave opportunity for fellowship or courting and parents felt good their youth were in a church setting.

The other thing that stands out in his mind so vividly took place after the services were over. A group of Republicans would get in one place and criticize the Democrats and the Democrats would be somewhere close by complaining about the Republicans. This never seemed to be an issue on church matters. (Shared on August 2007)

Abbotts Creek's Own Missionaries, Charles and Bonnie Wiggs

When we were appointed by the Foreign Mission Board (now the International Mission Board) of the Southern Baptist Convention in April of 1960, we were told that a church in High Point, North Carolina, wanted to support us. We did not know exactly how much monetary support this was because the amount went directly to the International Mission Board and we received a salary each month. We do know that the support that Abbotts Creek provided was much more than just the money sent to the International Mission Board. The prayers and personal support of our family were more important to us than the money.

We served in South Korea from 1960 until 1991, and during all those years we received many cards, letters, and gifts from members and organizations within the church. We appreciated the opportunity to share with the church on almost every furlough. Each time we visited, it was like coming home because we learned to love those in the church who were so kind to us. Most of all we appreciated their prayers, which sustained us through the years.

Of all the things that the church family did for us, I guess nothing meant as much to Bonnie as the gift made when Debbie, our first daughter, was leaving Korea to return to North Carolina to attend Wake Forest University. We were told that the RAs and GAs had done bake sales, car washes and many other things to collect the money sent for Bonnie to fly back to North Carolina with Debbie. Only recently have we learned that at the death of Perry Hayworth, his wife wanted the memorials made to help with this effort. We can never thank you, as a church family, enough for this gift. We are amazed that you thought to do this and actually did it! I am still overcome when I think of it!

Our three daughters, Debbie, Toni, and Lisa, all came to appreciate Abbotts Creek as they came back to attend Wake Forest and the church adopted each of them in turn. Not only did the church include them in the church's budget each year, which was used for their tuition expenses, but you also took them into your homes, invited them to special things at the church and took them gifts from time to time. As their parents, we really appreciated this procedure being done for them when we could not because we were so far away.

Your support and prayers for our girls brought great dividends. All three of them graduated from Wake Forest. Toni and Debbie went on to graduate from Southwestern Baptist Theological Seminary and married young men they met there. Their husbands are now Baptist pastors and have churches in Justin, Texas, and Henderson, Nevada. Lisa married a fellow student from Wake Forest who is senior manager of a Fidelity Investments office in Los Angeles, California. Your support and prayers had a big impact upon their lives. We are so grateful to you for that.

While we were in Korea, Charles served as administrator of the 550-bed, Bill Wallace Memorial Baptist Hospital, in Pusan. He was the first trained hospital administrator appointed by the Foreign Mission Board. Bonnie did lots of different things over the years. For a time she worked part time in the hospital business office. She was a deaconess and served in our Korean church as a Bible study leader, visitor, and worked with WMU. For about 10 years, she was director of Christian Home Ministries, an organization directing the work of the missionary women and for two years she was the treasurer of the Baptist Mission in Korea.

The mission work in Korea was very successful because people have answered the call of God to go there and churches like Abbotts Creek have provided prayer and financial support to the work of the Lord in Korea. Korea is now sending missionaries to other countries. They are second only to America in the number of missionaries that they have sent out.

We retired from the International Mission Board at the end of 1991 but three years later we went to Albania, a newly-opened field for the gospel, to serve two years with a team whose target group was the mountain villagers in this formerly Communist country. Following our "volunteer" service there we retired in Raleigh, North Carolina, where we find many opportunities to do missions. We will continue to serve as long as the Lord blesses us with good health.

Thanks again to Abbotts Creek Baptist Church for all you did for our family and continue to do to support the worldwide ministry of Christ.

Photos of Pastors

Elder William Turner
Jan. 1851–Dec. 1851
Feb. 1855–Nov. 1857
Sept. 1871–Dec. 1879
Jan. 1885–April 6, 1889
He died on the way home from New Friendship, where he served 18 years.

Elder John Robertson
Dec. 1851–Aug. 1853
Sept. 1861–Nov. 1863

Elder J. B. Jackson
Dec. 1863–Oct. 1868

Elder J. B. Richardson
Oct. 1868–Mar. 1871

Elder J. N. Stalling
May 1889–Nov. 1893

Rev. J. M. Hilliard
Nov. 1893–Dec. 1904
Jan. 1917–1923 (supply)

History, Heritage, and Memories

Pastors

Rev. Thomas Carrick
Dec. 1904–May 1917

Rev. E. F. Mumford
Apr. 1923–Jan 17, 1937
Supply Nov. 1940–Apr. 1941

Rev. Tom W. Bray
July 4, 1937–Nov. 1, 1940

Rev. B .A. Mitchell
May 4, 1941–May 29, 1949

Dr. A. B. Conrad
Supply, May 1949–Aug. 1949

Rev. A. R. Snipes
Aug. 21, 1949–Aug. 20, 1950

PHOTOS OF PASTORS

Pastors

Rev. W. H. Walton
Apr. 4, 1951–Oct. 14, 1962

Rev. Joe Coltrane
Apr. 14, 1963–Jan. 9, 1971

Rev. Charles Tanner
Aug. 16, 1971–Mar. 24, 1974

Rev. Roy Cantrell
Oct. 6, 1974–Oct. 24, 1998

Rev. Mark Hollar
June 21, 2001

Supply, Interim, Associate, and Intentional Pastors

Rev. Luther Morphis
Nov. 1950–Apr. 1951 (supply)

Rev. Jimmy Hinson
interim
Dec. 9, 1962–Apr. 14, 1963

Rev. Jack Rose
associate pastor
Aug. 4, 1992–Sept. 1, 2006

Rev. Lee Stocks
intentional interim
Mar. 1999–May 2001

Photos of Church Life

An Ariel View of the Church and Surroundings

1. Abbotts Creek Church Road
2. Browntown Road
3. Graveyard
4. Playground
5. Parking lot
6. Covered drive-through
7. Educational Building
8. Sanctuary and Fellowship hall
9. Parking lot
10. Primitive Church across road
11. Parsonage
12. Picnic Shelter
13. Ballfield

History, Heritage, and Memories

Congregation of Sunday School Classes in the 1970s

Church of 1928

PHOTOS OF CHURCH LIFE

Church of 1990

Church of 1990

Church Bell

Oil Lamp used along inside wall of old church

Hanging Chandler with old pulley used in old church

History, Heritage, and Memories

Inside new sanctuary

Beginning of new sanctuary, the inside view

Beginning of new sanctuary, the outside view

Photos of Church Life

New sanctuary

Stone monument

HISTORY, HERITAGE, AND MEMORIES

Marion Bodenheimer and Staley Bodenheimer (behind Marion) are shown using the scoop pan in the groundbreaking. This was the same scoop pan used in late 1920 to help dig the basement of the old church, which is still the area of the fellowship hall. Pictured on the left side of the rope, Clyde Spurgeon, Margaret Vogler, William Hayworth, Lee Davis, Violet Everhart, and Blanche Sechrest. On the right side, Daphne Motsinger, Ruth Spurgeon, Aileen Palmer, Charles Green, Wilson Hedgecock, and Kara Dean.

Pictured here is the graveyard across the road from our church.

PHOTOS OF CHURCH LIFE

Note burning: Molly Hedgecock, Bob Best, Evva Spugeon, Charlie Davis, Hugh Motsinger, Rev. Mark Hollar, Edith Bodenheimer, Kay Green, and Becky Sink.

Operation-In-As-Much: Rob Brasington, Billie Ann and J. C. Alcon, Betty Rose Alcon, and Evva Spurgeon.

History, Heritage, and Memories

Rev. Mark Hollar on horse on Old Fashion Day 2002.

This Christmon Tree is used every year. The tradition was started by Mrs. Pat Dawson.

Heritage Day 1999: Zane Hedgecock, Evva Spurgeon, Rev. Jack Rose, Lisa Hedgecock, Caroline Hedgecock (child), Daphne Motsinger (seated), Rev. Lee and Doris Stocks (seated), and Kara Dean (seated).

Abbott's Creek Records
from Liberty Baptist Association

Date	SS Enroll.	SS Director	Total Offering	Mission Gifts
1755–1758				
1756–1763				
1763–1783				
1819–1832				
Feb. 1833–1844				
1837–1842				
June 1842–1843				
1844–Oct. 1848				
1848–Dec. 1850				
1849				
Jan. 1851–Dec. 1851				
Dec. 1851–Aug. 1853				
1853				
Sept. 1853–Jan. 1855 (1854)				
1856				
Feb. 1855–Nov. 1857				
Nov. 1857–Nov. 1858				
Jan. 1859–Sept. 1861				
1860				
Mar. 1861–Aug. 1861				
1862				
Sept. 1861–Nov. 1863				
Dec. 1863–Oct. 1868				
1866				$2
1868				
1869				$2.50
1870				$1.15
Oct. 1868–Mar. 1871				
May 1871–Sept. 1871				$3.20
Sept. 1871–Dec. 1879				
1872			$2.55	$5
1874				
1875				
1876				
1877				$4.75
1878				$22.50
1879				$18
1879–Dec. 1880				$24.37
Dec. 1880–July 1882	40		$20.10	$22.20
Nov. 1882–Nov. 1884				
1882	31			$24.22
1883	62			$20.25
1884	62		$142	$31.43
Jan. 1885–April 6, 1889	32		$28.45	$26.75
1886			$139.65	$33
1887	66	N. W. Beeson		$25.50
1888			$113.69	$13.79
1889	59		$139.55	$29.15
May 1889–Nov. 1893				
1890	75		$663.42	$28.40
1892	72	N. R. Teague	$148.37	$17.47

History, Heritage, and Memories

Date	SS Enroll.	SS Director	Total Offering	Mission Gifts
Nov. 1893–Dec. 1904				
1894	95		$116.41	$13.46
1895	77		$146.53	$21.53
1896	90		$158.75	$41.75
1897	NL		$146.25	$33.25
1898	86		$142.15	$42.65
1899	97		$155.11	$39.11
1900	86		$176.15	$40.25
1901	80	N. R. Teague	$173.75	$27.25
1902	76		$251.71	$53.11
1903	77		$231.38	$50
1904	66		$201.61	$53.76
Dec. 1904–1916				
1905	67		$241	$50
1906	70		$232.75	$54.50
1907	75		$249	$66.50
1908	77		$260.80	$64.30
1909	71	N. R. Teague	$254.95	$64
1910	74		$237.95	$59.60
1911	68	N. R. Teague	$315.65	$69.50
1912	75		$270.10	$65
1913	89		$301.35	$66.50
1914	82		$318.65	$86.50
1915	87	W. D. Spurgeon	$304.50	$100.70
1916	82	W. D. Spurgeon	$301	$58.50
Jan. 1917–1923	61		$269.65	$61.25
1918	102	S. D. Hayworth	$367.25	$58.25
1919	106		$486.50	$159.50
1920			$1,099.57	$158.40
1921	84		$1,208.06	$460.92
April 1923–Jan. 1937	107		$970.10	$418.60
1924	87		$1,548.03	$888.58
1925	107		$1,179.25	$683
1926	125		$1,817.45	$625.05
1927	159		$19,503.59	$921.21
1928	175		$6,290.75	$1,284.65
1929	221		$4,244.97	$1,945.47
1930	289		$3,325.79	$1,786.27
1931	309	D. S. Hayworth	$2,787.31	$1,240.61
1932	336	Floyd Teague	$2,827.52	$1,133.52
1933	336	Floyd Teague	$1,141.21	$668.60
1934	359	Floyd Teague	$2,205.29	$1,336.88
1935	318	Floyd Teague	$1,867.16	$1,024.83
1936	316	Floyd Teague	$2,148.98	$1,282.24
Feb. 2–1937–May 9, 1937	311	D. S. Hayworth	$2,051.13	$1,126.54
June 1937–Nov. 1, 1940				
1938	304	D. S. Hayworth	$2,416.95	$1,301.82
1939	319	Floyd J. Teague	$2,637.14	$1,581.93
1940	303	Floyd J. Teague	$4,032.19	$994.28
May 4, 1941–May 29, 1949	258	T. C. Teague	$2,654.31	$859.34
1942	260	T. C. Teague	$3,171.89	$1,143.23
1943	265	T. C. Teague	$2,625.36	$1,353.84
1944	260	Carrick Teague	$4,413.54	$2,250.26
1945	306	D. S. Hayworth	$6,022.90	$2,083.13
1946	339	D. S. Hayworth	$7,164.42	$2,327.01
1947	338	D. S. Hayworth	$6,998.83	$1,778.11
1948	314	Floyd J. Teague	$8,440.35	$2,097.57
May 1949–Aug. 1949				
Aug. 1949–Nov. 1950	372	F. J. Teague	$5,947.09	$1,552.42

426

Abbotts Creek Records from Liberty Baptist Association

Date	SS Enroll.	SS Director	Total Offering	Mission Gifts
Nov. 1950-March 1951	376	F. J. Teague	$5,025.02	$3,246.24
March 1951-Oct. 1962	365	Wilson Hedgecock	$8,415.01	$3,281.41
1952	388	F. J. Teague	$10,830	$2,548
1953	411	F. J. Teague	$8,912.59	$3,640
1954	430	C. F. Moore	$10,520.95	$2,556.03
1955	489	C. F. Moore	$13,545.78	$2,219.64
1956	419	C. F. Moore	$13,068.33	$2,175.70
1957	370	Harry Cline	$13,239	$2,491
1958	406	Harry Cline	$12,089	$2,103
1959	469	C. F. Moore	$10,082	$2,048
1960	450	Earnest Burton	$10,722	$2,441
1961	408	Numa Everhart	$12,794	$2,201
Dec. 9, 1962-Apr. 14, 1963	351	Numa Everhart	$14,107	$2,258
April 14, 1963-Jan. 1971	431	Numa Everhart	$11,529	$2,678
1964	454	Numa Everhart	$12,816	$2,854
1965	458	Numa Everhart	$15,878	$3,688
1966	455	Numa Everhart	$15,416	$8,039
1967	458	Dwight Moore	$20,090	$5,127
1968	446	Dwight Moore	$18,677	$6,623
1969	410	J. C. Alcon	$20,233	$9,654
1970	402	J. C. Alcon	$63,553	$6,921
Aug. 1971-March 1974	363	J. C. Alcon	$21,262	$8,257
1972	367	Hugh Motsinger	$34,440	$7,176
1973	391	Hugh Motsinger	$36,885	$8,779
March 1974-Oct. 1974				
Oct. 1974-Oct. 1998	372	Hugh Motsinger	$39,206	$11,023
1975	373	Hugh Motsinger	$48,485	$11,500
1976	405	Hugh Motsinger	$55,306	$19,517
1977	391	Hugh Motsinger	$51,581	$12,921
1978	382	Hugh Motsinger	$51,658	$14,405
1979	386	Jeffrey Craver	$70,941	$17,801
1980	410	Jamie Williams	$88,422	$24,906
1981	407	Jamie Williams	$78,676	$24,484
1982	426	Jamie Williams	$75,881	$31,502
1983	415	Kenny Moore	$75,997	$27,099
1984	414	Kenny Moore	$91,046	$35,767
1985	438	Kenny Moore	$142,483	$56,203
1986	400	Charlie Davis	$110,599	$40,553
1987	390	Charlie Davis	$174,655	$36,726
1988	385	Charlie Davis	$216,923	$48,267
1989	405	Rick Cockrum	$1,163,062	$51,371
1990	478	Rick Cockrum	$1,027,228	$48,404
1991	492	Rick Cockrum	$230,163	$36,963
1992	479	Rick Cockrum	$357,080	$41,634
Aug. 4, 1992-Sept. 1, 2006				
1993	477	Rick Cockrum	$415,000	$37,922
1994	429	Pat Dawson	$337,083	$37,129
1995	502	Pat Dawson	$408,910	$40,438
1996	480	Pat Dawson	$437,392	$39,182
1997	471	Carl Alcon	$423,041	$399,994
1998	466	Ricky Delappe	$378,952	$53,913
Oct. 1998-March 1999				
March 1999-May 2001	447	Russell Fox	$458,063	$67,719
2000	490	Russell Fox	$467,236	$74,055
1-Jun	458	Russell Fox	$491,092	$71,592
2002	473	Russell Fox	$483,669	$83,010
2003	483	Perry Griffin	$675,082	$84,783
2004	520	Perry Griffin	$549,398	$82,951
2005	489	Perry Griffin	$569,168	$84,335
2006	460	PG & Tom Baity	$572,425	$74,921

History, Heritage, and Memories

Abbott's Creek Records from Liberty Baptist Association Records...

Date	Pastor	Clerk	Church Secretary
1755-1758	James Younger		
1756-1763	Daniel Marshall		
1763-1783	George Winfield Pope		
1819-1832	Ashley Swaim		
Feb. 1833-1844	Elder Eli Phillips	Philip Horney-1832	
1837-1842	Elder Josea Wiseman and Elder Enoch Crutchfield	Philip Horney Philip Horney	
June 1842-1843	Elder Benjamin Lanier	John Teague 1843-1879	
1844-Oct. 1848	Elder William Hamner	J. T. served 37 years	
1848-Dec. 1850	Elder Benjamin Lanier	John Teague	
1849	Benjamin Lanier	John Teague	
Jan. 1851-Dec. 1851	Elder William Turner	John Teague	
Dec. 1851-Aug. 1853	Elder John Robertson	John Teague	
1853	John Robertson	John Teague	
Sept. 1853-Jan. 1855 (1854)	Elder Benjamin Lanier	John Teague	
1856	Benjamin Lanier	John Teague	
Feb. 1855-Nov. 1857	Elder William Turner	John Teague	
Nov. 1857-Nov. 1858	Elder Amos Weaver (Supply)	John Teague	
Jan. 1859-Sept. 1861	Without a Pastor	John Teague	
1860	B. Lanier (Supply)	John Teague	
Mar. 1861-Aug. 1861	Elder Noah Richardson	John Teague	
1862	John Robertson	John Teague	
Sept. 1861-Nov. 1863	Elder John Robertson	John Teague	
Dec. 1863-Oct. 1868	Elder J. B. Jackson	John Teague	
1866	J. B. Jackson	John Teague	
1868	J. B. Richardson	John Teague	
1869	J. B. Richardson	John Teague	
1870	J. B. Richardson	John Teague	
Oct. 1868-Mar. 1871	Elder J. B. Richardson	John Teague	
May 1871-Sept. 1871	Elder G. W. Harmon (Supply)	John Teague	
Sept. 1871-Dec. 1879	Elder William Turner	John Teague	
1872	William Turner	John Teague	
1874	William Turner	John Teague	
1875	William Turner	John Teague	
1876	William Turner	John Teague	
1877	William Turner	John Teague	
1878	William Turner	John Teague	
1879	William Turner	John Teague	
1879-Dec. 1880	Elder R. R. Moore	John Teague	
Dec. 1880-July 1882	Elder S. F. Conrad	William Raper Hedgecock	
Nov. 1882-Nov. 1884 res	Rev. S. H. Thompson	W. B. Waff & Charlie Teague	
1882		Charlie elected 1882-1916	
1883	R. S. H. Thompson	Charlie Teague	
1884	S. H. Thompson	Charlie Teague	
Jan. 1885-April 6, 1889	Elder William Turner-	Charlie Teague	
		Charlie Teague	
1886	William Turner	Charlie Teague	
1887	William Turner	Charlie Teague	
1888	William Turner	Charlie Teague	
1889	William Turner	Charlie Teague	
May 1889-Nov. 1893	Elder J. N. Stalling	Charlie Teague	
1890	J. N. Stalling	Charlie Teague	
1892	J. N. Stalling	Charlie Teague	
Nov. 1893-Dec. 1904	Rev. J. M. Hilliard	Charlie Teague	
1894	J. M. Hilliard	Charlie Teague	
1895	J. M. Hilliard	Charlie H. Teague	

Abbotts Creek Records from Liberty Baptist Association

Treasurer	Deacon Chairman	Membership	Baptism & Letters
		43	B-5
		47	B-7
		85	B-37
		84	B-9 and L-1
Charlie Teague		85	B-4 and L-1
Charlie Teague		93	B-4 and L-1
		70	
		71	B-1
		69	B-4
		62	
		62	
		57	
		96	B-3
		93	
		132	B-41 and L-1
		130	
		126	B-8
		126	B-2
		121	B-3
		118	L-2
		117	B-2
		113	B-2
		119	B-9
		117	B-3 and L-1
		139	B-15
		141	B-11
		135	0
		134	B-5
		130	0
		129	0
		116	B-2 and L-1
		125	B-8
		144	B-27 and L-2
		134	B-3 and L-1
		132	B-2
		136	B-7

429

History, Heritage, and Memories

Date	Pastor	Clerk	Church Secretary
1896	J. M. Hilliard	Charlie H. Teague	
1897	J. M. Hilliard	Charlie H. Teague	
1898	J. M. Hilliard	Charlie H. Teague	
1899	J. M. Hilliard	Charlie Teague	
1900	J. M. Hilliard	Charlie H. Teague	
1901	J. M. Hilliard	Charlie H. Teague	
1902	J. M. Hilliard	Charlie H. Teague	
1903	J. M. Hilliard	Charlie H. Teague	
1904	J.M. Hilliard	Charlie H. Teague	
Dec. 1904-1916	Rev. Thomas Carrick	Charlie Teague	
1905	Thomas Carrick	Charlie H. Teague	
1906	Thomas Carrick	Charlie H. Teague	
1907	Thomas Carrick	Charlie H. Teague	
1908	Thomas Carrick	Charlie H. Teague	
1909	Thomas Carrick	Charlie H. Teague	
1910	Thomas Carrick	Charlie H. Teague	
1911	Thomas Carrick	Charlie H. Teague	
1912	Thomas Carrick	Charlie H. Teague	
1913	Thomas Carrick	Charlie H. Teague	
1914	Thomas Carrick	Charlie H. Teague	
1915	Thomas Carrick	Charlie H. Teague	
1916	Thomas Carrick	W. D. Spurgeon	
Jan. 1917-1923	Rev. J. M. Hilliard (Supply)	Willie D. Spurgeon	
1918	J. M. Hilliard	W. D. Spurgeon	
1919	J. M. Hilliard	Willie D. Spurgeon	
1920	J. M. Hilliard	W. D. Spurgeon	
1921	J. M. Hilliard	Willie D. Spurgeon	
April 1923-Jan. 1937	Rev. E. F. Mumford	Willie D. Spurgeon-1923-1932	
1924	E. F. Mumford	Willie D. Spurgeon	
1925	E. F. Mumford	Willie D. Spurgeon	
1926	E. F. Mumford	Willie D. Spurgeon	
1927	E. F. Mumford	Willie D. Spurgeon	
1928	E. F. Mumford	Willie D. Spurgeon	
1929	E. F. Mumford	Willie D. Spurgeon	
1930	E. F. Mumford	Willie D. Spurgeon	
1931	E. F. Mumford	Willie D. Spurgeon	
1932	E. F. Mumford	Willie D. Spurgeon	
1933	E. F. Mumford	Carrick Teague-1933-1937	
1934	E. F. Mumford	T. Carrick Teague	
1935	E. F. Mumford	T. Carrick Teague	
1936	E. F. Mumford	T. Carrick Teague	
Feb. 2-1937-May 9, 1937	Rev. V. M. Swaim-died 1937	Carrick Teague	
June 1937-Nov. 1, 1940	Rev. Tom W. Bray	Clarence Moore	
1938	T. W. Bray	Clarence Moore-1938-1947	
1939	T. W. Bray	Clarence Moore	
1940	T. W. Bray	Clarence F. Moore	
May 4, 1941-May 29, 1949	Rev. B. A. Mitchell	Clarence Moore	
1942	B.A. Mitchell	Clarence F. Moore	
1943	B.A. Mitchell	Clarence F. Moore	
1944	B.A. Mitchell	Clarence F. Moore	
1945	B.A. Mitchell	T. Carrick Teague	
1946	B.A. Mitchell	Clarence F. Moore	
1947	B.A. Mitchell	Clarence F. Moore	
1948	B.A. Mitchell	Robert Palmer-1948-1958	
May 1949-Aug. 1949	Dr. A. B. Conrad	Robert Palmer	
Aug. 1949-Nov. 1950	Rev. A. R. Snipes	Robert Palmer	
Nov. 1950-March 1951	Rev. Luther Morphis (Supply)	Robert Palmer	
March 1951-Oct. 1962	Rev. W. H. Walton	Robert Palmer	
1952	W. H. Walton	Robert Palmer	

Abbotts Creek Records from Liberty Baptist Association

Treasurer	Deacon Chairman	Membership	Baptism & Letters
		143	B-7 and L-1
		144	B-4 and L-3
		152	B-8 and L-11
		151	B-4
		151	B-5 and L-1
		149	
		169	B-22
		172	B-9 and L-1
		169	B-5
		176	B-9
		169	B-7 and L-2
		147	B-1 and L-5
		155	B-14 and L-1
		168	B-9 and L-3
		163	B-0
		164	B-2 and L-1
		165	B-1
		171	B-12 and L-1
		168	B-4
		179	B-12 and L-3
		176	B-2
		169	B-4 and L-2
		178	B-11
		179	B-3 and L-1
		195	B-18 and L-5
		173	B-1
		181	
C. E. Spurgeon		185	B-6 and L-1
C. E. Spurgeon		182	B-5 and L-1
C. E. Spurgeon		191	B-16 and L-1
C. E. Spurgeon		189	B-2
C. E. Spurgeon		206	B-18 and L-5
C. E. Spurgeon		218	B-15 and L-4
C. E. Spurgeon		227	B-13 and L-1
C. E. Spurgeon		232	B-16 and L-1
C. E. Spurgeon		245	B-17
Miss Mattie Teague		240	L-4
Miss Mattie Teague		278	B-26 and L-5
Miss Mattie Teague		275	0
Miss Mattie Teague		300	B-27 and L-1
Miss Mattie Teague		302	B-6 and L-2
Miss Mattie Teague		318	B-21 and L-7
Miss Mattie Teague		325	B-15
Miss Mattie Teague		327	B-1 and L-3
Miss Mattie Teague		326	B-3 and L-6
Grady Green		328	B-10
Grady Green		332	B-15 and L-1
Grady Green		354	B-25 and L-1
Grady Green		353	B-5 and L-6
Grady Green		347	B-3 and L-3
Grady Green		344	B-14
Fletcher Clinard		344	B-7 and L-1
F. J. Teague		338	B-5 and L-6
Charles Green		361	B-33 and L-4
		356	B-3 and L-8
Numa Everhart		361	B-11 and L-2

History, Heritage, and Memories

Date	Pastor	Clerk	Church Secretary
1953	W. H. Walton	Robert Palmer	
1954	W. H. Walton	Robert Palmer	
1955	W. H. Walton	Robert Palmer	
1956	W. H. Walton	Robert Palmer	
1957	W. H. Walton	Robert Palmer	
1958	W. H. Walton	Robert Palmer	
1959	W. H. Walton	Staley Bodenheimer '59-1970	
1960	W. H. Walton	Staley Bodenheimer	
1961	W. H. Walton	Staley Bodenheimer	
Dec. 9, 1962–Apr. 14, 1963	Rev. Jimmy Hinson (Interim)	Staley Bodenheimer	
April 14, 1963–Jan. 1971	Rev. Joe D. Coltrane	Staley Bodenheimer	
1964	Joe D. Coltrane	Staley Bodenheimer	
1965	Joe D. Coltrane	Staley Bodenheimer	
1966	Joe D. Coltrane	Staley Bodenheimer	
1967	Joe D. Coltrane	Staley Bodenheimer	
1968	Joe D. Coltrane	Staley Bodenheimer	
1969	Joe D. Coltrane	Staley Bodenheimer	
1970	Joe D. Coltrane	Pearl Hayworth-1970-1983	
Aug. 1971–March 1974	Rev. Charles Tanner	Pearl Hayworth	Kathy Green
1972	Charles L. Tanner	Pearl Hayworth	Kathy Green
1973	Charles L. Tanner	Pearl Hayworth	Pat Kanoy
Oct. 1974–Oct. 1998	Rev. Roy Cantrell—24 years	Pearl Hayworth	Pat Kanoy
1975	Roy Cantrell	Pearl Hayworth	Kathy Green
1976	Roy Cantrell	Pearl Hayworth	Kathy Green/Georgette Bullard
1977	Roy Cantrell	Pearl Hayworth	Georgetta Bullard
1978	Roy Cantrell	Pearl Hayworth	Wanda Beavers/Karen Wilson
1979	Roy Cantrell	Pearl Hayworth	Karen Wilson
1980	Roy Cantrell	Pearl Hayworth	Karen Wilson/Evva Spurgeon
1981	Roy Cantrell	Pearl Hayworth	Evva Spurgeon-10/80-3/89
1982	Roy Cantrell	Pearl Hayworth	Evva Spurgeon (first office)
1983	Roy Cantrell	Mrs. Kay F. Green	Evva Spurgeon
1984	Roy Cantrell	Kathy Green	Evva Spurgeon
1985	Roy Cantrell	Kathy Green	Evva Spurgeon
1986	Roy Cantrell	Kathy Green	Evva Spurgeon
1987	Roy Cantrell	Kathy Green	Evva Spurgeon
1988	Roy Cantrell	Sharyn Craven	Evva Spurgeon
1989	Roy Cantrell	Sharyn Craven	Evva Spurgeon & Patty Koontz
1990	Roy Cantrell	Joni Smith	Patty Koontz
1991	Roy Cantrell	Joni Smith	Patty Koontz
1992	Roy Cantrell	Evva Spurgeon	Stephanie Hall
Aug. 4, 1992–Sept. 1, 2006	"Rev. Jack Rose, Assoc. Pastor"	Evva Spurgeon	
1993	Roy Cantrell	Evva Spurgeon	Joann Chestnutt-1993-2001
1994	Roy Cantrell	Evva Spurgeon	Joann Chestnutt
1995	Roy Cantrell	Evva Spurgeon	Joann Chestnutt
1996	Roy Cantrell	Evva Spurgeon	Joann Chestnutt
1997	Roy Cantrell	Evva Spurgeon	Joann Chestnutt
1998	Roy Cantrell	Evva Spurgeon	Joann Chestnutt
Oct. 1998–March 1999	Rev. George Dowd (Supply)	Evva Spurgeon	Joann Chestnutt
	Rev. Leonard Rollins (Supply)	Evva Spurgeon	Joann Chestnutt
	Rev. Morris Hollifield (Supply)	Evva Spurgeon	Joann Chestnutt
March 1999–May 2001	Rev. Lee Stocks (Inten. Interim)	Evva Spurgeon	Joann Chestnutt-
2000	Rev. Lee Stocks (Inten.Interim)	Evva Spurgeon	Joann Chestnutt
June–2001	Mark Hollar	Evva Spurgeon	Linda Russell—May 2001
2002	Mark Hollar	Evva Spurgeon	Linda Russell
2003	Mark Hollar	Evva Spurgeon	Linda Rusell (First Full Time)
2004	Mark Hollar	Evva Spurgeon	Linda Russell
2005	Rev. Mark Holler	Evva Spurgeon	Linda Russell
2006	Mark Hollar	Evva Spurgeon	Linda Russell

The above information came from the Liberty Baptist Associational Minutes

Abbotts Creek Records from Liberty Baptist Association

Treasurer	Deacon Chairman	Membership	Baptism & Letters
Wilson Hedgecock		378	B-20 and L-7
Wilson Hedgecock		391	B-19 and L-4
Wilson Hedgecock		411	B-19 and L-11
Wilson Hedgecock		401	B-6
Wilson Hedgecock		405	B-10 and L-5
Wilson Hedgecock		399	B-6 and L-3
Wilson Hedgecock		419	B-27
Wilson Hedgecock		424	B-5 and L-8
Wilson Hedgecock		380	B-14 and L-5
Wilson Hedgecock		374	B-8 and L-2
Wilson Hedgecock		435	B-53 and L-10
Wilson Hedgecock		449	B-13 and L-8
Wilson Hedgecock		460	B-14 and L-8
Wilson Hedgecock		475	B-10 and L-10
Wilson Hedgecock		481	B-16 and L-10
Wilson Hedgecock	Numa Everhart	482	B-4 and L-5
Wilson Hedgecock	Dwight H. Moore	490	B-17 and L-2
Wilson Hedgecock	Dwight H. Moore	453	B-4 and L-2
Wilson Hedgecock	Dwight H. Moore	449	B-16 and L-8
Wilson Hedgecock	J. C. Alcon	467	B-27 and L-3
Wilson Hedgecock	John Sulger	475	B-5 and L-18
Wilson Hedgecock	Dwight H. Moore	466	B-6 and L-10
Wilson Hedgecock	Laurence H. Todd	507	B-28 and L-24
Wilson Hedgecock	Numa Everhart	523	B-9 and L-12
Wilson Hedgecock	Hugh Motsinger	524	B-4 and L-9
Wilson Hedgecock	John L. Hedgecock	545	B-20 and L-12
Hugh Motsinger	Donald Livengood	539	B-6 and L-15
Hugh Motsinger	Laurence H. Todd	578	B-38 and L-14
Hugh Motsinger	Dwight H. Moore	580	B-10 and L-8
Hugh Motsinger	Kay F. Green	598	B-8 and L-25
Hugh Motsinger	Kenny Moore	615	B-18 and L-15
Hugh Motsinger	Hugh Motsinger	616	B-6 and L-11
Hugh Motsinger	Wayne Bullard	636	B-26 and L-12
Hugh Motsinger	Charles Goad	646	B-18 and L-13
Hugh Motsinger	Laurence H. Todd	639	B-6 and L-8
Hugh Motsinger	John Sulger	641	B-7 and L-5
Hugh Motsinger	Carl Alcon	644	B-6 and L-10
Hugh Motsinger	Dwight H. Moore	634	B-3 and L-6
Hugh Motsinger	Laurence H. Todd	671	B-32 and L-21
Hugh Motsinger	Laurence H. Todd	700	B-24 and L-23
Beck Sink			
Becky Sink	Hugh Motsinger	722	B-16 and L-19
Becky Sink	Rick Cockrum	716	B-6 and
Becky Sink	Laurence H. Todd	712	B-16 and L-18
Becky Sink	Hugh Motsinger	707	B-4 and L-8
Becky Sink	Scott Ford	729	B-21 and L-24
Becky Sink	Carl Alcon	749	B-22 and L-17
Becky Sink			
Becky Sink			
Becky Sink			
Becky Sink	Laurence H. Todd	762	B-10 and L-16
Becky Sink	Patrick Moss	769	B-21 and L-6
Becky Sink	Don Myers	781	B-8 and L-22
Becky Sink	Ricky Robertson	820	B-22 and L-42
Becky Sink/Carl Alcon	John Hedgecock	846	B-22 and L-27
Becky Sink/Carl Alcon	Zane Hedgecock	864	B-12 and L-20
Becky Sink/Carl Alcon	Billy Hutchens	870	B-11 and L-19
Becky Sink/Carl Alcon	Wayne Bullard	883	B-18 and L-21

INDEX

Abbotts Creek Baptist Mission, 230
Abbots Creek Church,, 63, 66-68, 71, 96, 108, 230
Abbotts Creek Primitive Baptist Church, 6, 96, 102, 273, 350
Abbott, Henry, 28, 105
Abbott, John, 28
Abbott, William, 29
Alcon, Betty Rose, 9, 258, 307, 334, 370, 423
Alcon, Billie Ann, 238, 244, 246, 253, 307, 334, 357, 363, 370
Alcon, Bobby, 346, 348
Alcon, Carl, 286, 290, 292, 383,311, 320, 329, 332, 338, 340, 342, 356
Alcon, J. C., 209, 237, 238, 241, 246, 266, 268, 276, 282, 284, 286, 287, 296, 305, 332, 345, 371
Alcon, Jennifer, 249, 260, 272, 312
Alcon, Kim, 249, 259, 263
Alcon, Robert, 224, 228, 230, 235, 237
Alcon, Ray, 253
Alcon, Sonya, 290, 315, 324, 326, 330, 340, 353, 359-362, 381
Alexander, M. O., 181
Alice, Black, 93
Allen Jay Baptist Church, 237
Allred, Dorothy, 272
Allred, James, 258
Allred, John, 272
Amos, Ginger, 252
Andrews, Bill, 280
Anderson, Gaye, 362
Andrews, Connie, 280
Andrews, Terri Peele, 258
Ann, Margaret, 189
Anson Community College, 299
Anthony, Brianna, 362
Anthony, Brooke, 362
Anthony, Debbie, 362, 370
Appalachian State University, 259, 354
Armstrong, Elders Thomas D., 66, 108
Armstrong, George, 246

Arnold, Gary, 312
Arnold, Laura, 312, 315
Arnold, Larry, 312
Atkins, Blanche, 262
Atkins, Frances, 118, 141
Atkins, N. C. James, 262
Atkinson, Reverend C. B., 193
Atkinson, Sister Dinah, 112
Aulander Baptist Church, 279
Austin, Rebecca Holton Raper, 22
Avritt, Brother S. N., 161
Baity, Tom, 427
Baker, E. F., 185
Baker, Kelly, 353
Baptist State Convention of North Carolina, 12, 67, 175
Baptist Theological Seminary, 148, 211, 365, 412
272, 313, 325, 350
87, 90, 159, 168, 170, 182
Baptist World Alliance, 187, 194, 213, 260, 296, 330
Barbados Baptist, College, 279, 284, 286, 289
Barnes, Rebecca, 361, 369
Barron, Frances, 32, 74
Barron, William, 32, 74
Bates, Robert, 281
Beach, Holden, 287
Beavers, Mike, 269, 270, 279
Beavers, Wanda, 432
Beeson, Broadus, 236
Beeson, Clarence, 298
Beeson, E .E., 151
Beeson, Grace, 206
Beeson, Isaac, 99
Beeson, John, 236
Beeson, King C., 133, 141
Beeson, Lois, 223
Beeson, Marie, 206
Beeson, Monroe, 236, 245, 285
Beeson, N. W., 425
Beeson, Newell W., 129, 134, 140
Beeson, Paul, 206, 236
Beeson, Polly, 236
Beeson, Roxie, 223, 237, 238, 245, 246, 249, 263, 278, 283, 304
Beeson, Sister C. B., 150
Beeson, Thomas A., 138

Beeson, Thomas L., 136, 141
Beeson, Thomas, 130, 136
Bell, Becky, 249, 265, 269
Bellot, John, 348
Bennett, Elder J. M., 155
Bennett, Erin, 318
Berrier, Louis, 204
Berrier, Tempie, 204
Best, Bob, 286, 320, 358, 372, 423
Best, Brad, 311
Best, Camie, 377
Best, Nancy, 300, 378
Biggers, Hugh, 272
Billingsly, Captain James, 101
Binkley, Dr. Olin T., 243
Bisinton, Sarah, 32, 74
Blackwell, Bessie, 290
Blackwolf Baptist Church, 323
Blair, Colonel W. A., 25
Blake, Christi, 331, 340, 348, , 353-354
Blake, George, 331, 335, 346
Blake, Lori, 331, 335
Blevins, Jennifer, 325, 355, 360, 362, 370, 372
Bodenhamer, A. M., 167, 170
Bodenhamer, Andrew, 165, 173
Bodenhamer, Charley, 170, 173, 174
Bodenhamer, Charlie, 177
Bodenhamer, Crissa J., 142
Bodenhamer, D. H., 130
Bodenhamer, David A., 140
Bodenhamer, Debby B., 142
Bodenhamer, Dorothy, 183
Bodenhamer, Eliza, 155, 157, 158
Bodenhamer, Ester, 117
Bodenhamer, Jacob, 79
Bodenhamer, Jake, 177
Bodenhamer, Lucy, 124, 141
Bodenhamer, Mae Craven, 177
Bodenhamer, Margaret, 141
Bodenhamer, Martha, 142
Bodenhamer, Maude, 177
Bodenhamer, Mozell, 170
Bodenhamer, Nancy K., 142
Bodenhamer, Peter R., 133, 141
Bodenhamer, Phobe, 154

INDEX

Bodenhamer, R., 133, 141, 167
Bodenhamer, Sarah E., 133, 141
Bodenhamer, Sister Lucy, 124
Bodenheimer, Agnes, 22
Bodenheimer, Andrew, 160, 165, 188, 192, 398, 401-402
Bodenheimer, Bonnie, 272, 296
Bodenheimer, Burley, 178
Bodenheimer, C. H., 197
Bodenheimer, Cassie, 180, 182
Bodenheimer, Charity, 22
Bodenheimer, Charles, 173, 183, 190, 193-194, 397
Bodenheimer, Cleta, 397, 405
Bodenheimer, Clyde, 204, 322
Bodenheimer, Debbie, 236
Bodenheimer, Donald, 182
Bodenheimer, Dorothea, 234
Bodenheimer, Edith, 238, 270, 287, 423
Bodenheimer, Emma Hayworth, 408
Bodenheimer, Eric, 178
Bodenheimer, Gete, 178
Bodenheimer, Ivey, 192
Bodenheimer, Kristy, 272
Bodenheimer, Mae, 182, 222
Bodenheimer, Marion, 204, 299, 312, 392, 403, 422
Bodenheimer, Mildred, 193, 222, 296
Bodenheimer, Millard, 25
Bodenheimer, Norman, 236
Bodenheimer, Nikki, 245
Bodenheimer, Oren, 207
Bodenheimer, Patty, 217, 235, 241, 253, 318, 321, 329, 333
Bodenheimer, Perry, 194
Bodenheimer, Peter, 22
Bodenheimer, Randal, 183
Bodenheimer, Ruby, 180
Bodenheimer, Rusty, 245
Bodenheimer, Ruth, 194
Bodenheimer, Sadie, 178
Bodenheimer, Staley, 208-209, 227, 231, 234, 235, 237-238, 240-241, 245, 269, 272, 286, 288, 299, 301, 305, 311, 317, 392, 422, 432
Bodenheimer, Stanton, 182
Bodenheimer, Stella, 178
Bodenheimer, Tommy, 236, 245

Bolick, Reverend James, 246
Boone, Daniel, 24
Bowers, David, 259
Bowers, James, 241, 242, 256
Bowers, Jerry, 259
Bowers, Marie, 328
Bowers, Wilbur, 240, 241, 245, 252, 256, 257, 321, 332
Brasington, Robert, 381, 423
Bray, Tom W., 188, 398, 403, 408, 414, 430
Breed, Joseph, 46
Bridgelal, Amrit, 389
Bridgetat, Amrit, 294
Brissons, Carson, 314
Britt, R. A., 185
Brock, J. C., 185
Brookie, Jean, 258, 260
Brown, Absolom, 25
Brown, Ann, 32, 74
Brown, Brother E. D., 125
Brown, Elder J. B., 137, 156
Brown, Elizabeth, 25, 65, 68, 107, 141
Brown, Ephraim, 122
Brown, Ester, 129, 141
Brown, George W., 133, 141
Brown, Elizabeth, 65
Brown, Jane, 133, 141
Brown, Jean Davis, 25
Brown, Jones H., 138
Brown, Lety, 141
Brown, Levi, 134, 142
Brown, Mary A., 126, 141
Brown, Peter, 137
Brown, Sarah, 141
Brown, Sister Eliza, 128
Brown, Susan, 236
Brown, W. A., 148
Bryant, Elizabeth, 230
Bryant, Joe, 227-230, 268
Bryant, Robbie, 370, 377, 378
Bryant, Roy, 228-230
Buffey, Elder Charles, 46
Bullard, Denise, 269. 272, 303, 304, 310
Bullard, Georgette, 261, 263, 269, 270, 289, 294, 296, 311, 332, 387, 432
Bullard, Wayne, 272, 278. 285, 288, 292, 299, 304, 311, 346, 348-349, 352, 356, 359, 361, 377, 433
Buller, Mary, 32, 74
Bunce, Darrel, 295

Burch, William, 61, 100, 108
Burlington, Vernon Lewis, 291
Burris, Bobbie, 329, 343, 363, 370
Burris, Craig, 332, 336, 339, 343, 351, 369
Burton, Ernest, 193, 195, 201, 226, 228, 232, 237, 427
Burton, Fleta Motsinger, 177, 226, 306
Busch, Elder Wm, 66
Butcher, Andrew, 236
Butcher, Clifford, 236
Byrd, Sherri, 350, 357, 362
Cadell, John, 133, 141
Calvary Baptist Church,, 293, 311
Campbell College, 277
Campbell, Sister Polly Ann, 93
Canada, Bobby, 243, 252, 254, 256, 257, 258, 272, 285, 299, 305, 308, 312, 321, 328, 332, 342, 345, 346, 351, 362, 372, 378, 382
Canada, Dorothy, 249, 252, 256, 299, 307, 378
Canada, Lynn, 259, 322, 324
Canipe, Brother J. C., 174
Canipe, Mae, 262, 306
Cantrell, Beth, 260, 290, 311, 339, 340, 389
Cantrell, Chet, 276, 279, 282-284, 286, 289, 339-341, 388
Cantrell, Chris, 282, 285, 289, 290, 292, 339
Cantrell, David, 279, 339, 341
Cantrell, Linda, 259, 261, 263, 266, 270, 272, 278, 291, 307, 329, 344
Cantrell, Michelle, 305, 339, 340
Cantrell, Reverend Roy, 1, 3, 13, 257, 201, 310, 383, 400, 406, 408, 410, 415, 432
Carey, Both, 241, 266
Caribbean, 13, 14, 284
Carie, Brother, 132, 134
Carmichael, Charlie, 199, 219, 224, 234
Carmichael, Flossie, 234, 235, 306
Carmichael, Richard, 226
Carolina Memorial Baptist Church, 231
Carrick Teague, 430

435

Carrick, Brother Thomas, 155, 165, 183, 196, 199, 395
Carroll, Eli, 110, 116
Carter, Crissa, 134, 142
Carter, Jane, 141, 147
Carter, Mary, 136
Carter, Phebe A., 132
Carter, William, 130, 140
Cartledge, Dr. Tony, 384
Cartswell, Elener, 32, 74
Cary, William, 51, 52
Cassels, Andrew, 332
Castalia Baptist Church, 202
Cedar Lodge Baptist Church, 312, 337
Center Hill Baptist Church, 290, 335
Chadwich, Wheeler, 78
Chadwick, Wheeler, 81
Chaipman, J., 61
Chandler, Hanging, 419
Chaplin, Dillen, 32, 74
Chappell, Amber, 362, 380
Chappell, Andy, 352, 362, 377
Chappell, Tarinda, 359, 361, 362, 378
Charles, Addison, 193
Charles, Ann, 117
Charles, Brother G. W., 118, 148
Charles, Clarissa, 142
Charles, Destimones R., 141
Charles, Eleanor, 133, 142
Charles, Elsie G., 133, 141
Charles, George W., 130, 140, 148
Charles, Huldak, 141
Charles, Joseph, 134, 142
Charles, Larkin, 133, 141
Charles, Lena G., 142
Charles, Mary Lee, 168
Charles, Melissa C., 141
Charles, Melissa J., 130
Charles, Melssa J., 141
Charles, Poan C., 140
Charles, Roan, 130
Charles, Sarah, 141
Cherokee Baptist Church, 222, 257, 258, 339
Chestnutt, David, 330, 352
Chestnutt, Joann, 316, 318, 319, 329, 339, 355, 432
Chestnutt, Leann, 340
Chewning, Crystal, 265
Chipman, Margaret, 32, 74

Chow, Edward, 193
Chris, 9, 269, 276, 282, 285, 289, 290, 292, 339, 348
Christ Wesleyan Church, 381
Christian, Michael, 283
Churchland Baptist Church, 321
Churton, William, 102
Clambet, Brother George, 87
Clarence Moore-1938-1947, 430
Clegg, Robert, 291
Clemens, David, 271, 290, 291, 339, 345, 355, 358, 359, 389
Grove Baptist, 209, 264
Clinard, Angela, 313
Clinard, Beverly, 20
Clinard, Brother Wm., 131
Clinard, C. J., 130
Clinard, Catherine, 206
Clinard, Crissa J., 141
Clinard, Desdemona R., 142
Clinard, Eliza J., 142
Clinard, Elizabeth H., 142
Clinard, Fletcher, 202, 223, 224, 430
Clinard, Hyram, 133, 141
Clinard, Jacob A., 141
Clinard, Jesse, 134, 136, 142
Clinard, Kasey, 20
Clinard, Kelly, 246, 287, 291, 301-303, 305, 309, 312
Clinard, Kirk, 272
Clinard, Kristin, 20
Clinard, L. F., 130
Clinard, Laura, 236, 279, 410
Clinard, Loreta F., 141
Clinard, Louisa, 141
Clinard, Lucinda, 142
Clinard, Maggie, 228, 306
Clinard, Margaret J., 142
Clinard, Mary, 133, 141
Clinard, Michael, 230
Clinard, Patty, 197, 218
Clinard, Sarah Lou, 133
Clinard, William, 130, 131, 140, 155
Clinard, Wilson, 141
Cline, Ashley, 303
Cline, Ben, 329, 353
Cline, Christy, 303, 311
Cline, Harry, 223, 227, 427
Cline, Kathy Green, 258
Cline, Margaret, 387
Clodfelter, Dot, 222
Clodfelter, Jerry, 182

Clodfelter, Ollie, 178
Coart, Samuel, 32, 74
Cobb, Ty, 291
Coble, Mary Jane Kanoy, 258
Cockrum, Linda, 332
Cockrum, Nathan, 332, 353
Cockrum, Richard, 317, 427, 432
Coffey, Richard, 381
Coggins Memorial Baptist, 295
Colby College,, 51
Coltrane, Joe, 235, 238, 239, 241, 259, 278, 312, 355, 393, 406, 408-410, 415
Coltrane, Zemma, 387
Columbian College,, 51
Compton, Bobby, 288
Compton, Peggy, 288, 298
Conrad, Dr. A. B., 181, 414, 430
Conrad, S. F., 139, 147, 428
Cook, Carl, 228, 229
Cook, Christi, 260
Cook, Cindy, 241, 242, 278, 287
Cook, Linda, 246
Coon, Dr. Hoke, 302
Cooper, D. W., 261
Copeland, Dr. Luther, 322
Couch, Richard, 117
Counts, David, 339, 341
Counts, Jennie, 9
Covington, B. G., 134
Cradelboh, Sara, 74
Cradleboh, Sarah, 32
Cranen, Sary, 32
Craner, Moses, 32, 74
Craven, Austin, 353
Craven, Betty, 3, 8, 265, 272, 307, 380, 381, 383, 393
Craven, Brother Thompson, 93
Craven, Christy, 303
Craven, Gene, 293
Craven, Harry, 283, 297, 308, 317
Craven, Jane, 236
Craven, Jay, 246
Craven, Jeff, 314
Craven, Joe, 330, 331, 337, 342, 345
Craven, Paul, 207
Craven, Samuel, 94
Craven, Sharyn, 299, 432
Craven, Tony, 321, 323, 334, 339, 340, 363, 370, 372
Craver, Howard, 206

INDEX

Craver, Ida, 178
Craver, Jeffrey, 427
Craver, Sarah, 141
Craver, Sary, 74
Creek, Leonard, 18
Crews, David, 332
Crews, Doris, 330, 371
Crews, Heather, 329
Crickenberger, Jackson, 380
Cridlebough, E. E., 170
Cridlebough, Thomas, 156
Crocack, Anderson, 141
Crouch, Ann, 117
Crouch, Brother James, 123
Crouch, Elizabeth, 124, 130, 141
Crouch, James, 123
Crouch, Mary, 141
Crouch, Pam, 259
Crouch, Sister A., 123
Crutchfield, Enoch, 136, 428
Culler, Audrey, 237, 238
Culler, Joan, 237
Culler, Lester, 240
Curlee, Keith, 290, 317, 389
Curry, Faye, 336
Daniels, E. J., 263
David, Carey, 227
David, John, 11, 381
Davidson County Community College,, 259, 290
Davis, Amanda, 328, 340
Davis, Aviation Cadet Lee W., 204
Davis, Bill, 226, 228
Davis, Brethren Joseph, 94
Davis, Clay, 207
Davis, Joseph, 91, 94
Davis, Brother Solomon, 86
Davis, C. W., 151, 153, 155, 158
Davis, Captain William, 101
Davis, Carey, 187, 192, 197, 199, 214 219, 226, 228, 230, 231, 235, 237, 239, 241, 267, 396, 398
Davis, Charles H., 236
Davis, Charles W., 204, 267
Davis, Charles, 263, 270, 293, 304, 317, 330, 350, 353, 372, 377, 384, 393
Davis, Charlie, 35, 356, 362, 423, 427
Davis, Della, 193
Davis, Elijah, 381
Davis, Garfield, 209
Davis, Grace, 230

Davis, Henry, 19
Davis, Jacky, 19, 241, 265, 266, 268
Davis, Jean Ann, 234
Davis, John Roe, 395
Davis, Joseph, 91, 94
Davis, Kisha, 381
Davis, Lee, 182, 240, 256, 257, 272, 286, 297, 422
Davis, Margaret, 32, 74
Davis, Sary, 32, 74
Davis, Shirley, 199, 218, 405
Davis, Solomon, 86, 91, 92
Davis, Vickie, 358-359, 361
Davis, W. P., 218, 223
Davis, Wilbur, 245
Davis, William, 19, 101
Davis, William, III, 19
Davis, Carey, 398
Dawson, Debbie, 256
Dawson, Dianne, 246
Dawson, Pat, 242, 246, 253, 263, 282, 315, 321, 343, 353, 358, 387, 427
Dawson, T., 332, 353
Dawson, Tom, 238, 240, 244, 245, 251, 252, 272, 392
Deal, Helen, 183
Dean, Betty Lou, 194
Dean, Howard, 192, 199, 200, 221, 223, 226, 227, 238, 241
Dawson, Pat, 315, 424
Kara, 166, 177, 278, 306, 395, 422, 424
Delap, Alexander, 117
DeLappe, Ashley, 340, 353
DeLappe, Kyle, 362, 380
DeLappe, Pam, 353
DeLappe, Ricky, 323, 340, 359, 361, 364, 427
Dieator, Daniel, 163
Dillard, Dr. George, 141
Dillard, Meranda, 134, 142
Dills, Dot, 363, 374
Dills, Ginger, 236, 241, 242
Dills, Norma, 252, 299
Dills, Vivian, 306
Dills, Walter, 374
Dixon, Russ, 359
Dobbins, Gary, 370
Dobson, Elder E., 122
Doss, Hugh, 339
Doss, Nancy, 339
Dowd, William, 62-64, 67, 70, 95, 97, 98, 114

Dowd, George, 272, 294, 308, 310, 311, 330, 335, 432
Dowd, P. W., 97
Dowd, William, 59, 62-64, 66, 67, 70-72, 95, 97, 108
Drage, Therodorus S., 103
Drake, Hannah, 41
Dull, Perry, 248, 249, 254, 259, 265, 268
Dunn, Angellee, 258
Dunn, Angie, 297
Dunn, Mathew, 254, 261, 290, 292, 294, 297-298, 304, 314, 327, 334, 337, 342-343, 349, 353, 356, 358, 387, 424, 427
Dunn, Missionary Wayne, 286, 289
Durso, Keith E., 49
Druso, Pamela, 49
Earnhardt, Jerry, 279
East Grimes Street Baptist Church, 294
East Taylorsville Baptist Church, 374
Eaton, Herb, 22
Eberhardt, David, 314
Eberhardt, Mike, 290, 298, 314
Eberhardt, Robin, 290, 298
Eberhart, Robin, 296
Echols, Beth Hayworth, 11, 14, 209, 389
Echols, Beth, 5, 298
Echols, M. Patton, 213
Eddins, Dr. John, 244
Edwards, Jonathan, 39
Edwards, Kenneth, 221, 222, 273
Edwards, Morgan, 33, 102
Eliza, Julia, 35
Eller, Pauline Stewart, 6
Elmer, James, 207
Embler, Jack, 240, 243
Embler, Ricky, 294
Emily, Rebekah, 354
Emmanuel Baptist Church, 289
Emmons, Brenda, 312
English Road Baptist Church, 316, 317, 389
Enon Baptist Church, 265
Essee, David, 140
Essick, Angie, 362, 364
Essick, Betty, 189, 235, 333
Essick, Dale, 260, 366
Essick, David, 353, 357

437

History, Heritage, and Memories

Essick, Larry, 305
Essick, Libby, 3, 8, 351, 383, 397
Essick, Melissa, 330
Essick, Willie, 227
Ester, Mike, 351, 410
Evans, Ann, 35, 68
Evans, Anna, 65, 79, 107, 119
Evans, Architect Bud, 301
Evans, Betty, 117
Evans, Christiana, 117
Evans, Christina, 141
Evans, Elizabeth, 80, 86, 94
Evans, James, 34, 35, 65, 68, 74, 79, 86, 87, 89, 93, 94, 107, 112, 118
Evans, Mary, 65, 68, 74, 107, 141
Evans, Pastor Ken, 325
Evans, Sister Anna, 119
Evans, Sister Elizabeth, 94
Evens, Anna, 32, 74
Everhart, Annette, 272, 290
Everhart, Junior, 206
Everhart, Karen, 234
Everhart, Numa, 201, 208, 217. 220, 222, 224, 226-229, 231,233, 235, 240-241, 245, 248, 251, 261, 278, 294, 300, 308, 323, 427. 433,
Everhart, Velecia, 265
Everhart, Violet, 223, 320, 324, 334, 397, 410, 422
Eythe, Johann Bernhart, 20, 21
Fant, Elder J. K., 154
Ficklin, Parnell, 344
Field, Barksdale, 406
Fielder, Brother, 154
Fields, Ann, 32, 74
Fields, Tim, 8
Fields Publishing, 3, 4, 8
Filbour, Harold, 204
First Congregational Church of Windsor, 41
First Reformed United Church of Christ, 389
Fitzgerald, E. B., 156
Floyd Baptist Church, 254
Folger, Dr. Alfred M., 25
Ford, Ashley, 340
Ford, Pam, 299, 313, 353
Ford, Scott, 312, 327, 335, 345, 372, 377, 432
Ford, Tanner, 328, 438
Foreign Mission Board, 198, 239, 281, 282, 284, 288, 289, 296, 298, 314, 411, 412
Fork Baptist Church, 188, 290, 292, 325
Foster, Barbara, 290
Foust, Sue, 3, 8, 101, 383, 398
Fowler, Ken, 260, 290, 295
Fowler, Tony, 348, 354, 356, 377
Fox, Christy, 353, 370
Fox, Russell, 344, 350, 357, 427
Frances, Leslie, 378
Frances, Mary, 193, 219, 408
Frank, Benji, 343, 345
Frank, Jonathan, 356
Frank, Kim, 299, 303, 336
Frank, William, 395
Freedman, Mathew D., 112, 116
Freeman, Elder, 117
Fruitland Bible Institute, 221
Fulk, Lincoln, 185
Gaither, Gloria, 270
Gallimore, Brother, 179
Gallimore, Keith, 358
Gann, Danny, 274, 278, 317, 322, 324, 326, 329, 330-331, 346, 367
Gann, Lee, 334
Gann, Mary, 293, 318, 327, 331, 334, 368, 387
Gann, Megan, 367
Gann, Michael, 262, 288, 290, 292, 296, 315, 323, 334, 358, 368, 377, 381
Gann, Nellie, 306
Gann, Sharon, 269, 291, 304, 324, 326
Gann, Taylor, 324, 368
Gann, Tracy, 362, 368
Gano, John, 19, 32, 37, 43
Gardner Webb University, 375
Gardner-Webb College,, 261
Garner, Charles, 243, 244, 253, 254, 270, 373
Garner, Marilyn Everhart, 254, 344
Garner, Tim, 311
Garret, Brother J. A., 158
Garrison, Billy, 194
Garrison, Hobert, 177
Garrison, Margaret, 183
Garrison, Mary, 252
Garson, Mary, 32, 74
George Washington University, 51, 212
Gibbons, Molly, 134
Gibson, Steve, 372, 377
Gilbert, Sherri, 378
Gilum, Elizabeth, 74
Glascoe, Monroe, 206
Glass, Dr. Victor, 270
Glassco, Mat, 178
Glassco, Rosie, 178
Glisson, Debbie, 236
Glusseck, Elizabeth, 141
Goad, Charles, 291, 432
Goad, Debbie, 289, 387
Grace, Negro, 32, 74
Graham, Franklin, 380
Grand Backlet Baptist Church, 290
Grassum, Ann, 32, 74
Grassy Creek Church, 42
Green Street Baptist Church, 389
Green, Annie, 178
Green, Charles, 219, 246, 256, 257, 269, 308, 311, 422, 430
Green, Clarence, 207
Green, General Nathaniel, 26, 105, 326
Green, Grace, 307, 321, 329, 333
Green, Grady, 153, 160, 181, 188, 190, 192, 196, 200, 214, 249, 251, 398200
Green, Hanar, 32, 74
Green, J. L., 190
Green, Jo Ann, 236
Green, Joanne, 236, 259
Green, Julie, 269
Green, Kathy, 244, 246, 249, 252, 258, 260, 270, 285-286, 299
Green, Kay, 251, 266, 267, 278, 285, 287, 288, 305, 423, 432
Green, Kermit, 192
Green, Lee Ray, 362
Green, Lester, 399
Green, Mae Bodenheimer, 222
Green, Mary, 32, 74, 75
Green, Minnie, 174, 187
Green, Ray, 188, 192, 196, 362
Green, Robert, 178
Green, Thomas, 32, 74
Gregory, Bliss, 204
Gregory, Lucian, 229, 400
Griffin, Perry, 359, 361, 427

INDEX

Grissom, Richard, 32, 74
Grissom, Sary, 32, 74
Grove, Clifton, 178, 207, 209, 263, 264, 284, 285, 401
Guesford, Sarah, 65, 68, 107
Guesford, Stephen, 65, 66, 68, 95, 107, 108
Guilford College,, 179
Gutrugs, Widow, 32, 74
Gwaltney, John, 330
Hale, Dustin, 380
Halker, Alicia, 304, 311
Halker, Chris, 348
Halker, Vicki, 283, 289
Hall, Stephanie, 432
Halton, Guy, 329
Hamby, Lorie, 336, 339, 343, 353, 362
Hamby, Roger, 332
Hammer, Ida, 280
Hammer, William, 120, 132, 428
Hanes, W. F., 161
Handy, Buddy, 245
Hardin, R. N., 342
Harenton, Lary, 32, 74
Harman, Valentine, 141
Harmon, G. W., 135, 428
Harmon, Rebeca, 142
Harris, Henry, 133, 141
Harrod, Donice, 330
Harry, Benjamin, 43
Hartsook, Jamie, 282
Harvard Divinity School, 283
Hasty Baptist Church, 339
Hatcher, David, 313
Hattie, 401
Haworth, Jane, 141
Hayes, Alvin, 236
Hayes, Dorothy, 291
Hayes, Judy, 236
Hayes, Martha, 236
Hayes, Rayford, 251, 308, 311, 313, 323, 325, 340
Haymore, Jim, 181
Haynes, James, 183
Hayworth, Alverta, 178
Hayworth, Anna Laura, 206
Hayworth, Anna, 362, 380
Hayworth, Athel W., 207
Hayworth, Aunt Mabel, 12
Hayworth, Baxter, 209
Hayworth, Beth, 11, 14, 194, 209, 284, 296, 299, 330, 389
Hayworth, Chairman D. S., 196

Hayworth, Charles E., 320
Hayworth, Charles, 353
Hayworth, Clarence, 178
Hayworth, Dan, 151, 209, 211, 246, 308, 396, 397, 408
Hayworth, Doris, 222
Hayworth, Dorothy, 183, 192
Hayworth, Douglas, 237, 245, 259
Hayworth, Dwight, 206
Hayworth, Earl, 194
Hayworth, Elizabeth, 183, 399
Hayworth, Esther, 141
Hayworth, Eva, 193, 385
Hayworth, Fred, 178
Hayworth, Grace, 226
Hayworth, Harvey, 177, 182
Hayworth, Jerome, 267, 273
Hayworth, Johnie, 199, 206
Hayworth, Joseph, 182
Hayworth, Kenneth, 209
Hayworth, Lessie, 204
Hayworth, Lillian, 164
Hayworth, Loucinda, 154
Hayworth, Louis, 177
Hayworth, Lucile, 183
Hayworth, Mabel, 12, 178,192-193, 201,226, 228, 236, 222, 387
Hayworth, Marie, 203, 226
Hayworth, Mary Frances, 182, 193
Hayworth, Mary, 340, 386, 405
Hayworth, Maxine, 194
Hayworth, Minnie, 12, 168-170, 172, 174, 210, 386, 392, 395, 396, 399, 402, 404, 405
Hayworth, Minnie, 12, 210, 386, 392, 396, 399, 402, 404, 405
Hayworth, N. S., 168
Hayworth, Nina, 193, 236, 386
Hayworth, Pauline, 320
Hayworth, Pearl, 3, 8, 235, 246, 263, 265, 285,-86, 383, 399, 432
Hayworth, Perry, 172, 177, 192, 269, 411
Hayworth, Roy, 182, 188, 203, 206, 221, 226-228
Hayworth, S. D., 426
Hayworth, Sharon, 234
Hayworth, Uncle Sanford, 392
Hayworth, W. L., 162, 163
Hayworth, W. S., 165, 168, 173, 196, 198

Hayworth, Wesley Paul, 204, 236
Hayworth, William, 204, 257, 305, 422
Heare, Mary, 142
Heart, J. L., 179
Hedgcock, Ruth, 405
Hedgecock, Ada F., 163
Hedgecock, Alonzo, 237
Hedgecock, Ansel, 95
Hedgecock, Art, 25, 263, 265, 269, 278, 279, 318
Hedgecock, Arthur, 173, 400
Hedgecock, Ashley, 329
Hedgecock, Bettie J., 142
Hedgecock, Blanche, 183
Hedgecock, Carl, 175
Hedgecock, Carol, 378
Hedgecock, Caroline, 383, 424
Hedgecock, Chairman Wilson, 197, 266
Hedgecock, Charlie, 178
Hedgecock, Cherrie, 272
Hedgecock, Cletus, 183, 202, 222, 224, 229, 230, 235, 240, 243, 331
Hedgecock, Debra, 258
Hedgecock, Early, 178, 204
Hedgecock, Ella, 194
Hedgecock, Elva Motsinger, 177, 400
Hedgecock, Elva, 193, 306
Hedgecock, Emaline, 141
Hedgecock, Ezekiel, 25
Hedgecock, Frank, 352
Hedgecock, Jason, 260
Hedgecock, Jimmy, 226
Hedgecock, John L., 130, 140, 236, 252, 254, 261, 266, 432
Hedgecock, Julian, 141
Hedgecock, Lee, 275
Hedgecock, Lesha, 332
Hedgecock, Lisa, 370, 424
Hedgecock, Lori, 290, 305, 311, 318
Hedgecock, Lynne, 241-242
Hedgecock, Madison, 380
Hedgecock, Mary, 189, 306
Hedgecock, Mildred, 203
Hedgecock, Molly, 283, 336, 362, 371, 378, 423
Hedgecock, Pauline, 140, 307
Hedgecock, Reitzel, 308
Hedgecock, Roger, 274, 280, 284, 287, 311

439

History, Heritage, and Memories

Hedgecock, Ruth, 226, 235, 246, 387, 405
Hedgecock, Scott, 260, 369
Hedgecock, Sister Juliann, 129
Hedgecock, W. T., 224
Hedgecock, William R., 130, 141, 147
Hedgecock, William Raper, 428
Hedgecock, Willie Paul, 173, 226, 273, 275
Hedgecock, Wilson, 193, 197-198, 209, 219-220, 222-224, 228, 231, 237, 240, 256, 266, 274, 308, 400, 403, 422, 427, 432
Hedgecock, Zane, 3, 8, 314, 316-317, 321, 325, 340, 343, 345, 347, 348, 354, 364, 371, 377, 424, 433
Helton, James, 32, 74
Helton, Mary, 32, 74
Helton, Rebecca, 32, 74
Hemphill, Carl, 231
Henderson, Boyce, 206
Hephzibah Baptist Church, 219
Hepler, John, 140
Herndon, John, 43
Herring, Doctor Ralph, 197
Herron, Reverend James, 269
High Point University, 375
Hill, Donny, 236
Hill, Lois, 307
Hill, Lynn, 236
Hill, Vance, 236
Hillcrest Baptist Church, 231, 232, 233, 235, 239, 240, 278
Hilliard, J. M., 400
Hilliard, Elder J. M., 160
Hilliard, Joseph Marcellus, 403
Hilliard, Reverend J. M., 160
Hilton, Barri, 317, 318
Hilton, Eddie, 265, 291, 311, 313
Hilton, Glenn, 209
Hilton, Vicki, 254, 263, 293, 337, 342, 343, 345, 347, 387
Hincle, Anthony, 80
Hines, Blanch, 178
Hines, Brother, 169
Hines, W. C., 169
Hinson, 235, 236, 344, 380, 406, 410, 416, 432
Hinson, Jimmy, 235, 380, 406, 410, 416, 432

Hinson, Margaret, 344
Hinson, Reverend Jimmy, 235
Hitchcock, Elijah, 80, 82
Hitchcock, Isaac, 23
Hitchcock, John, 23
Hodges, Charles, 256, 259
Holder, Elmo, 226
Holder, Ruth, 226-228, 387
Hollar, Anita, 362, 378
Hollar, Laura, 362
Hollar, Mark, 134, 354, 367, 375, 376, 390, 406, 408, 410, 415, 423, 424, 432
Hollar, Rebekah, 362, 380
Hollifield, Morris, 328, 339, 432
Hollon, Levi, 125
Holston Association, 103
Home Mission Board, 249, 257, 270, 305, 317
Hood, Edith, 331, 350, 352, 361, 362, 369, 371, 375, 378, 382
Hood, Harry, 331, 352
Hope, Spring, 196
Horney, Brother Phillip, 109
Horney, Jane, 141
Horney, P., 111
Horney, Phebe W., 133
Horney, Phebe, 65, 68, 107, 141
Horney, Philip, 111, 428
Horney, Phillip, 109, 110, 112, 116
Horney, Phoebe A., 141
Horney, Pleasant, 133, 141
Horney, Rebecca, 141
Bill Wallace Memorial Baptist Hospital, 412
The North Carolina Baptist Hospital, 218, 342
Houston, Sandra Jean, 315
Howard, Chief Justice, 104
Howard, Peter, 334, 336, 348, 354
Howell, Dr. Ray, 331
Hudson, Billy, 226, 230, 235
Huger, General, 106
Huggins, M. A., 102, 106
Hundley, Hope, 378
Hunt, Dr. Brooks, 312
Hunter, Terri, 324
Hutchens, Amy, 260
Hutchens, Billy, 352, 377, 432
Hutchens, Dawn, 378
Hutchens, Lori, 272
Hutchens, Matthew, 380

Hutchens, Nicole, 340
Hutcherson, Guy, 282
Hutcherson, Jeff, 282
Hutchinson, Guy, 279
Hyatt, Donna, 224
Hyatt, H. B., 222
Hyatt, Haywood, 221, 222, 316, 388
Hyatt, Elizabeth, 141
Hyatt, Verta, 226
Hyde, Barbara, 312, 324, 326, 362
Hyde, Radford, 362, 380
Hyde, Tony, 327, 339, 358-361
Idol, Barnet, 21, 94
Idol, Elizabeth Meier, 21
Idol, Elizabeth, 141
Idol, Emerson, 175
Idol, Grady, 183, 190, 192, 193, 196, 217, 221, 224, 227
Idol, Hesak, 141
Idol, Hester, 193
Idol, Jacob, 32, 74, 78, 79, 101
Idol, Lori, 362
Idol, Louisa, 141
Idol, Mary G., 141
Idol, Mattie Ruth, 21
Idol, Mister, 21
Idol, Mr., 101
Idol, Nancy, 226
Idol, Staley, 206
Idol, W., 130
Idol, Wade, 206
Jackson, R. R., 193
Liberty Piedmont Institute, 164, 169, 409
International Mission Board, 282, 356, 389, 411, 412
Israel, Cynthia, 236
Israel, James, 236
Israel, Noah Moses, 368
Israel, Rebecca, 236
Jackson, A. P., 140
Jackson, A. R., 130
Jackson, J. B., 78, 128-129, 130-131, 413, 428
Jackson, Eli, 130
Jackson, Isaac, 82, 428
Jacobs, Elder A., 122, 4
Jamaica, Island of, 290
James, Margaret, 293, 296, 299, 315, 327
James, Marie, 204
James, Osbert, 279, 289, 290, 299, 329, 338
Jamestown Baptist Church, 61

INDEX

Jenkins, Joel P., 255-256
Jennings, Gary, 374
Jersey Baptist Church, 98, 104, 328
Jester, Dr. John, 172
Jilcott, Angela, 330
Joann Chestnutt-1993-2001, 432
John Wesley College,, 316
Johnson, Archabald, 78-79
Johnson, Calhoun, 253
Johnson, David, 311
Johnson, Kirby, 296, 304, 311
Johnson, Mary, 79
Johnson, Sandra, 304, 311
Johnson, Steve, 276
Johnson, Suzanne, 332
Jone, Elizabeth, 74
Jones, Alethe, 141
Jones, Archie, 276
Jones, Cad, 73
Jones, Cadvolender, 32, 74
Jones, Caroline, 280
Jones, Debbie, 265
Jones, Elder H., 138
Jones, Elder, 138
Jones, Elizabeth, 32
Jones, Evie, 226, 306, 334
Jones, F. W., 137
Jones, Glaster, 224, 237, 238, 240, 255, 269, 272
Jones, J. J., 130, 141
Jones, Jan, 116
Jones, Jane, 35, 109
Jones, Jesse, 140
Jones, Philip, 296
Jones, Ruth, 306
Jones, Sarah A., 141
Jones, Sarah, 32, 74
Jones, Tom, 267
Jones, W. G., 223, 224
Jordan, Bessie, 234, 253, 307
Jordan, Brother F. M., 133
Jordan, Charles, 268, 272, 278, 283, 294, 314, 322
Jordan, Chip, 332
Jordan, Deacon Charles, 322
Jordan, Dot, 234
Jordan, Elder, 133
Jordan, Everett, 237, 240, 308
Jordan, Janet, 236, 259
Jordan, Jeff, 315, 377
Jordan, Jill, 259
Jordan, Sandy, 300, 325, 362
Joseph, Jimmy, 337, 356

Joyce, Ann, 292, 294, 313, 314, 321, 339, 343
Justice, B. W., 133
Kanoy, Charles, 178
Kanoy, Charley, 190, 193
Kanoy, Keith, 256
Kanoy, Mary Jane, 252, 258, 260
Kanoy, Mary, 193, 306
Kanoy, Norman, 177
Kanoy, Pat, 252, 253, 256, 257, 261, 432
Kanoy, Richard, 197, 253-255
Kanoy, Vera, 178
Kearns, Becky, 226, 258
Kearns, Beth, 260, 305
Kearns, Brad, 290
Kearns, Carlye Bodenheimer, 401
Kearns, Lee Roy, 235, 270, 285, 315
Kearns, Paul, 267
Kearns, Randy, 246, 259
Kehukee Baptist Association, 52
Keiner, Bill, 21
Kennedy, Jimmy, 261
First Baptist Church of Kernersville, 185
Key, Bessie, 236
Kiger, Ellen, 206
Kiger, Stacy, 304, 311
Kimbro, Mabel, 74
Kimbro, Susannah, 32, 74
Kimery, N. R., 197
King, Beth, 8, 371
King, John, 81, 85
King, Louise, 206
King, Pegg,y 296
King, Servilas, 141
King, Walter, 296
Kingswood Baptist Church, 388
Kirby, Isaac, 97
Knight, Calvin, 343
Koch, Elizabeth, 332
Koltash, John, 206
Kook, Ann, 32, 74
Kook, Lille, 32, 74
Kook, Thomas, 32, 74
Koontz, Patty, 310, 317, 432
La Union Baptist Church, 288
Lakeview Baptist Church, 313, 381
Lambeth, J. H., 153
Lanier, Benjamin, 119, 137, 428

LaPoint, Jerry, 381
Lawson, Dr. Eual, 249
Leach, Betsy, 343, 354, 359, 261, 368
Ledbetter, Henry, 37, 42
Ledford, Brother, 73, 74
Ledford, Hatharane B., 141
Ledford, John, 32, 73, 74, 80, 82
Ledford, Sister, 124
Ledford, Squire, 94
Ledford, Tabitha, 80
Leinbach, Ella Marie, 226
Leonard, Dr. J. C., 19
Leonard, The Reverend, 317, 342
Lewis, W. L., 182, 183
Lewis, Barbara, 370
Lewis, Dapathana, 183
Lewis, Kim, 269
Lewis, Vernon, 291, 297, 301
Liberty Baptist Association, 317
Liberty Baptist Church, 62, 110, 272
Lick Creek Baptist Church, 180, 286, 388
Lifter, Burden, 192
Lightford, William, 75
Linnville, Dewey, 368-369
Linnville, Hazel, 368
Livengood, Andrew, 140
Livengood, Don, 242, 249, 257, 261, 268, 272, 276, 278, 279, 291, 305, 320, 334
Livengood, Marty, 293, 344, 353
Livengood, Tammy, 290, 291, 305
Lodge, Masonic, 123, 124
Loggins, Doris, 3, 8, 383, 404
Loggins, Janet, 246
Loggins, Shane, 260
Lolley, Dr. Tom, 348
Lopp, Captain, 101
Lovelace, Dorothy, 182
Lovelace, William, 182
Low, Margaret, 74
Lowe, Tamer, 32, 74
Lower, 29, 66, 83, 96, 168, 383, 404
Lowery, Eve, 32, 74
Lucinda (Colored), 113
Luck, W. S., 184
Luck, Michelle, 265
Lumpkin, William A., 40

441

Lumpkin, William L., 49
Lusk, Mary, 32, 74
Lyda, B. B., 209, 234, 235, 308
Lyda, Joy, 246
Lyda, Peggy Stewart, 6
M., Moses, 395
Maarten, St., 304, 311
Mabe, C. R., 219, 224, 229
MacClaren, Beth Hayworth, 330, 389
MacClaren, Robert H., 212
Maddry, Charles, 174, 175
Mann, Charles, 308
Marion, Francis, 21
Mars Hill Baptist Church, 194
Mars Hill College,, 210, 284, 294
Marsh, Tom, 257, 269
Marshall, Abraham, 41, 44
Marshall, Dale, 310, 332, 353, 354, 381
Marshall, Daniel, 7, 19, 35-37, 39-48, 101, 388, 428, 432
Marshall, Denise, 310-311, 332
Marshall, Elder Abraham, 41
Marshall, Eunice, 46
Marshall, John, 46
Marshall, Joseph, 46
Marshall, Levi, 46
Marshall, Martha Stearns, 7, 15, 46-48
Marshall, Mary, 46
Marshall, Moses, 46
Marshall, Solomon, 46
Martin, Amber, 331
Martin, Governor Josiah, 103
Martin, Steve, 321
Martinoff, Reverend Clovis, 314
Mash, Jane, 32, 74
Mash, Roda, 74
Mash, Ruth, 32, 74
Matthews, Luther J., 187, 204
McBrayer, Carolyn, 378
McClaren, Beth Hayworth, 296, 299
McClellan, Aubrey, 256
McCuistion, Walter, 187, 192, 202
McDowell, Tebin, 279
McGuire, Andrea, 332
McGuire, Christina, 362, 380
McGuire, Dean, 296, 348, 356
McLean Baptist, 212, 389
McLellan, Shirley Davis, 405

McMillan, John Arch, 181
McRae, Dr. J. T., 406
McRae, Jane Carroll, 406
Mendenhall, Bleka, 236, 238
Mendenhall, David, 237, 278, 288, 305
Mendenhall, Montalva, 133, 141
Mendenhall, Phebe, 133, 142
Mercer University, 4, 49, 309
Meredith College,, 157
Meredith, Christopher, 353
Meredith, Thomas, 51
Merrill, Benjamin, 104
Merrill, Merrell 104, 105
Messer, Guy, 268
Metro Baptist Association, 296
Mill, Evans, 26
Miller, Benjamin, 28, 32
Miller, Brittany, 340
Miller, John R., 160
Miller, Polly, 117
Miller, Ted, 227
Mills Home Baptist Church, 183, 189
Mills, Brother J. H., 150
Mills, David, 364, 365, 377
Mills, Ellen, 359
Minerva (Colored), 133
Mitchell, Dr. John, 155
Mitchell, Margaret Ann, 189
Mitchell, Pastor B. A., 195, 198, 202, 219, 403, 406
Mock, Hannah E., 112
Mock, Hannah, 117
Montgomery, Elizabeth, 80
Montsinger, Brooks, 251
Moody, A. C., 231, 232
Moore, Aaron, 375, 379, 382
Moore, Burch, 204
Moore, Chairman Dwight, 235, 258
Moore, Clarence F., 190, 195, 201, 221-223, 427, 430
Moore, Daphne, 8, 63, 183, 245, 408
Moore, Della, 203
Moore, Donna, 258, 260
Moore, Dot, 203, 217, 218, 234
Moore, Dwight H.,182, 229-230, 235, 240-241, 243,-244, 254, 256, 258, 263, 278, 283, 288, 305,-306, 346, 406-407, 427 432
Moore, Elder R. H., 138, 428

Moore, Fred, 207
Moore, Harold, 204, 240
Moore, Isaiah, 381
Moore, Kenny, 236, 265, 279, 287, 291, 292, 297, 301, 312, 427, 432
Moore, Laura, 245, 251, 408
Moore, Michael, 223, 236, 259
Moore, Myra, 234, 241, 242
Moore, Pansy, 9, 63, 235-237, 271, 280, 295, 307, 314, 317, 332, 339, 349, 387, 406
Moore, Sara, 378
Moore, Seth, 262, 346
Moore, Ty, 375, 376
Moorefield, Roger, 227, 243, 247
Morey, Joseph, 32, 74
Morgan, 32, 33, 74, 93, 94, 102
Morgan, Brother, 32, 74
Morgan, David, 93, 94
Morgan, Ezekiel, 93
Moriarty, Donald James, 246
Moris, Elizabeth, 74
Moris, Hanah, 32
Moris, Rachel, 32, 74
Moris, Sary, 32, 74
Morphis, Luther, 219, 406, 416, 430
Morris, Elizabeth, 32
Morris, Jane, 55
Morris, Keyah, 381
Morris, Paul, 55
Morrow, Bill, 339
Morton, Brother, 156
Morton, Elder H., 156
Moss, Amanda, 364, 365
Moss, Jenilee, 340, 363
Moss, Kim, 313, 339, 353, 359, 383
Moss, Patrick, 323, 329, 339, 340, 343, 345, 352, 354, 357, 364, 370, 432
Moss, Rebecca, 362
Motsinger, Becky, 236
Motsinger, Betty Jo, 265, 274, 311, 320, 323, 334, 363, 387
Motsinger, Brian, 260, 290, 295
Motsinger, Brooks, 202, 222, 231, 238, 240, 2651-252, 255, 258, 267, 269
Motsinger, C. R., 209, 285, 287
Motsinger, Carrie Elizabeth Hines, 395

INDEX

Motsinger, Chris, 276
Motsinger, Curt, 178
Motsinger, Daphne, 8, 63, 220, 225, 227, 238, 245, 253, 256, 257, 263, 287, 290, 307, 408, 422, 424
Motsinger, Elizabeth, 141
Motsinger, Elsie, 234
Motsinger, Ethel, 229, 231
Motsinger, George, 35
Motsinger, Hugh., 261, 270, 273, 297, 314, 327, 337, 342-43, 345, 352, 354, 356-57, 364, 372, 377, 383, 423, 427, 433
Motsinger, Huldah, 117, 395
Motsinger, Jessie, 178
Motsinger, Kara Lee, 166
Motsinger, Kevin, 295
Motsinger, Mary Francis, 219, 410
Motsinger, Mary Jane Hedgecock, 395
Motsinger, Mike, 287, 330, 348, 350, 351, 354, 358
Motsinger, Nolan, 236
Motsinger, Richard, 236
Motsinger, Rick, 283, 293, 377
Motsinger, Robert, 236
Motsinger, Solomon, 117
Motsinger, William Frank, 395
Motzinger, Felix, 21
Motzinger, Jacob, 21
Mount Holly Baptist Church, 345
Mount Olivet Baptist Church, 339
Mulkey, Phillip, 43, 45
Mumford, E. L., 169
Mumford, Mattie Teague, 294
Myers, Charles, 353, 375, 376
Myers, Crystal, 350, 357, 359, 361, 362, 378
Myers, Don, 345, 358, 381, 432
Myers, Evan, 352, 381, 383
Myers, Franklin, 287
Myers, Rev. Gary, 313
Myers, Tyler, 362
Nancy, Black, 94
Neck, Welsh, 28, 34
Negrin's, The, 240, 386
New Friendship Baptist Church, 63, 92, 135, 201, 204
Newport Baptist Church, 246

Newsome, Fanny, 178
Newsome, Florence, 178
Nickles, Brother John, 124
Nicole, Laura, 354
Nisen, Brother, 137
Nooe, Jarred, 380
Nooe, Lee, 346, 348, 364
Nooe, Susan, 378
North Kenia Baptist Church, 363
North Lexington Baptist Church, 342
North Main Street Baptist Church, 203
Oak Hill Baptist Church, 313
O'Connor, Linda, 335
Odell, Isaac, 61, 87
Odell, James, 65, 68, 107, 117
Odle, James, 125
Odom, Dr. Dave, 342
Oliver, Elliott, 376
O'Rourke, Teresa, 339, 341
Orrel, Charlema L., 141
Orrel, N. B., 130, 141, 154, 156, 163
Orrell, Calvin, 209
Orrell, Christina, 130
Orrell, D. D., 155, 163
Orrell, Dan, 162
Orrell, Ivey, 166, 170, 172, 173, 183, 184, 199, 200, 394, 402
Orrell, Marry Willie, 261
Orrell, Mary Willie, 153, 160, 169, 173, 402, 403, 409
Osbert, 279, 289, 290, 293, 295, 299, 315, 327, 329, 338
Owens, Loulie Latimer, 45, 49
Pace, John, 135, 291
Packard, Brother T. H., 149
Pain, Barnabas, 125, 140
Pain, David Raper Elizabeth, 65
Pain, Elizabeth, 65, 107
Pain, Mary J., 141
Pain, Ruth, 117
Palmer, Aileen, 193, 210, 229, 230, 252, 305, 322, 405, 410, 422
Palmer, Charles Edward, 194
Palmer, Elder Wait, 39
Palmer, Robert, 187-188, 190, 192, 200, 218, 224-225, 228, 234, 254, 261, 273, 278, 288, 430, 432

Park, Reynolds, 407
Parks, Dr. Keith, 282
Parnell, Lynn Smith, 258
Parr, Mary, 32, 74
Paschal, George W., 34, 48
Patterson, Dorothy, 306
Paul, Andrew, 312, 313
Paul, Debra, 315, 318, 374, 378
Paul, Doug, 320
Paul, Nicholas, 332, 353
Payne, Catherine, 229
Payne, Elizabeth, 95, 130
Payne, Helen, 230
Payne, John, 318
Payne, Mrs. A., 137
Payne, Roger, 230
Payne, Ruth, 92, 117
Payne, Sister Elizabeth, 93, 95
Payne, Wilson, 141
Peacock, Frances, 327, 349
Peacock, Francis, 356, 378
Peacock, Lewis, 320-322, 326-327, 329, 333, 348, 349, 356
Peake, Elizabeth, 133
Pearce, Alexander, 65
Pearce, Raymond, 78
Pearer, Meredith, 108
Peasons, Thomas L. F., 141
Peele, Fred, 249
Peele, Phyllis, 258, 260
Peele, Terri, 256, 258, 260
Peele, Tony, 246, 279, 282
Perry, Brothers, 195
Perry, Give, 198
Pharbee, William, 186
Phifer, Paul, 110, 116
Philip Horney-1832, 428
Philips, Mary, 141
Phillips, Annie Lou, 192, 225
Phillips, Eli, 62, 66, 67, 97, 108, 110, 114-116, 118, 428
Phillips, Ivey V., 183
Phillips, J. R., 165, 173
Phillips, John, 188
Phillips, Larry, 314
Phillips, Paul, 116
Piedmont Liberty School, 164
Pilot Mountain Baptist Association, 225, 228
Pine Stump School, 176
Pines, Spruce, 374
Pitts, Emory E., 130, 141
Pitts, Flora T., 141
Pitts, Flora, 130

Pitts, John, 94
Pitts, Lotitia, 141
Plummer, Charlie, 209
Poehlin, Dr. Gary, 352
Point, Dr. Conrad of High, 201, 202
Point, Reverend R. R. Jackson of High, 193
Poole, Emma, 228
Pope, Catron, 74
115
Pope, George, 15, 32, 58, 61, 74-80, 83-84, 115, 428
Pope, James, 85, 86
Pope, Mary, 32, 74, 77, 84
Pope, Oliva, 32, 74
Pope, Shawn, 292
Potts, Lena L., 142
Presley, Elvis, 260
Preto, Rio, 297, 299, 311, 314
Price, Kathy, 261
Primitive Baptist Church, 29, 34, 52, 67, 168, 272, 274, 392, 395, 400
Proctor, Bessie, 183
Proctor, Lucille, 183
Proctor, Raymond, 194
Proctor, Susanna, 141
Proctor, Tom, 183
Profile, Congregational, 358, 377
Purdle, Preacher, 394
Purefoy, Elder George, 45
Raleigh, Brother J. M. Page of, 196
Raper, A. O., 156
Raper, Austin, 25
Raper, Brother Davis, 109
Raper, Brother J. M., 149
Raper, Brother William, 58, 86-87, 109, 120
Raper, Charlie, 170
Raper, Cora E., 142
Raper, Davis, 68, 107, 109
Raper, Elijah, 74
Raper, Eliza, 117, 141
Raper, Flora C., 151, 168
Raper, Hannah, 109, 116
Raper, Heziah, 65, 68, 117, 141
Raper, Joseph M., 22, 133, 141, 148-149
Raper, Keziah, 107
Raper, Laura K., 1130, 41
Raper, Lula, 154
Raper, March Heziah, 117

Raper, Margaret, 141
Raper, Martha, 122
Raper, Mister, 22
Raper, Orville W., 141
Raper, Orville, 133
Raper, P. W., 131
Raper, Phillip W., 140
Raper, Rose, 142
Raper, Sarah, 133, 141-42
Raper, Selina, 142
Raper, Sister Martha, 122
Raper, W. M., 150
Raper, William Raper Heziah, 65
Raper, William, 22, 58, 65, 68, 86, 87, 95, 97, 107, 109, 112, 114, 119, 120, 137, 140, 428
Ray, Dr. Cecil, 283
Read, James, 42
Red Bank Church 135
Red Springs Baptist, 287
Reece, Evelyn, 337
Reece, Rachel, 206
Reed, Clive, 343
Reed, D. S., 153
Reeds Baptist Church, 289, 291, 331
Reid, Frank, 209
Reid, Sally, 197
Reid, Scott, 381, 391
Reunion, Raper, 22
Rich Fork Baptist Church, 188, 290, 292
Rich, John, 32, 74
Richards, Elder, 32, 74, 116-117, 197, 226, 236, 253-255, 261, 317, 381
Richards, Carolina E., 142
Richardson, Alice, 133, 142
Richardson, Brother J. B., 131, 138
Richardson, J. B., 117, 128-132, 134, 138, 139, 413, 428
Richardson, Noah, 128
Richardson, Pastor J. B., 134
Richason, Frana, 74
Richie, Zach, 376
Rickard, Cheryl, 265, 290
Rickard, Jeremy, 289
Rickard, Rodney, 258, 283, 285, 286, 288, 289
Ridge, Timber, 87, 91, 97, 98
Ridgecrest, 210, 256, 293, 334
Rigans, Martha, 141
Right, Ann, 32, 74

Rinehardt, Michael, 331-334, 337, 342, 360, 382
Rio Preto Association, 314
Ritchie, Zach, 353, 375
Riverwood Baptist Church, 284
Roach, Joe F., 219
Road, Barney, 334, 398
Road, Browntown, 417
Road, Curry, 176, 409
Road, Horneytown, 176
Road, Moore, 245
Robarge, Karen, 282
Robbertson, John, 128, 129
Robbins, Daniel, 61, 86
Robbins, Eliza, 24
Roberson, John, 26, 32, 74, 79
Robertson, Carma Ann, 309
Robertson, John, 26, 125, 129, 413, 428
Robertson, Ricky, 358, 432
Robinette, T. E., 265
Robins, Elizabeth, 32, 74
Rogers, Becky, 378
Rollins, Leonard, 237, 239, 260, 288, 301, 312, 339, 342, 410, 432
Rollins, Polly, 317
Rominger, C. A., 138
Rominger, Haritha S., 138
Root, Willie H., 141
Rorex, Drew, 358, 360, 362, 370
Rosalind Hills Church, 350
Rose, Jack, 321, 327, 329, 344
Rose, Leslie, 329
Rose, Patsy, 327, 329, 344
Rose, Pete, 291
Rose, Reverend Jack, 316-317, 322, 326, 328-329, 332-334, 340, 342, 347, 353, 355, 360-361, 367, 379, 389, 408, 410, 416, 424, 432
Rothrock, P. F., 160-161
Rowan, Matthew, 29
Rowbottom, Levi, 284
Rowbottom, Shanti, 284, 327
Rowbottom, Wayne, 294, 299, 389
Rowe, Ben, 292, 301, 304, 310-313, 339, 375, 376, 381, 388, 410
Royal, Dave, 226
Royal, Davis, 204
Royal, Flay, 200

INDEX

Royal, Grayson, 182
Rudd, Donna, 282
Rudd, Leon, 331
Rumble, Jethro, 105
Rush, Dorcus, 32, 74
Russell, Linda, 359, 360, 432
Sabbath Home Baptist Church, 287
Saintsing, Gretchen, 330
Sandy Creek Association, 45, 58, 97-100, 127
Sandy Creek Baptist Church, 33, 36, 41, 43, 44, 102, 384
Sapp, Jeanette, 141
Scheem, Pam, 286
Schlotfeldt, Louise, 318, 329
School, Charles, 92
School, Delane, 177
Schultz, Tom, 346, 348, 352
Sechrest, Blanche, 226, 256, 422
Sechrest, George, 219, 223, 226-227, 230, 235, 249, 252, 266, 270, 279, 291, 297, 300, 305-306, 320, 330, 372
Sells, Bernice, 194
Sells, Doris, 234, 321, 373, 376, 410
Sells, John, 141, 150
Sells, Lewis, 178
Sells, Shane, 260
Sells, Sula, 178
Sells, Susan, 141
Sells, Zane, 260
Semple, A. B., 40
Semple, Robert, 47, 48
Settles, Ben, 329, 330
Settles, Carol, 324, 326, 330, 334, 348, 375
Settles, Jamie, 329
Settles, Marshall, 337, 342, 343
Seven Springs Baptist Church, 194
Sexton, Azzie, 182
Sexton, Hanale, 182
Shackleford, Lee, 295
Shady Grove Methodist Church, 239
Sheets, Henry, 30, 54, 55, 62, 115, 120, 152, 154
Shelle, Jeremy, 32, 74
Shelton, Haarala, 403
Shields, Martha, 130, 141
Shields, William, 25
Shillinglaw, Mike, 291

Shocraft, Simeon, 141-142
Shoener, Patty, 290
Shoseraft, Simeon, 130
Shurden, Walter, 309
Siceloff, Lucy, 183
Silliven, Danniel, 32, 74
Silliven, Margaret, 32, 74
Simms, Brother A. M., 157
Sink, Albert, 320, 332
Sink, Becky, 287, 320, 324, 335, 337, 342, 345, 355, 423, 433
Sink, Mollie, 318, 329
Slone, Olive, 125
Smith, Baxter, 229, 242, 249, 261
Smith, Bernie, 241, 242
Smith, Bonnie, 272
Smith, Brian, 258
Smith, Chester, 178
Smith, Colonel, 102
Smith, Donald, 375
Smith, Dr. Leon, 295
Smith, Dr. Roy, 5, 11, 260
Smith, Emma, 324
Smith, Ester, 178
Smith, Floy, 177
Smith, Gene, 289
Smith, Gerald, 332
Smith, Ina, 194
Smith, Ivey S., 204
Smith, Joe, 240, 245, 251, 252, 254, 261, 300, 308
Smith, Joni, 312, 370, 432
Smith, Kanette, 269
Smith, Kenneth, 258
Smith, Lynn, 258-260
Smith, Martha Teague, 9, 35
Smith, Marvin, 178
Smith, Mary, 235, 237, 241, 246, 253, 259, 295, 299, 302, 304, 307, 314, 321, 332, 340, 387, 410
Smith, Michael, 235, 318
Smith, Minnie, 273, 405
Smith, Pamela, 258
Smith, Patrie Swaim, 24
Smith, Rachel, 32, 74
Smith, Tomson, 32, 74
Smith, Virginia, 206
Snipes, A. R., 202, 218, 406, 408, 414, 430
Snyder, Cathleen, 178
Snyder, Hosey, 178
Snyder, Jim, 269
Snyder, Vera, 178
Snyder, Willie, 178

South Elm Street Baptist Church, 291, 389
Southeastern Baptist Theological Seminary, 243-244, 255, 283, 284, 286, 299, 322, 354, 362, 365, 388
Southern Baptist Theological Seminary, 148
Southgate Baptist Church, 373
Southside Baptist Church, 232
Southwestern Baptist Theological Seminary, 412
Sowers, Louis, 142
Spainhour, Bessie, 178
Spainhour, Carvin, 178
Spainhour, Doris, 194
Spainhour, Grace, 259
Spaugh, Andrew, 241, 246
Spaugh, Ruth Holder, 226
Spergen, Joseph, 98, 100
Spigin, Joseph, 73, 75
Spirgin, Joseph, 79, 80, 91, 93
Spirgin, Samuel, 73, 74
Spirgin, Squire, 82
Spoolman, Sary, 32, 74
Spring Hill United Methodist Church, 217
Spring Hope Baptist Church, 196
Springs, Seven, 194
Sprinkle, Larry, 261
Sprinkle, Linda, 259
Spurgeon, Ara Green, 177
Spurgeon, Betty, 189, 193, 206
Spurgeon, Blanche, 164
Spurgeon, C. E., 165, 168, 169, 190, 192, 197, 430
Spurgeon, Charles, 184, 188, 368
Spurgeon, Chester, 178, 403
Spurgeon, Clell, 206, 397
Spurgeon, Clyde, 182, 422
Spurgeon, Colonel William, 20
Spurgeon, Daisy, 190, 193, 201, 210, 220, 223, 386, 387, 405
Spurgeon, Darren, 262, 290, 291, 294
Spurgeon, Evva, 3, 8, 9, 352, 271-272, 280. 288, 190, 300, 302, 311, 317, 329, 332-333, 334, 329, 343-344, 346-347, 350, 356-357, 359, 367,-368, 383, 387, 410, 423,-424, 432
Spurgeon, Frank, 170, 178, 182, 190, 192, 211

445

History, Heritage, and Memories

Spurgeon, Grace, 170
Spurgeon, Jamie, 259, 263
Spurgeon, Jimmy, 305
Spurgeon, Jodi, 269
Spurgeon, John, 20, 187, 190, 201, 203, 397
Spurgeon, Joseph, 20, 97, 294
Spurgeon, Lucille, 226
Spurgeon, Margaret, 235
Spurgeon, Marla, 234
Spurgeon, Mary, 106
Spurgeon, Minnie A., 242
Spurgeon, Minnie, 187
Spurgeon, Patty, 293, 300, 305
Spurgeon, Ruth, 234, 252, 422
Spurgeon, Susan, 223
Spurgeon, Tim, 262-263, 269, 296
Spurgeon, Tracy, 304, 305, 311
Spurgeon, William D., 19, 20, 24, 183, 184, 198, 396, 430
Spurgeon, W. R., 165
Spurgeon, W. S., 162
Spurgin, Alberta, 141
Spurgin, Brother Joseph, 109, 110, 122
Spurgin, C. E., 173
Spurgin, E. G., 155, 158
Spurgin, Eliza A., 130, 141
Spurgin, Emily, 141
Spurgin, Emma G., 134, 142
Spurgin, G. H., 130
Spurgin, Grace, 151, 158
Spurgin, J. S., 120, 124, 153
Spurgin, James, 142
Spurgin, John, 173
Spurgin, Joseph, 109-112, 114, 116, 120
Spurgin, Letty, 142
Spurgin, Louisa, 141
Spurgin, Louiza N., 142
Spurgin, Nevada, 138
Spurgin, Samuel, 32, 74
Spurgin, Sanford, 133, 141
Spurgin, Sarah, 141
Spurgin, Sary, 32, 74
Spurgin, William, 130, 141
Stack, Debran, 32, 74
Stallings, J. N. , 152, 154, 155, 313, 428
Stanley, Kirk, 279
Starnes Cove Baptist Church, 257
Stearns, Shubal, 28, 32, 36, 37, 39, 40, 42, 48

Steed, Sister, 153
Steele, Elizabeth Maxwell, 105, 106
Stevens, Herman, 175
Stewart, Clifton, 6, 299
Stewart, Lou, 6
Stewart, Loyde, 6
Stewart, Luther, 138
Stewart, Pauline, 6, 183
Stilley, Jimmy, 327, 334, 343, 345, 349, 354, 358
Stilley, Kandi, 350, 357
Stocks, Doris, 344, 348, 350, 355, 424
Stocks, Lee, 343, 347, 354, 367, 381, 408, 410, 416, 432
Stocks, Tom, 350
Stokes, Steward, 254
Stokes, Stewart, 253, 256
Stone, Jr. Ransome, 183
Stone, Leona, 183
Stone, Wanda, 318
Storey, Charles, 326
Stoughton, Dr. William, 51
Stratton, Kim, 272
Stratton, Wayne, 272, 291, 294
Strauhorn, Elizabeth, 32, 74
Strauhorn, Moses, 74
Stoughton, Sally, 51
Sulger, Betty, 256, 307
Sulger, Dawn, 249
Sulger, Debra, 249, 257, 259, 290
Sulger, Dianne, 249, 272, 293
Sulger, John, 237, 254-256, 258, 261, 273, 286, 297, 303, 305, 308, 311, 314, 327, 371, 378, 433
Summerville Baptist Church, 290
Supurgen, Colonel, 105
Surely, 12, 30, 110, 127, 137, 162, 184, 396
Surgeon, Charley, 193
Swaim, Anne, 32, 74
Swaim, Ashley, 25, 50, 58, 61, 63-65, 87, 91, 97, 98, 108, 114, 388, 428
Swaim, Charity, 24, 32, 74
Swaim, Elders M., 99
Swaim, Gladys, 206
Swaim, Hyram D., 24
Swaim, John, 24, 32, 74
Swaim, Martha, 24, 74
Swaim, Mary, 24, 32, 74, 234

Swaim, Michael, 98
Swaim, Rachael Bess, 24
Swaim, V. M., 185
Swaim, V. M., 430
Swaim, William, 24, 32, 74
Swepsonville Baptist Church, 339
Sykes, Rom, 183
Sylva-Webster High School, 258
Takoma Park Baptist Church, 212
Tanner, Charles, 247, 251, 259, 278, 312, 406, 408-410, 415, 432
Taylor, Crystal, 246
Taylor, Daniel, 136
Teague, A. C., 153
Teague, A. O. T., 140
Teague, Abraham, 32, 35, 74
Teague, Almira, 141
Teague, Ann, 142, 394
Teague, Anna, 35, 141
Teague, Aquilla, 140
Brother Carrick, 183, 199
Teague, Brother J., 120
Teague, Brother James, 86
Teague, Brother John, 148
Teague, Brother N. R., 164
Teague, Carrick H., 151, 156, 167, 171, 172, 174, 183-184, 199, 299, 388
Teague, C. W., 165
Teague, Cassie Bodenheimer, 180, 182, 434, 445
Teague, Charles, 125, 140, 178
Teague, Christian Jane, 35
Teague, Crissa J., 142
Teague, Deacon John, 55, 115
Teague, Eliza I., 141
Teague, Eliza J., 133
Teague, Emaline, 141
Teague, Ethel Swaim, 24
Teague, Ethel, 387
Teague, Ettie, 164
Teague, Eudora B., 142
Teague, Eudora Bell, 35
Teague, Ezekiel, 78, 79
Teague, F. J., 426, 427, 430
Teague, Flora Augusta, 35
Teague, Floyd J., 172, 180, 184, 187, 192, 196-200, 219, 220, 426
Teague, H. Banks, 142
Teague, Hannah E., 141

INDEX

Teague, Isaac, 32, 73-75
Teague, Isaiah, 32, 74
Teague, J. C., 151
Teague, Jacob, 87
Teague, James, 86
Teague, Jane E., 134, 142
Teague, Jason, 32, 74
Teague, John Q., 133
Teague, John T. A., 141
Teague, Joseph C., 140
Teague, Julia, 151
Teague, Kathleen, 182
Teague, Linda, 246
Teague, Lou Ann, 142
Teague, Lou, 178
Teague, Maggie, 178
Teague, Martha J., 141
Teague, Martha, 9, 35, 65, 68, 107, 141
Teague, Mary E., 141
Teague, Mary J., 32, 74, 130, 142
Teague, Matilda C., 141
Teague, Mattie, 179, 181, 182, 190, 196, 216, 294, 386, 400, 405, 430
Teague, Milton, 178, 180, 182, 189, 230, 299
Teague, Mose, 134
Teague, Moses F. T., 299
Teague, Moses, 35, 131, 137, 140
Teague, N. R., 155, 164, 165, 167-170, 385, 386, 425, 426
Teague, Nancy, 91, 141
Teague, Nathan, 89
Teague, Noah Richardson, 35
Teague, O. P., 35, 162
Teague, P. T. A., 141
Teague, Phebe, 117
Teague, R. I. A., 140
Teague, R. L., 130
Teague, R. Quincy, 129
Teague, Ray W., 249
Teague, Robert, 410
Teague, Sister Jane, 162
Teague, Solomon, 140
Teague, Sophia A., 141
Teague, Thomas Carrick, 202, 35, 426, 430
Teague, Turner, 236
Teague, Velma, 178, 182
Teague, Victoria Richardson, 386

Teague, Victoria, 35, 172, 395
Teague, William, 78, 79
Tesh, M. A., 153
Thomas, Alexander, 65, 66, 68, 76, 91, 107-109
Thomas, Brother, 114, 155
Thomas, Debbie, 290
Thomas, Elder John, 43
Thomas, Hannah, 65, 68, 107
Thomasville Female College, 162
Thompson, R. S. H., 428
Thompson, S. H., 93, 149, 150, 428
Tise, Emma Lee, 177
Tobago Baptist Association, 294, 389
Todd, Jimmy, 380
Todd, Laurence, III, 287, 315
Todd, Laurence, Jr., 230, 255, 257, 259, 264-265, 272, 283, 287, 301, 311, 316, 323, 326, 340, 347, 357 432
Todd, Maxine, 226, 252, 256, 257, 307, 319
Todd, Patricia, 249, 254
Todd, Sandi, 339, 379, 381
Tom Creek Church, 72
Towsen, Brother B., 173
Traynham, Blanche, 192, 234, 238, 386, 387
Traynham, Breed, 209
Traynham, Coy, 263, 401
Traynham, Crissie, 394
Traynham, Dora B., 158, 162
Traynham, Doris, 194
Traynham, E. L., 130
Traynham, Elizabeth T., 141
Traynham, Eudora, 206
Traynham, Flora Banks, 409
Traynham, Flora, 164
Traynham, George, 134, 142
Traynham, Gil, 408
Traynham, Henry, 133, 141, 182, 192
Traynham, J. P., 150, 153, 155, 162, 165, 167, 192, 196
Traynham, Jeffrey, 35, 130, 140-141, 161, 170, 239, 265, 395
Traynham, Lucy A., 130, 141
Traynham, Margaret, 285
Traynham, Mary Banks, 133, 142
Traynham, Dora B., 162

Traynham, Ruth, 182
Traynham, Sarah T., 142
Tryon, Governor, 102, 103
Tucker, Carrie, 272, 289, 290
Tucker, Donna, 357, 387
Tucker, Katie, 304, 311, 329
Tucker, Marcus, 269, 291 413, 428
Turner, J. Clyde, 175
Turner, Pastor, 175
Turner, William, 150, 152, 413, 428
Tuttle, Shannon, 331
Union Baptist Church, 288, 291
University of Washington, 317
Vaden, Ruth, 230
Valero, Andrea, 360, 374
Vann, P. S., 161
Vickery, Christopher, 32, 74, 76, 87
Vickery, Nancy, 112, 117, 141
Vogler, Margaret, 422
Waff, W. B., 149, 428
Wait, Samuel, 39, 50, 51, 59, 63, 69, 71, 108, 114
Wait, William Cary, 51
Wake Forest College, 52, 139, 198, 203
Wake Forest Manual Labor Institute, 52
Wake Forest Medical College, 193
Wake Forest Seminary, 241
Wake Forest University, 56, 63, 67, 254, 279, 349, 384, 411
Walker, Dora Mae, 206
Walker, Martha J., 142
Walker, Saunders, 43
Wall, Arlan, 269
Wall, Arlyn, 262
Wall, C. M., 154
Wall, Christina C., 154
Wall, Dale, 262
Wall, Emma E., 154
Wall, Judy, 262
Wall, Minnie M., 154
Wall, Sara J., 141
Wallace, Steve, 278, 291
Wallburg Baptist Church, 21, 201, 290, 310, 312
Walls, Christenie C., 141
Walton, W. A., 219
Washington, George, 51, 105, 212

447

History, Heritage, and Memories

Waterfalls Baptist Church, 259
Waterville College,, 51
Watkins, C. J., 130
Watkins, Charles T., 140
Watkins, Charles, 130
Watson, Charity, 32, 74
Watson, Elder John M., 54
Waughtown Baptist Church, 225
Wearenton, Sary, 74
Weaver, A., 128
Weaver, Elder Amos, 428
Weavil, Blanch, 183
Weavil, Evans, 206
Weavil, Homer, 183
Weavil, Ina, 182
Weavil, Jay, 194
Weavil, Rachael, 141
Weavil, Roland, 206
Weeks, Reba, 306
Welborn, John, 402
Welborn, Aaron, 34
Welborn, Billie Ann, 194
Welborn, Brother James, 77
Welborn, Carol, 194, 225, 230
Welborn, Charlie, 229
Welborn, Cora May, 154, 180, 182
Welborn, David Wall, 182
Welborn, Gene, 24
Welborn, Gladys, 166
Welborn, Glenn, 224
Welborn, Isabel, 23, 32, 74
Welborn, J. W., 218
Welborn, James, 23, 24, 32, 34, 74-78
Welborn, Jimmy, 229, 230
Welborn, John, 166,181
Welborn, Johnny, 398
Welborn, Junior, 225, 308
Welborn, Maggie, 166, 188, 190, 259, 405
Welborn, Margaret, 193
Welborn, Sara, 230
Welborn, Wayne, 230
Welborn, William, 74, 78
Welborne, Donnie, 193
Welborne, Beth, 293
Welborns, 24, 34
Welch, 114, 117, 173, 381
Welch, Bud, 381
Welch, Jonathan, 114, 117
Welch, Polly, 117
Wesley Memorial Church, 228
West Hickory Baptist Church, 292, 388

West, James, 32, 74
Western Carolina University, 259
Weston, D. W., 179
Wetherton, Elizabeth, 32, 74
Wheeler, Ada, 177
Wheeler, Bessie, 200, 203
Wheeler, Darell, 302
Wheeler, Henrietta, 299, 303, 311
Wheeler, Heziah, 117
Wheeler, Kara, 302
Wheeler, Sonni, 291
Wheeler, Tonia, 269, 296, 297, 299, 302, 304, 311
White, Brenda, 237
White, Patricia, 237
White, Stuart, 370
Whitfield, George, 38
Wiggs, Bonnie, 269-271, 293, 295, 333, 411
Wiggs, Charles, 277, 314, 333
Wiggs, Debbie, 269, 271-272, 277, 293, 295
Wiggs, Lisa, 295
Wiggs, Toni, 287, 290
Wilkerson, Ron, 294
Wilkes Community College, 375
Willard, Elder V. V., 241
Willard, Pauline, 177
Willard, Ronald, 206
Williams, Betty, 252, 289, 318, 320, 321, 320, 324, 334, 349, 356, 405
Williams, C. B., 28
Williams, Cody, 362
Williams, Dawn, 362, 370
Williams, James, 227, 230, 235, 237-238, 240-241, 243-245, 252, 254, 259, 266, 282, 285, 289, 292, 294, 305, 311, 317-318, 321=322, 326-330, 349
Williams, Jamie, 278, 348, 358, 359, 427
Williams, Ken, 235
Williams, Mary, 32, 74
Williams, Roger, 228
Williams, Ted, 228, 231, 232
Williams, William, 75
Williamson, George, 278
Wilson, Eric, 269
Wilson, Karen, 432
Wilson, Wayne, 332
Wingate University, 284, 292-293

Wiseman, Elder, 110, 118, 119, 428
Wiseman, Joseph, 116
WMU Training School, 211
Womble, Kathleen, 183
Wood, Ester, 117
Wood, Manerva, 142
Woodard, John, 384
Wright, Christy, 304
Wright, Marie Hayworth, 226
Wright, Will, 150, 294
Yadkin Association, 97, 127
Yates, Doris, 290
Yokely, Willie M., 204
Yokley, Early, 178
Yokley, Myrtle, 177
Yokley, Willie, 178
York, Troy, 231
Young, Alicia, 327, 329-332, 371
Young, Allen, 318, 329, 332, 340, 353
Young, Betty, 223, 236
Young, Ronnie, 274, 286, 297, 314, 327, 345, 364, 366, 372
Young, Sammy, 231, 232
Young, Scott, 330, 332, 343, 364, 375
Young, Sherri, 304
Young, Sue, 330, 353, 361, 371
Younger, Anna Nash, 34-35
Zion Baptist Church, 31